TEACHER'S MANUAL

THE SUPREME COURT AND THE CONSTITUTIONAL STRUCTURE

by

ERNEST A. YOUNG

Alston & Bird Professor of Law
Duke University School of Law

FOUNDATION PRESS
2012

THOMSON REUTERS

© 2012 by THOMSON REUTERS / FOUNDATION PRESS
    1 New York Plaza, 34th Floor
    New York, NY 10004
    Phone Toll Free (877) 888-1330
    Fax (646) 424-5201
    foundation-press.com

Printed in the United States of America

ISBN: 978-1-59941-741-7

Mat #40880264

INTRODUCTION

This teacher's manual is simply a very lightly annotated version of my own class notes. Having taught the course for many years now, I'm increasingly willing to stray from the script, but I find it helps to *have* a script in any event, principally to provide a quick but relatively comprehensive review immediately before class. I have tried to purge the document of the worst of my jokes, but in over 400 pages I may have missed a few. If so, you have my apologies.

The principal complaint about this book from students is likely to be that the reading assignments are quite long. I usually point out that the reading assignments at Sullivan & Cromwell, Covington & Burling, or any of the other places they're trying to get jobs will generally be much longer, so they might as well get used to it. But I do think that longer readings make sense in this course for two reasons. First, I don't think we always do students a favor by cutting opinions way down. Much material that is often cut would have actually made it easier to understand the Court's reasoning, so that students may prefer to read longer but suffer shorter bouts of confusion. Second, I think Constitutional Law becomes easier to understand the more background one has— especially in history, but also in philosophy and political science— in a way that may not be true of some of the other first-year subjects. So again, students are asked to read longer but may have a better sense of what's going on. My students have generally proved willing to drink the kool-aid on both these points, for which I am eternally grateful.

I have not included in this volume any sample exams or review problems, although I hope to do so in future versions. My general approach is to do a review problem, which basically looks like an issue-spotter exam, at the conclusion of each of the doctrinal units in the second half of the course. As for exams, I generally try to give a midterm when I teach the course in the Fall semester of the first year, because I think that law students desperately need some meaningful practice and evaluation on issue-spotter exams before they play for all the marbles at the end of the semester. The problems with this are twofold: First, grading any sort of midterm is a ton of work, and it has to be done in the thick of the semester. And if you meet with individual students to talk over their answers—which I do—then this effort to grade and confer will eat about a month of your life. The second problem, which is unique to these materials, is that the first half of the course is historical in its organization and teaches doctrine somewhat incidentally. That makes it hard to write an issue-spotter midterm exam without resorting to cheesy devices like: "The year is 1915, and you should evaluate the Plaintiff's arguments under the doctrines in effect at that time." I do think there's enough doctrine sprinkled through the first half of the course to do a credible midterm (e.g., standing, political question, commerce clause analysis under *Wickard* that basically hasn't changed all that much), but it's not easy. Nonetheless, I would urge you to consider a midterm. Students are desperate for feedback in the first semester, and you will get better final exams if you've taught the students how to take them. I think you'll find the benefit is worth the pain.

My final exam is generally 75% issue-spotter and 25% a more thematic question, dealing with topics like the role of history in constitutional interpretation, the Dead Hand problem, theories of constitutional interpretation, and the like. There is a lot of such material in the book, and students are unlikely to take it seriously if it is not tested (or to be resentful if they *did*). I get better results on the thematic question if I give it out on the last day of class, allow the students to draft an answer, and then have them paste it into the remainder of their final exam on the appointed day. My exam is always open-book, open-note, open-Internet—that is, they can use anything but a friend. I generally tell them that there is a technical term for thinking you know the answer to a complex legal question off the top of your head: "malpractice."

I hope that these materials are helpful to you. If you are in fact using these materials (or considering doing so) and I can be useful to you in any way, I hope you will not hesitate to contact me at young@law.duke.edu.

Ernie Young

SAMPLE SYLLABUS (SPRING 2011)*

This course is an introduction to American constitutional law. The first half of the course is a study of the United States Supreme Court and judicial review from 1789 to the present time. Combining historical and analytical approaches, we will examine the Court's landmark constitutional decisions, explore the theory and techniques of judicial review, and relate the Court's authority to the wider political-societal context of American government. We will consider both structural and individual rights issues as illustrations of the development of judicial review.

The second half of the course focuses on the structural aspects of the Constitution–federalism and separation of powers. Although we will hardly ignore history, the emphasis will be on current doctrine in these areas. These areas have seen extensive and exciting developments in recent years, from the Rehnquist Court's revival of judicially-enforceable federalism limits on national power to the Roberts Court's grappling with the War on Terror. One of the themes of this course is to show how the issues of 1789 and 1868 are still very much with us today.

Texts

The primary text for this course is the draft of a casebook that I have been working on for some years now. Because casebooks are always works in progress, any suggestions you may have for changes in future editions are welcome.

The introduction to the casebook has some suggestions for further reading. A good historical supplement is ROBERT G. MCCLOSKEY, THE AMERICAN SUPREME COURT (4th ed. 2004). Our former colleague Erwin Chemerinsky's hornbook, CONSTITUTIONAL LAW: PRINCIPLES AND POLICIES (3rd ed. 2006), offers a clear and concise overview of the doctrine. Further suggestions are included in the Introduction in the text.

Logistical Issues

Class Meetings: We meet from 3:30 to 4:30 pm, Monday through Thursday, in room 3043. We will occasionally schedule a makeup or review session on Friday, but we will not do this often.

---

* I have included the full syllabus, including silly logistical issues, on the theory that some users of this guide may be first-time teachers who might find it useful to see examples of what might go in a syllabus. I have omitted page numbers because they corresponded to a pre-publication version of the materials.

Office: My office is 3.177. The phone number is 613-8506, and I can also be reached by e-mail at young@law.duke.edu. (I check e-mail considerably more faithfully than voice mail.) I will be available in my office from 10-11:30 am on Tuesdays and Wednesdays, but please feel free to make an appointment or simply stop by at other times.

My assistant is Ms. Tia Williams, who lives in Room 3.207. Her phone number is 613-8585. Extra copies of class handouts, etc., will be available from Ms. Williams.

Blackboard: We will use Blackboard for several purposes:

- *Announcements*: You should check Blackboard at least once every few days for announcements about the course, such as scheduling changes or alterations to the assigned reading.

- *Documents*: I will post class handouts and other materials for download as we go along.

- *Discussion Boards*: Blackboard has a discussion area where anyone can post and respond to comments and questions about the course. I will occasionally attempt to start threads here, but I encourage you to start your own.

- *Links and Documents of Interest*: I may post documents and links that relate to the course in the "External Links" section of Blackboard. These arc for you interest only – you are not required to look at them.

Lunch: Although this law school has a bad tendency to schedule events in the lunch hour, I will try hard to be available for lunch on Mondays and Wednesdays with students. This is totally optional; if interested, you can sign up in groups of 3 to 5 by e-mailing Ms. Williams.

Exams, Grading, and Class Participation

The exam is an 8-hour take-home exam. In the past, the exam has consisted of issue spotter questions (75% weight) and a "big-picture" essay concerning broader themes in the course (25% weight). I will give you the latter essay question on the last day of class, in order to allow you to think about the question and (preferably) prepare an answer in advance. The overall word limit will be somewhere around 3000 words, and it will be strictly enforced. You must type the exam. You will be permitted to use any materials other than a friend.

Your grade will also be influenced by class participation. Each session will be a mix of traditional lecture and Socratic questioning. It is very important that you have read the material and be prepared to discuss it in class. We will not be using panels this year; everyone is "on call." Each student is entitled to four "opt out" days of immunity from being called upon; please contact Ms. Williams at least one hour ahead of class in order to use an opt out. If you volunteer regularly (and competently) in class, you will be eligible for a modest boost to your final exam grade. This boost represents essentially free points—don't neglect them.

The ABA's accreditation standards require regular class attendance. I do not intend to take roll this semester, and I understand that almost everyone has to miss class from time to time. But I want to stress that you will almost certainly find this course much more difficult if you do not attend regularly, and in any event you will be in default of your obligations to contribute to class discussion for the benefit of your classmates. If I call on you and you are not present, you will be charged with one of your opt-outs. If you have already used them all, I reserve the right to impose a penalty on your final grade in the course. If you have special circumstances requiring a more extended absence, please do not hesitate to speak with me about it.

A Note on Laptop Computers

A significant number of professors at this and other law schools have chosen to ban laptop computers from the classroom. Two different reasons are generally given: Many students use their laptops to surf, hone their Minesweeper skills, etc. during class. Equally important, students taking notes on a laptop tend to attempt to transcribe the class rather than writing down the most significant points.

I believe both these concerns are significant. At this time, I am not banning laptops from my classroom. But I do want to stress two points:

1. Using your laptop for non-class activities during class time is rude and disrespectful to the faculty, and it is distracting to your fellow students. To the extent that it keeps you from participating in class discussion, it deprives your classmates of the vibrant class experience that they (and you) are paying for.

2. One of the most important aspects of note-taking is *filtering* the lecture and class discussion to sort out the most important points. Simply transcribing eliminates this filter and, as a result, may well undermine comprehension of the material.

My aim is simply to bring these matters to your attention, without imposing a policy. If you are willing to use your laptops for note-taking, and you have made a considered judgment about what is the most effective note-taking technique for you, then you are welcome to use them. A word to the wise is sufficient.

Reading Assignments

The assignments below are numbered but not dated. Many of them will take more than one day to complete, but it will usually help if you read the whole thing ahead of time. Please stay a reasonable distance ahead of wherever we get to in the preceding day's class. This will enable me to "catch up" occasionally without leaving anyone behind.

The notes following the cases in the casebook should generally reflect the questions upon which we will focus, so pay attention to them.

Part One – The Constitution and Judicial Review

Assignment 1 – The Constitution and the Dead Hand

Constitution of the United States; Raz, *On the Authority and Interpretation of Constitutions*; Note on Constitutional Functions; *District of Columbia v. Heller*; McConnell, Textualism and the Dead Hand of the Past; Note on *Heller* and the Dead Hand

Assignment 2 – *Marbury* and the Case for Judicial Review

Federalist No. 78 (Hamilton); Note on Hamilton's Argument for Judicial Review; Marbury v. Madison; Note on *Marbury* and the Legitimacy of Judicial Review

Assignment 3 – Cases and Controversies

Correspondence of the Justices; Note on Advisory Opinions; *Warth v. Seldin*; Note on the Justiciability Doctrines

Assignment 4 – Political Questions

Baker v. Carr; Nixon v. United States; Note on the Political Question Doctrine and Other Limits on Judicial Review

Part Two – A History of Judicial Review

Assignment 5 – The Marshall Court and the Federal Balance

Introductory Note on the Bank of the United States; *McCulloch v. Maryland*; Note on *McCulloch* and the Scope of National Power; *Gibbons v. Ogden*; *Willson v. Black Bird Creek Marsh Co.*; Note on the Commerce Clause as a Limit on State Power

Assignment 6 – The Taney Court and Slavery

Prigg v. Pennsylvania; Note on *Prigg* and the Relation Between Slavery and Federalism; *Dred Scott v. Sandford*; Levinson, Would You Sign the Constitution?; Note on Slavery and the Constitution

Assignment 7 – Reconstruction and the Fourteenth Amendmen

Barron v. Baltimore; *Slaughterhouse Cases*; *Civil Rights Cases*; Note on the Effect and Interpretation of the Reconstruction Amendments

Assignment 8 – The *Lochner* Era and Freedom of Contract

Lochner v. New York; Note on *Lochner* and Judicial Review of Economic Regulation; *Adkins v. Children's Hospital*; *Nebbia v. New York*; Note on the Heydey of Economic Substantive Due Process

Assignment 9 – Federalism in the *Lochner* Era

United States v. E.C. Knight Co.; *Hammer v. Dagenhart*; *The Shreveport Rate Cases*; *A.L.A. Schechter Poultry Corp. v. United States*; Note on Dual Federalism in the *Lochner* Era

Assignment 10 – The Judicial Revolution of 1937

Roosevelt, *Fireside Chat on Reorganization of the Judiciary;* Note on Court-Packing and the "Switch in Time"; *West Coast Hotel Co. v. Parrish*; *NLRB v. Jones & Laughlin Steel Corp.*; *Wickard v. Filburn;* Note on the Constitutional Revolution of 1937

Assignment 11 – Judicial Deference and the Double Standard

United States v. Carolene Products; *Williamson v. Lee Optical of Oklahoma, Inc.*; Ely, Policing the Process of Representation; Baker & Young, Federalism and the Double Standard of Judicial Review; Note on the "Double Standard" after 1937

Assignment 12 – *Brown* and the Problem of Racial Segregation

Plessy v. Ferguson; Note on the Application of "Separate but Equal"; *Brown v. Board of Education (Brown I)*; *Bolling v. Sharpe*; Wechsler, Toward Neutral Principles in Constitutional Law; Black, The Lawfulness of the Segregation Decisions; Note on Neutral Principles and the Segregation Decisions

Assignment 13 – Segregation Remedies and the Judicial Role

Brown v. Board of Education (Brown II); Note on Desegregation Remedies; *Cooper v. Aaron*; Note on *Cooper* and the Allocation of Authority to Interpret the Constitution; Rosenberg, The Hollow Hope; Note on the Efficacy of Judicial Decisions

Assignment 14 – Incorporation and the Nationalization of Criminal Procedure

Adamson v. California; Duncan v. Louisiana; Note on Incorporation of the Bill of Rights into the Fourteenth Amendment

Assignment 15 – The Rebirth of Substantive Due Process

Griswold v. Connecticut; Note on *Griswold* the Right to Privacy; Bork, Neutral Principles and Some First Amendment Problems; Bork, The Original Understanding; Note on Originalist Approaches to Constitutional Interpretation

Assignment 16 – Abortion, Act One

Eisenstadt v. Baird; Note on *Eisenstadt* and the Transformation of Marital Privacy; *Roe v. Wade*; Note on *Roe v. Wade*; Grey, Do We Have an Unwritten Constitution?; Note on *Griswold, Roe,* and the Unwritten Constitution

Assignment 17 – Abortion, Act Two

Planned Parenthood of Southeastern Pennsylvania v. Casey; Note on *Casey* and the Abortion Debate; Scalia, Common Law Courts in a Civil-Law System; Note on *Stare Decisis* and Common Law Development

Assignment 18 – The Court and the Political Process [SKIPPED]

Intro to Chapter 8; *Bush v. Gore*; Note on *Bush v. Gore* and the Court's Role in Disputed Presidential Elections

Part Three – Federalism

Assignment 19 – The Federal System and Dual Sovereignty

Federalist Nos. 10 & 51 (Madison); Note on the Political Theory of the Federalist; *U.S. Term Limits, Inc. v. Thornton*; Note on Sovereignty, Representation, and the *Term Limits* Case; Note on the Values of Federalism

Assignment 20 – Judicial and Political Safeguards of Federalism

Garcia v. San Antonio Metropolitan Transit Authority; Federalist Nos. 39, 45, 46, & 62 (Madison); Note on the Political, Judicial, and Procedural Safeguards of Federalism

Assignment 21 – The Commerce Clause

United States v. Lopez; Note on *Lopez* and the "Federalist Revival"; *Gonzales v. Raich*; Note on *Raich* and the Future of the Commerce Clause

Assignment 22 – Congress's Power to Enforce the Reconstruction Amendments

Katzenbach v. Morgan; *City of Boerne v. Flores*; Note on the Section Five Power

Assignment 23 – The Spending Power

South Dakota v. Dole; Baker, *Conditional Federal Spending after* Lopez; Note on the Spending Power

Assignment 24 – Clear Statement Rules

Jones v. United States; *Gregory v. Ashcroft*; *Solid Waste Authority v. U.S. Army Corps of Engineers*; Note on the Clear Statement Cases

Assignment 25 – The Anti-Commandeering Doctrine

New York v. United States; *Printz v. United States*; Note on the Anti-Commandeering Doctrine

Assignment 35 – Powers Incident to the Conduct of War

Ex parte Merryman; Rehnquist, *All the Laws but One*; *Hamdan v. Rumsfeld*; Note on Presidential Power and Executive Detention and Trial

CONSTITUTIONAL LAW – CLASS NOTES

PART TWO – A HISTORY OF JUDICIAL REVIEW   76

PART ONE – THE CONSTITUTION AND JUDICIAL POWER

I. Chapter One – The Constitution and the Dead Hand

I generally try to do four things in the first class:

- *First, I talk a little about the constitutional document itself, as well as the distinction between the document and the caselaw which has grown up around it;*

- *Second, I jump right into District of Columbia v. Heller, which we read not so much to become Second Amendment experts but as an illustration of some basic questions in constitutional theory—especially the "dead hand" problem;*

- *Third, we discuss some of the functions of constitutions more generally;*

- *At the end of the hour, I try to give an overview of where we're headed in the course and talk a little bit about how the course is going to work.*

These notes have a good bit of introduction to constitutional theory—probably more than one can sensibly fit in without taking too much time and distracting from the issues in Heller. *I generally truncate this discussion and then pick up the particular issues later in the course.*

A. The Constitution

The leading casebook in Constitutional law is by Professor Kathleen Sullivan of Stanford, who took it over from Gerald Gunther. A recent edition of that book—which is a great book—prints the Constitution as Appendix A, immediately following p. 1395.

(So if the Constitution doesn't start until p. 1396, what do you think is on the preceding 1395 pages?)

Judicial decisions construing the Constitution. Oh, there's some other stuff—scholarly commentary, even some executive and legislative materials. But it's overwhelmingly what people, mostly judges, have said about the Constitution—not the Constitution itself. And in fact, that's what the 1300-odd pages of my book are mostly about, too.

There are two points here:

- The first is the reality that, while we start with a foundational text and purport to be interpreting that text throughout the course, Constitutional Law is in many ways a common law subject, dominated by court decisions and evolving in at least somewhat the same way Torts and Contracts evolve.

- But the second point is that we *do* start with a central text and it's good to remember that. The Constitution itself is the law; what the judges have said about it is derivative.

In January 2011, the House of Representatives read the Constitution aloud on the House floor to open the new session. A lot of commentators thought this was a political stunt by the new Republican leadership, and perhaps on some level it was. But it gives us an opportunity to think about what it means to commit ourselves to a common text.

(What do you think of reading the Constitution aloud? Especially on the floor of the House?)

I think it's salutary, for a couple of reasons.

- For one thing, most people don't actually know what the darn thing says.

(How many of you had ever read it all the way through before this class?)

I think most people haven't. And even purported experts are confused about some of its provisions.

- A second salutary effect is that reading the Constitution affirms a common political culture.

Some nations are united by race or ethnicity or religion; we're too diverse for that. What unites us is a commitment to constitutionalism, and in particular to *our* Constitution. Even though the House reading started out as an arguably partisan exercise, most Democrats seem to have embraced it. Gabrielle Giffords, who was shot in the Arizona tragedy just a week or so later, was elated at being chosen to read the First Amendment.

(When you read it for yourself, did anything in the document surprise you?)

Some of the most surprising things are omissions:

- There's no right to vote.

- There's no rule for what vote it takes to pass a law through Congress.

- There's no mention of political parties.

Today and tomorrow we'll be talking a good bit about what constitutions *do*. You have a somewhat longer list from Professor Raz in the book, but they do basically three distinct things:

- Constitute the Government

- Confer rights on individuals

- Entrench certain structures, principles, and rights

I want to start with entrenchment—the idea that the Constitution makes certain principles permanent, or at least so difficult to change that they might as well be. This creates what we call the "Dead Hand" problem— that is, that we're forced to live with these entrenched principles because various distinguished but *dead* people thought they were important, even if we the living might prefer to do things differently. That issue is put pretty acutely, I think, in *Heller*.

B.   ***District of Columbia v. Heller*, 554 U.S. 570 (2008)**

(Who's the plaintiff in this case?)

Dick Heller is a police officer in the District of Columbia.

(What's he mad about?)

He wants to keep a gun in his house, but he can't under D.C. law.

(What does the law say?)

It does two things:

- It prohibits the possession of handguns.

   Technically, it a) prohibits carrying an *unregistered* firearm, and b) prohibits registering any handguns.

- It requires any lawfully-possessed firearm to be kept in the home in a disabled state.[1]

(And what's Heller's problem with the law?)

He says it violates the Second Amendment.

(What does the Second Amendment say?)

"A well regulated Militia, being necessary to the security of a free State, the right of the people to keep and bear Arms, shall not be infringed."

(What does Justice Scalia think this language means?)

It confers an individual right to bear arms for a variety of purposes, including self-defense.

(And what does Justice Stevens think?)

He thinks the amendment confers a right to bear arms only as part of a militia.

1.   **The Operative and Prefatory Clauses**

(What's a militia?)

---

[1] These provisions are part of the D.C. Code, which is enacted by Congress exercising its constitutional power under Art. I, § 8, cl. 17, "to exercise exclusive Legislation in all Cases whatsoever, over" the District of Columbia. Congress enacted the legislation in response to a recommendation from a District committee.

It's a body of citizens coming together to defend the community. They were the primary armed forces in the early Republic, when we largely lacked a standing army.

(Do we have militias anymore?)

Not really. The National Guard probably comes closest.

(Is the Government likely to forbid members of the National Guard to carry guns in connection with their National Guard duties?)

No.

(So in what way would Justice Stevens's view of the 2nd Amendment constrain the Government?)

I don't see how it would. Perhaps it would constrain the federal government's ability to interfere with *state* control of the national guard, but I can't imagine these dissenters upholding that sort of thing. As you'll see later on, they generally don't believe that the Court should limit national power on behalf of the States.

(What's the best argument for Stevens's view?)

That the text says militias are the point of the amendment. The Court divided the language into two clauses—a "prefatory clause," and an "operative" clause.

- The "prefatory clause" says "A well regulated Militia, being necessary to the security of a free State . . . ."

- The "operative clause" says "the right of the people to keep and bear Arms, shall not be infringed."

I think it's fair to say that the prefatory clause says *why* the amendment was enacted; the operative clause says what it does. The question is the extent to which the former should constrain the latter.

(What's Justice Stevens' argument that the prefatory clause controls?)

He says, Look, the meaning of the operative clause is ambiguous: We don't know how broad "keep and bear arms" is meant to be. The prefatory clause answers that question.

(And what's Justice Scalia's response to that?)

Well, he says the prefatory clause can't limit or expand the operative clause, but he also thinks that's a false conflict, because the core purpose of the Amendment is to protect the *general* militia—the armed body of the citizenry—from being disarmed by the Government.

(Did everyone catch the difference in how they're thinking about the militia?)

Justice Stevens is thinking about the "organized" or "select" militia, controlled by the Government; Justice Scalia is focused on the "general" or "people's" militia, which is armed as a safeguard *against* the government as well as external threats.

2.   Sources of Constitutional Meaning

I want to stop for a minute and think about the different sources of constitutional meaning that the Court is relying on.

(What sources have we talked about so far?)

- constitutional text

- history

Now, there are lots of different kinds of history being thrown around here:

- pre-constitutional – e.g., the English Bill of Rights, Blackstone

(Why care about this stuff? Didn't we fight a revolution to get away from those people?)

There's still lots of ways in which the English experience influenced us. It's like parents – you rebel against them, but they still profoundly shape your life.

- constitutional drafting history

(What sorts of evidence do we have here?)

There is, for instance, the record of various proposals Madison considered in drafting the Amendment.

(Why is that relevant?)

It's kind of a double-edged sword. The text of the Second Amendment might have been meant to convey the same meaning of those earlier proposals—or it might be a deliberate departure from those proposals. It's hard to tell which, unfortunately.

- parallel state provisions

(Why do we care about these?)

It may illuminate the meaning of particular words; it may also help show what the Founders were trying to achieve.

- post-ratification interpretation and practice

(Why is this relevant? Isn't meaning fixed at ratification?)

It helps to know what smart people closer in time thought about the original meaning.

We may also believe in an *evolving* meaning.

(What do we know, for instance, about the right to bear arms during Reconstruction?)

It sounds much more like a right of individual self-defense.

(What's the impact of that evidence? I asked this in the notes – suppose the right to bear arms is an individual right by 1868. What does that tell us?)

It means the "living constitution" arguments for the result in *Heller* may actually be strongest. That's a problem for both sides, right? After all, the conservatives are usually the strong originalists, and the liberals generally favor a more evolving meaning. But those methodological commitments tend to push in unusual ways in *Heller*.

Besides history, there's also:

• judicial precedent

The Court generally spends more time analyzing precedent than anything else. And so will you.

(What's the leading case here?)

United States v. Miller, 307 U.S. 174 (1939).

(What happened in *Miller*?)

The Court rejected a second amendment challenge to a ban on sawed-off shotguns.

(Why?)

Because possession of such weapons was unconnected to militia service.

(What does that mean for this case?)

For Justice Stevens, it means that the Second Amendment is just about militias. For Justice Scalia, it means that the Amendment only protects *weapons* you're likely to use in a militia.

Apart from who's right about *Miller*, there's the question of how much weight should it get?

(Why does Justice Scalia discount *Miller*?)

Because the opinion wasn't careful and one side didn't show up.

(Is that the only consideration?)

Even if it wasn't careful, people might have relied on it.

(Let's consider the more fundamental question I asked in the notes, though: If Scalia's right about the amendment itself, but Stevens is right about *Miller*, what should the Court do?)

This is a hard one, and we'll come back to it when we do *Planned Parenthood v. Casey*, in which the Court considers the *stare decisis* weight of *Roe v. Wade*. In essence, the question is whether it's ever OK for the Court to prefer what it's *said* the Constitution means (i.e., its precedent) to the best reading of the Constitution itself.

3.   The Relevance of Policy:

I want to shift gears and focus on Justice Breyer. His opinion has a different feel to it, doesn't it?

(How would you characterize Breyer's dissent?)

He's much more interested in contemporary policy arguments. Dueling experts and studies contend that strict handgun bans will increase/decrease gun crime and accidents. This evidence raises several questions, including:

- To what extent can policy gains justify incursions on constitutional rights?

- Who decides—the court or the legislatures—how to weigh conflicting evidence about policy?

I want to take the second one first: Who decides?

(What do you think?)

It's a pervasive problem. Generally, the more "fundamental" a right is, the more the courts will resist deference to the political branches of the Government.

The first problem—policy interests versus rights—is also pervasive. But in this case it has a particular temporal dimension, as the policy arguments have surely changed over time. That leads to:

C.   The Dead Hand Problem

Let's say that the *New York Times* was right when it opined that "[*Heller*] is a decision that will cost innocent lives, cause immeasurable pain and suffering and turn America into a more dangerous country." And let's stipulate that this is true because of *changes* in society since the Founding. I suspect the gun control lobby would have been a lot smaller, and a lot less persuasive, in frontier America in 1791.

This gives rise to the Dead Hand Problem: If adhering to the Second Amendment requires the Government to forego policies that would save significant numbers of lives, why do it? Why do the wishes of the (very dead) Framers trump the wishes of contemporary elected officials, which presumably reflect not only contemporary political preferences but also contemporary policy realities?

This problem is a function of the Constitution's entrenchment function. It's really hard to change the Constitution. So Article V is a terribly important section of the Constitution, because it makes change extremely difficult. It's remarkable that we have only 27 amendments after two and a quarter centuries. The Texas Constitution, by contrast, has been amended over 300 times, because the amending procedure is considerably more easy.

(Could you have a constitution that *wasn't* entrenched?)

Sure. It would be called "Great Britain, circa 1972."

I say "circa 1972," because in 1973 Britain became a part of the European Community and subject to certain aspects of European law that raise very thorny issues about Parliament's power to change them. The important point remains, however, that one can – in both principle and practice – have a "constitutive" constitution without "entrenching" it against ordinary legislation.

Ours, however, is pretty darned entrenched. To answer the dead hand problem, we need a theory of constitutional *obligation*. We'll also need two other kinds of theories: A theory of *judicial review*, and a theory *interpretation*. These three kinds of theories will keep cropping up, so it's worth a minute to get them straight at the outset. Before we do that, though, I want to talk just a bit about what we mean by constitutional *theory*.

1.   Theory vs. Doctrine

(What's the difference between "theory" and "doctrine"?)

The type of theory that we'll focus on raises general questions of methodology; there are also substantive theories of, say, personal autonomy or executive power. Theories are general organizing ideas, whereas doctrines are the more local rules and principles that guide decision in particular cases.

In *Heller*, for example, Justice Breyer's dissent criticized the majority for not formulating a particular *test* for when the Second Amendment would be violated. Justice Breyer did offer such a test—an exceptionally mushy balancing test—and that test is an example of a judicial *doctrine*. Similarly, the notion that any restriction on abortion rights must be justified by a compelling state interest is also an example of a particular doctrine. The "black letter" rules that you see in *Gilbert's* or *Emanuel's* study aides are doctrine.

I love doctrine, and we'll spend a lot of time on it. But I also want to make a case for thinking a bit about theory. If you happened to watch, for example, the confirmation hearings of both John Roberts and Samuel Alito, you may recall that they were just as much about the general *theory* of constitutional law as they were about specific issues of constitutional doctrine. Each confirmation process raises a lot of talk about whether the nominee is likely to follow the "original intent" of the Framers of the Constitution, or the "plain text" of the document itself, or whether he or she believes in a "living constitution" that evolves over time. This focus on theory is in part because the nominees are properly reluctant to talk about how they'd decide specific questions that might come before them in the future, but it's also because *no one* really knows what specific issues the Court will have to face five or ten years from now.

The same thing is true for us in law school, by the way: I could teach you a ton of specific doctrinal rules – and I will, in fact, teach you a ton of doctrinal rules – but it's actually very difficult to know what kind of constitutional questions you may actually confront over the course of your legal careers. (I don't think anybody expected, five years ago, that we were all going to get interested in the Second Amendment all of a sudden.) That's why it's so important to think about the way in which we approach constitutional problems generally – the *method* of interpretation that the nominees for the Court and that you as lawyers will bring to the table. Part of what learning to "think like a lawyer" means is developing a theory or a methodology for approaching new legal problems, and we'll spend a fair amount of time on those questions in this class.

To answer the dead hand problem, we need a theory of constitutional *obligation*. As I said, we'll also need two other kinds of theories: A theory of judicial review, and a theory *interpretation*. These three kinds of theories will keep cropping up, so it's worth a minute to get them straight at the outset.

2.   Three Kinds of Constitutional Theories

Theories of *obligation* explain why we *obey* the Constitution. Some examples:

- Divine Right – the Judaeo-Christian tradition gives authority to the Mosaic law on the ground that it came straight from God.

- Consent – the Lockean "social contract" grounds legal obligation in the consent of the governed.

- Morality – finally, we might obey the Constitution simply because it's morally good.

We'll come back to theories of obligation in a minute – this is by no means a complete list.

Theories of *judicial review* explain why *judges* get to interpret it, as opposed to other governmental officials. Some examples:

- judicial job description (i.e., courts have to apply the highest law in cases before them).

- institutional capacity – courts might just be better than other governmental actors at enforcing a constitution.

- representation reinforcement – judicial review might be necessary to correct for defects in the ordinary political process.

Theories of *interpretation* tell *whoever* is enforcing the Constitution how to figure out what the Constitution *means*. Some examples:

- textualism

- originalism

- common law development

- moral theory

It turns out, as the McConnell reading suggests, that these different kinds of theories are related; which theory of obligation you choose, for instance, may have strong implications for your theory of interpretation. *Heller* raises all three theoretical questions, but today I want to focus on obligation.

3.   Constitutional Obligation

Obviously, the *policy merits* in *Heller* – that is, whether gun control saves lives – are highly controversial. But the majority is largely uninterested in that problem (as is Justice Stevens). They focus on historical meaning. But why should *we*, living in 2011, prefer the legal product of dead people in 1791 to the product of democratic processes operating in the present day?

Judge McConnell quotes a great statement of the problem from Noah Webster, who said that making a "perpetual constitution" amounts to "legislat[ing] for those over whome we have as little authority as we have over a nation in Asia."

McConnell gives a number of possible answers to this problem:

- **It's a Good Constitution**

We obey the Constitution because we – now – agree that the principles it embodies are attractive for moral and/or practical reasons.

This is the most attractive reason in a way – it means we never have to choose between our moral principles and constitutionalism.

(Is there a problem?)

I think so: It's not clear this is really constitutionalism at all. After all, we're basically saying we'll depart from the constitutionalism whenever we think we ought to. So what drives our decisions is our view of what's right and wrong *now* – not any commitment to the document ratified in 1789.

- **Constitutionalism is Enabling**

Sticking with a set constitution enables us to practice self-government.

(What does McConnell mean by that?)

This argument has a lot going for it, and I think McConnell's metaphor of the rules of a game is a good one. The rules of basketball constrain the players – but they also make the game possible.

(Any problems?)

Well, it locates the legitimacy of the constitution in what we might call *conventionalism*, which is simply the fact that we need a set of rules and this is the one we can agree on. But if we could agree on a different set of rules, there's no obvious reason why we couldn't go with that instead. And I think there are some instances where that best describes what has in fact happened.

Another version, though, is a bit stronger because it commits us more directly to agreement over *time*. The analogy frequently given is Odysseus and the Sirens.

You all remember the story where Odysseus wants to hear the Sirens' song, but also wants to live to tell about it. So he ties himself to the mast of his ship in order to save himself from the temptation to jump overboard. The Constitution also serves to protect us from short-run temptations to change the basic qualities and values of our governments.

This idea may even start us toward an account of why *courts* have a special role (that is, toward a theory of *judicial review*). Maybe there's something about courts – in particular, their independence – that makes them well-suited to protect democratic majorities from themselves.

(Can you think of an example where this would be true?)

The flag-burning case[2] in the late 1980s is a good example. Gregory Johnson burned a flag in Dallas to protest the illegitimacy of the Government. The overwhelming popular sentiment is to throw flag-burners in jail; most of us, however, also have long-term preferences for a system of open political debate. The Constitution's function in that case is the make it impossible for the majority to yield to the short-term temptation to throw that value out the window.

- **The Dead Hand Rules**

---

[2] *Texas v. Johnson*, 491 U.S. 397 (1989).

The Framers (and Ratifiers) of the Constitution in 1789 were invested with popular authority that holds until the People speak again in some fundamental way and change it.

(Any problems here?)

Well, this theory is, I think, where you have to confront the non-representativeness of the Framers. No women; no African-Americans; no poor people; etc. You might doubt whether the group that *did* ratify had the right to speak for all of us as "the People."

- **Implied Ratification**

The Constitution "derives its continued authority from the implicit consent of the people in each subsequent generation."

(What about this one?)

There are all kinds of problems with implied consent. It's often a fiction. After all, it's hard to just pick up and leave to show you don't consent.

At the same time, I think you can defend implied consent as a fairly accurate summary of people's actual attitudes. Most of us *like* the Constitution.

- **Self-Government Over Time**

One key aspect of being human is the ability to commit to temporally-extended projects – that is, lasting commitments that endure across generations. The Constitution is that kind of project. This is another kind of argument that the Dead Hand just isn't a problem – it suggests that to *deny* the dead hand is to deny part of what makes us human beings.

(That sounds nice, but what does it mean?)

You might remember the fish Dory from Finding Nemo, who had severe memory problems. Marlin, the protagonist, is continually having to re-establish his relationship with Dory and fill her in on what they're trying to do, because she keeps forgetting. Dory's really frustrated, because she can't really get on with her life if she has to keep starting over. The point is that Jefferson's idea – that "the earth belongs to the living" and the present generation can't be bound by what's gone before – would make us a little like that.

This is a complicated idea that we'll talk about more when we do precedent.

4. Judicial Review

A theory of obligation establishes that the Constitution is binding. But it *doesn't* tell us anything about who enforces it. Who decides whether the Constitution contains a right to abortion? Who has the last word as to the powers of the President? In our system, we tend to assume that *courts* will have the last word.

(Could you have a binding constitution without relying on *judicial* enforcement?)

Sure. Lots of other countries have written constitutions without judicial review. And it's critical to remember that other gov't officials have an obligation to interpret and follow the constitution to their best ability even if there's no judge looking over their shoulder.

We'll want to approach the judicial review question from several different directions:

- What *legal* support is there for judicial enforcement? (That's the question in *Marbury*.)

- Are the courts a good institutional choice for enforcement? This is a *functional* criterion. Are courts likely to be better at interpreting and enforcing the Constitution than other governmental actors?

- How *effective* is judicial enforcement? (Here, we'll particularly look at the frustrating story of the courts' attempt to force the South to desegregate its schools.) The answer, I think, is that courts can't do much on their own.

The clearest historical evidence favoring judicial review is from Hamilton's Federalist No. 78. I want to hold discussion of Hamilton's argument, however, until after *Marbury*.

5. Constitutional Interpretation

Finally, there's the question of interpretation, which applies to *any* actor charged with enforcing the Constitution. As you saw in *Heller*, the meaning of the Second Amendment doesn't exactly leap off the face of the text. A theory of interpretation tells the interpreter how to determine constitutional meaning in circumstances when that meaning isn't obvious. Lots of constitutional provisions are ambiguous, so interpretive methodology matters a great deal.

Obligation to Interpretation: Judge McConnell argues that your theory of obligation will powerfully affect your theory of interpretation.

- **Moral Approval**

(How do you approach interpretation if you're following the constitution because it's *good*?)

You look for the morally best result, right?

- **Convention**

(What about the conventionalist theory of obligation – that is, that constitutional constraint enables government?)

Here I can imagine two tacks. One is the one McConnell takes: You look to enhance the functioning of government through something like representation reinforcement – that is, courts should interpret the constitution in such a way as to maximize the representation of diverse groups in society.

On the other hand, I'd say that convention should point you in the direction of whatever interpretive theory can best secure widespread agreement. That probably points you toward something of a hybrid—attention to text and history, but also a reluctance to disrupt expectations by overruling precedent.

- **Authority of the Framers (or Ratifiers)**

(What about here?)

Originalism, right? The Constitution derives its force from their will, so their understanding is key.

- **Implied Ratification**

(And here?)

Traditionalism – evolving consensus over time.

- **Self-Government Over Time**

I think the implications here are basically similar to implied ratification: The key question is continuity with what's gone before.

Other Considerations in Choosing an Interpretive Theory: I don't mean to suggest that your theory of obligation is the *only* factor in deciding on an interpretive theory. Two other key factors:

The Costs of Interpretation: We need to think about the institutional consequences for courts of adopting a particular theory of interpretation. Two costs are central:

- **Error costs**: How *hard* is the method in terms of time and resources. E.g., do judges have to do extensive historical research?

- **Decision costs**: How likely are judges to make *mistakes* if they pursue a particular method? E.g., are judges likely to get the history wrong?

Determinacy of Results: By determinacy, we mean the likelihood that a particular method or test will yield a single right answer. For instance, if we tell judges in *Heller* to use the interpretation of the Second Amendment that will make the best policy sense, well, people disagree about that. On the other hand, if we say interpret the right only to extend to the circumstances clearly articulated in the text (e.g., militia service) that would yield a much narrower range of possibilities.

We care about determinacy for two reasons:

- We want the law to be predictable, so that people who have to comply with it can know in advance what their obligations are. Determinacy enhances predictability.

- The more determinate constitutional doctrine is, the more it seems like "law" rather than "politics" or "policy choice." That is important in legitimating judicial review, for reasons we'll talk about more in the next section.

D.   The Constitutive and Rights-Creating Functions

I promised I'd come back to the other constitutional functions. Besides making it really tough to do the smart policy thing, what a Constitution does two other things:

- A Constitution constitutes the Government – that is, it creates the institutions of government and specifies their powers and obligations;

- It creates rights that individuals can assert against governmental action. These rights are really just the flip side of the constitutive function; they specify where government powers *end*; and

1.   The Constitutive Function

Let's take the constitutive function first. We often take this function for granted, simply because it's so basic. But think about the old "I'm Just a Bill" sketch from Schoolhouse Rock. That's the constitutive function: Article One of the Constitution establishes a Congress and sets out how it produces authoritative legislation.

The constitutive aspect of the constitution doesn't show up in court opinions that often, simply because parties don't often dispute it. You don't see too many cases, for instance, about whether both houses of Congress have to sign off before a bill becomes a law (although we'll read one).

(Is the Constitution the *only* thing that constitutes our government?)

No way. How a bill becomes a law is powerfully affected not only by the provisions of Article One, but also by internal House and Senate rules setting up committees that consider legislation, voting rules like the filibuster, etc. And think how much federal law isn't even made this way. The Communications Act of 1934, for instance, sets up the basic framework for telecommunications regulation in this country. The most important aspect of it is to set up an administrative agency, the Federal Communications Commission, and it's then the FCC that makes most of the important policies governing broadcasting, phone service, etc. So the Communications Act is itself *constitutive* – it establishes a new government institution and specifies its powers and the procedures by which it has to operate. So it's probably more accurate to say that the Constitution supplies the foundational principles of the government, but leaves a lot to be filled in through legislation and regulations.

2.   Conferring Rights

A constitution also creates rights. The Bill of Rights is probably the most familiar part of the Constitution to most of you, even though it was kind of an afterthought to the Framers. Free speech, equal protection of the laws, the right to remain silent – these are what constitutional law is *about*, right?

I want to quibble here, too, about whether the Constitution is really a *complete* or most fundamental list of our rights.

(What if I say you have to choose between your right to burn the flag and your right to drink clean water? To income support and healthcare in old age? To not be discriminated against on the basis of race if you go work for a private company?)

So once again, the Constitution isn't *exclusive*, but it's surely an important catalog of our rights.

Rights vs. Structure: We might think of the constitutive function as creating a *structure* of government, in contrast with the *rights*-bearing provisions of the Constitution. And this dichotomy is one of the basic divides in Constitutional Law. Focusing on it for a minute will help in giving you a preview of what the course is about.

Let's think about, for instance, two concrete constitutional issues that get a lot of airtime every time the Senate holds hearings to confirm a new supreme court justice: the constitutional right to an abortion, and the scope of executive power to do things like detain suspected terrorists and conduct wiretaps without statutory authorization from Congress.

These are two good issues to illustrate a way in which we frequently divide the subject matter of Constitutional Law: Abortion is a question of individual *rights*, while executive power is a matter of government *structure*.

Rights questions are probably more familiar. They require us to determine the limits of governmental authority to say what individuals can and cannot do.

Structural questions may be less familiar. It's easy to think of the wiretapping dispute, for instance, as a question of whether the President has the authority to invade your privacy. That would turn it into a *rights* question, probably under the Fourth Amendment's "search and seizure" clause. But the primary dispute today starts with the proposition that the Government *can* tap your phone in certain instances relating to national security; the question, instead, is whether a particular part of the Government – the President – can do that on its own authority without getting the approval of another part – the Congress. This is a question of constitutional *structure*.

(Are these two kinds of questions completely independent in the examples I've given?)

Incidentally, it's easy to see how rights and structure are related. Obviously it's going to be harder for the President to invade people's privacy if he has to get the approval of a potentially hostile Congress first.

Much of this course will be about constitutional structure, with only a secondary emphasis on rights. We will spend roughly two-thirds of our time on issues of federalism (the balance of power between the national government and the states) and separation of powers (the division of national power between the Executive, Legislative, and Judicial branches).

This emphasis on structure is pretty standard in the first-year curriculum, but it sometimes comes as a surprise to people who expected to spend lots of time talking about abortion, flag-burning, and the like. We *will* cover a number of important rights issues – racial segregation, privacy and abortion, gay rights – as part of the first big unit in the course, which is a general history of judicial review. And the Law School offers a broad array of con law electives, most of which focus on issues of rights. But there are very good reasons to emphasize structure at the outset:

(Do we have any clues about how the Framers viewed the relative importance of these two sets of issues?)

(1)   The Framers thought that structure was all that really mattered. That's why there was no Bill of Rights in the original constitution. The view was that the best way to protect individual freedom is to set up the institutions of government in such a way as to prevent tyranny from developing in any part of it. That insight that federalism and separation of powers are basic to individual liberty remains true today.

(2)   Structure is where much of the action is in Constitutional Law today. The Supreme Court is embarked on a basic reexamination of federalism the likes of which we haven't seen since 1937. And the War on Terror (as well as fights surrounding the financial crisis, the 2000 election and the impeachment crisis of the late 1990s) have given rise to all kinds of interesting separation of powers issues. So while some people used to find structure boring, it's hard to say that anymore.

E.   **A Last Word About Entrenchment**

I want to circle back to entrenchment just for a moment, to finish off this dead horse I've been beating about the *exclusivity* of the Constitution.

(Is the difficulty of amending the Constitution the *only* thing that entrenches a given governmental structure? Think about the Social Security program, for example. Sure, Congress could eliminate them both tomorrow by passing an ordinary statute. But is that likely to happen?)

No way, right? Social Security is the third rail of American politics. Likewise, the FCC's been around a long time; it employs a lot of people, carries out a lot of important functions; it has a lot of powerful interests invested in it. That makes it really hard for anyone to snap their fingers and get rid of it. So it's important to understand that there's such a thing as institutional inertia, and it's very powerful. Article V isn't the *only* thing that entrenches our institutions.

II.   **Chapter Two – Judicial Review**

A.   ***Marbury v. Madison*, 5 U.S. (1 Cranch) 137 (1803**

When I have to teach a somewhat shorter version of the course, I start with Marbury *on the first day. It's a tough case for the first day, because the jurisdictional and procedural issues that one must understand in order to reach the basic question of judicial review are themselves complex, and may be especially difficult for 1Ls who have not yet had Civil Procedure. I have generally found 1Ls equal to the task, although it is sometimes difficult—especially for someone who also teaches Federal Courts—not to get sucked into a long discussion of federal question jurisdiction, etc.*

Marbury *is also a good window on the politics of the Founding and the Early Republic. It's worth spending some time here, especially if your class contains non-liberal arts majors who may have last taken history in high school. That politics frames the basic issues that recur throughout the course. It also may be reassuring for students to realize that politics has always been messy and discordant. I like to point out that no matter how uncivil Washington, D.C. may seem today, Nancy Pelosi has not yet shot John Boehner.*

The first half of the course is concerned with the institution of judicial review – that is, the power of the federal courts to strike down laws or actions by the other branches of government when those actions are contrary to the Constitution. This is the part of the course that makes the rest of it possible; if the courts didn't have the power to examine the constitutionality of governmental action, we'd have a very short set of materials.

Marbury is the case that explicitly recognizes, for the first time, this power of judicial review. It's also one of the more difficult cases in the course.

1.   Factual Background

(Who's the plaintiff in this case?)

William Marbury, who's just been named a justice of the peace for the District of Columbia.

(Who appointed him justice of the peace?)

President John Adams.

(Why's Marbury upset?)

Because the Jefferson administration hasn't honored the appointment.

(Why not?)

Because Marbury's commission was signed but never delivered.

(Why do you think the Jefferson administration is being difficult about this?)

Because Marbury is part of a last-minute plan by the outgoing Federalist party to pack the courts before they leave office.

(Who are the Federalists?)

The Federalists formed half of the first two-party system in American politics. The ins and outs of this are a little confusing, because in the early republic political labels mean different things at different times, and prominent people tend to jump around a little bit. Basically there are two periods that you need to keep straight:

1)   The debate over the Constitution itself; and

2)   The political parties that form after George Washington leaves office.

During the first period, we use "Federalists" to describe proponents of the new Constitution. Washington, Madison, Hamilton, John Adams, and James Wilson are all leaders of this group. The opponents of the Constitution are the "Anti-Federalists" – people like Patrick Henry and George Mason. The debate between them tends to be – and here we're oversimplifying dramatically – between those who favor a stronger central government than under the Articles of Confederation and those who fear that the new Constitution will result in a centralized and tyrannical national government.

The second period begins largely after George Washington leaves office. There's a reason George Washington gets to be on the one-dollar bill. Like no one else in American politics, he was able to command so much respect and deference that he could hold a consensus government together without political parties. After he goes, however, things fall apart a little.

The split tracks previous quarrels within the Washington administration between Alexander Hamilton (Washington's Secretary of the Treasury) and Thomas Jefferson (Washington's Secretary of State).   After Washington leaves, political parties begin to form around both these men. Hamilton's party retains the name "Federalist" and remains the party of strong national government.   They are also the party that is most interested in industrialization, with all the social change that entails.

The Jeffersonians, on the other hand, form what is called the "Republican" party. Note that this is *not* the predecessor of today's Republican party – that party is formed just before the Civil War and is the party of Lincoln, not Jefferson. The Jeffersonian Republicans are the intellectual heirs of the Anti-Federalists, although they've accepted the Constitution and are simply committed to keeping the central government in bounds.   The Republicans tend to be agrarians resistant to industrialization, and they favor strong states' rights as a counterweight to the federal government.

One interesting aspect of the Hamilton-Jefferson split is that James Madison – the "Father of the Constitution" and Hamilton's co-author on the Federalist Papers – sides with Jefferson. There's disagreement about why this happened. Some think Madison was simply inconsistent in later life; others think Hamilton and the Federalists simply pushed too far in favor of centralized government and Madison jumped off the bandwagon. In any event, by the time of *Marbury* Madison is serving as Jefferson's Secretary of State.

(That's the basic background to the political controversy. Why did the Federalists try to appoint all these judges at the end of Adams's term?)

The Federalist had just lost – and lost badly – the election of 1800. They've lost the Presidency and control of Congress. All that's left, they think, is the judiciary. So if they can consolidate their control of the courts, they can hope to prevent the Republicans from undoing the Federalist accomplishments under Washington and Adams.

They do this in two ways through legislation passed in January of 1801, just before Jefferson takes office:

(1)   by creating a lot of new judgeships and appointing Federalists to fill them; and

(2)   by dramatically expanding the scope of federal jurisdiction.

(How do the Republicans respond, besides by making trouble for Marbury?)

By repealing the Circuit Court Act of 1801 – the act appointing most of the new judges and expanding federal jurisdiction. They also do some other nasty stuff:

- They abolish the 1801 Terms of Court, so that the Supreme Court can't even sit to decide the *Marbury* case, and

- They start impeaching Federalist judges, starting with district judge John Pickering and moving on to Supreme Court justice Samuel Chase. (This strategy fizzles after the effort to impeach Chase narrowly fails in the Senate.)

So it's important to recognize that the *Marbury* case is a single battle in a much wider war over the federal judiciary.

2.   Procedural History

(Did Marbury file this case in the original or appellate jurisdiction of the Supreme Court?)

Original.

(What's the difference?)

Original means that the case *starts* in the Supreme Court – this isn't an appeal from the ruling of a lower court.

(Why did Marbury file in the Supreme Court's original jurisdiction?)

He *has* to file there. The Republicans had just repealed the 1801 Judiciary Act's provision that would have allowed him to file in a lower federal court.[3] It's possible he could have filed in state court, but that's a very complicated question.

(What's Marbury asking for in this suit? What's the procedural relief he seeks?)

A writ of mandamus, ordering Madison to give Marbury his commission.

(What's a writ of mandamus, anyway?)

It's a common law procedural vehicle – basically an order to a lower court judge or to a government official commanding him to perform a duty which he is required by law to perform.

---

[3] This is a federal question case – that is, a claim based on a violation of federal law. The 1801 Act provided for general federal question jurisdiction, but a new statute won't be enacted again until 1875; federal question suits have to be brought in the state courts unless there is diversity of citizenship. And Marbury and Madison are both citizens of Virginia.

(What's likely to happen if the Court gives Marbury his writ of mandamus?)

Jefferson and Madison will probably refuse to obey the order.

(What means does the Court have to force Jefferson and Madison to obey such an order?)

The Court doesn't have any. It's a critical point that the Court's power depends entirely on the respect that other people have for its orders. The Court doesn't have any means of coercing compliance on its own.

So you can see the bind that Chief Justice Marshall finds himself in. He doesn't want to confess that the Court is powerless to stand up to the Republicans. On the other hand, he can't afford a political confrontation because he'll probably lose.

(By the way, who's the joker who forgot to deliver Marbury's commission?)

John Marshall, who was Adams's Secretary of State at the time. John Marshall entrusted the commissions to his brother James, who didn't get them all delivered. So one important lesson of this case for young lawyers is, Don't give important documents to your brother.

(In light of these facts, should Marshall even be hearing this case?)

Probably not – at least under modern standards of propriety. He should probably have recused himself. On the other hand, it would be awfully hard to sit this one out. And it's not like his personal relationship to the case causes him to help Marbury out in the end.

3.   Marshall's Opinion

Marshall says he's setting out to answer three questions. They are:

(1)   Does Marbury have a right to the commission he demands?

(2)   If he has a right, and that right has been violated, do the laws of his country afford him a remedy?

(3)   If they do afford him a remedy, is it a mandamus issuing from this court?

a.   Does Marbury have a right to the commission?

(What's the Court's answer to the first question?)

That the commission is final when the President signs it, and withholding it now violates a vested legal right.

b.   Does the law give him a remedy?

(Why *wouldn't* Marbury have a remedy?)

Because the President and his agents might not be accountable for this sort of conduct.

(What's Marshall's answer to this argument?)

He has two – one general, one specific.

The general answer is that "[t]he very essence of civil liberty certainly consists in the right of every individual to claim the protection of the laws, whenever he receives an injury."

This is pretty sweeping, and it's not totally true.　There are lots of situations in which one might have a right but no remedy.　For instance, we'll talk a little about the idea of "sovereign immunity," which is the government's immunity from suit in certain circumstances.　In some cases, for example, the State of North Carolina might have breached a contract with you but it might be immune from suit.

(What's Marshall's more specific answer?)

He distinguishes between "discretionary" and nondiscretionary or ministerial duties of government officials.

(What's a discretionary duty?)

It's a decision like whether to recognize a foreign government, or negotiate a treaty, or sign a law.

(Can a court order the President or a cabinet officer to perform that kind of duty?)

No.

(Does that mean that the President is unaccountable for those kinds of acts?)

No – He's still accountable to the voters.　Just not to courts.

This refusal to intrude on the political duties of the Executive is the root of the modern political question doctrine, which we'll talk about more next week.

(What about nondiscretionary duties?　How are they defined?)

They are duties that the law specifically directs an official to perform, without allowing any leeway or discretion.

(What kind of duty are we dealing with here?)

That the duty to deliver the commission is nondiscretionary, and that therefore the law can require executive officials to perform it.

(There's also a second aspect of this duty that makes it subject to judicial command.　What is that?)

The fact that individual rights – Marbury's right to his job – depend on the performance of the duty.

So once Marshall holds that Marbury has the right to his commission, and that he's entitled to a remedy, we're ready for:

c. Is that remedy a mandamus from this Court?

(What's the first issue the Court confronts here?)

Whether the defendant here is subject to mandamus.

(Why wouldn't he be?)

Because he's the Secretary of State. Marshall is worried about courts trying to order around senior executive officials. "Questions in their nature political, or which are, by the constitution and laws, submitted to the executive, can never be made in this court."

This is basically the same point that the Court decided under question two: The Court is just re-emphasizing that its claim of authority to review executive conduct is very limited.

Remember: This claim – that the Court can review executive conduct – is the most controversial aspect of *Marbury* at the time.

(What's the second issue?)

Whether the writ can come from the Supreme Court here.

(Is this purely a constitutional question?)

No – Marshall has to construe the jurisdictional authority that Congress has conferred on the Court in the 1789 Judiciary Act. It's important to know that legislatures usually have to give jurisdiction to the courts in *statutes*. Why that's true is something we can talk about when you take the Federal Courts class.

(What does the statute say?)

The Supreme Court may "issue writs of mandamus, in cases warranted by the principles and usages of law, to any courts appointed, or persons holding office, under the authority of the United States."

(Does this cover Madison?)

It appears to. He's a "person[] holding office, under the Authority of the United States."

(What's the next question?)

Whether the statute is constitutional, that is, whether it is consistent with Article III.

Article III does two things that are relevant here. In Clause 1, it defines the limits of the subject matter jurisdiction of the federal courts – that is, what kinds of cases the federal courts can hear.

(You have Art. III reprinted in the handout.[4] Does this case fall within the subject matters discussed in Clause 1?)

Yes – Marbury's right to the commission is a question of federal law because it deals with the internal operations of the federal government. So this is what we call a "federal question" case: a case "arising under this Constitution [or] the laws of the United States."

(So if Clause 1 of Art. III lays out the different kinds of federal subject matter jurisdiction, what does Clause 2[5] do?)

It allocates the Supreme Court's jurisdiction between appellate and original jurisdiction.

(Is Marbury trying to bring his case within the appellate or original jurisdiction?)

Original.

(Does the case fit within the original jurisdiction under Clause 2?)

It doesn't seem to. You might think Madison's a "public minister," but it seems pretty clear from historical materials that "public ministers" refers to *foreign* ministers.

So there's the constitutional problem: The Judiciary Act, as Marshall reads it, permits the Supreme Court to exercise original jurisdiction in a case that isn't within the Court's original jurisdiction as defined in Art. III.

(Is there any other way to read Clause II to avoid this problem?)

You could read Clause II as setting up an allocation of jurisdiction between original and appellate without setting that allocation in stone – that is, as setting up a baseline which Congress is free to modify in the future.

---

[4] Section 2, Clause 1: "The Judicial Power shall extend to all Cases, in Law and Equity, arising under this Constitution, the laws of the United States, and Treaties made, or which shall be made, under their Authority; -- to all Cases affecting Ambassadors, other public Ministers and Consuls; -- to all Cases of admiralty and maritime Jurisdiction; -- to Controversies to which the United States shall be a Party; -- to Controversies between two or more States; -- between a State and Citizens of another State; -- between Citizens of different States; -- between Citizens of the same State claiming Lands under Grants of different States, and between a State, or the Citizens thereof, and foreign States, Citizens or Subjects."

[5] "In all Cases affecting Ambassadors, other public Ministers and Consuls, and those in which a State shall be a Party, the supreme Court shall have original Jurisdiction. In all the other Cases before mentioned, the supreme Court shall have appellate Jurisdiction, both as to Law and Fact, with such Exceptions, and under such Regulations as the Congress shall make."

Note that the Court did later adopt this sort of reading about the appellate jurisdiction – that is, the Court has held that cases that *do* fall within the original jurisdiction under Art. III can be farmed out to lower federal courts, and the Supreme Court can then exercise appellate jurisdiction over those cases.

(But wait – Does the *statute* really tell Marbury to bring this case as an original suit in the Supreme Court? The statutory language is reprinted in the handout.[6])

(How does Marshall read this provision? Does that make sense?)

He reads it to say Congress is conferring original jurisdiction on the Supreme Court over any case asking for a mandamus against a public official.

(Any alternative ways to read this?)

Two alternatives to Marshall's reading:

- The Supreme Court can exercise mandamus as part of its *appellate* jurisdiction.

- The Supreme Court can exercise mandamus in any case in which it would *otherwise* have jurisdiction.

Either one of these interpretations eliminates the constitutional problem, and requires dismissal of Marbury's case on *statutory* grounds.

The fact that there's an *available* interpretation that doesn't contradict Art. III is important, because there's a rule of statutory construction that you should always construe a statute to avoid potential constitutional problems.

(Why would we have a rule like that?)

Because it's a big deal for a court to strike down a law. We don't want it to happen too often, so any devices that avoid the necessity are welcome.

(Having concluded that the statute contradicts Article III, what's the next question?)

Whether the court must still follow the statute. In other words, is it the Court's job to tell Congress that the law it's passed is invalid, or is *Congress*'s judgment about constitutionality final?

---

[6] "The Supreme Court shall also have appellate jurisdiction from the circuit courts and courts of the several states, in the cases herein after specially provided for; and shall have power to issue . . . writs of mandamus, in cases warranted by the principles and usages of law, to any courts appointed, or persons holding office, under the authority of the United States."

This is the key question for us today, although there's reason to believe that it wasn't all that controversial back then. *See, e.g.,* Federalist 78.

(What arguments does Marshall make on this point?)

(1)   *The nature of a written constitution:* There's no point to having a written constitution if the courts can't enforce it.

It's worth dwelling on this point for a few minutes, because it gets us to a question even more fundamental than the issue of judicial review itself.

What Marshall is saying is that the Constitution must take precedence over the Judiciary Act – that's what written constitutions are for. But that in itself is something of an extraordinary assertion. After all, the Judiciary Act was enacted by democratically elected members of Congress, and it's more recent than the Constitution.

Remember, however, that we talked yesterday about the distinction between whether the Constitution is *binding* and whether *courts* can enforce it. The latter doesn't necessarily follow from the former.

(We'll talk more about why judges ought to be the enforcers throughout the course. But what's Marshall's answer?)

(2)   *The nature of the judicial function:* **"It is emphatically the province and duty of the judicial department to say what the law is."**

(Why is that true? Doesn't *Congress* say what the law is?)

Congress decides which laws to enact, but the courts generally interpret what they mean.

(Why separate the law*making* and the law *interpreting* functions?)

(What does Marshall mean by this?)

(Does he mean in *general* or in the course of litigation?)

He seems to mean simply that, in deciding a case, the Court must either apply the Constitution or the statute; it has to make a decision, and the nature of a Constitution is that it prevails over a mere statute.

(3)   *The "arising under" jurisdiction:* Article III extends the judicial power to all cases "arising under the Constitution"; how can courts not be empowered to *apply* the Constitution in such cases?

But the jurisdiction would not be null and void without judicial review of Congressional action. The Court might still, for example, review *executive* action or *state* laws.

(Why might it be particularly important to review executive action and state laws?)

Well, the old view of "due process" in English law was that the executive could act only as authorized by positive law, enacted by the legislature. And the executive branch includes the police and all government bureaucrats – they're the part of the government that comes into direct contact with the people most often, so they're the most likely to violate people's rights.

And a central part of the Federal Government's function in general (and the Court's in particular) is to rein in the states.

So it's not like there's no possible ground of distinction. But once you concede that any case "arising under the Constitution" involves *some* form of judicial review, however, there is no obvious basis in the text for stopping short.

(4)   ***Constitutional restrictions on Congress:***   A number of constitutional provisions – such as the prohibition on *ex post facto* laws – directly restrict what Congress can do. Marshall says it would be absurd to have these prohibitions without allowing courts to enforce them.

(Is there an answer to this argument?)

It seems to simply beg the question whether *Congress* is meant to be the final judge of whether it has violated these provisions.

(Why *not* let Congress be the judge?)

You'd have a severe fox-henhouse problem. Much of constitutional law can be reduced to the proposition that "foxes should not guard henhouses." But if the Court has the last word on what the constitution means, isn't *it* exercising unchecked power too?

(5)   ***The Judges' oath:***   Judges take an oath to follow the Constitution, and Marshall says this would be a cruel joke if their hands were tied when it comes to applying it.

But *all* government officials take this oath – not just judges.

(6)   ***The Supremacy Clause:***   Article VI says that "This Constitution, and the Laws of the United States which shall be made in pursuance thereof . . . shall be the supreme Law of the Land." Marshall says this means that the only federal laws made "in pursuance" of this Constitution should be given effect.

(Any holes in this argument?)

"[I]n pursuance thereof" might simply mean that the law has passed through all the requirements of Art. I, and that Congress's word is then final.

You could also argue that the Supremacy Clause is directed at the *States* – it mentions only that "the Judges in every State" are bound, and says that the "Constitution or Laws of any State" can't withstand federal law. Everyone does seem to agree this means judicial review of state laws. But as I've suggested, once you've taken that step, it's odd to leave out federal laws.

If we step back a minute, there are two important points about these arguments:

(*First*, what *kind* of arguments are they? What sources of authority is Marshall relying on?)

The first two are structural arguments – they're not based on any particular text, but rather the nature of the institutions that the Constitution creates.

The last four are textual arguments explicitly.

It's interesting that Marshall does *not* rely overtly on judicial precedent – there were some available, although nothing had confronted the issue so directly – or on explicit appeals to history.

This may have something to do with Marshall's need to justify judicial review to a wider audience. For that purpose, the broad appeals to structural principle are probably more effective than citing obscure precedents. And the history was familiar to all concerned.

The *Second* point is that all these arguments may work together more effectively than they do as stand-alone points. The broad structural points basically *assert* a relationship between the court and the other institutions of government which the textual references then confirm.

One last aspect of the opinion: The ultimate holding is that the Court lacks jurisdiction to hear this case. Ordinarily, courts check their jurisdiction *first*, and if they don't have it, they don't say anything about the merits.

(Has Marshall done this?)

No – He's gone out of his way to say that the Jefferson administration has acted illegally here. So you can see the political brilliance of the opinion:

Marshall starts in a position of weakness: The Jefferson Administration is attacking the federal courts, and it's clear that Jefferson will ignore any order that Marshall might issue against him.

Out of this, Marshall manages to:

(1)   avoid a political confrontation with Jefferson;

(2)   establish the power of judicial review; and

(3)   announce to the world that Jefferson has acted illegally;

all because Marshall is willing to sacrifice the immediate result – he doesn't give Marbury any relief – and therefore leaves Jefferson with no court order to defy. Jefferson is stuck with a minor victory but a pretty massive defeat in the broader war.

B. **Considering Judicial Review**

I said earlier that we need to approach the judicial review question from several different directions:

- What *legal* support is there for judicial enforcement?

- Are the courts a good institutional choice for enforcement? Are they likely to be better at it than other governmental actors?

- How *effective* is judicial enforcement?

We've already discussed the legal support for judicial review in *Marbury*. And we discussed John Marshall's worry about *effectiveness* in *Marbury* as well—that is, his concern that if he ordered Madison to give Marbury his commission, Madison would simply ignore the order.

Now I want to walk about institutional choice. There's a great deal of historical evidence that the Framers of the Constitution assumed that judicial review would occur—the Convention rejects other proposals, such as a separate "Council of Revision" the review federal laws, on the ground that judicial review is a better approach to the problem of legislative overreaching. The best reasoned defense of the institution, prior to *Marbury*, is Hamilton's Federalist No. 78.

Before we talk about Hamilton, though, I want to raise a principal criticism.

(What's Alexander Bickel's problem with judicial review?)

1. **The Counter-Majoritarian Difficulty**

Even if there's historical support for the power of judicial review, isn't all this undemocratic? Who elected these judges? The big debate in constitutional theory – which I just want to introduce here – arises from what Prof. Alexander Bickel called "the countermajoritarian difficulty": The presumption in a democracy is that the majority of the people rules, and any departures from that principle – like judicial review – have to be specially justified.

(What's Hamilton's answer to this problem in Federalist 78?)

He has two. One has to do with the independence of the courts from the political branches.

- **Judges as an "intermediate body"**

Hamilton says that "[n]o legislative act . . . contrary to the Constitution, can be valid. . . ." "It cannot be presumed that "the legislative body are themselves the constitutional judges of their own powers"; instead, "[i]t is far more rational to suppose, that the courts were designed to be an intermediate body between the people and the legislature, in order . . . to keep the latter within the limits assigned to their authority."

(What does Hamilton mean by describing the courts as "an intermediate body"?

You might sum this up a lot more efficiently by saying that the foxes shouldn't guard the henhouse. But that homey image assumes the foxes are more dangerous than the hens.

(What do you think of Hamilton's assertion that the Judiciary is the "least dangerous branch"? Would you say that today?)

- "Will" vs. "Judgment"

Hamilton's second argument has to do with the nature of the judicial function as professional interpreters of the law:

"The interpretation of the laws is the proper and peculiar province of the courts." It's crucial that a judge, deciding a case, does something entirely different from a legislator deciding whether to vote for a bill. "The courts must declare the sense of the law; and if they should be disposed to exercise WILL instead of JUDGMENT, the consequence would . . . be the substitution of their pleasure to that of the legislative body."

(What's the key thing that distinguishes "will" from "judgment"?)

It's the determinacy of the law. The law has a fixed meaning apart from the political or policy or moral preferences of the judge. The judge is *bound* to follow the law, not his own desires: "To avoid an arbitrary discretion in the courts, it is indispensable that they should be bound down by strict rules and precedents, which serve to define and point out their duty in every particular case that comes before them . . . ."

This is one of the basic questions we'll address in this course: Is what judges do in the process of judicial review really just applying the law, or do they *make* the law in the same way that other officials do?

- **Short-term vs. Long-term Values**

Bickel made a somewhat different argument similar to the Odysseus and the Sirens story, deriving from the fact that society has both short-run preferences and enduring values. That fact in itself might justify having a constitution, but you still face the *institutional* question: Which institutions are better at preserving those long-term values.

(Are legislators or Presidents good at this?)

53

Frequently not. Notice that we don't have to say they never are – in fact, since most cases never come to court, we're counting on politicians and government officers to interpret and follow the Constitution *most* of the time. But as long as we think they will slip up sometimes, we can ask if some other institution might be better.

(What's special about courts?)

Their insulation gives them the freedom to take a much more principled view: "Judges have, or should have, the leisure, the training, and the insulation to follow the ways of the scholar in pursuing the ends of government."

(Do you agree with this? Isn't it pretty elitist? Is that so bad?)

- **The "sober second thought"**

Bickel makes another argument about *time*: It's not just the fact that the judges are there for a long time, though this helps, but that judicial review comes *after* the political battles over getting legislation passed. This means courts can provide a "sober second thought" about governmental actions. It also means they get to examine the gov't act in the context of concrete case, where it's easier to gauge its consequences. This is an important reason for the justiciability doctrines we talked about earlier: The requirements of a particular plaintiff with a particular injury (standing), as well as a ripe controversy, ensure that this "sober second thought" gets to operate.

2.   Thayer's Critique

I want to highlight another criticism of judicial review – which is not so much an argument that we shouldn't do it as that we should be careful about doing it *too much*. That is Bickel's argument – drawing on the work half a century earlier of James Bradley Thayer – that "judicial review may, in a larger sense, have a tendency over time seriously to weaken the democratic process."

(Why would that be true?)

Because other actors – congressmen, presidents – start feeling like they can leave the Constitution to the courts. FDR says exactly that in his letter to Congressman Hill.

Bickel quotes Thayer's classic statement of this concern that the problem is that "the correction of legislative mistakes comes from the outside, and the people thus lose the political experience, and the moral education and stimulus that comes from fighting the question out in the ordinary way, and correcting their own errors." The result is to "dwarf the political capacity of the people, and to deaden its sense of moral responsibility."

So it's important to underline the point that the Constitution binds *all* officials: Congressmen should consider it when they vote for or against a statute; the President when he signs or vetoes legislation.

Finally, there's the basic question – which we'll return to when we do *Brown v. Board of Education* – of how much difference judicial review can actually make. It's worth remembering Judge Learned Hand's statement, that "a society so riven that the spirit of moderation is gone, no court *can* save; that a society where that spirit flourishes, no court *need* save."

(Is this a pessimistic or optimistic statement?)

It's both, right?

(Do you agree with Judge Hand?)

C.   Cases and Controversies

The unit on justiciability serves two functions: First, it explores the primary limit on the power of judicial review recognized in Marbury. *This is important in order to avoid giving the impression of unbridled judicial supremacy. Second, it injects a healthy dose of doctrine—even some black letter rules—early in the course. In my experience, the historical bent of the first half of the course makes students a little nervous, because they're afraid they aren't learning any current law. And if one likes to give a midterm (as I do, for the purpose of introducing first semester 1Ls to law school exams), then one needs some doctrine to test them on.*

We'll spend the next two classes on five justiciability doctrines – the prohibition on advisory opinions, and doctrines of standing, ripeness, mootness, and political questions. These go to the questions of who can challenge governmental action in court, when they can do it, and when the court can intervene. Political questions is something of a different animal, so we'll hold that to one side for now and focus on the first four.

(What's the textual basis for these doctrines?)

All of the first four justiciability doctrines are based on Article III's limitation of the judicial power to "cases and controversies."

But all four also have prudential components.

(What do we mean by a "prudential" limitation? Where do they come from?)

They are limitations on judicial power that the courts have imposed on themselves for policy reasons.

(Where do courts get the power to impose these rules?)

It's not clear. But courts are thought to have some basic authority to govern their own proceedings.

It's important to be clear about the difference between constitutional and prudential limitations. Prudential rules – unlike the ones that are derived from Art. III itself – can be overridden by Congress.

There are four key doctrines:

- **Advisory Opinions:** The general rule that the federal courts cannot issue advisory opinions is the precursor to all three justiciability doctrines. In essence, the doctrine holds that courts may only rule on legal issues when they are necessary to the decision of an actual dispute.

- **Standing:** Standing essentially asks whether the lawsuit is being brought by the right plaintiff.

The other two doctrines are about timing:

- **Ripeness:** Ripeness asks whether the lawsuit has been brought too soon, before the dispute between the parties has "ripened" into a case that the court can decide.

- **Mootness:** Mootness is the opposite problem; it asks whether the suit has been brought too late, after the dispute between the parties has ceased to exist.

1.   Advisory Opinions

During President Washington's administration, the President asked the justices of the Supreme Court whether he might request their views about legal questions arising from U.S. neutrality in the war between England and France.

The Justices say, "No, thanks. You're on your own."

(Why? This is George Washington asking. He's the Father of our Country, for gosh sake! And it seems like a pretty reasonable request.)

The Court cites separation of powers concerns, but also casts cold water on the idea of "extrajudicial" decisionmaking.

(What's the separation of powers concern?)

Judicial independence: By refusing to act as *counselors* to the President or Congress, the Court avoids any excessively cozy relationship between judicial and executive or legislative branch.

Note that you will find in our history instances of individual justices who have violated this norm. For instance, Justice Story drafted a new admiralty jurisdiction statute for Congress because he thought Congress would just mess it up otherwise. And after LBJ appointed his long-time lawyer Abe Fortas to the Supreme Court, he continued sometimes to treat Fortas like his personal legal advisor. But these examples are pretty few and far between.

There's also a more concrete concern about judicial *power*:

(Suppose the Court gives Washington the advice. Does Washington have to follow it?)

No – it's just advice, right? But publicly ignoring a court ruling isn't good for the Court's prestige or its power.

(The more important arguments today deal with extrajudicialness. What makes an advisory opinion "extrajudicial"?)

It doesn't settle a dispute between actual parties concerning a concrete set of facts.

(Why might we like to have advisory opinions?)

- resolve legal uncertainty before action is taken: Usually government officials want to comply with the law, but they may be uncertain about what the law actually requires. That's a fair description of Washington's request, I think. It's a hassle to pass a law or take Executive action, only to have some court come in years later and declare it all null and void.

- veil of ignorance: Sometimes it's helpful to approach an issue as a matter of abstract principle before you find out whose ox is actually being gored.

(What are some reasons why courts shouldn't issue advisory opinions?)

- concreteness of issues: Courts usually do a better job of deciding legal issues if those issues are presented in the context of a concrete case, where the parties are involved in a real dispute. This is thought to give the court a better sense of how the legal rules it adopts will play in the real world.

- adversary presentation: Our system depends on the parties to zealously present both sides of an issue to the court. We usually think this is more likely to happen if both parties are litigating based on their concrete self-interest.

- judicial restraint/separation of powers: The "case or controversy" requirement is an important limit on judicial power. Courts can't act *proactively* -- they have to wait for an actual case and a plaintiff with standing before they can decide any issue. This inability of courts to set their own agenda is a pretty important limitation on their power.

Note that some of the advantages of the advisory opinion are captured by the declaratory judgment procedure, which requires an actual dispute but allows suit prior to taking action or incurring injury.

Note also that the Office of Legal Counsel at the Justice Department has taken over the advisory opinion function, at least for the Executive Branch.

State Practice: Many state courts are empowered to issue advisory opinions. Two important points:

- state governments aren't limited by separation of powers concerns, except for any limitations in their own *state* constitutions; and

- in particular, Art. III's "case or controversy" requirement doesn't apply to state courts.

Implications for the Federal Courts

- Much of justiciability doctrine -- under standing, ripeness, and mootness -- derives from the idea that federal courts can't issue advisory opinions.

- The advisory opinion bar is also the reason that courts ordinarily don't reach issues that are not necessary to the decision. After all, portions of an opinion that don't affect the outcome of the case are essentially advisory.

This describes much of *Marbury*, doesn't it?

2.   Standing: *Warth v. Seldin*, 422 U.S. 490 (1975)

This is a case challenging discriminatory zoning rules for residential housing. The claim is that the town of Penfield – which seems to be a suburb of Rochester, NY – has designed its zoning ordinances to exclude poor people. There's a further claim that, by excluding poor people, Penfield may really be trying to exclude racial minorities.

The Court holds (Powell, J.) that the plaintiffs lack standing to bring their claims.

(Is the Court interested in the merits of these claims?)

Not on the surface at least. (Justice Brennan disagrees, and we'll consider his view in a minute.) The important point for now is that the majority *assumes* for the sake of argument that these zoning rules are illegal. That doesn't mean, however, that anyone can walk in off the street and challenge those rules in court. Standing is about whether we have the *right plaintiff* to challenge these laws.

(Why do we need to worry about this? As long as this law is in fact illegal, why doesn't the court simply thank the plaintiffs – whoever they are – for bringing it to the court's attention and strike down the law?)

The standing requirement is thought to protect basically the same values as the prohibition on advisory opinions:

- concreteness of issues

- adversary presentation

- judicial restraint/separation of powers

a.   The Basic Rules

The Court begins its discussion by distinguishing between prudential and constitutional standing rules.

(How much of the standing rules are mandated by the Constitution itself?)

The Court says the core requirement is that the plaintiff must himself have suffered "some threatened or actual injury resulting from the putatively illegal action." The Court later breaks this out into three questions:

(i)   concrete injury: Is the injury too abstract, or otherwise not appropriate, to be considered judicially cognizable?

(ii)   causation or traceability: Is the line of causation between the illegal conduct and injury too attenuated?

(iii)   redressability: Is the prospect of obtaining relief from the injury as a result of a favorable ruling too speculative?

(What's the difference between the traceability requirement and the redressability requirement?)

Traceability "examines the causal connection between the assertedly unlawful conduct and the alleged injury," while redressability "examines the causal connection between the alleged injury and the judicial relief requested."

(What are the prudential aspects of the standing rules?)

Standing doctrine incorporates several prudential ideas:

* **no third party standing:** the "general prohibition on a litigant's raising another person's legal rights,"

* **no generalized grievances:** "the rule barring adjudication of generalized grievances more appropriately addressed in the representative branches," and

* **zone of interests:** "the requirement that a plaintiff's complaint fall within the zone of interests protected by the law invoked."

Remember: These prudential rules can be overridden by Congress, but there's no statute that purports to do so in *Warth*.

b.   The *Warth* Plaintiffs

(Who are the plaintiffs in this case that are asserting standing to challenge Penfield's discriminatory zoning ordinance?)

We have several different kinds:

* Ortiz, Reyes, Sinkler, & Broadnax – individuals of low or moderate income

- Taxpayers of the City of Rochester

- The Associations – Metro-Act and Home Builders

The Low Income Individuals

(What's the injury claimed by these plaintiffs?)

They claim to have been excluded from living in Penfield because of the zoning ordinance.

(What's the problem with this allegation of injury? Does the ordinance cover individuals like this at all?)

No – It doesn't say who can live in Penfield and who can't.

(Then how does the ordinance affect these individuals?)

The claim is that it affects what sort of housing developers can build, which drives up prices to the level that these individuals can't afford housing.

(Why isn't that a plausible injury?)

It's too indirect. There's no demonstrated causal link between the denial of particular projects and the plaintiffs' inability to find housing. And there's no indication that striking down the ordinance would suddenly make housing available to these plaintiffs.

(So which of the three requirements for a cognizable injury – concrete injury, traceability, and redressability – haven't been met here?)

The problem is traceability and redressability.

The Rochester Taxpayers

(What about the Rochester taxpayers? What's their injury?)

They allege that because Penfield excludes poor people, those people live in Rochester instead. This causes Rochester to have to spend more money on services for these people, which leads to increased taxes.

(What's the problem with this claim?)

One problem is that causation also runs through the actions of third-parties not before the court. That is, taxes may have gone up, but only because officials in Rochester decided to raise them. They may have been motivated by factors that Penfield's ordinance helped bring about, but the fact that Rochester officials had a free choice breaks the causal chain.

(But the Court doesn't really rely on this argument. What's the more important problem?)

(Whose rights are the taxpayers asserting? Is anything illegal being done to them?)

No. They're asserting the rights of people who want to live in Penfield. So this falls within the prudential standing rule holding that parties can ordinarily only assert their *own* rights – not those of third parties.

The Associations

Finally we have the associations – Metro-Act and Homebuilders.

(Are the associations asserting their own rights?)

No – they're asserting the rights of their members. This is a very important point: An organization can have standing if:

- its members would otherwise have standing in their own right;

- the interests it seeks to protect are germane to the organization's purpose; and

- neither the claim asserted nor the relief requested requires the participation of individual members in the lawsuit.[7]

Here, the two different organizations assert different sorts of injuries.

(What's the injury asserted by Metro-Act?)

Metro-Act appears to be some kind of citizens' advocacy group. Some of its members are just like the individual low-income plaintiffs, who didn't have standing for the reasons we've already talked about.

But some of the members are actually residents of Penfield.

(What's their injury?)

They claim to be deprived of the benefits of living in a racially and ethnically integrated community.

(Have these residents been deprived of any constitutional rights?)

No – they're asserting that the denial of the rights of others has injured them. But that is the rights of third parties problem that we talked about with respect to the Rochester taxpayers.

(What about the Home Builders association? What's its injury?)

They claim that they've been denied business opportunities by the Penfield ordinance.

(What's the problem with this claim?)

It's generally not concrete enough. There's only one alleged instance where a member specifically applied for a permit to construct a housing project in Penfield, which was denied because of the ordinance. And that instance was several years ago, with no indication that the controversy is still live.

---

[7] *See Hunt v. Washington Apple Advertising Comm'n*, 432 U.S. 333 (1977).

c.   Standing and the Merits

(What's Justice Brennan's general take on this case?)

He thinks the majority is using the standing doctrine to mask its hostility to the plaintiffs' claims on the merits.

(Does he think the plaintiffs have been given a fair shot to prove a cognizable injury?)

No – He thinks they should get discovery in order to develop the causal link between Penfield's ordinance and the market conditions that make it impossible for the plaintiffs to get housing.

(What's the drawback to allowing discovery?)

It means you incur a lot of time and expense before you know whether the case is viable or not.

(What kind of effort is it going to take in order to get standing to challenge this kind of governmental action?)

You probably need cooperation from some builders – which these plaintiffs have – and a more careful documentation of particular requests for permits and denials, as well as concrete plans to build in Penfield.

The concrete allegations made in the *Arlington Heights* case[8] are a good example.

(Is there any alternative to this kind of effort?)

The federal government itself frequently brings suit to challenge these sorts of practices.

3.   Ripeness

The question with ripeness is, Has the plaintiff sued too soon?

The notes illustrate this with the *Mitchell* case,[9] in which some government employees are challenging the **Hatch Act,** which provides that federal executive branch employees can't take "any active part in political management or in political campaigns."

(Had the plaintiffs violated the statute yet when they filed suit?)

No. This is a case about "pre-enforcement review" – that is, a challenge to a law before the law is enforced against you.

(What's the alternative to pre-enforcement review? What is the Court telling these folks to do if they want to get their case heard?)

---

[8] *Arlington Heights v. Metropolitan Housing Corp.*, 429 U.S. 252 (1977).

[9] *United Public Workers v. Mitchell*, 330 U.S. 75 (1947).

They can always violate the law, wait for the law to be enforced against them, then challenge it as a defense to the enforcement action.

(What's the drawback to that?)

Well, it means the plaintiffs have to risk losing their jobs if they want to challenge the law.

(So can you think of any reasons *not* to let them have pre-enforcement review?)

If nobody's violated the law yet, then we don't have much of a factual context to evaluate the legal issues. We don't know what kind of activities the plaintiffs will engage in, or what kind of interests the government may be able to assert in response. You can imagine some cases in which the government would have a stronger interest than others.

This concern for concrete facts is much like what we saw behind the injury requirement for standing – in fact, you can think of ripeness as just another name for the fact that the plaintiffs don't have an injury *yet*.

So we have two factors that seem to dominate these cases:

- Does the Court have enough information to decide the issues, or does it need to know more?

- Are the plaintiffs presently suffering any harm?

These factors cash out into the doctrinal test for ripeness developed in a case called *Abbott Labs* and reproduced in the handout:

(1)   Are the issues fit for judicial resolution? That is, does the Court know enough to decide?

(2)   Will the parties suffer hardship if pre-enforcement review is denied?

The courts tend to weigh these two considerations together: If the issues are clearly fit for resolution, for example, the court may not require much of a showing of hardship. But you need to argue both.

4.   Mootness

Has the plaintiff sued too late? Or have the issues in controversy gone away due to events occurring after the plaintiff filed suit?

Mootness has been described as "standing in a time frame" – the idea is that the injury that gives the plaintiff standing at the outset of the litigation has to continue through to the end.

There are several reasons a claim might become moot:

- Changes in the underlying legal framework

- The challenged government action is of limited duration

- The opponent provides full relief

One good way to *prevent* mootness is to include a claim for damages for whatever the government did to you in the past. That way, even if they stop, you still have a live claim for the money. But even that claim will become moot if they write you a check.

The *Friends of the Earth* case[10] in the notes illustrates one important exception to mootness. In that case, the plaintiff has sued to enjoin a factory owner from polluting a stream. The factory stops polluting, but the Court says the case isn't moot because it has ceased polluting *voluntarily*, and could resume in the absence of a court judgment barring it. Ordinarily the plaintiff has a continuing interest in a *judgment* vindicating his position unless there is some serious impediment to the resumption of the defendant's activities.

(What do we do with a case like *Roe v. Wade*? You all know the basic facts. What's the plaintiff's injury in *Roe*?)

She's being required to carry a baby she doesn't want. That becomes moot when the baby is either aborted – as a result of winning in a lower court – or born.

(Could you ever get a Supreme Court ruling in a case like this without some kind of exception?)

No – It will always take more than 9 months to get to the Court.

That's why the Court holds in *Roe* that an issue is not moot if it is "capable of repetition, yet evading review."

The plaintiff must show that:

(1)   the challenged action is in its duration too short to be fully litigated prior to its cessation or expiration; and

(2)   there is a reasonable expectation that the same complaining party will be subjected to the same action again.

The second requirement is not *that* strict. Jane Roe doesn't have to file an affidavit that says, "I'm likely to become pregnant and seek an abortion again in the near future."

D.   The Political Question Doctrine

The political question doctrine serves much the same pedagogical function as the other justiciability doctrines: it highlights limits on judicial power, and it introduces some doctrine early on. Most students find it fairly confusing, in part because I do not gloss over the controversy as to whether there is, in fact, a

---

[10] *Friends of the Earth v. Laidlaw Environmental Services, Inc.*, 528 U.S. 167 (2000).

political question doctrine at all. (My own view is that Louis Henkin was right, and most political question holdings can be explained as simply cases in which there was no constitutional violation on the merits because the relevant constitutional provisions confer discretion on the relevant government actor.) One virtue of continuing to teach this material, however, is that Baker *is a helpful illustration for other points, such as the historical role of the Warren Court and also John Hart Ely's "representation reinforcement" theory of judicial review.*

Finally, note that if you are teaching the chapter on the Court and the electoral process, one could easily move the political question doctrine to that part of the course. Under the current arrangement, of course, you may want to revisit the political question doctrine when you get to Bush v. Gore.

Remember in *Marbury*, when Chief Justice Marshall said that "[q]uestions, in their nature political, or which are, by the constitution and laws, submitted to the executive, can never be made in this court." That's the root of the modern political question doctrine, which holds that there are some constitutional questions that courts just can't decide. As I said, that's a doctrine of broad applicability—it's not just a question that arises in election cases.

The leading case on that is *Baker v. Carr.*

1.   *Baker v. Carr*, 369 U.S. 186 (1962)

Tennessee voters challenged a 1901 state statute apportioning state general assembly seats. They argued that by 1961, the apportionment was wildly out of sync with the present distribution of voters.

Plaintiffs sought an injunction prohibiting elections under the old law and requiring either a reapportionment in accord with federal census figures or an "at-large" election.

The Court holds (Brennan, J) that the courts can hear a challenge to the TN setup, although it's not until later that they establish the principle of "one person, one vote." The key question in this case is whether the Court can decide the case at all.

(Why wouldn't the Court be able to decide the case?)

The state and the dissenters argue that the Court should refuse to consider the case under the political question doctrine.[11]

---

[11] The classic example of a political question case is *Luther v. Borden*, 7 How. 1 (1849) [discussed in the *Baker* opinions]:

During Dorr's rebellion, Rhode Island citizens who had been disenfranchised under the colonial charter tried to force the adoption of a more democratic state constitution. Soldiers of the charter government broke into plaintiff's home at a

(The dissenters have a more expansive view of this doctrine than the majority. Why do they feel so strongly about it?)

The dissenters feel pretty strongly about the need to maintain the Court's "complete detachment, in fact and in appearance, from political entanglements" is necessary to preserve its legitimacy.

(What do the dissenters mean by legitimacy?)

Public confidence necessary to maintain the Court's authority. (Remember Hamilton's distinction between judgment and will.)

I don't think Brennan is nearly as worried about legitimacy – he thinks the Court has a lot of it, and he's willing to spend it to get things done.

(One question is whether the political question doctrine is a function of separation of powers or federalism. What would the *federalism* argument for a political question doctrine look like?)

It would say that you can't interfere in the basic political structure of a state's government. That's basically Justice Frankfurter's position in dissent: "The Court has been particularly unwilling to intervene in matters concerning the structure and organization of the political institutions of the States."

(What does Justice Brennan think?)

Nonjusticiability is primarily a function of separation of powers. It's about the role of courts vis a vis the political branches of the government.

(Does Justice Brennan offer a hard and fast rule for identifying nonjusticiable political questions?)

No. A case-by-case inquiry is required. We can, however, identify important factors in finding a political question:

---

time when the rebels had proclaimed a new government. Plaintiff sued for trespass, which claim depended upon which government was the "real" one at the time.

The Court (Taney, CJ) holds the case nonjusticiable. "[It] rests with congress to decide what government is the established one in a State," and "its decision is binding on every other department of the government."

One could read the Guaranty Clause cases as referring these basic questions of state sovereignty to Congress, in which the States have a direct political voice. This resonates with the "political safeguards of federalism" argument that we'll discuss next week. In general, the Court has been extremely reluctant to try to enforce the Guaranty Clause.

1) "textually demonstrable constitutional commitment of the issue to a coordinate political department";

2) "lack of judicially discoverable and manageable standards for resolving it";

3) "the impossibility of deciding without an initial policy determination of a kind clearly for nonjudicial discretion";

4) "impossibility of a court's undertaking independent resolution without expressing lack of the respect due coordinate branches of government";

5) "unusual need for unquestioning adherence to a political decision already made"; or

6) "potentiality of embarrassment from multifarious pronouncements by various departments on one question."

Some examples:

- *Foreign relations*: Often no judicial standards; discretion committed to executive or legislature; necessary to speak with one voice. But not every foreign affairs case is nonjusticiable.

- *Validity of enactments*: Respect for coequal branches; need for finality.

You could divide the six criteria into three categories:

1. **The Textual Criterion:** Whether the issue is committed to another branch of government.

2. **Functional Criteria:** Lack of judicially manageable standards; necessity of an initial policy determination. These go to the institutional *capacity* of the courts to decide the case.

3. **Prudential Criteria:** Respect for coequal branches; need to adhere to a political decision already made; embarrassment from different branches reaching different conclusions. These go to the institutional *consequences* of an adjudication.

(What sort of criteria are most important to Justice Frankfurter, in dissent?)

I think it's a combination of the second two: For the dissenters, legitimacy requires that the Court needs to avoid becoming embroiled in political controversy (the prudential criteria) and that it should only decide cases where it can come up with principles that will seem *legal* rather than political in nature (the functional criteria).

(Let's take the pure prudential issue first. You can imagine a version of the doctrine that would turn simply on how controversial a decision will be. Do we have a doctrine like that?)

I don't think so. If that were true, the Court wouldn't have decided *Marbury, McCulloch, Dred Scott, Brown, Roe, Lawrence* – or most of the other cases we'll read in this course. "The doctrine of which we treat is one of 'political questions,' not one of 'political cases.'"

(But what about the functional criterion: Why are we so worried about whether there are "manageable standards"?)

Because if there aren't clear legal rules to apply, the Court looks like it's behaving just like any other political branch of government. If that's true, there's no reason for the public to support the Court's resolution of a particular political conflict than the resolution offered by Congress or a state legislature.

(Are there workable standards here?)

Well, it's hard to tell in advance. But one-man, one-vote turns out to be pretty workable.

(How easy is it to get one-man, one-vote out of the Constitution?)

Not completely easy, right?   After all, the U.S. Senate violates that principle. And in fact, in a subsequent case,[12] the Court actually does strike down Colorado's *state* senate, which is apportioned by county exactly the same way the U.S. Senate is apportioned by state. It's a bit awkward, yes?

On the other hand, one-man one-vote has the virtue of relative clarity – it's not that hard to apply. It's a little like *Miranda* – it's a relatively easy rule to live with, and so it hasn't been attacked.

(Does this suggest that it's less important how firmly a rule is grounded in the Constitution than how "law-like" it seems in operation?)

Yes, I think it does.

(How do Justice Brennan's other factors play out in this case?)

Here, the factors are not present. The question is consistency of state action with the equal protection clause of the federal constitution. No coequal branch has acted. There are no foreign affairs considerations.

(What's the best case for judicial intervention in this area?)

Ely: distorted political process, which is unlikely to fix itself since the incumbents have strong incentives to keep the districts the way they are.

---

[12] *Lucas v. Forty-Fourth General Assembly*, 377 U.S. 713 (1964).

2.   Is The Political Question Doctrine Consistent with *Marbury*?

Baker ends up *not* applying the doctrine, and in general the Court has been pretty leery of holding that there are constitutional questions that it can't answer. It's more willing to do so in the area of foreign affairs, although the Supreme Court itself hasn't weighed in on such a question since the 1970s. I want to ask, however, whether we should have this kind of doctrine *at all*:

Marbury says it is the Court's duty to "say what the law is." And in *Cohens v. Virginia*, Chief Justice Marshall made it even clearer that "[w]ith whatever doubts, with whatever difficulties, a case may be attended, we must decide it if it be brought before us." So it's not clear where the Court gets off not deciding these cases.

Two possible ways out of this problem:

a)   Textual exception to *Marbury*. If the Constitution really does commit something to another branch, then judicial review would not be required.

b)   Distinguish between "strong" and "weak" theories:

- **Strong:** A *strong theory* of the political question doctrine would say that even though there might be a constitutional violation, the Court is powerless to do anything about it because the question is committed to another branch.

- **Weak:** A *weak theory* would simply use "political question" as a way of explaining why there is no substantive violation, i.e., that the other branch has broad discretion to act in a particular area under the Constitution.

The weak version is completely consistent with *Marbury*, right? But note that on either view, there's not much room for "functional" or "prudential" criteria.

3.   *Nixon v. United States*, 506 U.S. 224 (1993)

This case is about the *other* Nixon, a former district court judge who was convicted of making false statements to a grand jury and subsequently impeached. He challenged the procedure by which the Senate "tried" him: he was permitted to make an appeal to the full Senate, but only a committee actually heard the evidence.

The Court says (Rehnquist, CJ), that the case is nonjusticiable.

(Which of Justice Brennan's factors is the Court relying on here?)

It's primarily the textual commitment argument.

(Can we draw a sharp line between this and the other factors?)

69

Not really. "[The] concept of a textual commitment to a coordinate political department is not completely separate from the concept of a lack of judicially discoverable and manageable standards for resolving it; the lack of judicially manageable standards may strengthen the conclusion that there is a textually demonstrable commitment to a coordinate branch."

(What does the relevant text say here?)

Here, Art. I, § 3, cl. 6 says that "[t]he Senate shall have the sole power to try all Impeachments." "Sole" indicates that the Senate has the final say on this.

The Framers understood "try" broadly -- it implies no particular procedure. And the Constitution does impose three specific requirements -- that the members are under oath, a 2/3 vote is required to convict, and the Chief Justice presides when the President is tried." These limitations suggest that they are the *only* requirements.

(Are there any functional arguments here?)

Judicial review here would be inconsistent with checks and balances. Impeachment is the *only* check by the legislature on the judicial branch; judicial review of impeachment would eviscerate this check.

The need for finality and difficulty of fashioning relief also counsel against justiciability.

I want to shift focus, for a minute, to Justice White's concurrence:

(What's a concurrence in the judgment?)

It means you agree with the result but not the rationale.

(Trivia question: What's Justice White's claim to uniqueness as a justice?)

He's the only Supreme Court Justice to hold the NCAA collegiate football rushing record, comin in second for the Heisman trophy, and lead the NFL in rushing (for the Detroit Lions).

(How would Justice White resolve the case?)

The case is justiciable, but there is no violation. Checks and balances requires that there be some judicial check on the freedom of the legislature in impeachment proceedings.

(How different is this, really, from the majority's position?)

This goes back to the strong/weak approach to the political question doctrine.

(What about Justice Souter: How does he differ from the majority?)

He thinks judicial review might be appropriate in extreme cases. If the Senate convicted "say, upon a coin-toss, or upon a summary determination that an officer of the United States was simply 'a bad guy,' judicial interference might well be appropriate" despite "the prudential concerns that would ordinarily counsel silence."

I want to finish by focusing on a broader issue, which is whether the political question doctrine goes to the nature of the government *function* being exercised—e.g., impeachment—or the nature of the *claim* made against it—here, a claim under the Impeachment Clause itself.

The way to test this is if we hold the function constant, but change the claim. Consider, for instance, the case of Judge Alcee Hastings, the first African-American federal district judge in Florida. Hastings was impeached about the same time as Judge Nixon, for similar corruption-related reasons. But he claimed that he was being pursued on account of his race. Imagine if *he* had challenged his impeachment, but done so on grounds of discriminatory prosecution under the Equal Protection Clause.

(Is that claim nonjusticiable?)

I'd be surprised if the Court didn't hear it. After all, we have judicially-manageable standards for discriminatory prosecution claims. And the Equal Protection Clause governs *all* government functions.

If that's right, what makes *Nixon* a political question is that the claim is brought under the Impeachment Clause itself, which doesn't provide such standards. So nonjusticiability inheres in the nature of the *claim*, not the *function* being challenged.

4.   Is There A Political Question Doctrine?

An influential article by Professor **Louis Henkin** questions whether there really is a "political question" doctrine at all.

Henkin says the cases all fall into one of three categories:

1)   **The Constitution commits the act at issue to the discretion of** Congress or the Executive, and that branch's decision is final. In these cases, there is no constitutional violation on the merits because the other branch has acted within its authority.

2)   The act at issue is reviewable by the Courts, but the Congress or Executive still has broad discretion and has not violated any limitation on that power in this case. Again, this is a decision on the merits.

I think we can safely group these first two situations. There's one more:

3)   The Court simply applies traditional limits on the equitable powers of courts. These limitations give the courts broad discretion to deny injunctive relief where there is no workable way to fashion a remedy, for example, or where there is no pressing need for

equitable relief. This is *not* a special exception to judicial review. For one thing, the court might still choose to issue a declaratory judgment that the challenged act violates the Constitution. For another, equitable factors are specific to the case; in different circumstances, the same constitutional claim might permit entry of an injunction.

So Prof. Henkin is really arguing for a *weak* version of the doctrine.

5.   What You Need to Know

- Federal courts sometimes declare cases nonjusticiable on the ground that they present "political questions."

- The six factors listed by Justice Brennan in *Baker v. Carr*, and the fact that the two most important are: textual commitment to another branch of government, and lack of manageable judicial standards for deciding the case.

- The political question doctrine is primarily a function of separation of powers, not federalism.

- The application of the political question doctrine is (a) very rare, and (b) highly dependent upon the circumstances of the case -- in particular on the institutional consequences of judicial review.

- In many -- if not all -- cases, application of the "political question" doctrine will either be (a) a finding that there is no constitutional violation on the merits, or (b) an exercise of the court's equitable discretion not to issue an injunction.

- The political-ness of a question turns on the nature of the plaintiff's *claim*, not on the government *function* that's being exercised. So you can't say categorically that impeachment cases are never justiciable, etc.

E.   Other Limits on Judicial Review

Each of the topics in the note at the conclusion of Chapter One could warrant extended discussion, but most of them—especially Congress's control over federal court jurisdiction and the right/remedy distinction—are better reserved for courses on Federal Courts. Still, I think it's helpful to at least introduce those concepts in the first year.

The notes at the end of this first Part of the readings briefly mention a few other limits on the power of judicial review. We won't go into any of them in any depth, but it's important to know they're out there so you can keep the extent of judicial power in perspective.

Four important limits:

1.   Congress's Control over Federal Court Jurisdiction

Courts are highly independent in how they resolve the cases that come before them, but Congress has a lot of power to restrict which cases those are. The power comes from two places:

- Article III specifically provides that Congress can make "exceptions" to the Supreme Court's jurisdiction; and

- Article I confers power on Congress to create lower federal courts, but Article III gives them the option of *not* doing so. From the fact that Congress doesn't have to create lower federal courts, the Court has inferred that Congress has the lesser included power of limiting the jurisdiction of those courts in various ways.

Congress doesn't exercise these "jurisdiction stripping" powers very often. There are perennial proposals to strip federal jurisdiction in areas where the federal courts are doing things that members of Congress don't like – e.g., abortion, school prayer – but they rarely pass. The Military Commissions Act and the Detainee Treatment Act are two recent examples, but even those statutes preserve a great deal of judicial review.

Also, don't forget that Congress exerts subsidiary control over budgets, staffing, etc., for the courts. This can be important. Consider, for instance, the leverage that Congress's authority to grant or withhold a pay raise gives the political branches over the courts.

2.   Rights vs. Remedies

Chief Justice Marshall said in *Marbury* that for every right, there's a remedy. But that's not always true. There are often limits on the remedies that courts can grant that constrain judicial power. These include:

- Rights to sue (e.g., sometimes there aren't any)

- Limits on injunctive relief: Sometimes these are a matter of the traditional standards for equitable relief, but sometimes they're imposed by Congress (e.g., the Prison Litigation Reform Act).

- Immunity provisions and doctrines: Especially for government defendants, establishing your legal rights is often just half the battle. Both government entities and the officers that serve them enjoy significant immunities and defenses in suits by private individuals.

Both jurisdiction stripping and the limitations on remedies for constitutional rights claims are important topics in the course on Federal Courts (which you should take, of course).

3.   Constitutional Amendment

Obviously you *can* overrule the Court's interpretation of the Constitution if you can change the Constitution itself.   But passing a constitutional amendment is *really* hard – especially if it's about anything remotely controversial.

Only four constitutional amendments have overturned Supreme Court rulings:

- XI (1789) overturned *Chisholm v. Georgia's* holding that states may be sued by private individuals in federal court.

- XIV (1868) overturned *Dred Scott's* holding that African Americans may not be citizens.

- XVI (1913) circumvented *Pollock v. Farmers' Loan & Trust's* holding barring a federal income tax.

- XXVI (1971) reversed *Oregon v. Mitchell's* refusal to require the states to let 18-yr-olds vote.

Some good stats on this:

- Over 11,000 proposed amendments have been introduced in Congress, but

- Only 33 have been approved by 2/3 of both houses and submitted to the States, and

- Only 27 have actually been ratified by the States, of which just about half came either in the initial Bill of Rights or during Reconstruction.

If you look at the recent amendments, you'll see their mostly government housekeeping stuff – presidential succession and the like.   That doesn't bode well for recent proposals on flag burning and gay marriage.

One interesting comparison is to the state constitutions, which have been amended nearly 6000 times.   The TX constitution alone has over 300 amendments.

(Is the federal constitution too hard to amend?)

One reason we haven't had more amendments is that the Supreme Court has exercised pretty wide latitude to interpret the document flexibly and keep it "in tune with the times."

(Is that a good thing or a bad thing? Would it be better to require explicit amendments on things like abortion, school desegregation, or the scope of Congress's power to regulate the economy?)

The other point to note here is that the difficulty of changing a supreme court decision through amendment affects the doctrine of *stare decisis*. When the Supreme Court interprets a statute, that ruling has nearly absolute precedential effect; the reason is that, if it turns out to be wrong, *Congress* has the power to change the statute and fix the mistake. But when the Supreme Court interprets the *Constitution*, there are only two ways to fix it. One is constitutional amendment, but that's almost impossible. So the Court has to be a little more willing to fix its own mistakes in constitutional interpretation by overruling its precedents.

4.   The Power of Judicial Appointments

The average tenure for Justices is about 15 years, with a new Justice being appointed to the Court about every 22 months. That means most presidents will get two appointments per term. This keeps the Supreme Court from getting too out of touch with political trends in society generally.

PART TWO – A HISTORY OF JUDICIAL REVIEW

The introduction that follows explains the historical focus—I think it helps to make this pitch explicitly, since students may be uncomfortable with an approach that does not focus on the black letter law. I do find it important to highlight, throughout this unit, which principles remain good law today and which do not. This can also lead to a discussion of the influence of opinions that are not good law—either dissents that pave the way for future majority opinions, or later-rejected opinions (e.g., Dred Scott*) that serve as cautionary tales or "counter-precedents."*

Today we dive into the second part of the course, which will take up almost half the semester. That unit is a History of Judicial Review. We already started the story with *Marbury*, in which the Court seizes the power of judicial review; now we basically explore what the Court's used that power for over the last two centuries. We'll finish the course with an intensive unit on constitutional structure.

It may help to begin by identifying four distinct Eras of Supreme Court History:

- Founding to the Civil War: Central preoccupation with allocation of authority between the States and the Nation.

- Reconstruction through the "New Deal Revolution": Central preoccupation with governmental authority to regulate the economy.

- Post-New Deal Court through Burger Court: Central preoccupation with enforcement of non-economic individual rights.

- Rehnquist-Roberts Courts: ???? It's too early to tell. Conventional wisdom suggests that the Rehnquist Court will be known for reviving constitutional limits on national power vis-à-vis the States; I'm more partial to broadening that conception to a renewal of interest in constitutional structure generally, which would include separation of powers as well as the electoral process.

It's fair to ask why the first part of the course is organized in a historical way. Two reasons:

- Constitutional literacy: This historical survey is a good way to work in some real basics, like *Brown v. Board of Education* and *Roe v. Wade*. You shouldn't be released into the wild at the end of three years without knowing these cases.

- History influences doctrine: You simply can't explain why the doctrinal debates in the second part of the course – about federalism and separation of powers – come out the way they do unless you have an appreciation of the Court's earlier struggles, even in areas that seem far afield substantively. For instance, the Court's modern federalism doctrine is pervasively influenced by the Court's bad experience with the Due Process Clause in the period leading up to the New Deal.

I.   **Chapter Three – The Marshall Court and the Federal Balance**

These cases introduce the basic issues of federalism—both the scope of Congress's affirmative regulatory power and the "dormant" preemptive effect of that power on the States. I want students to understand both the Marshall Court's broad doctrinal construction of the Commerce and Necessary and Proper Clauses and that Court's more general institutional role as an engine of nationalization in the early Republic.

McCulloch *is important not just for its own sake but also as our first illustration of a doctrinal "test"—and, indeed, a paradigm case of the standard two-part analysis of (1) the nature and strength of the government's objective and (2) the "fit" between that end and the means chosen to pursue it. It is well to give students practice applying this sort of analysis, as it will be pervasive in the individual rights cases throughout the course.*

Finally, Willson *illustrates both the doctrinal limits of the Dormant Commerce Clause and the more general problem of drawing a bright line between state and federal authority. This allows me to introduce Larry Lessig's notion of the "Frankfurter Constraint"—that is, that the Court needs doctrine to be sufficiently determinate to look like law rather than policy (or, in Hamilton's terms, "judgment" rather than "will"). This is an issue that will crop up with respect to virtually every doctrinal construction in the course.*

Our first era covers the Marshall and Taney Courts – basically from 1800 until the Civil War. During that period, the Court's central preoccupation is with defining the relationship between the national government and the states. This is the question of federalism.

Remember that the central difference between the Articles of Confederation— that is, the *first* "constitution" of the U.S. written after independence—and the new Constitution drafted at Philadelphia in 1787 was to strengthen the central government significantly. The Articles of Confederation created a very weak central authority with several crucial characteristics:

- No centralized President or administrative apparatus;

- No power to raise its own revenues;

- No power to act directly on private actors—instead, the national government had to depend on the States for law enforcement; and

- Quite limited enumerated powers.

All the Framers of the new Constitution—including many Antifederalists— agreed that the new central government had to be stronger and more independent of the states. But they disagreed about *how much*.

This basic question of the allocation of power between the nation and the states remains with us. It was the subject, for example, of the Supreme Court's decision on medical marijuana just a few years ago, and it's at the heart of current debates over the Obama healthcare law. We'll spend a great deal of time on current doctrine in the second part of the course. But for now, we need to consider the Marshall Court's early cases on the subject.

Here's one crucial fact to keep in mind. The new Constitution of 1789 doesn't have to create the *state* governments; they're already up and running, with lots of employees, lots of money, and lots of people who feel their primary loyalty to Virginia or Massachusetts or New Hampshire. The national government, by contrast, is brand new and untested. You can understand the Marshall Court's jurisprudence as centrally concerned with carving out a place in the world for this new government. And *McCulloch v. Maryland* is the key case on that subject.

A.   *McCulloch v. Maryland*, 17 U.S. (4 Wheat.) 316 (1819)

McCulloch involves the constitutionality of the Second Bank of the United States. The First Bank's charter had expired in 1811, and Congress chartered the Second in 1816. Both banks are part of an effort by the federal government to facilitate the development of a national financial infrastructure that could regulate the currency and help fund the development of the new nation. Remember that the constitutionality of the Bank had been a basic question dividing the Hamilton's Federalists from Jefferson's Republicans, beginning with dueling memos that the two men wrote for President Washington. (This is an important example of constitutional interpretation outside the judiciary.)

Once the Second Bank is chartered, it establishes branches in many different states. One branch is in Baltimore, MD, where the legislature starts to worry about competition between the national Bank and the banks that the state government has chartered itself.

(What does the state legislature do?)

They impose a tax on any bank not chartered by the State.

(Who's McCulloch?)

He's the cashier of the Baltimore branch of the bank.

(Why is his name on the case?)

Because the state has sued him, as the cashier, for payment of a statutory penalty for failure to pay the tax.

The Court holds (Marshall, CJ) that the Bank is constitutional, and Maryland's attempt to tax it is invalid.

Marshall divides the opinion into two questions:

1) Has Congress power to incorporate a bank?

2) Whether Maryland can tax a branch of that bank?

Both these questions are pretty important.

1.   Congress's Power to Incorporate a Bank

(Marshall observes pretty early on in the opinion that "[t]his government is acknowledged by all to be one of enumerated powers." What does he mean by that?)

He means that the federal government has only those powers that the Constitution affirmatively gives to it.

(Are the *states* governments of enumerated powers?)

No – except that maybe yes. As far as the federal Constitution is concerned, they are not. The states have all the powers that are left over after the Constitution delegates some powers are delegated to the federal government.

The "maybe yes" stems from the fact that the people of each state are still free to choose whether they want their governments to be ones of general powers or enumerated powers. But this is a question of *state* constitutional law. It depends on what the state constitution says.

(What part of the Constitution makes these relationships clear?)

The 10th Amendment, which provides that "[t]he powers not delegated to the United States by the Constitution, nor prohibited by it to the States, are reserved to the States respectively, or to the people."

(Does the Constitution expressly delegate to Congress the power to create a bank?)

No.

(So what's the question in this case? Why isn't it just obvious that this is a power reserved to the States?)

We still have to ask whether this is an *implied* power.

(Is the notion of implied powers consistent with that of enumerated powers?)

Marshall says it is.

(What kind of sources does he rely on?)

He has a textual argument and a practical or structural argument.

(What's the textual argument?)

The 10th Amendment omits the word "expressly" in describing the Union's enumerated powers. The prior Articles of Confederation *had* provided that each state "retains" every power not "expressly delegated" – therefore shutting off any talk of implied powers. So Marshall interprets the omission of the same wording from the 10th Amendment as an effort to expand federal power.

(What about the practical argument?)

Marshall says it would be impossible to enumerate all a government's powers in the text. "A constitution, to contain an accurate detail of all the subdivisions of which its great powers will admit, and of all the means by which they may be carried into execution, would partake of the prolixity of a legal code, and could scarcely be embraced by the human mind. It would probably never be understood by the public. . . . In considering this question, then, we must never forget, that it is *a constitution* we are expounding."

This last bit may be the most frequently quoted phrase in constitutional law.

(Why *not* make the document bigger and more detailed?)

Consider, for example, the proposed constitutional treaty for the European Union, which ran to over 300 pages. Sure, it's a doorstopper and maybe less people would read it. But would that be worth the cost if it could more determinately answer important questions?

(Does Marshall think that *any* power can be implied?)

No – He's arguing for a somewhat narrower proposition: that when the Constitution specifies a particular *end*, we should be able to imply the *means* by which this end is to be accomplished.

(What are the enumerated ends for which a bank might serve as a means?)

Marshall says a bank is useful for all kinds of stuff: "Throughout this vast republic, from the St. Croix to the Gulf of mexico, from the Atlantic to the pacific, revenue is to be collected and expended, armies are to be marched and supported."

Basically, Marshall is saying, it's a busy country, and everything costs money, so a bank is really useful for raising, borrowing, and distributing the funds we need to do everything else that government is supposed to do. (This is the Richard Scarry passage of *McCulloch* – it's a busy, busy country . . . .)

(Marshall has another textual ace up his sleeve: What other constitutional provision does he rely on?)

The Necessary and Proper Clause, which gives Congress the power to make "all laws which shall be necessary and proper for carrying into execution the foregoing powers, and all other powers vested by this constitution, in the government of the United States, or in any department thereof."

The problem, obviously, is how to allow for implied powers without making the idea of enumeration meaningless. How do you tell what's in and what's out?

(What rule is Maryland arguing for?)

That necessary means "essential" or "absolutely necessary."

(How does Marshall answer that argument?)

He has several answers:

- "Necessary" need not mean "essential" -- it can also mean "convenient." We have to figure out what the Framers meant.

- The Framers couldn't have meant to dramatically restrict Congress's freedom of action. "This provision is made in a constitution intended to endure for ages to come, and, consequently, to be adapted to the various *crises* of human affairs."

- We have accepted non-essential means in other areas: For instance, the power to punish those who steal letters from the post office is hardly "essential" to establishing post offices and post roads.

- There would be no need to add the restriction "proper" if "necessary" meant "essential."

- The clause is placed among the powers of Congress, not among the limitations, and its terms purport to *enlarge* those powers.

(What's Marshall's test, instead of "essential"?)

Marshall's test: "Let the end be legitimate, let it be within the scope of the constitution, and all means which are appropriate, which are plainly adapted to that end, which are not prohibited, but consist with the letter and spirit of the constitution, are constitutional."

This test really has three key elements:

(1) Is the *end* within the enumerated scope of the Constitution?

(2) Is there some minimal degree of fit between the *means* and the *end* – that is, is this means "appropriate" to the end?

(3) Is there no other part of the Constitution that *prohibits* what Congress is trying to do?

The first two elements here have become a template for doctrinal tests that occur across a wide spectrum of constitutional law. Those tests—which are called things like "strict scrutiny" or "rational basis" review—tend to combine these same elements but apply them with differing degrees of rigor. We tend to always look at (1) what is the government's interest that's being advanced, and (2) how well do the means that the government has selected fit that interest.

To see how the "fit" part might operate in another case, consider one of the ends that the Court relies on in *McCulloch*, which is to "coin money and regulate the value thereof" – that is, to establish a national currency.

(Suppose that instead of just establishing a national bank, the Government bans possession of foreign currency by private citizens?)

That would be a tougher case for "fit," right? It's excessive and disproportionately draconian. We can think of a lot of less burdensome means to achieve the same objectives. So "fit" tests are not just about whether the means adopted will further the selected end, but also whether those means are disproportionate to the end. But again, *McCulloch's* version is not a very strict test.

(Can someone give me an example of something that would be OK under the first two elements but unconstitutional under the third?)

Suppose Congress wants to regulate interstate commerce in newspapers. It passes a law bars the use of the public mails to distribute newspapers. This would probably pass (1) and (2) but violate the freedom of the press guaranteed by the First Amendment.

2.   Maryland's Power to Tax the Bank

OK, so Congress has power to create the Bank in the first place. But we're only halfway home. We still have to figure out why Maryland can't *tax* the Bank.

(Does the Constitution preempt the States' taxing powers altogether?)

Marshall says no -- they retain a concurrent taxing power. This is a very important idea because it introduces a fundamental distinction between *concurrent* and *exclusive* powers:

- *Exclusive* powers means that some substantive areas within the power of one level of government are off limits to the other. For instance, you'll see arguments that foreign affairs is the *exclusive* province of the federal government, or that family law is the exclusive province of the States.

- *Concurrent* powers means that either level of government can regulate something, and both state and federal regulation are valid as long as there's no conflict. If there *is* a conflict, then federal law prevails under the Supremacy Clause. So, for instance, both federal and state governments regulate pollution. But if federal law says you can't use dioxin or some other chemical in manufacturing, state law can't come in and say it's OK.

One of my basic views that I'll stress throughout the course is that there really aren't any areas of *exclusive* federal or state authority anymore, and that everything is pretty much concurrent.

(So if both the federal and state governments have concurrent taxing authority, what's wrong with Maryland's tax?)

Marshall says it interferes with the federal effort to establish the Bank. Federal supremacy preempts all obstacles to the operation of federal law. Here, "the power to tax involves the power to destroy."

(Would *any* tax destroy the bank?)

Of course not. Marshall is worried about malicious and excessive taxation.

(Is that a realistic worry here?)

Maybe – Maryland's tax may be designed to put the Bank out of business in Baltimore. Although some historians suggest that there was less hostility to the Bank in MD than elsewhere at the time.

(What's Marshall's more general argument for why we can't just *trust* the States not to destroy federal programs like the Bank?)

Marshall says that we can't trust the States because the rest of us aren't represented there -- a government of the part oughtn't to have the power to mess up things created for the good of the whole.

This is an important flavor of argument that you'll see a lot of later on in the course. The gist of it is that judicial intervention is more appropriate when we can't trust the political process to sort things out for itself. Here, we worry that politics at the *state* level won't appropriately take into account *national* concerns. So the Court intervenes to protect those interests.

Think about *Baker v. Carr* in the last unit: There, we can't trust the political process in TN to fix itself, because mal-apportionment of legislative seats means that the legislature has a strong interest in *not* fixing the problem. So a court intervenes on behalf of the unrepresented persons in the big cities.

Now, *McCulloch's* basic holding that the state can't regulate federal entities has to be qualified somewhat for the modern world. I asked you in the Notes to think about four situations that might raise similar issues:

- A federal officer employed by the Social Security Administration, busted for speeding on his way to work;
- A teacher employed in a federal worker-training program, who's subject to a state income tax;

- A nationally-chartered bank that wants to open a branch in a residential neighborhood but is precluded from doing so by local zoning rules; and
- A marine recruiter barred from recruiting at a state university because the university opposes the military's position on homosexuality.

(How does *McCulloch* bear on these situations?)

I think the first two are clearly constitutional. When I was a federal employee working at the appeals court in Boston, for instance, I had to pay state income taxes to Massachusetts. And when I drove to work, I had to abide by the state speed limit. So notwithstanding the "power to tax is the power to destroy" language in *McCulloch*, it's not true that states can't tax federal officials.

The third is arguably harder because state regulation falls on the federal entity itself, not just on individuals that work for the entity. But I think it's still OK. It's important that the state law falls on federal and non-federal entities alike; the state hasn't singled the feds out for unfavorable treatment.

The fourth instance, though, is probably barred under *McCulloch*. For one thing, the state is restricting a federal entity based on a disagreement with national policy. (It's probably true, though, that the university is treating private employers who discriminate the same way.) It also doesn't help that there's a strong national security argument here.

In any event, the extent to which states can and can't regulate federal entities turns out to be a complicated question. But the basic point is that state governments can't regulate federal things in a way that thwarts important federal interests, and that's a function of the supremacy of federal law.

B.   The Commerce Clause

The first issue in *McCulloch* concerned the scope of Congress's *enumerated powers*, and that issue has continued to be important ever since. The most important of these powers is the power "[t]o regulate Commerce with foreign Nations, and among the several States, and with the Indian Tribes." Art. I, § 8.

That power has two aspects that we might call *affirmative* and *negative* or "dormant."

- The affirmative commerce clause is simply the scope of Congress's own authority to pass laws regulating interstate commerce.

- The negative or dormant commerce clause is a judicial doctrine concerning the extent to which *states* can regulate interstate commerce, at least in areas where Congress hasn't acted yet. (That's why we call it *dormant*.)

There's also a third issue lurking here, which is the preemptive effect of laws that Congress *does* pass on state regulation dealing with the same subject matter. It's clear that federal law prevails over state law under the Supremacy Clause, but it's not always clear to what *extent* a federal law ousts state regulation.

The Founders plainly viewed this national power over commerce as crucial to building a unified nation and a healthy economy. Madison said that, under the Articles of Confederation, "want of a general power over Commerce led to an exercise of this power separately, by the States, which not only proved abortive, but engendered rival, conflicting and angry regulations."

So the Commerce Clause is usually viewed as an attempt to promote two kinds of unity:

- Economic Unity: The Framers aimed to achieve economic prosperity by creating a national market free of internal trade barriers.

- Political Unity: The Framers also thought that economic barriers went hand in hand with political barriers, and that interstate trade wars would lead inevitably to political conflict that might threaten the Union.

The rationale here is very similar to the thinking behind the contemporary European Union. Forget about the Greek debt crisis: the success of the EU over the past fifty years can be evaluated by asking one question: "Has Germany invaded France?" The point was to integrate everyone's economy so much that no one could afford to go to war anymore. And it's worked beautifully. The Commerce Clause had a similar purpose: create a single national market in order to ensure peace and prosperity.

C. *Gibbons v. Ogden*, 9 Wheat. (22 U.S.) 1 (1824)

New York granted a monopoly to Robert Livingston and Robert Fulton – who pioneered the steamboat – to operate steam boats on waters within the State. Fulton & Livingston in turn licensed Ogden to operate a ferry between NYC and Elizabethtown, NJ.

At the same time, Gibbons acquired a *federal* license to operate steamboats and began competing with Ogden. Ogden sued for violation of his monopoly.

The Court (Marshall, CJ), held that Ogden's state-granted monopoly is invalid.

Gibbons is a useful case for us because you see the seeds of all three of the different kinds of federalism cases I just mentioned:

- Affirmative Commerce Clause: Is regulating steam boats within the affirmative power of Congress under Article I?

- Dormant Commerce Clause cases: If regulating steam boats is within *federal* commerce power, does that mean the states are *excluded* from regulating it?

- Preemption cases: Where Congress *has* acted – here, to grant a license to Gibbons – does that affirmative act exclude the states' concurrent regulatory power?

We'll spend a good bit of time on each of these in our unit on federalism.

1.   The Affirmative Commerce Clause Question

Chief Justice Marshall starts with the first question: Is this case within Congress's affirmative regulatory power?

(What does Marshall think "commerce" means?)

It's not just buying and selling – it's "intercourse," including navigation.

(So would it matter if Gibbons offered steam boat rides for free?)

Probably not – it's the back-and-forthing that counts.

(What about the phrase "commerce among the several states"? What does that mean? Does it include commerce within the borders of a state?)

It can – after all, it's hard to find a place to stand (or float) in this country that's not within the border of some state. "Among" means "intermingled with," so it includes commerce within state borders.

(Does that mean Congress can regulate *all* commerce? Is there any limit?)

Marshall says Art. I covers only "commerce which concerns more states than one."

(Why stop there? Isn't there a sense in which *all* commerce concerns "more states than one"? We often talk about how integrated the economy is nowadays, but don't you think that even in the early 19th century, the price of wheat in Pennsylvania affected the price of bread in New York City?)

The problem is that if we go too far down that road, Congress's power would be unlimited. "The enumeration presupposes something not enumerated; and that something . . . must be the exclusively internal commerce of a state."

So notice one important point: Constitutional law is often an exercise in line-drawing. And Marshall knows that for a particular line to be persuasive, it has to have meaningful cases on *both* sides of the line. So he defines commerce pretty broadly here, but he's careful to point out that some things are excluded – there *is* some limit on federal power.

By contrast, if you have a definition that doesn't leave anything on the other side of the line, that's a big problem with your definition – it proves too much.

This becomes a terribly important point in the modern federalism cases, where the proponents of broad national power frequently argue for definitions of Congress's powers that fail to exclude anything. That's why they keep losing the cases in the Supreme Court.

(Is this doctrinal line-drawing the *only* limit on Congress's power?)

No – Marshall acknowledged that within the scope he's set out, Congress's power is still pretty broad. But he says there's still a safeguard based on "political safeguards" for state autonomy. "The wisdom and the discretion of congress, their identity with the people, and the influence which their constituents possess at elections, are, in this, as in many other instances, . . . the sole restraints on which [the Framers] have relied, to secure them from [Congress's] abuse [of the commerce power]."

(What does he mean by that?)

Primarily that the states are represented in Congress, and they can vote down laws that intrude too much on their prerogatives – without requiring a court to draw further lines. These power allocation problems generally get hashed out *politically*. This becomes a terribly important argument in the modern era.

2.   State Authority to Regulate

The rest of the case is about the *dormant* commerce clause argument and the preemption argument.

(Is there any challenge to *federal* regulation in this case? That is, is anyone saying that Gibbons's federal steamboat license is unconstitutional?)

No.

(Then what was all that stuff we just went through for? Why did we have to determine the scope of Congress's own power?)

Because Gibbons wants to say that Congress's power is *exclusive* – that is, that if steamboat navigation is within Congress's commerce power, then the states *can't* regulate it. (Remember the distinction between exclusive and concurrent powers that we mentioned toward the end of *McCulloch*.)

(Does the Court accept this argument?)

Marshall's very tempted by it. He says, "[t]here is great force in this argument, and the court is not satisfied that it has been refuted." But the Court doesn't finally resolve that question.

(Can you think of a reason *not* to accept the notion that the federal commerce power is exclusive?)

Well, it would wipe out a bunch of state regulation. Suppose, for instance, that New York doesn't want to bar Gibbons from operating his boat, but instead simply wants to impose a speed limit in New York waters.

(Should New York be able to do that?)

Surely yes.

(*Can* New York do that, if federal power is exclusive?)

Maybe they can – but only if you say that they're not *really* regulating commerce but instead using their "police powers" – that is, their general regulatory authority over public safety, health, and morals. That is in fact the line the Court ends up drawing, but it's not very illuminating.

(In any event, how does the Court resolve the case?)

It holds that New York's monopoly grant to Ogden has to yield before the *federal* grant of a license to Gibbons. They're not saying New York can't regulate – or even that they can't grant their own licenses – but simply that any *restriction* on licenses is preempted by the force of supreme federal law.

(What's the textual warrant for that?)

The Supremacy Clause. We'll come back to this notion of federal *preemption* later in the course. But for now it's important simply to understand the difference between the "dormant" exclusionary force of the Commerce Clause itself and the affirmative force of an actual federal law enacted by Congress.

D. *Willson v. Black Bird Creek Marsh Co.*, 27 U.S. (2 Pet.) 245 (1829)

The Supreme Court ultimately *does* adopt the notion proposed in *Gibbons* that national power to regulate interstate commerce is exclusive of the states. *Willson* is a good case for showing the *limits* on that principle. Here, the State of DE has authorized the Marsh Co. to build a dam on Black Bird Creek. Willson argues that the dam obstructs interstate commerce by cutting off a navigable stream.

The Court (Marshall, CJ) holds for the Marsh Co.

(Why did DE authorize the Marsh Co. to build the dam? Is it trying to regulate interstate travel and commerce?)

No – It's trying to drain the swamp, to improve the health of the residents and their property values.

(So what is the State allowed to regulate? And what is prohibited?)

The Court tries to distinguish between regulation of interstate commerce itself, which is barred, and "police" regulations designed to enhance public health, safety, and welfare. It's much the same as Marshall's discussion of quarantine regulations and similar measures in *Gibbons*.

E.   **The Rest of the 19th Century**

For most of the 19th century, the commerce clause cases that come to the Court are cases like *Gibbons* and *Willson* - not about the scope of *Congress*'s power, but rather about the scope of *state* power to regulate interstate commerce. The reason for this is primarily that Congress didn't do much in the way of national economic regulation during this century.

This begins to change toward the end of the century, especially with the passage of the Interstate Commerce Act of 1887 and the Sherman Anti-Trust Act of 1890. For now, though, I'd like you to have some sense of the evolution of this doctrine of *dormant* exclusionary force under the Commerce Clause. The main reason is that is shows how the Court will often come up with a test, then, when it becomes hard to apply, try a new test, and so forth.

Three doctrinal frameworks prior to 1937:

1.   "Commerce" vs. "Police" Regulation: The Marshall Court suggested that Congress's power over "commerce" regulation might be exclusive, *see Gibbons v. Ogden*, 9 Wheat. (22 U.S.) 1 (1824), but that the States retained authority to engage in "police" regulation, *see Willson v. Black Bird Creek Marsh Co.*, 2 Pet. (27 U.S.) 245 (1829).

2.   "Local" vs. "National": The Taney Court holds that federal and state powers are concurrent with respect to "local" issues, but federal power is exclusive over "[w]hatever subjects of this power are in their nature national, or admit only of one uniform system [may] justly be said to be of such a nature as to require exclusive legislation by Congress." *Cooley v. Board of Wardens*, 12 How. (53 U.S.) 299 (1851).

3.   Direct vs. Indirect: Between the late 19th century and the New Deal, the Court applied a direct/indirect distinction to adjudicate *both* the questions in *Gibbons*: the scope of Congress's own power, and the scope of the field from which the states are excluded. This didn't work out so great because it was really hard to apply in a principled way, and it all breaks down during the New Deal.

These trends are important in their own right, but they're also important in that they show the Court grappling with a basic problem in the formation of judicial doctrine. That is the problem of **indeterminacy**.

Can you formulate a rule in such a way that it produces predictable results?

(Why is this so important?)

Because it distinguishes judicial from political decisionmaking. That's what Larry Lessig means in the Notes when he talks about the "Frankfurter Constraint." When he was still a law professor, Justice Frankfurter wrote a book about the Commerce Clause in the 19th century, and his basic argument was that the Court had a hard time drawing a determinate line between national and state concerns, and that this indeterminacy made the doctrine ultimately untenable.

Remember the Court's basic need to maintain—and to be *seen* to maintain—the distinction between law and politics. This is done primarily through trying to keep the doctrine as *determinate* and predictable as possible. Each of these doctrinal solutions – commerce vs. police, national vs. local, direct vs. indirect – comes to seem fuzzy and indeterminate as it's applied to particular cases, and in each case the Court ultimately abandons the doctrine. You'll see this in action when we get to the *Lochner* period in a week or so.

II.   Chapter Four – Slavery, Civil War, and Reconstruction

A.   The Taney Court and Slavery

This section has several objectives, many of which will challenge students' preconceptions about the Supreme Court and constitutional law. It explores the relationship between the Constitution and morality by focusing on the original sin of American constitutionalism and asking (1) whether a moral person could sign the original constitution and (2) whether a moral judge could enforce it in a case like Prigg. *We also explore the relationship between slavery and federalism by complicating the conventional wisdom that "states' rights" were always on the side of slavery. In* Prigg, *Congress had become an instrument of the "slave power," and in* Dred Scott, *individual states' broader conception of citizenship were stamped out in favor of a narrow national definition. Methodologically,* Dred Scott *introduces both originalism as a method of constitutional interpretation and the notion of unenumerated constitutional rights (e.g., the substantive due process principle that strikes down the Missouri Compromise). Finally,* Dred Scott *illustrates why the Supreme Court was not considered a primary protector of individual liberties until fairly late in our history—a point which may cause students to question judicial review itself.*

A lot of constitutional law casebooks leave out slavery; I think this is a lot like teaching German history without the Holocaust. As always, though, there are multiple dimensions along which you need to think about these cases:

- Moral – These cases raise most directly the possible conflict between law and morality. Professor Levinson's essay raises the basic question whether, in light of the Constitution's commitment to slavery, it's moral to *sign* the constitution.

- Structural – These are not only cases about slavery, but also cases about federalism. Who decides how to handle escaped slaves? Who decides who can be a citizen? The Nation or the States? People associate a pro-states position with pro-slavery, but cases like *Prigg* show that the issue is considerably more complicated.

- Methodological – *Dred Scott* in particular raises two methodological questions:

1) to what extent should courts be bound by the Framers' intentions, and

2) to what extent should courts be free to infer unenumerated individual rights from the Constitution?

1.   Slavery in the Constitution

Slavery is pretty explicitly recognized several places in the Constitution:

- **The "Slave Trade" Clause,** Art. I, § 9, cl.1: "The Migration or Importation of such Persons as any of the States now existing shall think proper to admit, shall not be prohibited by the Congress prior to the Year one thousand eight hundred and eight, but a Tax or duty may be imposed on such Importation, not exceeding ten dollars for each Person."

- **The Fugitive Slave Clause**, IV, § 2, cl. 3: "No Person held to Service or Labour in one State, under the Laws thereof, escaping into another, shall, in Consequence of any Law or Regulation therein, be discharged from such Service or Labour, but shall be delivered up on Claim of the Party to whom such Service or Labour may be due."

- **The "Three-Fifths" Clause**, Art. I, § 2, cl. 3: "Representatives and direct Taxes shall be apportioned among the several States . . . according to their respective Numbers, which shall be determined by adding to the whole Number of free Persons, including those bound to Service for a Term of Years, and excluding Indians not taxed, three fifths of all other Persons."

(Here's a good question to get you thinking about the political dynamics of slavery and the legislative structure. Would black slaves prior to 1860 have been better off if the last of these clauses had counted slaves as whole people, or not at all?)

Not at all, right? The point of counting them – even at a 3/5 discount – is to magnify the power of the Southern states in Congress. It effectively gives the South credit for voters that they're not, in fact, allowing to vote. The travesty isn't really that black people are being counted as 3/5 of a human being, but that they're being counted at all in this provision.

2.   *Prigg v. Pennsylvania*, 41 U.S. 539 (1842)

Prigg's an awful story about Margaret Morgan, a slave in Maryland who was allowed by her master to live in virtual freedom, to get married, and eventually to move to Pennsylvania with her husband and children. Years later, the good master dies, and the heirs send slave catchers to PA to kidnap Margaret.

No one knows for sure what happened to Margaret and her children – they were never recovered – but PA tried to prosecute the slave catchers under its personal liberty law.

The case raises three separate issues of federalism:

- Is federal power to regulate fugitive slaves and the process of their apprehension exclusive?

- If not, is PA's statute providing procedural safeguards for alleged fugitive slaves preempted by the federal fugitive slave law?

- Can PA state officials be required to participate in the enforcement of the federal statute?

a.   The Fugitive Slave Clause

These questions arise under the Fugitive Slave Clause, Art. IV, § 2, cl. 3, which I've reprinted in the handout.

"No Person held to Service or Labour in one State, under the Laws thereof, escaping into another, shall, in Consequence of any Law or Regulation therein, be discharged from such Service or Labour, but shall be delivered up on Claim of the Party to whom such Service or Labour may be due."

(Why is this Clause in the Constitution?)

Because the Southern states are worried about their slaves escaping to the Northern states, and that the Northern states – disagreeing about the morality of slavery – won't give them up.

This is what the economic literature on federalism calls an *externality*. By that we mean that a particular policy in one state – say, PA offering a sanctuary to escaped slaves – may undermine a policy adopted by another state, such as MD's allowance of slavery.

The classic example is that Ohio's failure to regulate really tall smokestacks means that pollutants are discharged into the upper atmosphere and come down as acid rain in New Hampshire – so NH's policy of trying to protect the environment is undermined by OH's more lax policy.

(What's the best way to correct for an externality like that?)

We regulate at the *national* level, so that both the state that is the *cause* and the state that feels the *effect* are brought under the same authority.

That's what the Fugitive Slave Law does, right? Uniform regulation at the national level minimizes the externalities created by PA's liberty law. One nice thing about *Prigg*, though, is it shows that sometimes externalities are *good*.

(Here's another question: Is there any express grant of authority for Congress to *legislate* here?)

No. It just says that fugitives "shall be delivered up."

(Whom does the Clause seem to be addressing?)

Whomever has the fugitive, right? You might even imagine that the slaveowner would have a right to *sue* a state government or private person who had access to a fugitive but failed to turn them in. It wouldn't be crazy to say that the Clause could operate without federal legislation.

(So how does Justice Story find that there *is* federal legislative power?)

He makes the same kind of "necessary and proper," end implies the means argument that you saw in *McCulloch*. Hopefully you can see why a 19th century civil libertarian might *worry* about *McCulloch*: The Feds won't always use this broad implied power to do nice things.

(But this is just a predicate to the first question I identified: Once we find Congress has power, is that power exclusive?)

Story says it is – that the right wouldn't be meaningful if it were subject to a different regime of regulation in every state.

The dissenters all disagree with this holding. Three justices say Congress's power is not exclusive, because a State could always pass laws that were *helpful* to slave hunters. For them, the federal law is a floor, but states are free to go above and beyond.

(What does Justice McClean say?)

He says that federal law requires delivering up *slaves*, but a state should be able to regulate how we figure out who's really an escaped slave and who's not.

(Would *any* such procedural statute be OK? For instance, supposed they required proof beyond a reasonable doubt and 5-years' worth of state judicial scrutiny before handing a fugitive over. Would that be OK?)

That would probably eliminate the right to recover the fugitive, as a practical matter. The difficult question is what sort of state laws might go too far and thwart vindication of slaveowners' rights. The point, though, is that if Congress's power isn't exclusive then we have to analyze the case as a matter of *preemption* – the second question I identified.

Note how similar this structure of analysis is to *Gibbons*: There, once the Court found the case within the Commerce Power, it then had to ask whether the Commerce Power was exclusive. Once the Court declined to decide that Congress's power was exclusive, it then had to ask whether what Congress had actually done – licensing the ferry to Gibbons – preempted the state law in question.

b.   The Commandeering Question

Now, one thing to know about *Prigg* is that Justice Story considered himself an abolitionist. That raises two interesting questions. The first has to do with the purposive approach to interpretation that he takes:

"How, then, are we to interpret the language of the [Fugitive Slave] clause? The true answer is, in such a manner, as, consistently with the words, shall fully and completely effectuate the whole objects of it."

(Now, is that the *only* way to proceed? If you think the Clause's objects are morally repugnant, does a good judge have any other options?)

Well, you could interpret it narrowly: Don't do violence to the language, but don't magnify its impact any more than you have to.

(Which of these is more consistent with the proper judicial role?)

(You know, of course, that the next question will be about a judge personally opposed to abortion . . . .)

So here's the other question: Story insisted to the end of his days that *Prigg* was actually a *good* decision from the abolitionist point of view.

(How could he possibly have thought that?)

Because he said it would be unconstitutional to require *state* and *local* officials to enforce the Fugitive Slave laws.

(What effect would nonparticipation by state and local law enforcement have?)

It would make it difficult to have public enforcement at all. Remember that even today, state and local law enforcement personnel outnumber federal law enforcement by a factor of over 10 to 1.

Alas, I'm not convinced, since the real threat to fugitives (and people wrongfully accused of being fugitives), is self-help by the owners and their agents. *Prigg* itself defeats state efforts to crack down on that.

But the basic point about federal vs state enforcement is terribly important – it's the first instance of the modern anti-commandeering doctrine. That doctrine, which we'll study in depth in Part Three, holds that the Federal Government cannot require state and local officials to enforce federal law if they don't want to. It requires the national government to bear the full implementation costs of its programs – which will also be a pretty significant check on what Congress can do.

c.   Two Kinds of Threats to State Autonomy

I also want to use *Prigg* to make a broader point about the dynamics of federalism. There are two sorts of ways in which broad national power can threaten the autonomy of the states.

- Vertical Aggrandizement: The national government seeks to impose its own will on the state governments.

In this scenario, the national government has a policy preference that's just different from that of a given state. So, for instance, politicians at the national level might want to expand their control over public education so that they can have more power and get credit for reforming an important area of policy.

There's another kind, however:

- Horizontal Aggrandizement: A powerful group of states uses the national government as an instrument to impose its preferences on another group of states.

The Fugitive Slave Law in *Prigg*'s an example of this, right? I don't think the Federal Government as a whole is just salivating to be the fugitive slave police; rather, one powerful group of states that favors slavery is using the national government as an *instrument* to impose its policy preferences on the group of states that opposes slavery.

We generally assume that, in the debate over slavery, the doctrine of "states' rights" was exclusively a tool of the slave states. But that's not really so.

Here's Henry Adams, writing in his 1882 biography of John Randolph:

"Between the slave power and states' rights there was no necessary connection. The slave power, when in control, was a centralizing influence, and all the most considerable encroachments on states' rights were its acts. . . . Whenever a question arose of extending or protecting slavery, the slaveholders became friends of centralized power . . . . Slavery in fact required centralization in order to maintain and protect itself . . . . Thus, in truth, states' rights were the protection of the free states, and as a matter of fact, during the domination of the slave power, Massachusetts appealed to this protecting principle as often and almost as loudly as South Carolina."

Adams cites the following examples of national action that helped slavery: the Louisiana Purchase, the annexation of Texas, the Mexican war, the Fugitive Slave Law, and the *Dred Scott* decision.

The relationship is equally complicated in *Dred Scott*.

3.   *Dred Scott v. Sandford*, 60 U.S. (19 How.) 393 (1857)

Marbury v. Madison was the first case in which the Supreme Court held that part of an Act of Congress was unconstitutional. *Dred Scott* – decided 54 years later – is the second. That fact alone ought to tell you something about the Supreme Court's role in the early Republic. It doesn't mean the Court wasn't exercising the power of judicial review; it struck down a number of *state* laws during this time. (*McCulloch* is a good example; *Gibbons* is another.) But the important point for present purposes is that there are very few direct confrontations between the Court and the *federal* political branches during this early period.

Now, on the other hand, judicial invalidation of federal laws is a lot more common. We have had several instances lately in which the Court has struck down 2 or 3 federal statutes in a single one-year term of court. But keep in mind that federal invalidations are hardly a complete measure of judicial activism. Statistics on how often the Court strikes down laws that you see today in our current debates often make the mistake of only counting invalidations of *federal* laws.

a.   Facts

The Missouri Compromise of 1820 barred slavery in the Louisiana Territory north of 36°30', except for the state of Missouri which was admitted as a slave state. Dred Scott was a slave who was taken by his master, Dr. Emerson into the Minnesota territory and the State of Illinois – lands made "free" by the Compromise. He argued that because he would be free under the laws of those jurisdictions, his current master – Sandford – was not entitled to hold him as a slave in Missouri.[13]

(What's the narrow legal question that the Court is supposed to be deciding?)

Whether the federal trial court had jurisdiction over the case. That jurisdiction would exist if there was diversity of *citizenship* between the parties. That criterion would, of course, require that Scott be a "citizen" in the first place.

(Are we asking whether a *slave* is a citizen?)

No – the Court has to assume for purposes of deciding the jurisdictional issue that Scott's claims on the merits are correct. So it effectively

---

[13] Scott claimed to be emancipated under MO law. He sued in MO state court first but lost, then refilled in federal court. The federal court would not have been bound to follow the state court if the question were one of "general" common law under *Swift v. Tyson*. Scott claimed to be a citizen of MO; Sandford was a citizen of NY.

assumes that he is a *free* black person.   That means the question is whether the free jurisdictions that Scott traveled to had the authority to confer citizenship on a free black person.

b.   The Citizenship Holding

The Court holds (Taney, CJ) that Scott cannot become a citizen. The Court says that "We think [black people] . . . are not included, and were not intended to be included, under the word 'citizens' in the Constitution, and can therefore claim none of the rights and privileges that that instrument provides for and secures to citizens of the United States."

(In part, this is a case about federalism.   What's the federalism angle here?)

Whether a state can say who is a citizen of the United States and who is not.

(How does the Court answer that?)

It holds that U.S. citizenship is a function of federal law – the states can't make black people citizens on their own. That's still good law.

Note how federalizing the issue raises the stakes on this question: If you don't federalize, then some states will make blacks citizens and some will not. If you *do* federalize, then you might stomp out those bad states that don't make blacks citizens – *or* you might stomp out the good ones that did.

Think of a prior question: Let's say we'd federalized the question of slavery in general in 1789.

(How would that have gone, do you think?)

Well, remember that 4 of the first 5 presidents were slaveholders from Virginia.

(Back to the citizenship question in *Dred Scott:* What does the case turn on?)

Whether the Framers of the Constitution intended to include free blacks within the meaning of "citizens."

(What kind of evidence does the Court cite?)

It's a very originalist opinion – lots of historical evidence.

In terms of our framework from the first day, originalism is a theory of *interpretation:* It's a way of determining the meaning of the Constitution. There are two flavors of originalism:

- Original *intent*: What did the drafters of the Constitution's text intend to accomplish?

- Original *understanding* or *meaning*: What would the public have understood the text to mean at the time that it was ratified?

Consider a hypothetical where the drafters of the citizenship clause secretly intend to make black people citizens, and they write this down in secret memos to one another, but they don't tell anyone and the ordinary reader at the time would not have understood blacks to be covered. Original *intent* would say that blacks are citizens; original *meaning* would say they're not.

There's still some debate about which of these approaches is better – assuming we're going to be originalist at all – but I think this is one where there's actually a pretty clear right answer. We can get there by thinking about our underlying theory of obligation.

You may remember from the McConnell reading that the root of most forms of originalism (not all) is the notion that the Founding Generation was vested with authority by the People to establish the Constitution. So if that's our theory of obligation, then we need to ask *who* had the authority.

(Did the Drafters of the Constitution have any legal authority?)

No. They simply drafted a proposal.

(Who *did* have authority?)

The ratifiers. So the important thing is to understand what the ratifiers would have understood the document to mean. That's a matter of original public *meaning*.

(So how would you characterize Chief Justice Taney's method in *Dred Scott*? Is it original *intent*? Or original *meaning*?)

I think it's most fair to characterize Taney as asking whether an ordinary reader of the Constitution in 1789 would have understood "citizen" to include free blacks. He asks "who were citizens of the several States when the Constitution was adopted"?

So he cites

- Evidence of English practices toward blacks pre-dating the Revolution;

- State legislation forbidding racial intermarriage or the education of blacks, in both the slaveholding states and more "enlightened" states like Massachusetts and Connecticut; and

- Early acts of Congress restricting the right of becoming citizens to "aliens being free white persons."

One of the most interesting arguments he makes is to cite the Declaration of Independence.

(How in the world does he turn the statement that "all men are created equal" into support for his holding that black people *can't* be equal?)

He says, Look, if that language was meant to include black people, then Thomas Jefferson and George Washington and most of the rest who signed it were hypocrites, because they sure didn't *treat* black people as "created equal." He insists that "the men who framed this declaration were great men . . . high in their sense of honor, and incapable of asserting principles inconsistent with those on which they were acting." So they *can't* have meant to include black people.

(Do you buy that?)

(How does Justice Curtis, in dissent, respond to this argument?)

He says that "the great truths [that Jefferson and the rest] asserted on that solemn occasion, they were ready and anxious to make effectual, wherever a necessary regard to circumstances . . . would allow."

In other words, it's hard enough to found a new country and fight a war for independence – you can't be expected to right every wrong in society at the same time. Jefferson and the rest knew that they were articulating "universal abstract truths" which would be only imperfectly realized at the beginning, but they wanted to set up that ideal at the outset to give us something to strive for in the future.

(What do you think of that argument?)

We'll come back to this in a minute. First, though, I want to look at what may be Taney's strongest argument, based on the provisions of the Constitution itself.

(What provisions does he cite?)

The first is Art. I, § 9, cl.1, which provides that "[t]he Migration or Importation of such Persons as any of the States now existing shall think proper to admit, shall not be prohibited by the Congress prior to the Year one thousand eight hundred and eight, but a Tax or duty may be imposed on such Importation, not exceeding ten dollars for each Person."

The second is the Fugitive Slave Clause, Art. IV, § 2, cl. 3,[14] which we already discussed in *Prigg*.

Taney describes this latter clause a "the States pledg[ing] themselves to each other to maintain the right of property of the master."

---

[14] "No Person held to Service or Labour in one State, under the Laws thereof, escaping into another, shall, in Consequence of any Law or Regulation therein, be discharged from such Service or Labour, but shall be delivered up on Claim of the Party to whom such Service or Labour may be due."

(Aren't these clauses just about slaves? What do they have to do with free blacks?)

Taney says look at the Preamble, which says "We the People of the United States, in Order to . . . secure the Blessings of Liberty to ourselves and our Posterity . . . ." Taney asks, do you really think "We the People" could include *black* people, when the same document explicitly protects the slave trade and includes a fugitive slave clause?

(Can you make a *legal* argument that his conclusion doesn't follow?)

Sure – You could draw a bright line between slaves and free blacks, and say that the Framers meant to accept free blacks into the political community. Nothing in the text really slams the door on that reading.

But at the same time, isn't there something to Taney's point? He's essentially saying, Look, the Founding Generation was *racist*: Black people "had for more than a century before been regarded as beings of an inferior order, and altogether unfit to associate with the white race, either in social or political relations; and so far inferior, that they had no rights which the white man was bound to respect . . . . [The Negro] was bought and sold, and treated as an ordinary article of merchandise and traffic . . . . This opinion was at that time fixed and universal in the civilized portion of the white race."

In other words, Taney's claim is that the Founders were so racist that it's simply not plausible that they understood "citizen" to include *any* black people – free or slave – and the slave provisions of the Constitution are pretty conclusive evidence of that.

Now I don't want to suggest that Taney has a knock down argument on the narrow question which he frames, which is whether free blacks in the founding period were thought to be citizens in the sense of having some basic civil rights, like the right to sue in a federal court. Justice Curtis has some evidence on his side, too; for instance, many states *did* make free blacks citizens. But it seems to me that Taney's historical case is strong enough that we have to take it seriously.

(If you disagree with how he comes out, is it because you think he's wrong on the history, or for some other reason?)

Well, you might challenge his originalist premise.

(Does Taney argue that the *current* view – in 1854 – is that free blacks can't be citizens?)

No – He seems at least implicitly willing to acknowledge that there's a contemporary dispute about this, arising from the abolitionist movement. But Taney says that "No one, we presume, supposes that any change in public opinion or feeling, in relation to this unfortunate race . . . **should** induce the court to give to the words of the Constitution a more liberal construction . . . than they were intended to bear when the instrument was framed and adopted. Such an argument would be altogether inadmissible in any tribunal called upon to interpret it." In other words, if you don't like the Constitution's original meaning, use the amendment process.

(Do you agree? Should contemporary morality be more relevant here?)

(If your answer is "yes", how do you link that to a theory of interpretation? Taney says that any effort to import contemporary morality "would abrogate the judicial character of this court, and make it the mere reflex of the popular opinion or passion of the day." How would you answer that argument?)

(In any event, is contemporary morality – in 1857, mind you – clearly the other way? Did we have a consensus in 1857 that African-Americans could be citizens?)

If we can't come up with a *legal* theory that makes *Dred Scott* come out the other way, then I think we confront an even more basic question:

c.   Would You Sign the Constitution?

If we think that Chief Justice Taney is right about what the Constitution means, then maybe you agree with William Lloyd Garrison – who was one of the leading white abolitionists at the time – that the Constitution was "A Covenant with Death and an Agreement with Hell."

At the very least, I think we have to really wrestle with Prof. Levinson's question, which is whether a founding document that permits and even protects slavery – and that embodies the kind of racial attitudes that Taney articulates – is worthy of our allegiance.

(What do you think? Would you sign it?)

Now one easy way out would be to say that Taney's constitution – or Madison's – is not *our* constitution. Our constitution has a 13th Amendment, banning slavery, and a 14th Amendment, guaranteeing equal citizenship and equal protection of the laws.

I don't find that answer terribly satisfying, however, for a couple of reasons:

First, I think we're used to thinking of ourselves – at least in this course – as heirs to a political tradition that begins with Jefferson, Madison, and John Marshall. If we're embracing the pre-1868 constitution – that is, the Constitution as it existed prior to the 14th Amendment – then I think we have to grapple with this fairly substantial blot on the historical record.

Second, I think this dilemma has resonances with other issues of loyalty that are very much alive today. For instance:

- The Constitution protects private property. Should someone who believes that capitalist economic institutions perpetuate the subjugation of the poor sign the Constitution?

- The Constitution protects abortion. Should someone who believes that life begins at conception sign a document that protects the murder of unborn children?

- The Constitution protects hate speech. Should someone who believes that cross burnings, epithets, and the like perpetuate violence and oppression of racial minorities, gays and lesbians, or women sign a Constitution that prevents effective regulation of hate speech?

So I don't think there's any way to avoid Prof. Levinson's question: Is the unvarnished, unexpurgated Constitution of 1789 worthy of our allegiance?

(What does Levinson do in the end?)

He signs. But note that he revisited the question in a second essay in 2003,[15] where he said he'd changed his mind. But *not*, mind you, because he'd reconsidered the slavery question. Rather, he decided not to sign because of structural provisions in the Constitution that make it "deeply dysfunctional."

So in other words, he could get past slavery, but the malapportionment of the Senate – now, that's a dealbreaker. Sheesh.

If you find any of this interesting, you might want to look at the answer of Professor Randall Kennedy, a prominent black legal academic at Harvard.[16] (It appears in the same volume as Levinson's essay.) Prof. Kennedy invokes Dr. King's statement that the Constitution and the Declaration of Independence "were signing a promissory note" for future generations to *someday* provide equal rights. King said that "America has defaulted on this promissory note," but he "refuse[d] to believe that there are insufficient funds in the great vaults of opportunity of this nation."

(Is that too optimistic?)

I think the basic point is sound. A more instrumental version of it is this: If you are an oppressed minority and you don't have the power to get change on your own, you have to *persuade* the majority to change. And in order to persuade, you have to be able to appeal to some moral

---

[15] Sanford Levinson, *Why I Did Not Sign the Constitution: With the Chance to Endorse It, I Had to Decline*, Findlaw's Writ, Sept. 23, 20003 (available at http://writ.news.findlaw.com/commentary/20030923_levinson.html).

[16] Randall Kennedy, *Afro-American Faith in the Civil Religion: Or, Yes, I Would Sign the Constitution*, 29 WM. & MARY L. REV. 163 (1987), available at (http://scholarship.law.wm.edu/wmlr/vol29/iss1/15).

commitment that you share with the majority – to show them that their own beliefs support what you're asking for. That's the secret of Dr. King and the Civil Rights Movement, who I think were successful in large part because they grounded their claims for racial justice in the Declaration of Independence, the Constitution, and the Bible.

Without that common moral ground, I think the movement would have failed. You could have made the same arguments by invoking abstract theories of equality – like John Rawls' Theory of Justice – but it would never have had the same appeal. And the Constitution also provided a lot of practical support, by guaranteeing the right to protest in the first place.

So Prof. Kennedy and Dr. King are in effect saying that the same Constitution that protected slavery also carried within it the seeds of slavery's destruction. Whether that destruction would have come sooner without a national Union, or whether anti-slavery forces should have granted fewer concessions in 1789, is one of those historical imponderables that it's generally impossible to resolve.

The bottom line for me, at least, is that the Constitution contains enough of the right values, and is open to enough different interpretations, that most people striving for justice are better off embracing the constitutional framework than trying to work outside it.

d.   The Missouri Compromise Question

We still have the **second issue** in *Dred Scott* to go: The Court didn't stop after finding that it had no jurisdiction. It says it has to determine whether, if it had jurisdiction, Scott would be correct that bringing him into free territory made him a free man. (Just as an aside, it's unclear why the Court needs to reach this – as in *Marbury*, once you decide you don't have jurisdiction, you're supposed to pack up and go home.)

(What does the Court say about that?)

It holds that the Missouri Compromise – the federal statute that outlawed slavery north of 36 30' – was unconstitutional.

(Why?)

Chief Justice Taney says that "an act of Congress which deprives a citizen of the United States of his liberty or property, merely because he came himself or brought his property into a particular Territory of the United States, and who had committed no offence against the laws, could hardly be dignified with the name of *due process of law*." (p. 203)

(Is that a natural reading of the Due Process Clause?)

Not to our modern eyes, at least. It looks to us like the Clause simply guarantees fair procedure. But in fact, the Clause has been read to have two different components:

- *procedural* due process, which *is* in fact concerned with the procedural safeguards that government provides when it deprives you of life, liberty or property. Those cases are about things like whether you're entitled to some kind of hearing before you're fired from a government job.

- *substantive* due process, which restricts the government from burdening or violating certain rights no matter what procedural safeguards are provide. That's the basis, for example, of the constitutional right to privacy.

Justice Taney's argument is that the government simply can't take your property – Mr. Scott – under these circumstances, not that they should have had a hearing first.

This is the first time that the U.S. Supreme Court struck down a law based on substantive due process, but it won't be the last. The argument figures prominently in the *Slaughterhouse Cases* for next time, and we'll see it again in *Griswold v. Connecticut* and *Roe v. Wade*.

e.   The Court's Ability to Resolve Social Controversy

One last point: In *Dred Scott*, it's clear that Chief Justice Taney really thought he was saving the Union by ruling the way he did.

(Why would that be true?)

Because he thought that *legislative* controversy over slavery was tearing the Union apart. By placing the issue off limits to politics – by constitutionalizing it, essentially – he hoped to end that controversy.

(How'd that work out for him?)

Not so great, right? Over 600,000 people died in the Civil War. The Civil War probably would have come with or without this decision, but most seem to agree that *Dred Scott* worsened the crisis and hastened the conflict.

(But what would have happened if *Dred Scott* had gone the other way?)

It's not necessarily all sugarplums and puppies. Professor Powe points out that the South might have left in 1857, rather than 1860 and 1861. The President in 1857 was James Buchanan, who was on record to the effect that while secession would be illegal, the President lacked any power to prevent it. So he might have simply let the South go.

(Would black people have been better off then?)

(More generally, what do you think about the Court's ability to resolve these basic social controversies?)

In a week or two we'll read *Planned Parenthood v. Casey*, which is the case in which three conservative justices join the liberals in order to reaffirm

Roe v. Wade. Those justices make the argument that they are also resolving a bitter social controversy by "calling the contending sides of a national controversy to end their national division by accepting a common mandate rooted in the Constitution." This claim is enough to turn Justice Scalia purple with rage in dissent, and he squarely invokes *Dred Scott* as an analogy to what the majority is doing. On the other hand, I think it's fair to say that there *are* deep social controversies where the Court has played an important role in facilitating settlement and helping the nation move on. This is an issue we'll wrestle with throughout the course.

B.   Reconstruction and the Fourteenth Amendment

This section is often somewhat confusing for students. My goals are generally to (1) explore the ways in which the Civil War and the Reconstruction Amendments changed the Constitution, as well as the historical factors (such as the compromise that ended Reconstruction after the 1876 election) that made many of those changes slow to be realized; (2) introduce the issue of incorporation of the Bill of Rights against the States, which will come up again in Chapter Six on the Warren Court; (3) convey the doctrinal interpretations of privileges and immunities and the state action doctrine articulated in the two principal cases (note that this is really the only place they'll get state action, although it comes up again in United States v. Morrison *in Chapter Ten); (4) highlight the structural relationship between rights and national power under Section 5 of the Fourteenth Amendment; and (5) foreshadow the expansion of the Due Process Clause in the* Lochner *era that immediately follows.*

The next set of cases continue a shift in focus that began with the second holding of *Dred Scott*, from structure to individual rights. It's logical to start with the Bill of Rights and the Fourteenth Amendment, which contain the Constitution's most prominent provisions dealing with rights. This assignment is about the relationship between those two parts of the document.

We start with *Barron*, which holds that the original Bill of Rights did not apply to the States. This is a prelude to a discussion we'll have a bit later on about the doctrine of incorporation, which holds that the Fourteenth Amendment – adopted in 1868 just after the Civil War – effectively overruled *Barron* and "incorporated" the Bill of Rights into its provisions, which *do* apply to state governments. But more broadly, you can't understand the Fourteenth Amendment without understanding the antebellum notion of the Federal Government's role with respect to rights. That notion viewed the Federal Government as a threat to rights, which is why the Bill of Rights was directed against the national government only. This understanding fundamentally changes with the War, when we begin to see the States as a primary threat to rights, and the Federal Government as the great defender of rights.

The next case, *Slaughterhouse*, is the Court's first major statement on the meaning of the Fourteenth Amendment. It considers whether the Privileges and Immunities Clause of the Fourteenth Amendment protected a broad set of substantive rights—including but not limited to the specific provisions of the Bill of Rights—against state encroachment, or whether its focus was much more narrow. We'll then turn to the *Civil Rights Cases*, which further limited the Fourteenth Amendment's scope by recognizing a critical limitation on constitutional law generally—the state action doctrine..

1.   ***Barron v. Mayor and City Council of Baltimore*, 32 U.S. (7 Pet.) 243 (1833)**

Barron sued the City for diverting the flow of a stream in a way that ruined his wharf. He argued that this was a taking without just compensation.

(What's the critical question?)

The issue is whether the 5th Amendment applies to the States.

The Court holds (Marshall, CJ) that the 5th Amendment does not apply to state governments.

(There are two arguments here: a textual argument and a historical argument. What are they?)

The textual argument: Art. 1, § 10 includes limitations that are binding on state governments. These include the "no state shall" language. It's clear that other provisions, such as those in Art. I, § 9, don't bind the states, and they simply use general language.

(What kind of restrictions are in Art. I, § 9?)

Things like no bill of attainder or no ex post facto laws.

(How do we know the Art. I, § 9 stuff doesn't apply to the states?)

We know that the § 9 stuff doesn't bind the states because § 9 has its *own* bill of attainder and ex post factor limitation, which is then repeated in § 10 vis a vis the states.

So given the contrast in wording in Art. I, it makes sense to read general language in the Bill of Rights the same way.

(What about the historical argument?)

The historical argument: The Bill of Rights was a concession to antifederalists who were worried about the powers of the *national* government. It's clear these anxieties weren't aimed at the states.

(Does this mean that state governments don't have to respect people's rights, except for the few restrictions in Art. I, § 10?)

No.

(Where do rights against the States come from?)

State governments are limited primarily by the provisions of *state* constitutions.

2.   The Fourteenth Amendment

The big question for the rest of this assignment is whether and to what extent the Fourteenth Amendment changes the situation articulated in *Barron*. The most obvious way in which that amendment might change it is through the Privileges and Immunities Clause.

Section 1 of the 14th Amendment provides that "[n]o State shall make or enforce any law which shall abridge the privileges or immunities of citizens of the United States."

There are really two issues arising out of this provision:

(1)   Does it incorporate the Bill of Rights?

(2)   Does it protect unenumerated rights?

This clause seems like the best textual candidate anywhere in the Constitution for either of these kinds of rights. But the *Slaughter-House Cases* nipped that in the bud.

3.   *The Slaughter-House Cases*, 83 U.S. (16 Wall.) 36 (1873)

Louisiana granted a monopoly over the slaughterhouse business to a private company. The plaintiffs were butchers whose businesses were restricted by the statute. They argued that the statute deprived them of the opportunity to pursue their lawful calling, which was a privilege or immunity of citizens of the United States.

The Court holds (Miller, J) that the plaintiffs' claim does not invoke a "privilege or immunity" of U.S. citizens within the meaning of the 14th Amendment.

(The Court starts by invoking that "pervading purpose" of the 14th Amendment. What's that purpose?)

Helping black people. The Court says that the Amendment is designed to guarantee "the freedom of the slave race, the security and firm establishment of that freedom, and the protection of the newly-made freeman and citizen from the oppressions of those who had formerly exercised unlimited dominion over him."

(What does Justice Bradley's dissent say about that?)

He thinks the purpose is broader than that: He says that "the African race . . . . may have been the primary cause of the amendment, but its language is general, embracing all citizens, and I think it was purposely so [expressed.]"

This is an important question, for a number of debates under the 14th Amendment. For example:

a)   Do provisions of the Amendment like the Equal Protection Clause protect other people besides blacks, such as women?

b)   Is the purpose to make black people better off, or can white people sue under the 14th Amendment when the government arguably discriminates in their favor? This is one of the keys to the whole affirmative action debate.

Current law is much closer to Justice Bradley's position.

(Is Justice Miller's majority opinion correct in arguing that expanding the amendment's coverage would pervert its purpose?)

a.   Privileges and Immunities

(The basic holding of *Slaughter-House* is that the privileges and immunities protected by the 14th Amendment are different than those protected by the privileges and immunities of Article IV. What's the difference?)

Article IV protects the privileges and immunities of *state* citizenship, which are defined in *Corfield v. Coryell*. These are "fundamental" rights, which include

- protection by the government

- the right to acquire and possess property

- the right to pursue and obtain happiness and safety

(Would the right claimed by the plaintiffs here fit within one of these categories?)

Sure: Justices Field & Bradley both argue that the right to pursue a lawful calling is fundamental. Yhe Court later holds explicitly (in *Camden*) that "pursuit of a common calling" is one of the fundamental privileges protected by Art. IV.

(How does the Court define the "privileges or immunities" of *national* citizenship?)

Rights that "owe their existence to the Federal government, its national character, its Constitution, or its laws."

The Court lists a few:

- the right to come to the seat of government to assert any claim against the government

- free access to seaports

- right of access to the institutions of state government, such as the state courts

- protection by the federal government when on the high seas or in a foreign country

- the right to peaceably assemble and petition for the redress of grievances

- the right to use navigable waters

- all rights secured under U.S. treaties

- rights secured by the 13th and 15th amendments, as well as other articles of the 14th.

(How does Justice Field respond to this listing of *national* privileges and immunities?)

He says that these could not have been violated by states anyway. That's probably right – you can read *McCulloch v. Maryland* for the broad proposition that states aren't allowed to interfere with federal rights.

(So what does Justice Field think that "privileges and immunities" means?)

The 14th Amendment protects the same privileges and immunities as Art. IV.

(Wouldn't that make the 14th Am. redundant?)

No.   Art. IV provides an antidiscrimination principle – the 14th Amendment makes this a substantive protection.

(Do you understand the difference?)

Article IV doesn't say that a state government has to allow anyone to pursue a common calling – to be a butcher, for instance. It just says that if a state lets *anyone* be a butcher, then it can't deny that privilege to out-of-staters.

(Justice Miller makes 2 arguments for his distinction between Art. IV and the 14th Amendment. What are they?)

The *textual* argument: Section 1 of the 14th Amendment distinguishes between U.S. citizenship and state citizenship. The privileges and immunities clause, which is in the very next sentence, must have presumed this distinction.

The *structural* argument: Holding the 14th Amendment to encompass all the Art. IV privileges and immunities would vastly broaden the powers both of Congress and the Courts. That would "radically change[] the whole theory of the relations of the State and Federal governments to each other and of both these governments to the people."

(What does Justice Miller mean by that? How would holding that the 14th Amendment's P&I clause incorporates the privileges and immunities of *state* citizenship "change the whole theory of the relations of the State and Federal governments"?)

The problem is that the substantive provisions of Section 1 of the amendment are coupled with Section 5, which gives Congress the authority to *enforce* the amendment by appropriate legislation. So every expansion of a substantive right under the 14th Amendment is an expansion of Congress's power.

Here's the key portions of *Corfield*'s catalogue of the privileges and immunities of state citizenship again:

- protection by the government
- the right to acquire and possess property
- the right to pursue and obtain happiness and safety

(Can somebody give me an example of a statute Congress could pass if these are all rights protected under the 14th Amendment?)

Congress could do almost anything: It could rewrite state property law, for instance, on the theory that the state governments weren't adequately protecting the right to acquire and possess property law.

Or it could take over state public education (although there wasn't any when this case was decided) on the ground of enforcing the state's obligation to provide "happiness and safety" for its citizens. Pretty sweeping, yes?

This is an important point, and we'll come back to Congress's enforcement power under the 14th Amendment shortly, in the *Civil Rights Cases*. The important thing to remember for now is that every substantive expansion of individual rights protected under the 14th Amendment is also an expansion of Congress's power, potentially at the expense of the states. So it's impossible to totally extricate individual rights concerns from concerns about federalism.

b.   Due Process & Equal Protection

(Do the plaintiffs rely only on the Privileges and Immunities Clause?)

No. They've got two other arguments:

(1)   due process

(2)   equal protection

(The plaintiffs' claim is that they've got a right to work as butchers. What does this case have to do with procedure?)

Nothing – this is a *substantive* due process claim.

Remember the difference from our conversation about *Dred Scott*: *Procedural* due process is concerned with the procedural safeguards that the government is obligated to provide when it takes away rights that stem from some other aspect of the law – so "life," "liberty," or "property." The due process clause doesn't itself create those rights – that may be done by state law, or other provisions of the Constitution. It just means, for instance, that the government has to provide notice and a hearing before it takes your property away.

Substantive due process actually *creates* or recognizes fundamental rights and bars government interference with those rights. That's where we get the right to privacy, for example.

So here, the claim is that the right to work is a fundamental substantive right protected by the due process clause.

(What does the Court say about this claim?)

It gives it the back of the hand – Justice Miller says that no prior construction of the due process clause had protected this kind of right.

(Is that right?)

No – remember that *Dred Scott* had recognized substantive aspects of the Due Process clause. But you can understand why, in 1873, nobody's psyched to rely on *that* case.

(How does Justice Bradley answer the majority's argument in dissent?)

He says that "a law which prohibits a large class of citizens from adopting a lawful employment, or from following a lawful employment previously adopted, does deprive them of liberty as well as property, without due process of law."

Again, it's important that Justice Bradley locates these general rights under the Due Process clause rather than the "privileges and immunities" clause.

(Where do these rights come from? How do we know which rights are protected and which aren't?)

(What sources does Justice Field rely on?)

He talks about "the most sacred and imprescriptible rights of man" – which suggests kind of a natural law view. He also cites works of political and economic theory.

The Court's rejection of substantive due process doesn't hold up; in the cases for tomorrow, you'll see the Court embrace the idea that the Due Process Clause protects economic rights, like the right to work or enter into contracts. And Justice Field's citation to Adam Smith's *Wealth of Nations* in support of the notion that the right to pursue a calling is fundamental foreshadows the Court's use of substantive due process to protect the free market from government regulation.

For next time, compare Justice Field's assimilation of economic philosophy into the Constitution with what Justice Holmes accuses the majority of doing in *Lochner*.

4.   *The Civil Rights Cases*, 109 U.S. 3 (1883)

The opinions here deal with several cases consolidated together, all of which concern discrimination on the basis of race in access to public accommodations. The *Ryan* case is a good example: Ryan was charged with a criminal offense for denying a black person a seat in the dress circle of Maguire's theatre in San Francisco. (It's worth noting that these cases come from both North and South: The *Singleton* case, for instance, comes from the Grand Opera House in New York City.)

(Are these defendants being prosecuted under the Constitution itself?)

No.

(What's the law they're being prosecuted under?)

The Civil Rights Act of 1875, which banned by statute discrimination on the basis of race in public accommodations.

(What do we mean by "public accommodations"?)

Any business or facility that's open to the public: Theatres, street cars, stores, lunch counters, etc.

(So what does the Court do with these cases?)

It says (Bradley, J) that the prosecutions are no good because the Civil Rights Act is unconstitutional.

(In *Slaughterhouse*, the claim was that the statute in question was unconstitutional because it interefered with various individual rights. Is that the claim here?)

No. The claim is that Congress lacked *power* to enact the statute.

(OK, so this is an enumerated powers case. What power did Congress rely on to enact the Civil Rights Act?)

Its power to enforce the Reconstruction Amendments – particularly the Thirteenth and the Fourteenth.

a.   The Fourteenth Amendment Argument

(What does the Fourteenth Amendment say about Congressional power?)

It says, in Section 5, that "The Congress shall have power to enforce, by appropriate legislation, the provisions of this article."

So what would the predicate for Congressional power be here? Remember, for instance, that the predicate for Congressional power under the Commerce Clause would be economic activity or travel that affects more states than one.

(What would you have to have as a predicate for Congress to act under Section Five?)

A violation of the Fourteenth Amendment, right?   So even though the defendants here aren't being prosecuted under the Fourteenth Amendment itself, the case comes down to whether they've *violated* the provisions of that Amendment.

(Have they?)

The Court says no.

(Why not?)

Because they *can't* – they're not *States*. The amendment says "No *State* shall" do various things – not private entities.

Let's compare the public accommodations provisions of the Act with another provision – Section 4 of the Act – that the Court recognized has been upheld as OK.   That provision says "no citizen . . . shall be disqualified for service as grand or petit juror in any court . . . on account of race, color, or previous conditions of servitude."

(Why's that OK, if the public accommodation part isn't?)

Because it deals with state action. The *government* runs the courthouse and qualifies jurors.

(Let's give an example a little closer to home: When I was in college at Dartmouth, the College was in a constant fight with a student newspaper called the Dartmouth Review. If the College had simply banned the paper from campus and threatened to expel any student who wrote for it or read from it, would that have violated the First Amendment?)

No – Again, the College is a *private* actor, and therefore not bound by the Constitution. Duke is too. But UNC's obligations, on the other hand, are considerably different.

(Justice Harlan, in dissent, thinks that all this is nuts: How would he read Section 5?)

He sees it as conferring on Congress the power to enforce equal civil rights for black people. And he thinks its ridiculous that Congress should have to wait until the states *affirmatively* deny such rights before legislating.

(Is he necessarily denying that some state action is required?)

I don't think so. I think it's simply sufficient for him that the state may violate the Constitution through *inaction* – that is, if the states *fail* to protect the civil rights of black people, Congress can step in to remedy that defect. The Court, to repeat, requires some affirmative act of discrimination by the states.

Now, it's important to understand that this "state action" requirement is a *general* principle of constitutional law and not just a quirk of the Fourteenth Amendment's text. With only one exception, *all* constitutional provisions bind the *Government*, not private individuals.

(Why do you think that is?)

Because the Constitution is a charter of *Government*, and that's who it is addressed to. Another way of saying this is that the Constitution is generally a set of secondary rules – of rules for *making* rules. The Government makes laws that regulate individuals all the time, but the Constitution is concerned with the process by which that happens and the limit on its scope. Its rights provisions are primarily concerned with protecting the People from the Government, not from one another.

(Would the world be better if it were otherwise? Would it be a good thing if the individual rights provisions, say, applied to private individuals? If the College couldn't silence the Review, for instance?)

It would actually be pretty intrusive, wouldn't it? Suppose I had to give my son Michael a due process hearing, with counsel, before grounding him for a week. Or *Miranda* warnings before interrogating him about who spilled root beer all over the floor. Or – here's a more plausible example – suppose every small landlord had the same obligation to rent his spare room equally without regard to race, gender, or religion that public employers do. (Note that the Civil Rights statutes have generally made exceptions for individual homeowners and the like, but it's easier to fine tune things like that if it's a statute than if it's in the Constitution itself.) A lot of rights are imposed to limit the government precisely because it's the government – it has more power over us than most private entities, and it employs legitimate coercion against us.

b.   The Thirteenth Amendment Argument

(What about the Thirteenth Amendment argument? Does it encounter the same problem of state action?)

No – The Thirteenth is the only provision in the Constitution without a state action requirement. It simply says slavery shall not exist – that applies not only to the Government but to you, me, Duke, and General Motors. (When you experience the working conditions at Sullivan and Cromwell, you may want to remember that.)

(So what's the problem here, then?)

Discrimination in access to public accommodation isn't the same thing as slavery. The Court says that "It would be running the slavery argument into the ground to make it apply to every act of discrimination which a person may see fit to make as to the guests he will entertain, or as to the people he will entertain, or as to the people he will take into his coach or cab or car . . . or deal with in other matters of intercourse or business."

They go on to say that, at some point, the freed slave "takes the rank of a mere citizen, and ceases to be the special favorite of the laws."

(How does Justice Harlan, in dissent, read the Thirteenth Amendment?)

He says it's the power to erase the inferiority that came with slavery. Congress "may enact laws to protect that people against the deprivation, because of their race, of any civil rights granted to other freemen in the same State."

That's a lot broader, right? It makes the Thirteenth into an Equal Protection Clause, for race at least, without a state action requirement.

(What do you think of these arguments? Who's right?)

Some of the majority's rhetoric seems to sweep a little far for me. It's not like Reconstruction had achieved equality and was now being pressed too far. But it's not necessary to the core argument that the Thirteenth Amendment is special. One might make a breadth/depth point here: The Thirteenth is very strong within its scope, because there's no state action required. But that means we may need to confine that scope relatively narrowly.

(Let's step back a minute. Justice Harlan's basic complaint is that the Court has hamstrung the Reconstruction Amendment by reading them too narrowly. What do you think of that criticism?)

Well, it's true that these decisions probably undermine the broad vision that many of the Framers of those amendments had. On the other hand, it's not clear that this is, in fact, why Reconstruction failed to achieve equality for black people. The Jim Crow laws, for instance, were certainly state action that impacted black equality directly – neither *Slaughterhouse* nor the *Civil Rights Cases* would have blocked Congress from enforcing these Amendments against those laws.

Keep in mind that Reconstruction ended after 1876, with the withdrawal of federal troops from the South. This resulted from the political compromise that resolved the 1876 election deadlock; the South acquiesced in the election of the Republican candidate, and the Union troops withdrew. The decision in the *Civil Rights Cases* may be reflecting the fact that the country very much wanted to move on from the War/Reconstruction era.

It may be worth stopping to summarize some of the key results of the War in Constitutional Law:

- The question of secession is now off the table – probably forever;

- The war creates a new sense of nationhood in the North as a result of the mobilization and industrialization that the War required; and

- The War and the Reconstruction Amendments, along with accompanying legislation expanding the jurisdiction of the federal courts and empowering private individuals to sue when their rights are violated, establishes the national government as the primary guarantor of human rights in the constitutional system.

But this last point is not immediately apparent—as *Slaughterhouse* and the *Civil Rights Cases* make clear. It doesn't really come to fruition until the Warren Court. It's no accident that Eric Foner, the leading historian of Reconstruction, called it "America's unfinished revolution." But the groundwork is laid for that shift in the War and the period immediately afterward.

(Let's return for a moment, though, to our focus on *private* discrimination. What's the contemporary version of this law, banning discrimination in public accommodations?)

The Civil Rights Act of 1964. That law has been upheld – not because the *Civil Rights Cases* have been overruled, but by relying on Congress's power under the Commerce Clause. So it's important to understand, as we turn to the scope of that power in the next few classes, that we're not just talking about economic regulation, but also federal power to guarantee human rights and the like.

III.   Chapter Five – The *Lochner* Era and the New Deal Crisis

Much of contemporary constitutional law can be understood as a reaction against the Lochner *era, in which the Court aggressively reviewed regulatory legislation, at both the state and federal level, in order to preserve the free market against encroachments by the regulatory state. When courts express reluctance to second-guess government policy judgments or recognize unenumerated rights, these anxieties often stem from a desire to avoid repeating the mistakes of this period. So even though many of these cases are not "good law," they can tell us more about modern constitutionalism than many cases that are. Students don't like learning cases no longer state the law, so it is important to explain this to them.*

The cases in this section are arranged to show (a) how the Due Process/freedom of contract decisions and the Commerce Clause decisions worked in tandem to limit government regulation of the market. and (b) how within each area of doctrine there were competing strands of decisions, one of which invalidated regulatory action and one which tended to uphold it. The latter point is important to show that not only was the Court not uniformly hostile to regulatory legislation, but that each line of cases had to wrestle with serious doctrinal inconsistency. This fact provides an "internal" explanation for the Court's "switch in time" in 1937 that competes with the "external" explanation—that is, that the Court switched in response to President Roosevelt's court-packing plan. These materials do not purport to resolve the controversy over these two competing explanations, and my own view is that it was probably a little of both. But one of the themes of this course involves the quest for doctrinal coherence, so it is important to convey the role that that quest played in the Court's ultimate change in direction.

The next two classes involve two lines of cases that are different doctrinally but very closely connected historically. And since this large unit is basically about the Court's experience doing constitutional interpretation, I think it makes sense to do both strands together.

We're talking about a period from the late 19th century to 1937, in which the Court was increasingly willing to strike down efforts by both state and federal government to regulate the economy. That era culminates with a showdown between the Court and the President over the constitutionality of the New Deal. After 1937, the Court backs down and is much more permissive in reviewing this sort of regulation, and that shift frames much of the current debate over constitutional interpretation.

There are two strands of cases:

(A)   Substantive Due Process: The Court struck down a lot of legislation – enacted by both state and federal governments – on the ground that it violated economic rights – like "freedom of contract – that the court read into the Due Process Clauses of the Fifth and Fourteenth Amendments. *Lochner* itself is the paradigm case here.

(B)   Commerce Clause: A second group of cases – which we'll cover tomorrow – invalidated federal legislation as beyond the scope of Congress's enumerated power to regulate interstate commerce. *E.C. Knight* and *Hammer v. Dagenhart* are classic examples here.

These are very different theories doctrinally – one is an individual rights approach, the other is derived from federalism concerns. We'll come back to the Commerce Clause cases when we focus on federalism in the third part of the course. But both strands are part of a historical story about the rise and fall of one era of judicial activism, and I think you'll better be able to appreciate that story if you read them together.

Finally, to complete the story, we'll spend two classes on the collapse of this period of activism, which was prompted at least in part by FDR's attack on the Supreme Court's institutional independence in 1937. We'll then touch on the post-1937 case law so you'll have a sense of the restrained doctrines that the Court has applied in subsequent cases. What you'll see is that, after 1937, the Supreme Court seems to simply stop enforcing some parts of the Constitution – like economic substantive due process and limits on the Commerce Clause – while continuing and even increasing its enforcement of others – like free speech or the right to privacy. So the final question of this section will be whether this "double standard" can be justified.

A.   Freedom of Contract

1.   The Road to *Lochner*

Substantive due process can be traced all the way back to the founding era.

Calder v. Bull, 3 Dall. (3 U.S.) 386 (1798),[17] is probably the most important case here, where Justice Chase argues that "an Act of the Legislature . . . contrary to the great first principles of the social compact, cannot be considered a rightful exercise of legislative authority."

Likewise, the Marshal Court's landmark decision in *Fletcher v. Peck*, 6 Cranch (10 U.S.) 87 (1810),[18] hinted at recognizing some unenumerated protection for property rights.

But there's a strong counter-current in this period as well, illustrated by Justice Iredell's response to Chase in *Calder*, which argued that a court can strike down legislative acts only based on an explicit constitutional provision.

Iredell rejected the natural law approach on the ground that it was too indeterminate and controversial. "The ideas of natural justice are regulated by no fixed standard: [and] the ablest and the purest men have differed upon the subject."

---

[17] In *Calder*, the CT legislature had enacted a statute that had the effect of setting aside a prior probate court decree rejecting a will; a new hearing was required, in which the court approved the will. The people who would have inherited if the will had been rejected claimed that this was an *ex post facto* law – a claim the court rejected on grounds that the clause applied only to criminal matters – and also made arguments based on natural law.

[18] *Fletcher* is primarily a contracts clause case invalidating a GA effort to revoke a land grant. But Marshall invokes "general principles" as an alternative ground.

So most of the Marshall Court decisions, as well, rely on express constitutional provisions and not natural law. This probably stems from *Marbury*, which rests the whole institution of judicial review on the idea that courts are enforcing a *written* constitution.

The other important antecedent is *Dred Scott* in 1857, which we've already discussed. A key thing about *Dred Scott* is that it, for the first time, explicitly grounds these transcendent, natural-law-type rights in the Due Process Clause. "An Act of Congress which deprives a citizen of the United States of his liberty or property, merely because he came himself or brought his property into a particular Territory of the United States, and who had committed no offense against the laws, could hardly be dignified with the name of due process of law."

Finally, note that there's some important state court decisions in the 19th century that recognize substantive due process-type rights as well.

The *Lochner* era really begins, however, with a series of cases in the late 19th century, starting with *Munn v. Illinois* in 1877, upholding economic regulation but warning that there are limits beyond which the government can't go.

The first case in which an economic regulation is actually struck down is *The Minnesota Rate Case* in 1890.[19]

And the liberty of contract is first recognized in 1897 in *Allgeyer v. Louisiana*, 165 U.S. 578 (1897).[20] That's where Justice Peckham – who wrote the majority opinion in *Lochner* eight years later – gives a broad definition to "liberty" in the due process clause: "The liberty mentioned in [the 14th] amendment means not only the right of the citizen to be free from the mere physical restraint of his person . . . [but] the right of the citizen to be free in the enjoyment of all his faculties; to be free to use them in all lawful ways; to live and work where he will; to earn his livelihood by any lawful calling; to pursue any livelihood or avocation, and for that purpose to enter into all contracts which may be proper, necessary and essential to his carrying out to a successful conclusion the purposes above mentioned."

---

[19] *Chicago, Minneapolis & St. Paul Ry. Co. v. Minnesota*, 134 U.S. 418 (1890). The Court struck down a provision for administrative ratemaking without judicial review – hence, the case is primarily a *procedural* due process case. But the Court also said that the "reasonableness" of the rates was "eminently a question for judicial investgation."

[20] *Allgeyer* invalidated a LA law prohibiting people from insuring LA property from unlicensed insurance carriers; by prohibiting this sort of insurance transaction, the statute violated freedom of contract.

Note how much this sounds like the broad definition of Art. IV "privileges and immunities" that Justice Washington set out in *Corfield v. Coryell*. We've come full-circle from the *Slaughterhouse Cases* 25 years before: now the Due Process Clause is doing exactly the work which Justices Bradley and Field wanted the 14th Amendment's Privileges and Immunities Clause to do.

2.   *Lochner v. New York*, 198 U.S. 45 (1905)

A New York statute limited bakery workers to sixty hours per week, or ten hours per day.

The Court (Peckham, J) holds the New York law unconstitutional.

(What's the basis for the Court's holding?)

The statute unconstitutionally interferes with the freedom of contract of bakery workers and their employers. Freedom of contract is part of the individual liberty protected by the Fourteenth Amendment.

(Does the Court think that the states have *no* right to regulate business conditions?)

No -- The Court upheld a maximum hours law for mine workers in *Holden v. Hardy*.

(How does the Court distinguish *Holden*?)

Mining is particularly dangerous and debilitating, so as to make such regulation appropriate.

(What's the standard for drawing the line between legitimate and illegitimate regulation?)

The question is: "Is this a fair, reasonable and appropriate exercise of the police power of the State, or is it an unreasonable, unnecessary and arbitrary interference with the right of an individual to his personal liberty . . . ?"

In essence, the Court identifies legitimate *ends* that government may pursue, and then analyzes whether the *means* pursued has a "direct relation" to those legitimate ends.

(What are the "ends" that the statute might pursue here?)

The Court considers two ends that the statute might serve:

• The "labor law" justification: By "labor law," the Court seems to mean an attempt to equalize bargaining power between employers and employees.

(What's the Court's view on this argument?)

This is not a legitimate end. There's no reason why bakers can't take care of themselves in negotiating their hours. Bakers are not "wards of the State."

- The "health" justification: The Court considers two: the *public* health, and the health of the bakers.

(What does the Court say about *public* health?)

The hours worked don't affect the bread, so the *public* health is irrelevant here.

The cleanliness argument looks pretextual here – the court thinks a motive other than the public welfare is at work. Although it turns out there were substantial concerns about sanitary working conditions at the bakeries that worked the longest hours. It might have been better to make this as a *fit* argument – that is, even if the working conditions are unhealthy, NY could always just regulate that directly. Hours legislation is a weird way to get at working conditions.

(What about the health of the *bakers*?)

The health of the bakers also won't fly. Baking isn't an inherently unhealthy trade, so there's no justification for state intervention. If the government can regulate this, they can regulate anything.

All the State may do is require proper drainage, plumbing, painting, bathrooms, etc.

(Which part of this analysis does Justice Harlan disagree with?)

Justice Harlan wants to say that there *is* a substantial relationship between this law and the health of the bakers. Baking is actually a grueling job, performed under harsh conditions. For instance, inhaling flour dust is bad for you. Bakers tend not to live very long. (Your nose turns red!)

(Does he just disagree with the Court's view of the facts? Or does he have a problem with the way the majority approaches the case?)

He also disagrees about the *standard of review* – that is, the level of deference that the Court should give to the legislative judgment.

The standard of review is a critically important issue in the law. Often courts aren't asked to decide a question in the first instance – they're asked to *review* the decision that someone else already made. That could be a lower court, or it could be a legislature or administrative agency. In any event, the question is, How much deference should that initial decision get, simply because that's the decision that was already made. The majority doesn't give it much deference at all.

(How does Harlan analyze the case?)

It doesn't matter who's ultimately right about the health effects -- if there is "room for debate" then the Court should defer to the legislature.

(Does Justice Holmes take the same tack as Justice Harlan? Note that this is one of Justice Holmes' most famous dissents.)

No – he focuses on the Court's decision that the "labor law" justification is an illegitimate "end" for government regulation.

(What does he think the majority is doing?)

The Court is simply imposing their laissez faire economic theory on the rest of us. "The Fourteenth Amendment does not enact Mr. Herbert Spencer's Social Statics."

(Who was Herbert Spencer?)

A popular proponent of *laissez faire* economic policy and social Darwinism.

(Why shouldn't the court enforce a substantive idea of economic liberty?)

Holmes says: "[A] constitution is not intended to embody a particular economic theory . . . . It is made for people of fundamentally differing views. . . . I think that the word liberty in the Fourteenth Amendment is perverted when it is held to prevent the natural outcome of a dominant opinion, unless it can be said that a rational and fair man necessarily would admit that the statute proposed would infringe fundamental principles as they have been understood by the traditions of our people and our law."

(Is Holmes totally against substantive due process?)

No -- but he seems to have a narrow view, grounded in tradition. And he sees no real tradition of unlimited freedom of contract: The government regulates all kinds of things that interfere with freedom of contract. *E.g.*, usury laws. And there are all sorts of limits on individual freedom, even where the rights of others are not implicated. *E.g.*, school laws.

But note the basic thrust of Holmes's position, which is that within certain very narrow limits, the majority should get to do whatever it wants.

(How many people think Holmes is right here?)

See if you still think that when substantive due process starts being used to protect non-economic liberties like the right to privacy. In order to begin asking that question, it's important to ask:

3.   Where Did the Court Go Wrong in *Lochner*?

(Where do *you* think the Court went wrong?)

Some possibilities:

- **"Liberty" under the 14th Amendment doesn't include "liberty of contract."**

  But what *is* it, if it doesn't include liberty of contract? Simply freedom from physical restraint?

  There's pretty good historical evidence that the 14th Amendment was intended to constitutionalize the Civil Rights Act of 1866, which did protect a broad range of rights -- including the right to make contracts.

  (Can you distinguish between freedom of contract and other kinds of freedoms?)

  From a practical perspective, economic liberty is arguably just as important as the other kinds.

- **Even if "liberty" includes "liberty of contract," the Due Process Clause guarantees only fair *procedures*.**

  The problem with this view is that you have to junk a lot of law besides *Lochner*: For instance, much of the incorporation doctrine (at least for substantive rights, like free speech), and any protection for things like privacy.

  (Are you willing to do that?)

  You might take the hard line position and say that the 14th Amendment incorporates only *procedural* rights. That would get you most of the criminal law decisions, but leave out free speech, establishment, etc. Maybe for those you actually need a constitutional amendment.

- **Even if there is substantive protection for liberty of contract, the Court blew the means/ends analysis.**

  There are actually two possible objections here, both of which are raised in Justice Harlan's dissent:

  One is *institutional* -- that the appropriate role for the courts requires them to defer to the legislature when there is fair room for debate about the means/ends connection.

  (Why should the court defer to the legislature on these matters?)

  Either because the legislature is elected, or because the legislature has more expertise.

  The other is *substantive* -- that the evidence before the Court was sufficient to establish the necessary connection.

  (Which is more persuasive?)

  (If you buy the institutional objection, would you apply the same deferential standard to protection of non-economic rights?)

(If not, how do you distinguish between economic and non-economic rights?)

Note that this distinction is the key to the "double standard" debate in the next set of readings.

- **The Court inappropriately held that the "labor law" justification was an illegitimate end.**

The Court's ends analysis rules out redistributive legislation -- government can intervene to protect only the public good of everyone, not to promote the interests of particular groups.

(What do you think of the Court's position? Should the Constitution be read to disallow redistribution?)

That's not a completely easy question. The Takings Clause, for instance, clearly does limit certain kinds of redistribution. But just about everything government does redistributes to some extent.

One aspect of the Court's position here is that it seems to take the presently-existing distribution of legal entitlements as "natural" and "pre-governmental" in some sense. Therefore, we should limit Government "interference" with those entitlements.

(What's the best critique of that position?)

The status quo is arguably the product of governmental action already. Distributions of wealth reflect the tax code, government decisions to subsidize particular activities, etc. So you can't characterize this as a choice between government intervention and non-intervention.

(Is there an answer to this sort of argument?)

The problem is that this sort of reasoning erases all meaningful distinctions between different kinds of government actions. Do we really see no difference between a law that, for example, allows the public schools in different parts of a state to be locally funded – and therefore fails to do anything about geographic disparities in the value of the tax base – and a law mandating that everyone with an income over $75K will give $5K annually to people with incomes under $15K?

(Does anyone think the Court was actually right?)

(Is anyone *harmed* by this law?)

The statute in *Lochner* was arguably special interest legislation, procured by a set of well-established bakeries—mostly earlier German immigrants—who didn't need to work the longer hours, in order to disadvantage smaller, more economically marginal bakeries—usually owned by later immigrants, such as Southern Europeans—who worked longer hours and had worse conditions. Similar legislation is sometimes supported by labor unions who have an organizational advantage over two groups adversely affected -- consumers (who pay higher prices for bread), and non-unionized workers (who might prefer long hours to no job at all).

(Should that make a difference?)

You can see economic substantive due process as an attempt at representation reinforcement -- the Court is arguably seeking to offset the advantages of special interests by demanding that statutes serve a *public* purpose.

But perhaps all politics is inevitably the product of interest group deals, so that it's simply unrealistic to demand a public purpose.

These arguments mirror the arguments in Justice Sutherland's dissent in the milk case, *Nebbia v. New York*, which we'll touch on in a minute.

We'll go through the remaining freedom of contract cases more quickly. You have two in the materials: *Adkins* and *Nebbia*.

4.   *Adkins v. Children's Hospital*, 261 U.S. 525 (1923)

Adkins involves a minimum wage law for women in the District of Columbia.   The law is challenged both by an employer—Children's Hospital, the same hospital that fixed up my soon Alex back in 1996—and a 21-year-old woman who works as an elevator operator at a hotel, who has lost her job because the hotel's unwilling or unable to pay her the minimum wage.

The case is similar to *Lochner*. Let's do the means/ends thing again:

(What's the end in view here?)

The health and morals of the workers.

(Is that a legitimate end?)

Sure.

(What about the fit between the means and the ends?)

Not so much, right? The regulation is too blunt an instrument: There's no relation between the fixed minimum wage and the value of particular work, or the needs of particular women in particular circumstance.

Note that again we get tag-team dissents, as in *Lochner*. Chief Justice Taft somewhat plays the role of Harlan: His dissent is *internal* to the doctrine. He simply can't make the invalidity of minimum wages square with the validity of maximum hour laws, as in *Bunting*. This is the Frankfurter Constraint at work—his concern is that whatever principle the Court is operating under isn't being applied in a principled way.

Justice Holmes, on the other hand, is more skeptical of the very idea of freedom of contract, although he also replicates some of Taft's narrower arguments.

Beyond this, I want to stress just a couple of points:

- In this case, the Due Process Clause is being deployed against the *federal* government, not the States.

- The majority acknowledges that the Court has *upheld* a lot of regulatory laws against freedom of contract challenges; in fact, the Court upheld as many statutes as it struck down during this period. The *Adkins* majority categorizes the sorts of cases where this has occurred:

    → regulations setting rates for businesses impressed with a public interest;

    → regulation of the terms for performance of government contracts;

    → wage regulation other than amount—i.e., methods for time & payment, etc.

    → maximum hour laws, at least in particularly hazardous lines of work, and hours for women.

- There's an interesting discussion of feminism, because the big case that the majority has to distinguish is *Muller v. Oregon*, 208 U.S. 412 (1908), which upheld a maximum hours law regulating women working in laundries. The Court was willing to accept that women were less able to look out for their own interests, and were more vulnerable to debilitating work conditions.

    But the Court limited *Muller* in *Adkins*, where it struck down a minimum wage law for women. The Court cited the advances women had made toward equality as evidence that they no longer needed special protection.

    (If you're a feminist, do you like *Muller* or *Adkins* better?)

5.   *Nebbia v. New York*, 291 U.S. 502 (1934)

Nebbia is important for two reasons: It's an example of a case going the other way during this period, and it's a harbinger of the change that's going to occur three years later in 1937. In that respect, it casts some doubt on the causality of FDR's Court-Packing plan in forcing the Court to change direction.

New York is regulating milk prices—trying to keep them higher rather than lower. (Remember, the big economic problem in the Depression wasn't *in*flation but rather *de*flation—that is, dramatic drops in prices. Complain about rising gas prices all you want, but deflation is worse.)

Let's do the means/ends thing again:

(What's the end?)

Two: Protecting dairy farmers, and protecting public health by keeping prices high enough so that producers can afford to be vigilant against health risks.

(Are these legitimate?)

Health surely is.

(What about protecting producers?)

The dissenters say no, right? Why protect producers vis a vis grocers or consumers?

(What about means/ends fit?)

It's not clear this helps farmers, since it's not clear the prices will be passed through.

(How does the court evaluate this? How does it resolve disputes about facts and efficacy?)

It defers considerably to the legislature.

Note the other move, which concerns the "affected with a public interest" doctrine.

(How does the Court define this category?)

Broadly: Whatever the government considers to be affected with a public interest, *is* affected with a public interest.

6. *Lochner* and Non-Economic Rights

The Court's expansive reading of the Due Process Clause during this period doesn't include only economic rights like freedom of contract. Recall that Justice Peckhams' definition of "liberty" in *Allgeyer* was basically all those freedoms which make it possible for an individual to choose their own vision of the good life. That broad reading is borne out in two critical cases during the *Lochner* period involving non-economic rights:

- *Meyer v. Nebraska*, **262 U.S. 390 (1923):** The Court strikes down a state law forbidding the teaching of foreign languages to young children. Justice McReynolds uses the case to announce a very broad view of "liberty" as including "not merely freedom from bodily restraint but also the right of the individual to contract, to engage in any of the common occupations of life, to acquire useful knowledge, to marry, establish a home and bring up children, to worship God according to the dictates of his own conscience, and generally to enjoy those privileges long recognized at common law as essential to the orderly pursuit of happiness by free men."

The Court says that the foreign language rule interferes with "the opportunity of pupils to acquire knowledge, and with the power of parents to control the education of their own."

- **Pierce v. Society of Sisters, 268 U.S. 510 (1925):** Court strikes down a law mandating that children attend public schools on similar grounds.

A third case decided just after the end of the *Lochner* era for *economic* rights demonstrates that the Court's willingeness to protect non-economic rights persists:

- **Skinner v. Oklahoma, 316 U.S. 535 (1942):** Court uses equal protection to protect a fundamental interest in procreation and bodily integrity, striking down a mandatory sterilization law for persons convicted of a third felony involving moral turpitude.

B.   Federalism in the *Lochner* Era

This assignment develops the Lochner *era Court's federalism jurisprudence as complementary to its freedom of contract jurisprudence—that is, as a distinct doctrinal lever used for the same philosophical end of protecting the market from government interference. It's important to point out that the* Lochner *era federalism cases did not actually protect the freedom of state governments to regulate as they wished; rather, the states were prevented from regulating (in many cases, at least) by the freedom of contract cases. Although there are no "dormant" Commerce Clause cases in this section, it's worth noting that the Court was also quite strict in that area, giving it another lever to prevent active state regulation of the market. At the same time, and as in the previous section, it's important to stress that the Court was by no means categorical in its prohibition of federal regulation. This area reflects instead a tension between two lines of cases, one embodied by* Hammer *and one by the* Shreveport Rate Cases, *which did allow federal regulation of intrastate activity where it was necessary to facilitate interstate regulation.*

This assignment is also a good place to introduce the distinction between "formalist" and "functionalist" or "realist" approaches to constitutional doctrine. That contrast is particularly interesting here, because in one line of cases (e.g., E.C. Knight) formalism tends to restrict government power, while in another (e.g. Hammer) it tends to expand it—and vice versa for realism.

Remember we've already discussed the Commerce Clause in connection with *Gibbons* and *Willson*. Those cases were mostly about the "negative" or "dormant" Commerce Clause – that is, the restrictions that the Constitution imposes on *state* regulation of the national economy. That sort of limit is the Court's central concern in the 19th century, mostly because not much regulation is being undertaken at the national level. But with the advent of national regulation like the Sherman Antitrust Act and the Interstate Commerce Act at the end of the century, the Court begins to enforce some limits on the *affirmative* scope of the Commerce Clause – that is, the power of Congress to regulate.

These limits become an important tool for limiting governmental intrusions into the free market when undertaken at the national level. The Commerce Clause cases work in tandem with the substantive due process cases, and they follow a similar trajectory of judicial activism followed by retreat.

1.   Overview

Part of the story of the development of federalism jurisprudence in this country is a transition from "dual federalism" to "concurrent jurisdiction."

- *Dual Federalism* seeks to divide the world into two separate spheres of regulatory jurisdiction, with state and federal authority *exclusive* within their respective spheres.

  Ex: The Federal government has exclusive authority over foreign affairs; the States have exclusive authority over family law.

- *Concurrent Jurisdiction* recognizes both state *and* federal authority to regulate most subjects.   The question then is how to identify and resolve conflicts between federal and state activity.

  Ex: Both the States and the Federal government may regulate most commercial activity, but federal law prevails under the Supremacy Clause in the event of a conflict.

Gibbons and *Willson* were both "dual federalism" cases, and that trend basically persists until the Revolution of 1937. But the line between the federal and the state sphere becomes increasingly hard to draw over the course of this period.

There are basically two sets of cases:

- *Economic Regulation* cases, in which Congress is trying to regulate somewhat more broadly than strictly commercial transactions involving more than one state. Here, the classic examples are *E.C. Knight* and the *Shreveport Rate Cases.*

- *Social Regulation* cases, in which Congress is trying to achieve certain social or moral ends through banning interstate transportation of certain people or goods. Ex: *The Lottery Case; Hammer v. Dagenhart.*

It's important to recognize that even though the Court is more aggressive in striking down federal legislation in this period than they would be after 1937, there are also important lines of cases upholding broad national regulatory power.

Finally, it also helps to think about different *kinds* of legal rules here:

- *Formalism:* The Court examines the statute and the regulated activity to determine whether certain objective criteria are met. Actual economic effects or legislative motive are unimportant.

- *Realism:* The Court focuses on actual economic impact of the regulation or the actual motivation of Congress.

A lot of people tend to think "formalism = old, bad; realism = new, good." But I think the cases break down in a more complicated way than that. You see the old Court trying *both* formalist and realist approaches.

2.   The Economic Regulation Cases

In these cases Congress is trying to get at a particular economic problem, which it turns out extends somewhat beyond the bounds of strictly interstate commerce. The classic example is

a.   *United States v. E.C. Knight Co.*, 156 U.S. 1 (1895)

The American Sugar Refining Co. sought to acquire four other sugar refineries, which would give the company control over 97 percent of the sugar refining capacity in the U.S. The Government sought to set aside the merger under the Sherman Act, which bans monopolization of any part of interstate commerce. But the Supreme Court (Fuller, C.J.) says the Feds can't stop the merger.

(Is this a constitutional or statutory holding?)

Statutory. The Court held that the Sherman Act doesn't cover this case.

(Why not?)

The reason was that, in the Court's view, to define "commerce among the several states" in the Act broadly enough to include this case would make the statute unconstitutional. (Note that this is a good example of the principle I noted in our discussion of *Marbury*, which is that courts will read a statute narrowly in order to avoid constitutional problems.) The key point for present purposes, though, is that the analysis in the opinion is about the *constitutional* question – the limits of Congress's power.

(Why does the Court think Congress would lack power to regulate this merger?)

Two key distinctions are operating in cases like *Knight*. The first is:

- "Manufacturing" vs. "Commerce": The Court limits "commerce" to buying and selling; *making* the product (refining the sugar) is "manufacturing."

(Is that a satisfactory distinction?)

Well, the obvious answer is that a monopoly over production of a product will surely affect the price at which it's sold. The Court knows this, of course – they're not stupid or naïve.

(Why aren't they willing to look at the *effect* of the monopoly in production on the sale price for sugar?)

The Court employs a second distinction:

- "Direct" vs. "Indirect": The effect on price of a monopoly in production may be large, but it is *indirect* in nature. This turns out to be the key point, I think.

(Why not leave a situation like this to the States, anyway?)

Because American Sugar is so big, and operates in so many states, that no individual state is really in a position to regulate it.

Moreover, even if the acquired refineries were all in a single state, people in all states would be affected by a monopoly in sugar. So there's a clear spillover effect.

(Do these kind of practical considerations matter to the Court in *Knight*?)

No. That's why this case is a good example of *formalist* reasoning.

Knight is the sort of case that we generally associate with the Court's jurisprudence in this period. But it's important to understand that there are two strands of cases here, with considerable tension between them. The great counter-example is

> **b.   The *Shreveport Rate Case (Houston E. & W. Texas Ry. Co. v. United States*, 234 U.S. 342 (1914))**

Here, the Court upheld regulation of *intrastate* railroad rates by the Interstate Commerce Commission. The commission set a maximum rate for shipments from Shreveport to Texas, and also ordered the railway to charge no lower rates per mile on intrastate rates than on the interstate rate.

(The ICC's main task is to regulate *inter*state rates; why are they messing around with *intra*state rates?)

They did this because, otherwise, rates from Marshall to Dallas would be priced much lower than from Marshall to Shreveport, presumably to undercut Shreveport as a destination for shipments from East Texas. The Court holds (Hughes, J.) that the regulation is valid.

There's no problem whether this is commerce - it's travel, just like *Gibbons*. But one might think that the effect on commerce of the intrastate rates is an *indirect* one.

(Why isn't it an indirect effect?)

The Court finds that it's necessary to regulate the intrastate travel in order to effectively regulate the interstate travel: "the interstate and intrastate transactions of carriers are so related that the government of one involves the control of the other."

(Does this seem like a "formalist" or a "realist" approach to you?)

It's realist - recognizing the economic reality of an integrated interstate and intrastate economy, at least in some areas.

(Any way to distinguish *Knight* on the facts?)

Note that one distinguishing factor from *E.C. Knight* is that we're dealing with *trains* here, which are not only engaged in commerce but are actual *instrumentalities* of commerce.

I think that's at least somewhat important. But the Court's rationale seems broader than that. And throughout the *Lochner* period the *Shreveport Rate Case* serves as authority for upholding some kinds of economic regulation. This strand then becomes dominant after 1937.

Note - Federal Self-Denial: The Federal Communications Act, enacted during the New Deal Period and which created the Federal Communications Commission, explicitly denied the FCC the power to regulate intrastate communications. This provision was specifically intended to overrule the *Shreveport Rate Case* in the area of communications. Two points about this:

- It's an example of the political safeguards of federalism (mentioned by Marshall in *Gibbons*) at work. Sometimes Congress is more protective of state prerogatives than the Court.

- It's also an example of how the boundary between federal and state power is often set by *statute* rather than by constitutional doctrine.

3.   The Social Regulation Cases

The question in these cases is whether Congress can bar interstate shipment of goods in order to get at in-state activity that it doesn't like. A good example is *Champion v. Ames*,[21] which the Court decided in 1903 and has to distinguish in *Hammer*. In that case, Congress wanted to discourage lotteries on moral grounds, but it probably lacked power to simply ban lotteries directly. So the Federal Lottery Act of 1895 banned the *interstate transportation* of lottery tickets. Champion was indicted for shipping a box of Paraguayan lottery tickets from Texas to California in violation of the law.

---

[21] 188 U.S. 321 (1903).

Champion's best argument relied on Chief Justice Marshall's statement in *McCulloch* that "should Congress, under the *pretext* of executing its powers, pass laws for the accomplishment of objects not entrusted to the government; it would become the painful duty of this tribunal . . . to say that such an act was not the law of the land." But the Court in Champion's case upheld the federal law, concluding that since Art. I gives Congress the power to regulate interstate Commerce, it may do so for any *end* that it wishes.

Notice how this is the flip side of *McCulloch*. In that case, Congress wanted to pursue various *ends* that were enumerated in the Constitution (such as raising armies or borrowing money) by way of *means* that weren't enumerated (creating a national bank). In *Champion*, Congress is pursuing an *end* that's not in the Constitution (promoting morality by discouraging gambling) by a *means* that is enumerated in Art. I (regulating interstate commercial transactions).

During the first part of the 20th century the Court upheld a number of bans on interstate shipment or travel, even though the regulation is really directed toward health or morals concerns.

- Impure Foods: In *Hipolite Egg Co. v. United States*, 220 U.S. 45 (1911) the Court upheld a ban on interstate shipment of eggs with illegal ingredient after they had reached their final destination.

- Prostitution: *Hoke v. United States*, 227 U.S. 308 (1913), upheld the Mann Act's prohibition of transporting women across state lines for immoral purposes. (Keep that in mind the next time you fly in a date for a basketball weekend.)

In all these cases, the Court looks simply at the fact that what Congress is actually prohibiting is interstate commerce; it ignores the real *motive* of Congress to regulate public health and morals, which would ordinarily belong to the State police power. In this sense, these cases are an example of *formalist* reasoning.

The Court shifts course, however, in *Hammer*.

4.   *Hammer v. Dagenhart*, 247 U.S. 251 (1918)

Federal law prohibited transportation in interstate commerce of goods made with child labor. A father sued on behalf of his children to enjoin enforcement of the Act.

The Court (Day, J.) holds that the Act exceeds the commerce power.

(How does the Court distinguish *Champion* and the other interstate shipment cases?)

Champion is distinguishable because there, "the use of interstate transportation was necessary to the accomplishment of harmful results."

Here, the interstate transportation has nothing to do with Congress's purpose; the goods themselves are not harmful. (Really? I don't want to ride in a car built by my 13-year-old kid.) In the Court's view, Congress is simply using commerce as a hook to achieve a goal outside its enumerated powers.

(Was there any particular federal need to regulate in this area?)

There's a real race to the bottom problem. States may refuse to ban child labor for fear of business relocating to other states.

But the Court says that simply because interstate competition may discourage reforms like this is not a basis for Congress to act.

(Justice Holmes writes a famous dissent here. What's his position?)

"[I]f an act is within the powers specifically conferred upon Congress, it seems to me that it is not made any less constitutional because of the indirect effects that it may have, however obvious it may be that it will have those effects."

Note that this is the formalist approach again.

(What does he think the Court is really up to?)

Just enforcing its view of sound economics and policy. But if the Court is going to follow its own policy view, it should ban child labor.

This is a common charge throughout these years - that the Court is resisting economic regulation because of the Justices' personal commitment to laissez faire economics.

I'm a little skeptical here: After all, this is the same court that had upheld the other forms of economic regulation. And the distinction between this case and *Champion* does suggest that this case goes further - even if it's in a better cause. I think what the majority is really worried about is the litigation strategy point: Whether upholding this law would leave intact any principled limits on Congress's power.

On the other hand, it's worth stepping back and asking whether the Court is really protecting federalism in these cases.

(Is the Court protecting the autonomy of the states to do what they want in terms of economic regulation without federal interference?)

No way – When the states regulate, the Court strikes those regulations down under the due process clause.

The effect of the due process cases and the commerce clause cases, taken together, is to ensure that *neither* the federal nor the state level of government can regulate the economy. In other words, the Court is imposing its own national, uniform economic policy on all the states: *laissez faire*.

This is an important point, and its corollary is that when the Court shifts course and frees the federal government to establish the New Deal, that shift *also* empowers *state* governments to regulate the economy on behalf of their citizens. We'll come back to this point at the end of the next set of cases.

The last case in this sequence takes us into the New Deal period:

5. *A.L.A. Schechter Poultry Corp. v. United States*, 295 U.S. 495 (1935)

The National Industrial Recovery Act allowed boards of private businesses to develop "codes of fair competition," which were then approved by the President.

The Live Poultry Code promulgated under the NIRA regulated wages and hours in the slaughterhouse business, and required purchasers to buy an entire "run" of a coop, including sick poultry. (For that reason, this case is generally known as the "sick chicken" case.)

Schechter was convicted of violating the code in New York City. Virtually all the poultry in New York was shipped by railroad from other states.

The Court holds (Hughes, CJ) that the law is unconstitutional. There are two distinct problems:

• The law delegates too many lawmaking powers to the President and to private bodies. That's a *separation of powers* problem, and we'll see this case again in that unit.

• The law falls outside the limit of the Commerce Clause.

(What's the government's argument that the wages and hours of chicken vendors *affects* interstate commerce?)

Labor costs are about 50-60% of chicken prices, and allowing employers to charge really low wages and demand really long hours cuts those costs a lot and translates into lower prices for chickens. (Remember that a big part of the economic problem during the Depression is *deflation* rather than inflation.)

(What does Chief Justice Hughes say?)

Congress can't regulate indirect effects, which is all we have here. If they could do so, "the federal authority would embrace practically all the activities of the people and the authority of the State over its domestic concerns would exist only by sufferance of the federal government."

(Is the Court just being unsophisticated about the economics here? Do they not understand that prices and wages in different local markets are all tied together?)

I don't think so. Listen to Justice Cardozo's concurrence on this point: "[There] is a view of causation that would obliterate the distinction between what is national and what is local in the activities of commerce. Motion at the outer rim is communicated perceptibly, though minutely, to recording instruments at the center. A society such as ours 'is an elastic medium which transmits all tremors throughout its territory: the only question is of their size.'"

Now Cardozo is a pretty sophisticated guy; when you take Torts, you'll find his opinions on causation are still the classics in the field. His opinion in the *Palsgraf* case is probably the most famous discussion of proximate causation in American tort law. So it's not like he doesn't understand the mechanisms at work here.

His concern, though, is that we have to draw a line somewhere or else give up on the idea of limited and enumerated federal power. So he says: "The law is not indifferent to considerations of degree. . . . To find immediacy or directness here is to find it almost everywhere."

(Finally, does the Court care that there's a Depression on?)

Not really. The Court recognizes "the grave national crisis with which Congress was confronted. . . . But [extraordinary] conditions do not create or enlarge constitutional power."

Some observations on *Schechter*:

- The National Industrial Recovery Act, parts of which were struck down in *Schechter* as well as the *Panama Refining* case mentioned on p. 131, was an example of "corporatism" – a form a social and political organization in which government cooperates very closely with business in running the economy. It's a different model from having big regulatory bureaucracies run the economy; under the NIRA, Congress gave private companies the power to get together and regulate their own markets. (It's also not the socialist model either, which envisioned *public ownership* of the means of production—the NIRA is more like Mussolini's Italy.)

  This isn't a model we're very interested in anymore, and in fact most people agree that the NIRA was a failure. In fact, it was set to expire a few weeks after *Schechter* was decided. So the Court may have done FDR a favor in giving it the *coup de grace*. But his concern is that *Schechter* means that the Court's view of federal power is too narrow to permit other, more valuable programs.

- Note that the liberals join this opinion, and that the opinion below striking the law down was written by Judge Learned Hand. So *Schechter* indicates that the range of disagreement on the Court in this period is not all that dramatic; even the liberals agree that the Court ought to draw *some* lines limiting federal power. They differ mainly on questions of degree.

- Note finally that we'll see this case again: The Court also struck down the statute on the ground that it impermissibly delegated legislative authority to private entities. We'll study that holding when we get to separation of powers and the nondelegation doctrine.

C.   The New Deal Crisis

As did the units on Marbury *and* Dred Scott, *this section emphasizes the interplay between law and politics. We start with FDR's "fireside chat" in support of his plan to pack the Court. It's worth lingering on the question whether court-packing offends any constitutional norms, and whether other institutional alternatives— such as a constitutional amendment giving Congress power to reverse certain Supreme Court decisions—would have been preferable. The Court's "switch in time" obviated that discussion, of course, and the materials offer two theories about that switch—the conventional "external" account that the Court caved in to political pressure, and the revisionist "internal" account that the switch actually derived from the Court's resolution of tensions that existed in the doctrine all along. That question is probably unresolvable at the end of the day, but it affords an opportunity to talk about the extent to which the Court should be responsive to the other branches and to public opinion.*

> *Lochner* on the due process side and *Hammer* on the commerce clause side are probably our two paradigm cases of aggressive judicial review during the *Lochner* era. While you should keep in mind that there are departures from the pattern – that is, that the Court *upheld* a lot of statutes during this period under both theories – the story is one of increasing tension between the political branches and the federal courts through the nineteen-teens and twenties.
>
> There's also a lot of tension *within* the Supreme Court. Note that the Court was deeply divided during this period, with a lot of 5 to 4 decisions striking down federal legislation. The line-up in those cases tended to be a core of four conservative justices – Sutherland, McReynolds, Butler, and Van Devanter, collectively known as "the Four Horsemen" – joined by Justice Owen Roberts, who was more moderate. The "liberal" wing consisted of Chief Justice Charles Evans Hughes and Justices Cardozo, Stone, and Brandeis.
>
> But it's worth noting that not *all* these cases are 5-4, either prior to the New Deal crisis or during it. In *Schechter*, for instance, Hughes writes the majority opinion and Cardozo and Stone concur. These opinions are sometimes still cited as authority for various propositions, although their holdings are of pretty questionable validity today.

1.   **The Court Challenges the New Deal**

In any event, things really come to a head once FDR is elected president in 1932 and embarks on a program of radically restructuring the government to deal with the Depression.   The Court blocks a number of these initiatives, particularly on grounds of the commerce clause and non-delegation – the two grounds that are uniquely concerned with *federal* legislation.

We've already discussed one of the cases – *Schechter Poultry* – that FDR viewed as the "last straw" and that provoked to launch his effort to pack the Court with more favorable justices. *Schechter* was followed by *Carter v. Carter Coal Co.*, 298 U.S. 238 (1936), in which the Court struck down the Bituminous Coal Conservation Act of 1935 – a far more important statute than the NIRA – on Commerce Clause grounds.

Two other cases are important here:

- In *United States v. Butler*, 297 U.S. 1 (1936), the Court struck down the Agricultural Adjustment Act of 1933 – a major New Deal program, as outside Congress's *taxing* power, and the reasoning of the opinion suggested that the Social Security Act of 1935 – a centerpiece of the New Deal program – might also be in danger.

- On the Due Process/Freedom of Contract side, it had looked like things were looking up for economic regulation after *Nebbia v. NY*. But two years later in *Morehead v. New York ex rel. Tipaldo*, 298 U.S. 587 (1936), the Court reaffirmed its hard line freedom of contract stance from *Adkins* by invalidating New York's minimum wage law for women.

Put all these cases together, and the Roosevelt administration has reason to worry that the Court would strike down some of the truly critical components of the New Deal, such as the National Labor Relations Act.

2.   **The Court-Packing Scheme**

Following his massive victory in the 1936 election, Roosevelt proposed that one additional justice be added for each justice over seventy -- up to a total of fifteen justices. The claim was that the older justices needed help, but the clear intent was to pack the court with New Dealers.

I've given you FDR's "fireside chat" – a radio address in which he laid out his court-packing plan and the justifications for it to the American people. This is an extraordinary document, in that it's the President trying to talk to "the People" as a whole, directly, about constitutional law.

(How does FDR justify the need for change at the Supreme Court?)

There are three essential points, I think:

1) There's a national emergency that requires national action;

2) The Court's standing in the way;

and (crucially)

3) What the Court is doing is not mandated by the Constitution.

(How do we know that?)

Because the dissents in the cases say there's no basis for the holdings. FDR concludes that the Court is just doing politics. This is an example of the Frankfurter Constraint in action.

(What do you think of the court-packing plan? Is it an appropriate thing for a president to propose? Would it have been constitutional?)

The big alternative to court-packing at the time was a variety of proposed constitutional amendments that would have given Congress the authority to overrule Supreme Court decisions by supermajority vote.

Note that the proposed bill I passed out a couple weeks ago – proposed in the current Congress – would do much the same thing by 2/3 vote of both houses.

(What do you think of that as an alternative?)

One thing to note is that the court-packing plan isn't the first instance of efforts by the political branches to pack the Court. The Federalists, for instance, cut the number of justices from 6 to 5 in the Judiciary Act of 1801, in order to keep Jefferson from appointing a successor to a justice who had died.

The Jeffersonians engaged in equally dubious tactics, including canceling a term of court so that the Court couldn't hear particular cases and impeaching justices they disagreed with.

In the modern era, there have been lots of attempts to strip the court of jurisdiction over particular classes of cases in which the decisions have been unpopular.

(Are these alternatives better or worse than court-packing?)

Last point here is that the degree of public opposition to the court-packing plan is significant. This is true even though monstrous majorities backed the President on the substance of the laws being struck down. It tells you something about the well of legitimacy that the Court has to draw on as an institution, even if its results are unpopular. (This doesn't mean, though, that the plan would have failed if the Court hadn't switched.)

3.   The Switch in Time

Before the court-packing plan comes to a vote, the Court changes course. In *West Coast Hotel v. Parrish*, the Court abandons its economic substantive due process jurisprudence and upholds a state minimum wage statute, overruling a decision striking down such a statute the year before.

And in **NLRB v. Jones & Laughlin** -- decided during the Senate debates on the court-packing plan -- the Court upholds the National Labor Relations Act against a Commerce Clause challenge.

The swing vote in these two cases was Justice Roberts, who switched sides -- this was described as "the switch in time that saved Nine." But there is some evidence that the Court had already voted -- and Justice Roberts had switched sides -- in *West Coast Hotel* before the court-packing plan was unveiled.

After *West Coast Hotel* and *Jones & Laughlin*, the Senate rejected the court-packing plan.

And within a few years, the "Four Horsemen" all retired and were replaced by Roosevelt appointees. Roosevelt's appointments included Hugo Black, Felix Frankfurter, William O. Douglas, and Robert Jackson. These were united in their support for the New Deal and opposition to the old jurisprudence that blocked it; they went very different ways, however, when the issues changed to focus on individual rights.

> a.   **Substantive Due Process:** *West Coast Hotel Co. v. Parrish*, **300 U.S. 379 (1937)**

While *Nebbia* foreshadows the Court's turn away from resisting New Deal regulation in 1937, it's not until *West Coast Hotel* that the Court unambiguously repudiates the *Lochner* doctrines. Here we have another state minimum wage statute for women – the same sort of statute that the Court had struck down just a few years earlier in *Adkins v. Children's Hospital* and again in *Morehead*. The Court (Hughes, CJ) decides to overrule *Adkins* and uphold the statute.

(Recall the difference between Justice Harlan's and Justice Holmes's dissents in *Lochner*: Holmes questions the whole principle of freedom of contract, while Harlan simply seems to agree with the Court's application of the principle in that case. Which approach better describes *West Coast Hotel*?)

I think Holmes's. Chief Justice Hughes questions the very idea of freedom of contract:

"What is this freedom? The Constitution does not speak of freedom of contract. . . . Liberty under the Constitution is . . . necessarily subject to the restraints of due process, and regulation which is reasonable to its subject and is adopted in the interests of the community is due process."

He also embraces the notion that equalization of bargaining power between employers and employees is a legitimate purpose for legislation.

As we'll see tomorrow, the Court does *not* disavow the principle that economic legislation is subject to judicial review for its reasonableness. But that principle becomes so deferential to the legislative branches that it is truly exceptional to see the Court strike anything down on these grounds.

It's important to understand, however, that just as there were cases before *1937* upholding federal action under the Commerce Clause, there were also cases upholding federal and state action under the due process clause. The Court hasn't adopted a wholly new direction; it's just chosen between two conflicting strands of its precedent. It's chosen **Nebbia** over **Lochner**. The key point, though, is that it's chosen the one that is much more deferential to government regulation.

> **b.**   **Federalism: *NLRB v. Jones & Laughlin Steel Corp.*, 301 U.S. 1 (1937)**

West Coast Hotel is to the Due Process Clause as *Jones & Laughlin* is to the Commerce Clause: Each marks the end of the Court's attempt to use these doctrines as tools to protect the free market and strike down attempts at government regulation.

The National Labor Relations Act of 1935 set up a comprehensive system of labor-management relations. It guaranteed the right of organization and collective bargaining, and created a board to supervise elections and enforce prohibitions on unfair labor practices.

The NLRB found that Jones & Laughlin -- a vast steel company with subsidiaries in a number of states -- had engaged in unfair labor practices affecting commerce by discharging certain union members. Jones & Laughlin claimed that the NLRA exceeded the commerce power.

The Court (Hughes, CJ) upholds the statute. The practices here clearly affect interstate commerce, given the vast scope of Jones & Laughlin's enterprise. Congress has the power to regulate any activity that threatens to obstruct interstate commerce. This doesn't turn on a distinction between "manufacturing" or "production" and "commerce," but on the degree of the actual impact.

Here, the impact of a work stoppage at Jones & Laughlin's operation would be too massive to be described as "indirect." Jones & Laughlin has chosen to organize on a national scale -- it is crazy to think that Congress lacks power to regulate such an entity.

Justices McReynolds, Van Devanter, Sutherland, and Butler dissented – the critical switch is Justice Roberts.

(Is *Jones & Laughlin* consistent with the reasoning of the prior cases? Does it just reach a different conclusion applying the old rules to these facts?)

Note the strong reliance on the massiveness of Jones & Laughlin's own operation. That suggests that this case may be just factually distinguishable from something like *Hammer v. Dagenhart* (although *not* *E.C. Knight*). We get the other end of the spectrum in *Wickard*, which holds that Congress can regulate a single farmer who isn't even planning to *sell* his crop.

For 58 years after *Jones & Laughlin*, the Court refuses to strike down a federal statute under the Commerce Clause. Within five years of *Jones & Laughlin*, we get a string of cases indicating just how far the doctrine has moved.

c.   Federalism: *Wickard v. Filburn,* 317 U.S. 111 (1942)

The Agricultural Adjustment Act of 1938 imposed marketing quotas on all wheat farmers that included all crops available for marketing. Farmer Filburn grew more than his quota, although he consumed it entirely on his farm. He sued to enjoin enforcement of the Act against him.

The Court holds (Jackson, J.) that the Act is constitutional, even as applied to Filburn.

(How in the world is Farmer Filburn's extra-curricular wheat cultivation going to have a substantial effect on interstate commerce?)

There's actually two aspects to this question:

a)   Filburn is just one guy; and

b)   Filburn isn't going to *sell* his wheat.

Take the first one first: Filburn is not Jones & Laughlin Steel. In that case, it was plausible that Jones & Laughlin *alone* had a substantial effect on interstate commerce, just like regulating Microsoft would today.

(How in the world do we get from there to regulating one small farmer?)

The question is whether all similar activity affects commerce -- not just this case. "That [Filburn's] own contribution to the demand for wheat
      may be trivial by itself is not enough to remove him from the scope of federal regulation where, as here, his contribution, taken together with that of many others similarly situated, is far from trivial."

This is the *aggregation principle* – we aggregate all instances of similar activity in evaluating substantial effects.

(But what about the second point: Filburn isn't going to sell his wheat?)

Any wheat available for marketing -- whether marketed or not -overhangs the market and affects prices. If prices rise, that wheat flows into the market and holds prices down.

So note how the Court's rejected formalistic distinction; we look at a fairly sophisticated view of economic reality.

(Has the Court gone too far here? Is there anything that Congress *can't* regulate?)

Think, for instance, about backyard gardens. If 10 million people each grow one tomato instead of buying that tomato at the store, then that will surely affect the price of tomatos.

Or here's another example which we thought about putting in our brief in the marijuana case back in 2005: I'm ashamed to say that there's a market for sex in this country. When people stay home and sleep with their spouses, that "overhangs the market" in much the same way that the unsold wheat did in *Wickard* – that is, the non-commercial transaction trades off with a commercial transaction. So does that mean that the *national* government can pass a statute regulating sex (or to take a more likely example) banning gay marriage under the Commerce Clause?

There is one answer, which is that Farmer Filburn fed much of the wheat to his pigs, which he then sold on the market. So you don't have to read *Wickard* so broadly as to allow Congress to regulate any non-commercial activity that impacts commercial activity; instead, you can read the activity here as itself part of production of goods for market. But the case has generally understood more broadly.

We'll come back to *Wickard* when we do the 2005 medical marijuana case in the next unit.

4. The Next 50 Years

In subsequent cases, the Court consolidates the "New Deal Revolution." We run through the more modern due process cases in the next section. On the federalism side, the Court continues to build on *Jones & Laughlin* and *Wickard*:

- *Maryland v.* Wirtz, 392 U.S. 183 (1968): Congress amended the Fair Labor Standards Act to directly regulate wages and hours for every employee "of an enterprise engaged in commerce." The Court upholds this under *Wickard*.

- *Perez v. United States,* 402 U.S. 146 (1971): Court upholds federal criminal statute prohibiting loansharking. Court emphasizes findings that this class of activity has effects on interstate commerce.

- *Hodel v. Virginia Surface Mining Ass'n*, 452 U.S. 264 (1981): Court upholds federal regulation of strip mines. Question is whether Congress could *rationally* have found an effect on commerce.

So what's left after 1937 of the Court's prior jurisprudence? On the federalism side, the Court says in *Jones & Laughlin* that the national government is still one of enumerated powers and that it's applying the same standard as before. But the Court never strikes down another federal statute as outside the Commerce Clause until 1995.

On the substantive due process side, note that the Court never says, in *Nebbia, West Coast Hotel*, or the cases that come after, that the Due Process Clause simply doesn't protect substantive rights, or even economic rights.

Nor does the Court abandon the inquiry, pursued in *Lochner* itself, whether government regulation is rationally related to a legitimate state purpose. That test is still the law, even in cases challenging economic regulation.

The change is in the way the test is applied: After *West Coast Hotel*, judicial review under the rational basis test is so deferential that substantive due process challenges to economic regulation have no chance of success.

That *isn't* true of substantive due process challenges predicated on non-economic rights. *See, e.g., Griswold & Roe.* Whether this "double standard" is appropriate is the question in the next set of materials.

D.   Rationality Review and the Double Standard

This section concludes the New Deal "revolution" by laying out the structure of contemporary constitutional law. While the cases exemplify "rational basis" review, it is a good opportunity to lay out the general doctrinal structure of fundamental rights vs. other liberty interests, suspect vs. non-suspect classifications under the Equal Protection Clause, etc. The section is organized around the "double standard" in constitutional law – that is, the notion that the Court continues rigorously to review government action challenged under certain theories, but is much more deferential in other areas. The materials invite students to struggle with exactly how to define the boundary between these two forms of judicial review, as well as with whether the "double standard" can be justified.

After 1937, the dominant paradigm for judicial review of economic legislation is the "rational basis" test: We simply ask if there is a "rational basis" for the legislative judgment embodied in the statute.

1.   Rationality Review under the Due Process Clause

I've given you two paradigm cases of rationality review: *Carolene Products* and *Lee Optical*.

(How different is the Court's statement of its standard of review in *Carolene Products* or *Lee Optical* from its statement of the standard in *Lochner*?)

Not that different, right?

(Is the *application* different?)

Very much so – it's much more deferential. I think we can identify several particular ways in which it is different:

a.   Presumption in Favor of Legislative Factfinding – *United States v. Carolene Products Co.*, 304 U.S. 144 (1938)

The Court upholds the federal "filled milk" act, which banned mixing skim milk with non-milk fats. The Act was supported by legislative committee findings that filled milk is bad for you.

(Does the Court think that the legislative factfinding is conclusive?)

No – the Court says that the facts supporting the law may be challenged by putting other facts in the record.

(But how does the Court approach resolving that kind of factual dispute?)

It's very deferential. If "any state of facts either known or which could reasonably be assumed" supports the law, or if the question "is at least debatable," then the government wins.

So the Court is looking for actual facts, but willing to defer to the legislature on any close questions.

b.   Hypothetical Rationales and Facts – *Williamson v. Lee Optical of Oklahoma*, 348 U.S. 483 (1955)

The Court upholds a state law requiring that opticians fit or duplicate lenses only with a prescription from an opthalmologist or optometrist.

(Why do you think the legislature passed this law?)

It's special interest legislation – protecting the doctors' monopoly.

(If that were the only possible explanation, should the Court strike it down?)

Tough question. There's a lot of political science that suggests that almost *all* legislation is in some sense special interest legislation. On some theories of democracy – notably democratic pluralism – that's what politics is all about.

(Are there any facts in the record supporting more appealing rationales for the law?)

No.

(Then why doesn't the Court strike it down?)

The Court is willing to construct wholly hypothetical rationales – and hypothetical facts to support them.

(What's the rationale?)

For instance, the Court speculates that maybe it's just good for people to have to go to the opthalmologist or optometrist every so often and get an eye exam, and this statute promotes that.

c.   No Scrutiny at All – *Ferguson v. Skrupa*, 372 U.S. 726 (1963)

One last case that I haven't assigned, just to tell you about:

Justice Black's opinion for the Court upholds a Kansas law restricting the business of "debt adjusting" to licensed lawyers. Again, looks like special interest legislation to me. But the Court says that it has abandoned "the use of the 'vague contours' of the Due Process Clause to nullify laws which a majority of the Court believed to be economically unwise."

Justice Black makes it even clearer in another case from this period, where he says that "states have power to legislate against what are found to be injurious practices . . . so long as their laws do not run afoul of some specific federal constitutional prohibition or of some valid federal law." *Lincoln Federal Labor Union v. Northwestern Iron & Metal Co.*, 335 U.S. 525 (1949).

Contrast Justice Harlan's brief concurrence in *Ferguson*, where he says that the law is OK simply because "it bears a rational relation to a constitutionally permissible objective." (citing *Lee Optical*).

Harlan says there's still a constitutional *issue* here – it's just that the test isn't very tough for the legislature to meet. Black seems to be saying that there's not even a *question* – that absent some "specific federal constitutional provision" (like free speech or something) the Court exercises no review *at all*.

2.   The Double Standard

The Court hasn't invalidated a piece of economic regulation on substantive due process grounds since 1937. The Court almost never hears these cases, and doesn't take substantive due process claims particularly seriously.[22]

---

[22] Two possible blips on the radar screen:

- In *Eastern Enterprises v. Apfel*, 524 U.S. 498 (1998), the Court struck down a federal statutory provision imposing retroactive costs on companies that had been in the coal business. Four justices did this on Takings Clause grounds, but Justice Kennedy provided the crucial fifth vote on a substantive due process theory. About all you can say about this is "stay tuned."

- In *BMW of North America, Inc. v. Gore*, 517 U.S. 559 (1996), the Court struck down a state court punitive damages award as excessive on a substantive due

A similar withdrawal takes place with respect to federalism: After *Jones & Laughlin*, the Court doesn't strike down another law on federalism grounds until 1976, and that case is pretty quickly overruled. It's not until the 1990s that the Court really makes a sustained effort to start enforcing federalism again.

At the same time, you'll see that the Court has been quite activist – and I don't necessarily mean this in a pejorative sense – in enforcing other rights, such as rights to racial equality in *Brown*, or to free speech in a whole host of cases after WWII, or even *non*-economic substantive due process in cases like *Griswold* and *Roe*.

This contrast is what we mean by the "double standard" – there really seem to be, after 1937, parts of the Constitution that the Court is willing to enforce through judicial review and other parts that it isn't. This raises several questions:

(1)   Has the Court overreacted? Were the pre-1937 cases so far wrong that the Court should have abdicated enforcing these principles *entirely*? Do you really think, for instance, that *Schechter* was wrong?

(2)   What's in and what's out? In other words, a double standard between what and what?

(3)   If we can define this double standard, can we also *justify* it?

The first question you can answer for yourself – you've read the cases now, and can evaluate whether you think they're so abysmally wrong as to warrant the Court's withdrawal since. I want to focus on the second two questions:

a.   A Double Standard Between What and What?

We haven't read most of the post-1937 cases that fill out the other side of the double standard – that is, the constitutional principles that the Court remains willing to enforce. But I think you probably have enough common knowledge to know what they are:

- Racial equality – *Brown*, as well as cases limiting affirmative action on the other side;

- Personal right to privacy – *Griswold* (contraceptives) and *Roe* (abortion);

---

process theory. It's hard to describe *BMW* as anything other than economic substantive due process. And *BMW* promises to develop a fairly robust line of case law in the punitive damages area.

- Free speech – the Court has struck down lots and lots of laws on obscenity, flag burning, and the like; and

- Separation of Powers – these cases aren't quite as well known, but the Court continues to police the allocation of power between Congress and the President. It struck down, for instance, the Gramm-Rudman budget act and the Line-Item Veto.

- The Dormant Commerce Clause – the Court is still pretty aggressive about enforcing federalism-based limits on *state* legislation, although the nature of those limits has changed significantly since 1937.

(So how should we define what's in and what's out? What's our dividing criterion?)

> **b.** **Explaining the Divide – the *Carolene Products* Footnote**

One possible answer comes from the most famous footnote in Constitutional Law – footnote 4 of Justice Stone's opinion in *Carolene Products*. Recall that *Carolene Products* was mostly about describing a very deferential standard of review for laws implicating *economic* rights. In the footnote, Justice Stone says:

"There may be narrower scope for operation of the presumption of constitutionality when legislation appears on its face to be within a specific prohibition of the Constitution . . . .

"It is unnecessary to consider now whether legislation which restricts those political processes which can ordinarily be expected to bring about repeal of undesirable legislation, is to be subjected to more exacting judicial scrutiny . . . than are most other types of legislation. . . .

"Nor need we enquire . . . whether prejudice against discrete and insular minorities may be a special condition, which tends seriously to curtail the operation of those political processes ordinarily to be relied upon to protect minorities, and which may call for a correspondingly more searching judicial inquiry."

So three categories where judicial review should be more strict:

(1)   specific constitutional prohibitions, particularly those in the Bill of Rights;

(2)   restrictions on the political process itself – such as limits on free speech or the right to vote; and

(3)   "prejudice against discrete and insular minorities."

Let's take the first category first:

- **Textual vs. Unenumerated Rights**

The first paragraph of the *Carolene Products* footnote suggests that it should make a big difference whether something's actually in the constitutional text. It certainly makes sense of the contrast between *Lochner* itself and, say, the free speech cases.

(Can you think of any counter-examples, though?)

(What about *Blaisdell*? Isn't the Contract Clause pretty textual? Or the modern Takings Clause cases?)

(What about *Roe* on the other side?)

You might also draw a different line based on both the first and second categories in the FN:

- **Individual Rights vs. Structural Provisions**

You could explain the federalism cases by saying that it's the primary role of the court to protect *individual* rights, leaving institutional prerogatives to the political process.

(Does this explain the cases?)

Well, *Lochner* was an individual rights case. And the Court continues to enforce separation of powers, which is structural.

(How would Professor Ely explain the divide?)

- **Rights Entrusted to the Political Process vs. Political "Market Failure"**

(For Ely, what is the basic point of the Constitution?)

It's not to protect particular *values*, like property or privacy or free expression. It's to establish a *process* for democratic government. That process then ensures that conflicts over values are worked out in a fair and democratic manner.

(What does that have to do with judicial review?)

Ely's basic idea – based on FN 4 – is that, ordinarily, we expect the political process to work without a lot of judicial interference, and we think most groups can protect themselves through that process.

But sometimes we *can't* trust the political process, and that's when courts should step in.

(What sorts of political "market failure" is Ely worried about?)

Two kinds:

- when the government puts restrictions on the political process itself, which may skew outcomes or limit dissent, or
- when there's ganging up on minorities.

In these situations, more vigorous judicial checks are appropriate.

(What are some examples of restrictions on the political process itself?)

Restricting political debate is the classic example.

(What about minorities? Is any law that disadvantages a minority suspect? After all, majority rule does systematically disadvantage minorities.)

No. The thing about democracy is that minorities lose. But Ely points out that it oversimplifies to say that politics is about majorities vs. minorities. Rather, the electorate is made up of thousands of *different minorities*. (This will also be the point of Madison's essay in Federalist No. 10, which we'll read in the second part of the course.) Ordinarily, political majorities are simply coalitions of minorities that have decided to work together.

(So when should courts worry?)

When there are particular minorities that are systematically unable to form coalitions—for example, because of racial prejudice. This is what Footnote Four means by "discrete and insular" minorities.

(How well does Prof. Ely's account explain the "double standard"?)

That would explain both the free speech cases and all the cases protecting the rights of politically powerless minorities, as well as the federalism cases and economic substantive due process cases on the other side.

(But what about privacy? Is abortion a right of minorities?)

And there's also the problem of separation of powers.

- **Economic Regulation vs. All Other Kinds**

You might just say that 1937 was about legitimating the right of both national and state governments to regulate the economy.

Even here there are problems: E.g., Dormant Commerce Clause.

One last problem with this way of framing the double standard is that traditional *non*-economic rights are increasingly becoming big economic issues as well. Consider the **telecommunications** industry: Everything it does involves the communication of ideas, and it's all potentially subject to the First Amendment. But it's also a critical component of the economy that raises all sorts of antitrust and regulatory issues. Again, keeping these spheres separate is very difficult.

(How would you justify a line like this? What sort of arguments do Baker & Young identify?)

They distinguish three different kinds of arguments:

- Institutional: Judges have more expertise concerning our noneconomic rights, or they're more likely to come up with workable, determinate doctrine with respect to such rights.

- Necessity: Other, non-judicial actors are likely to protect disfavored rights (like federalism).

- Normative: Non-economic rights are simply more important.

(What do you think? Take the Institutional arguments first. Are judges really better at noneconomic cases?)

(Don't judges have to decide economic issues all the time?)

Sure – a couple of examples:

- Antitrust cases

- Contract cases – is a given provision unconscionable, commercially rational, etc.

(In fact, can we really say *at all* that federal judges are less familiar with economic rights claims? What's the proportion of business litigation to constitutional litigation in most federal courts?)

(What about the necessity arguments?)

(Do we really want judges making the judgment that judicial enforcement is sometimes unnecessary?)

(How would you handle, say, the Press Clause?)

(What about the normative arguments? Are disfavored rights less attractive?)

At the end of the day, I think it's fair to say that we have a double standard but that it's hard to define what's on each side of the line and what the justification for that line is. This doesn't mean we're hopelessly at sea—it's possible to know, at a more specific level of detail, that some rights and values enjoy strong constitutional protection (e.g., free speech, privacy) and that others do not (e.g., property, federalism). What's difficult is to come up with a rationalizing principle that can predict, at a higher level of generality, which rights and values will fall on which side of the line.

IV. Chapter Six – Civil Rights and the Warren Court

The majority of this chapter uses the school desegregation cases to accomplish a number of purposes: (1) Brown I *not only introduces modern equal protection doctrine but also demonstrates a profound shift in the Court's historical role; (2) the academic debate about* Brown I *between Professors Wechsler and Black addresses the question of what it means for judicial decisionmaking to be "principled"; (3)* Brown II *and the Rosenberg excerpts raise the question of judicial efficacy—that is, How much capacity does the Court have to effect social change?; and (4) Cooper raises the issue of the Court's interpretive authority vis-à-vis other government actors. The Chapter then turns to another signature Warren Court achievement, which was to largely complete the incorporation of the Bill of Rights against the States.*

A.　　**Brown and the Problem of Racial Segregation**

The big examples of judicial review that we've studied so far – *Dred Scott* and the *Lochner* cases – aren't exactly poster children for why judicial review is a good thing. These are the cases that the joint opinion in *Planned Parenthood v. Casey* will call "self-inflicted wounds."

Brown I is the poster child for judicial review. For most people, it's the great example of how judicial review can change the world for the better.

I have no wish to debunk *Brown* – I think the day it came down was a great day for America. But we *will* ask three big questions about this conventional wisdom.

- Principle: Are we any more confident about the Court's ability to distinguish between law and politics when we *like* what it's doing than when we don't? Here the critical readings are Herbert Wechsler's landmark article on "Neutral Principles in Constitutional Law" and Charles Black's effort to explain why *Brown* was, in fact, principled.

- Efficacy: We'll also question the conventional wisdom that *Brown* made a big difference. Gerald Rosenberg's book *The Hollow Hope* argues that nothing changed in the South following the *Brown* decision until over a decade later when the national political branches decided to force the South to end segregation. He has made similar arguments that judicial review doesn't make that much difference in other areas, such as abortion rights. So this material takes us back to the distinction between right and remedy, and asks us whether *judicial* remedies are really that meaningful.

- Interpretive Authority: Is the Court the last word on what the Constitution means? Do its rulings bind other government officials who are not parties to the case? This is the question in *Cooper v. Aaron*, but we'll reach back for other examples involving the Bank of the U.S. and the *Dred Scott* decision.

1.　　*Plessy v. Ferguson,* **163 U.S. 537 (1896)**

A LA statute required railroads to provide "equal but separate accommodations" for blacks and whites. Plessy was prosecuted when he failed to leave the coach reserved for whites.

The Court holds (Brown, J.) that the statute is constitutional.

"The object of the [fourteenth] amendment was undoubtedly to enforce the absolute equality of the two races before the law, but, in the nature of things, it could not have been intended to abolish distinctions based upon color, or to enforce social, as distinguished from political, equality, or a commingling of the two races upon terms unsatisfactory to either."

Laws separating the races "do not necessarily imply the inferiority of either race to the other."

(What's the Court's best example here?)

Segregated *schools* (!).

(Are there any limits on segregation?)

This doesn't mean that segregation can be taken to ridiculous extremes. "[E]very exercise of the police power must be reasonable, and extend only to such laws as are enacted in good faith for the promotion of the public good, and not for the annoyance or oppression of a particular class."

(What sort of limit is this?)

Substantive due process – which shows the libertarian potential of freedom of contract.

But – It's not unreasonable to enforce "established usages, customs, and traditions of the people."

(How does Justice Harlan's dissent respond to this argument – that segregation does not impose inequality on black people?)

He says, "Every one knows that the statute in question had its origin in the purpose, not so much to exclude white persons from railroad cars occupied by blacks, as to exclude colored people from coaches occupied by . . . white persons."

Compare Charles Black's "everyone knows" argument about *Brown*.

(Does Harlan think the races are really equal?)

No. He says that the white race will continue to be dominant "for all time, if it remains true to its great heritage."

(So what does "equal protection" mean for him?)

"But in view of the constitution, in the eye of the law, there is in this country no superior, dominant, ruling class of citizens. There is no caste here. Our constitution is colorblind, and neither knows nor tolerates classes among citizens."

(Is that the right interpretation? Is colorblindness what we should be shooting for?)

You'll want to think more about whether this is the right answer when the issue shifts to affirmative action and voting rights – which we unfortunately won't cover.

(How does the majority respond to Justice Harlan's argument about the stigmatizing effects of segregation?)

They blame the black plaintiffs. "We consider the underlying fallacy of the plaintiff's argument to consist in the assumption that the enforced separation of the two races stamps the colored race with a badge of inferiority. If this be so, it is not by reason of anything found in the act, but solely because the colored race chooses to put that construction upon it."

(What do you think of this argument?)

(If you think it's wrong, will *any* subjective belief suffice to show discrimination? What if I subjectively argue that segregated bathrooms are a badge of inferiority (especially since women's restrooms are always nicer)?)

Note how prophetic Harlan is. "What can more certainly arouse race hate . . . than state enactments which . . . proceed on the ground that colored citizens are so inferior and degraded that they cannot be allowed to sit in public coaches occupied by white citizens?"

It's only fair to say, though, that the majority is prophetic too:

"[The defendant's argument] assumes that social prejudices may be overcome by legislation, and that equal rights cannot be secured to the negro except by an enforced commingling of the two races. We cannot accept this proposition. . . . If one race be inferior to the other socially, the constitution of the United States cannot put them upon the same plane."

All this raises two critical questions:

(1)   What is the harm of segregation? Is it simply that the State is treating people differently on account of their race, or that it generates damaging results for black people?

(2)   What is the institutional capacity of courts to effect massive social change? Pay attention to whether the Court can simply order segregation to end, or whether it must depend on a shift in the political winds before its orders have any real effect.

2.   *Brown's* Precursors – The Big 12 Tetralogy

Three cases decided between *Plessy* and *Brown* prefigure the Court's shift in *Brown* from separate but equal to mandatory integration. (I haven't assigned the opinions themselves, but each is discussed in the *Brown* opinion.) Note that three are about law schools. (They're also all four Big 12 cases!)[23]

These decisions are also a good case study in how a doctrine that seems fairly determinate – separate but equal isn't a fuzzy balancing test, but looks like a bright line rule – can nonetheless fall apart when it comes in contact with the real world. This is how a doctrine dies.

a.   Missouri ex rel. Gaines v. Canada, 305 U.S. 337 (1938)

The Court strikes down Missouri's law school system, which required segregated education for whites and blacks. The all-white University of Missouri provided a law school, while the black university, Lincoln University, did not. Missouri law provided for sending black residents to law schools in neighboring states and paying their tuition there. The Court rules that the State must provide equal facilities within the state.

(Why would the Court insist on that? Let's assume the out-of-state school is just as good as the in-state one, by any objective measure.)

Well, why do so many of you turn down offers of admission to schools ranked higher than UT, in order to come here? Because you know that if you want to practice in Texas, it's better to have gone to law school here, made connections, learned local law, etc. (Believe me, I know this: I went to Harvard and then tried to get a job in Dallas, and it's clear I was no better off than if I'd gone to law school in Texas.)

b.   *Sipuel v. Board of Regents*, 332 U.S. 631 (1948)

The Court, relying on *Gaines*, orders the University of Oklahoma law school to admit a black student who had been excluded solely on the basis of race.

c.   *Sweatt v. Painter*, 339 U.S. 629 (1950)

The Court requires the UT law school to admit a black student, because the black law school was not in fact equal. I'm guessing the facilities were somewhat unequal, but the Court doesn't emphasize that. The Court does take into account intangible factors like reputation and networking in assessing "equality" of facilities.

Note also that this case amounts to a holding by the U.S. Supreme Court that the University of Texas is a great law school. Chief Justice Vinson's opinion says that "the University of Texas Law School possesses to a far greater degree those qualities which are incapable of objective

---

[23] Sadly, the University of Missouri is leaving the Big 12 beginning in the 2012 football season.

measurement but which make for greatness in a law school." (Take that, U.S. News!)

Now to say this is not to minimize the shame that the institution ought to feel for how Heman Sweatt was treated. Sweatt had an (understandably) hard time coping with the publicity and hostility that greeted him as a law student. He failed his first year and ultimately dropped out. (But George Washington, Jr., another black student, did graduate in 1952.)

d.   *McLaurin v. Oklahoma State Regents*, 339 U.S. 637 (1950)

This one's OU's case – McLauren is pursuing graduate school in Education at the University of Oklahoma. The Court strikes down a program segregating a black student within the white school – he was forced to sit in a special seat, prohibited from dining with other students in the cafeteria, and had to sit at a special table in the library. (Note the picture in the Handout—see why everybody hates Oklahoma?)

(So what's not equal here?)

The Court held that these restrictions "[impaired] and [inhibited] his ability to study, to engage in discussion and exchange views with other students, and, in general, to learn his profession."

Note that here the facilities are clearly equal. What the Court is recognizing is that segregation cuts black people off from the rest of society, and that that in itself is devastating to their prospects.

(What's left of separate but equal? Anything?)

With these rulings on the books, the Court is all set for Brown.

3.   *Brown v. Board of Education of Topeka (Brown I)*, 347 U.S. 483 (1954)

Black parents sued on behalf of their children to obtain admission to their local public schools on a non-segregated basis. The Court holds (Warren, CJ) that segregated schools are unconstitutional.

Professor Powe tells a wonderful story about the machinations that eventually produce the unanimous opinion in *Brown*. Remember that *Brown* is first argued in the 1952 Term, but not decided until the 1953 Term. (Terms of Court are identified by the year in which they start – e.g., *Brown* is decided in the Spring of 1954, but that's still the 1953 Term.)

Powe says the initial line-up of votes after the first argument was as follows:

- Black, Douglas, Minton, & Burton are inclined to hold segregation *per se* unconstitutional.

- CJ Vinson, Clark (our grad), and Reed are inclined to stick with *Plessy*.

- Jackson is ambivalent on race – unclear what he'll do.

- Frankfurter clearly agrees with the four good guys, but he doesn't think the Court can pronounce segregation unconstitutional in a 5-4 opinion.

So Frankfurter comes up with the idea to reargue the case in the following term. In the interim, CJ Vinson dies and is replaced by Earl Warren. Frankfurter supposedly said later that Vinson's death at that time was "the first evidence I've ever seen of the existence of God."

Warren, of course, wants to strike segregation down, and Clark likes to go with the Chief. That leaves Reed as the last holdout. Warren is said to have told Reed, "Stan, you're all alone in this, and you're going to have to decide what's best for the country." Ultimately, Warren gets his unanimous court. This is probably important: We've already talked about how John Marshall knew that sometimes it's important for the Court to speak with a unified voice. You'll see that again shortly in *Cooper v. Aaron*.

Enough inside stories; let's look at the opinion:

(What's the first source of law that the Court looks to? And what does it tell us?)

a.   The History

Remember that the ostensible purpose of the re-argument was to get the parties to brief the historical issues: Did the Framers of the Fourteenth Amendment mean to outlaw segregated public schools?

(Did they?)

Hard to say. Two problems with original intent here:

- It's indeterminate. Some supporters of the Civil War Amendments probably intended to desegregate the schools; others clearly did not.

  Remember that this is one of the problems with original intent generally: When you're dealing with the intent of a *collective* body, it's always possible that different members may have understood what they were voting differently, or voted for it with different objectives in mind.

  Remember also the difference between original *intent* or expectation and original public *meaning* of the words in the text.

- Conditions have changed. There was not widespread public education in 1868, particularly in the South. "Today, education is perhaps the most important function of state and local governments. . . . It is the very foundation of good citizenship. . . . In these days, it is doubtful that any child may reasonably be expected to succeed in life if he is denied the opportunity of an education."

b.   Separate is Inherently Unequal

(Having decided to look beyond original intent, what's the Court's basic argument here?)

"Separate educational facilities are inherently unequal." "To separate [children] from others of similar age and qualifications solely because of their race generates a feeling of inferiority as to their status in the community that may affect their hearts and minds in a way unlikely ever to be undone."

(What evidence is the Court relying on?)

Two bases:

- The District Court's finding of a "detrimental effect upon the colored children." According to the District Judge, "[s]egregation with the sanction of law . . . has a tendency to [retard] the educational and mental development of negro children and to deprive them of some of the benefits they would receive in a racial[ly] integrated school system." (Note how important the trial court's role is here – factual findings are very hard to overrule.)

- Social science data (in FN 11).

The Court also relies here on both *Sweatt* and *McLaurin* for the importance of intangibles in assessing equality.

Note how far we've come from *Plessy*, which blamed the victims of segregation for feeling stigmatized. Charles Black said of that comment in *Plessy* that the "curves of callousness and stupidity intersect at their respective maxima."

c.   What's the Rationale?

In thinking about this question, I want to direct your attention to Professor Herbert Wechsler's piece on "neutral principles."

Wechsler's central idea is that what makes judging different from politics is that "it must be genuinely principled, resting with respect to every step that is involved in reaching judgment on analysis and reasons quite transcending the immediate result." In other words, courts can act only based on reasons that are *general* and *neutral*. Otherwise, Wechsler says, the court is acting as a "naked power organ" – an image which has always seemed kind of gross to me – instead of as a *court*.

Wechsler says that *Brown* is the toughest test of our commitment to neutral principles. So it's worth looking at a few possible rationales for the Court's result in terms of Wechsler's critique:

1)   Education is too important to permit segregation.

Some of the opinion suggests we balance the state's interest in a policy of segregation against the importance of the educational function, i.e., the importance of access to education for excluded black people.

Problem: In a series of *per curiam* opinions after *Brown*, the Court struck down segregation in a wide variety of other public facilities, such as buses, municipal golf courses, and public beaches.

That means this rationale fails Wechsler's criterion of principled application. If the principle is in fact limited to education, then a "neutral" court would have to go the other way on these other issues.

2)   Segregated education hurts the educational development of black children.

(Any problems with this rationale?)

Note that most social scientists appear to agree nowadays that this data -- while not necessarily wrong in its conclusion -- was methodologically unsound.

That's a problem in its own right, because it raises the spectre that the Court would have to change its position if subsequent studies reach a different conclusion.

There may be a deeper problem. Note Justice Thomas's response to this rationale in a much later case: "[I]f separation itself is a harm, and if integration therefore is the only way that blacks can receive a proper education, then there must be something inferior about blacks. Under this theory, segregation injures blacks because blacks, when left on their own, cannot achieve."

(How would you answer him?)

Isn't *McLaurin* an answer to this? The idea there is that an education is inferior where it doesn't include interaction with others -- especially others that one may have to deal with in later life. The problem is *exclusion*, not particularly who's excluded.

But again, the emphasis is on education. This rationale doesn't get you desegregated swimming pools. And Thomas may be right in the context that he's addressing, which is de facto segregation that persists after the *de jure* system has been dismantled.

(How did Prof. Wechsler characterize the issue?)

3)   Segregation violates freedom of association.

The first amendment generall protects a right to associate, although its contours are unclear. But he questions whether there is a neutral principle that supports choosing blacks' freedom to associate over whites' freedom *not* to associate.

(How does Prof. Black respond to Wechsler?)

He doesn't have much patience with the argument: "[I]f a whole race of people finds itself confined within a system which is set up and continued for the very purpose of keeping it in an inferior station, and if the question is then solemnly propounded whether such a race is being treated 'equally,' . . . we ought to exercise one of the sovereign prerogatives of philosophers— that of laughter."

So Black's argument is very simple:

4)   Segregation stigmatizes black people.

The whole point of segregation -- *in the context of the post-slavery South* -- was to send a constant and pervasive message of black inferiority to keep black people in their "place."

- "Segregation in the South comes down in apostolic succession from slavery and the *Dred Scott* case."

- "[S]egregation was imposed on one race by the other race."

- "'Separate but equal' facilities are almost never really equal."

    He has my favorite line here: The fiction that white people tell themselves, i.e., that black schools are equal, is a "Molochian child-destroying lie." (You know who Moloch was, right?)

(Does this mean that separate education would *always* be unconstitutional? What about inner-city schools for at-risk black males?)

Probably not.   Context and history are everything.   "Our question is whether discrimination inheres in that segregation which is imposed by law in the twentieth century in certain specific states in the American Union."

(But what kind of evidence is necessary to prove this claim? Is Prof. Black really right that the Court can simply take judicial notice of it?)

Black says that these sorts of judgments are really at the bottom of *all* judgments about law. On the other hand, sticking to an evidentiary record is one way we constrain judges.

(Does Prof. Black's rationale meet Wechsler's "neutral principles" test?)

I think it actually does, although it's hard because Black's analysis is so much more concrete. But "neutral principles" themselves have to accept that sometimes provisions of law embody purposes that aren't themselves neutral. So it's fair to say that the 14th Am rejects all arguments that discrimination against a racial minority is "rational" or "legitimate." That means rejecting freedom of non-association for whites.

But note the tension in Black's argument. His focus on the *core* of equal protection may undermine a broader scope to the anti-discrimination principle.

d.   What Does *Brown* Mean?

At least two possibilities:

- State-enforced segregation is illegal.   Note that this violation can be remedied simply by repealing segregation and not considering race in school assignments.

- Educational equality can be achieved only if blacks and whites go to school together. This is the view Justice Thomas was objecting to. It requires more elaborate remedies.

4.   *Brown*'s Federal Cousin – *Bolling v. Sharpe*, 347 U.S. 497 (1954)

Plaintiffs challenged school segregation in the District of Columbia.

The Court holds this unconstitutional.

(What makes this a hard case?)

The Equal Protection Clause applies only to the States -- not to the Federal Government.

(What does the Court rely on?)

The Court holds that "discrimination may be so unjustifiable as to be violative of [the due process clause of the Fifth Amendment]."

(So what's the name we've been using for this sort of doctrinal theory?)

This is a substantive due process holding. So this ought to make you hesitate before you reject the idea of substantive due process altogether.

(What's the more basic subtext here?)

In light of *Brown*, it would be unthinkable that the same Constitution would impose a lesser duty on the Federal Government."

(What the heck does that mean? Are there really no good reasons to distinguish?)

Well, one would be that slavery wasn't really a *federal* policy (except that it *was*).

"Reverse Incorporation": *Bolling* is now read to stand for a principle of reverse incorporation -- that the Equal Protection Clause applies to the Federal Government through the Due Process Clause of the Fifth Amendment.

(Do you think the decision really supports a "jot for jot" principle of reverse incorporation?)

That's how it's been read, regardless. Probably for the very practical reason that it's hard to have two separate sets of equal protection rules in your outline – one for the states and one for the Feds.

B.   Segregation Remedies and the Judicial Role

The issue here is the *authority and efficacy* of judicial review. The story is that, on the day that *Brown I* came down, Thurgood Marshall said that implementation would be a snap: If they exclude our kids in the morning, we'll have them in court by noontime and in school by the next day. Didn't quite happen that way.

We have to confront three big issues:

- Constitutional Meaning: What is required to "implement" *Brown I*? Are we looking to end government interference with private choices? Or to produce integrated results?

- Authority: Where different government institutions read the Constitution differently, whose view prevails?

- Efficacy: To what extent can courts force real social change on an issue like segregation?

Brown II raises the first and third issues; *Cooper v. Aaron* raises the second.

1.   *Brown v. Board of Education of Topeka (Brown II)*, 349 U.S. 294 (1955)

Thurgood Marshall, right after *Brown I* came down, predicted that actually enforcing the ruling would be a same-day kind of deal. But after deciding *Brown I*, the Court set the case for reargument concerning the question of relief.

The Court (Warren, CJ) remands the cases for further proceedings in the District Courts, who are given authority "to take such proceedings and enter such orders and decrees consistent with this opinion as are necessary and proper to admit to public schools on a racially nondiscriminatory basis with all deliberate speed the parties to these cases."

Two aspects are critical:

a)   Remedies are guided by equitable principles. This means flexibility, a focus on the facts of each case, and broad discretion for each lower court.

b)   Toleration of *some* delay. The Court asks only for "prompt and reasonable start toward compliance," and acknowledges that full

162

compliance may take time.   Courts are authorized to consider administrative difficulties.

(What's the best case for delay?)

The purely administrative questions are huge: We're talking about moving millions of people around. And sensitivies are at their maximum: I don't know about you, but I'm just not rational when I think people are messing with my kids. So surely *some* degree of caution is called for here.

The Supreme Court issues only three opinions on school segregation in the ten years after *Brown*.   One is *Cooper v. Aaron*, which we'll discuss momentarily. The other two – *Goss* and *Griffin* – deal with attempts to maintain de facto segregation through various legal schemes, which the Court rejects firmly. But there's no case on remedies.

2.   Massive Resistance and the Trouble with *Brown II*

Brown was met in the South with a strategy of "massive resistance." It's reflected in the "Southern Manifesto" that I've reprinted in the Notes.

(What do you think of this Manifesto?   Is it an appropriate role for legislators to take on?)

They're interpreting the Constitution, right? Should legislators get to do that?

Of course, they're also encouraging—no matter what they say—people to defy the Court – which is exactly what happens.

Professor Rosenberg summarizes the results:

- In the border states and D.C., the Supreme Court does seem to have had an impact. Between 1956 and 1964, the number of black children In school with whites rose 15.2% throughout the border, and 28.1% if we exclude D.C. (which was less segregated to start with).

- But in the *real* South, it's a very different story. Ten years after *Brown*, only 1.2% are attending school with whites. And if we take out Texas and Tennessee (which had low percentages of black enrollment and probably don't really count as Deep South for these purposes), the percentage drops to less than half of one percent.

In other words, in the South, Judge Wisdom of the 5th Circuit observes that "the courts acting alone have failed."

(Does this history mean that *Brown II* was wrong? Should the Court have done something more aggressive? What?)

Most scholars have criticized *Brown II*'s "all deliberate speed" formula. But what precisely was wrong with it? Some possibilities:

- If segregation is unconstitutional, then *any* continued segregation is intolerable.

  (Doesn't this just ignore the practicalities of the situation?)

- *Brown II* encouraged white resistance by failing to demand an immediate remedy.

  (Would a head-on challenge have been worse? What if the States had simply refused to obey the order? Note that Arkansas did exactly that in *Cooper*.)

  (Was the Court really wrong to assume that the South would comply in good faith?)

- *Brown II* overstated the administrative difficulties of desegregation.

  (Does the difficulty turn on what you think the required result is? It's easy to take the laws off the books, but hard to make blacks and whites go to school together.)

- The Court should never have referred the task to the lower courts.

  Note that the Court starts getting more specific as it loses patience in the 1960s.

Maybe the real answer is not so much to bash the Court but to recognize that courts alone can't do it all.

3.   *Cooper v. Aaron* and Interpretive Authority

Cooper v. Aaron, 358 U.S. 1 (1958), arises out of the school desegregation litigation in Little Rock. The Supreme Court had ruled four years earlier, in *Brown* that segregated schools are unconstitutional. As we've discussed, *Brown* was a set of consolidated cases involving segregated education in Kansas, Virginia, South Carolina, and Delaware. Shortly thereafter, black parents in Little Rock brought a similar lawsuit to require desegregation there. After the district court ordered the school district to desegregate, the Governor of Arkansas announced that he was not "bound" by the *Brown* ruling and called out the National Guard to block black students from entering the high school. Ultimately, President Eisenhower had to send *federal* troops to Arkansas to enforce the black students' right to attend the white school.

In the midst of all this, the School Board decided that the children were unlikely to learn much with all the troops parading around and asked the district court to postpone its desegregation order. The district court granted this request and the case ultimately got to the Supreme Court.

In a unique opinion signed by all nine justices, the Supreme Court rejected the postponement.

One important holding of the case is that the Governor's intimidation tactics didn't justify compromising the desegregation remedy that the black families were entitled to: the Court says that "law and order are not here to be preserved by depriving the Negro children of their constitutional rights."

a.   Interpretive Authority

The part of the opinion that's relevant to the broader question of interpretive authority, however, addresses the Governor's contention that he was not *bound* by the *Brown* ruling.

(What's the Governor's best argument for why he shouldn't be bound by *Brown*?)

He wasn't a party to the case, so he shouldn't be bound by its ruling. You can see that there's something to this argument if you pretend for a minute that this is an ordinary tort case. Suppose you have a suit arising out of a car wreck, and the injured driver claims that the car was defective. She sues the dealer who sold her the car and gets a judgment in her favor.

(Does that mean that the *manufacturer* is bound by the judgment and has to pay his fair share of the damages?)

No.

(Why not?)

Because the manufacturer wasn't a party to the suit. If the dealer wants it to chip in, the dealer will have to sue the manufacturer in a second action for contribution.

To put this more generally, there are two distinct ways in which judicial decisions bind:

- As a judgment: If you litigate and win, the other party is bound by that judgment and it can generally be enforced without a new lawsuit. These matters are governed by the law of *res judicata* that you'll study in Civil Procedure. Basically, you don't get to relitigate an issue against the same party if you had an opportunity to litigate it before. But this principle basically extends only to the *parties* to the original suit.

- As a precedent: Non-parties are still bound by a prior judicial decision to the extent that that decision serves as a precedent in the new case. But non-parties to the original suit will be permitted to argue that the precedent was wrong and should be overruled. (We'll consider the rules of *stare decisis* when we get to *Planned Parenthood v. Casey*.)

In my hypothetical, the auto dealer is bound by the force of the initial judgment, but the manufacturer is bound only to the extent that the prior case serves as influential precedent in the second case.

So that's the Governor's argument: The State of Arkansas wasn't a party to the *Brown* litigation. That means that the Governor has both the responsibility and the prerogative to decide for himself what the Constitution requires in this context. He's still got to worry about the precedential force of *Brown* should the matter end up in court, but he's free in that scenario to argue *Brown* should be overruled.

(It's possible to make a fairly narrow, legal answer to the Governor's claim. What's that answer?)

The question isn't the relationship between the State of Arkansas and the *Brown* litigation – it's the relationship between the State, the Governor, and the desegregation litigation that is currently going on in Little Rock. Remember, the federal district court has issued an order in that case ordering that the schools be desegregated. The State isn't a party to that case either – it's between the School District and the private plaintiffs – but the State *is* trying to interfere with the implementation of the court's order. That's a no-no, even under a fairly modest view of the judicial power.

(But the Court makes a much broader answer. What does the Court say?)

The Court says that "the interpretation of the Fourteenth Amendment enunciated by this Court in the *Brown* case is the supreme law of the land, and [the Supremacy Clause] of the Constitution makes it of binding effect on the States."

(Everybody seems to agree that the result of *Cooper* was right, but this statement has been very controversial. Why?)

Because it seems to equate the Constitution itself with what the judges have said about it.

(What authority does the Court cite for this proposition?)

Marbury v. Madison – especially Justice Marshall's statement that "[i]t is emphatically the province and duty of the judicial department to say what the law is."

(Does *Marbury* necessarily mean that someone like Governor Faubus is bound by the Supreme Court's interpretation of the Constitution?)

Remember there's a lot in *Marbury* that suggests a more modest role: Marshall's strongest argument is basically: Look, we've got this case in front of us, and it's our job to decide who wins. That means we have to apply *some* law to it, so we necessarily have to decide which law applies.

In this case, the choice is between the Judiciary Act and the Constitution, and in that instance the Constitution controls.

This sort of argument suggests that the power of judicial review really is limited to the case before the court – i.e., the judgment doesn't have any effect beyond that.

b.   Some Presidential Views

We really have two questions arising out of *Cooper* (and *Marbury*):

(a)   Does the effect of the Court's judgment in a constitutional case extend beyond the parties to the litigation?

(b)   To what extent can other actors in the other branches of government implement their own interpretations of the Constitution when they disagree with the Court?

It's helpful to think about these questions by looking at statements by several presidents who've had rather profound disagreements with the Supreme Court. These are collected in the Notes. Keep in mind the three positions set out in the note about Walter Murphy:

• Legislative Supremacy

• Judicial Supremacy

• Departmentalism

One thing we'll see is that these positions aren't as clean cut as you might think.

(What's Thomas Jefferson's view on the authoritativeness of Supreme Court decisions?)

Jefferson takes a pretty broad view of the second question: Other actors – like the President or members of Congress – are free to pursue their own constitutional interpretations.

To accept this, however, you have either take a narrow view of the first question – i.e., only the parties are bound by a court's decision – or confine Jefferson's view to discretionary functions.

For example, the Supreme Court held that Congress had the power to incorporate a national bank in *McCulloch v. Maryland*, which we'll read in a week or two. But President Jackson still vetoed the second bank bill because *he* thought the bank was unconstitutional. In other words, no one seriously doubts that the President can veto a bill because he thinks it's unconstitutional, just like he could veto it simply because he thinks it's a bad idea for policy reasons.

You might also think of this in a slightly different way: *McCulloch* held that the Court must be very deferential to the political branches on what's "necessary and proper" to effectuate enumerated constitutional ends. But Jackson *is* a political branch—he's one of the people that the Court is deferring to. So why should he have to apply the same lenient test to the Bank that the Court did?

(How is Abraham Lincoln's view different?)

Lincoln seems to go a little further in his opposition to the *Dred Scott* decision. He says, not only will the President exercise his veto according to his own view, but also that the Executive will continue to challenge the decision in order to try to get it reversed. This is sometimes called non-acquiescence.

But this still doesn't mean that the President would defy a court order issued to him, or try to interfere with an order issued in a pending case.

Finally, FDR's statement raises two different issues. The first is really an extension of the second question that Jefferson and Lincoln addressed: Whether the President and Congress, in doing their jobs, must accept the interpretation of the Constitution adopted by the Court.

It's a little more difficult here, however. Jefferson and Jackson were both dealing with laws which they thought were unconstitutional, but the Court said were OK. In those cases, the Constitution didn't *require* these laws – it simply *permitted* them. And the President was free to veto them for any reason or no reason at all.

FDR, however, is operating in a situation where the Court has declared certain types of laws to be *un*constitutional, and FDR wants to propose similar legislation anyway.

(Should this make any difference?)

Maybe. His theory seems to be, we can get away with this for awhile before the Court strikes it down, which doesn't seem to show the sort of good faith needed if the government is to work.

FDR also raises another question in his letter to Congressman Hill. This is written just after the Court's decision in *Schechter Poultry*, which struck down the NIRA on Commerce Clause grounds. Hill's committee is considering another statute, the Bituminous Coal Conservation Act, that is similar in relevant principle to the NIRA, so Hill is worried the Court will strike this one down, too.

FDR says, Look, don't worry about whether or not the Court is going to strike this law down. Your job is simply to determine if the law is good policy, and you should let the Court worry about that legal stuff.

(What do you think of this view?)

It seems like a dangerous suggestion. Remember, all government officials take an oath to support the Constitution, and we're probably better off if everyone takes it as their obligation to interpret the Constitution as a guide to their own decisions in office, while respecting the Court's final say in litigated cases.

After all, a lot of issues simply never reach the Court at all.

(There's also a pragmatic reason to think about the Constitution before the litigation stage. Does anyone recall what happened to the law that FDR was trying to get Hill to support?)

It was passed, then promptly struck down by the Court. Big waste of time.

c.   Summing Up

So where do we stand in light of all this? A couple things are clear:

- Government officials can't disobey or interfere with the execution of a court order interpreting the Constitution, simply because they think the court got it wrong. (That's probably enough to take care of *Cooper* on its facts.)

  Marbury, after all, rejects legislative supremacy.

- There are some political branch functions that just aren't reviewable by courts – like the decision to veto a bill. Officials can do that based on their own interpretation of the Constitution, even if a court would most likely disagree with that interpretation.

  This is the aspect of Departmentalism that's clearly right.

- The hard questions arise when a political branch official has interpreted the Constitution in taking a measure which *is* subject to judicial review, and the Court then has to decide whether to respect that officials independent constitutional judgment.

  This is the aspect of Departmentalism that's harder to make sense of: Which department is this case really in?

We'll come back to the last question in *City of Boerne v. Flores* in the second part of the course.

4.   The Efficacy of Supreme Court Decisions

Recall Professor Rosenberg's statistics: In the *real* South – not the Border States – only 1.2% of black kids are attending school with whites ten years after *Brown*. So the first ten years represents an experiment to determine what courts can do *on their own*. Better yet, it's a *controlled* experiment, because after 10 years the federal political branches get into the act.

169

In 1964, Congress passes a major civil rights act that bans private discrimination in employment and public accommodations. It also has educational provisions, which provide

- The Justice Department can bring desegregation suits; and

- Any program or activity receiving federal financial assistance can't discriminate on the basis of race.

Then, in 1965, Congress passes the Elementary and Secondary Education Act, which for the first time provides a huge pot of money to school districts with lots of low income children. This is aimed at the South.

Finally, the Dept. of Health, Education, and Welfare eventually adopts regulations providing for the cutoff of federal funds to school districts that aren't desegregating.

The results of these developments are dramatic. You have the graph on p. 377 showing how desegregation took off after 1964.

- In the border states, the decrease in segregation is even greater than under the courts acting alone.

- In the South, the results are stunning. By 1972, we have 91.3 percent desegregation.

Again, note that we're using a very broad definition of "desegregation." But we were using that same measure for the 1964 figures as well, so the important point is the *change*.

Now, the results are somewhat mixed as to causes.

- The survey data does suggest that courts were perceived as an important cause of this increase in desegregation.

- It's important to keep in mind that these are also the years in which the Court gets tough. In cases like *Green* and *Swann*, the Court scraps all deliberate speed and eventually permits busing.

So recall the two views of the Supreme Court that Professor Rosenberg lays out:

- Dynamic Court: The Court's an important and efficacious engine for social change.

- Constrained Court: Courts are the "least dangerous branch," in Hamilton's terms – can't do anything on their own.

(What does this experience tell us about the two views of courts analyzed by Professor Rosenberg?)

(Is there any middle ground?)

I guess I'd make two points:

- The Court may act as a catalyst. Its holdings may mobilize social movements—Rosa Parks says the reason she refused to sit in the back of the bus was that she knew about the *Brown* decision. It may also mobilize the political brances—Eisenhower can't afford to let the Governor of Arkansas outright *defy* an order by the federal courts, so he has to send in troops in Little Rock.

- Courts may be more important in defensive contexts. For instance, any law requiring judicial enforcement can be more readily opposed by courts. E.g., *New York Times v. Sullivan*, in which Southern officials tried to de-fund the Civil Rights Movement by suing its supporters for libel. That suit had to go through courts, so courts could shut that strategy down. This is why the debate over whether suspected terrorists can be taken outside the judicial system and tried in military tribunals is so important.

  Courts can also protect the rights you need to push for social change. E.g., the courts did a lot to protect the free speech rights of civil rights protesters. Without that, a lot of these protests would have gone nowhere.

Nonetheless, Rosenberg's point is a necessary corrective, and we can restate it in a more positive way. *All* parts of the government must interpret and enforce the Constitution, and we make a mistake if we focus only on courts.

C.   Incorporation and the Nationalization of Criminal Procedure

The next assignment – which we'll go through very quickly – is primarily about the incorporation of certain basic individual rights into the 14th Amendment, notwithstanding the implicit rejection of that idea in *Slaughterhouse*.

I also want to use this assignment and the next one to think about the Warren Court's place in the story of Judicial Review that we've been developing all semester. You've already seen that Court, of course, in *Brown*, and we'll have one more day on it tomorrow with *Griswold*. But these criminal procedure cases were absolutely central to the Warren Court's place in the public consciousness. (Incidentally, Professor Powe's book on the Warren Court is the best thing out there on this period.)

In *Murray v. Hoboken Land & Improvement Co.*, 59 U.S. (18 How.) 272 (1856), the Court explicitly ties the phrase "due process of law" in the 5th Amendment to the English concept of "the law of the land," based in the Magna Charta. This concept, which is picked up in cases under the due process clause of the 14th Amendment, roots due process in traditional modes of proceeding. And it's frequently been thought to have some *substantive* content. There's also considerable historical evidence that the

Framers of the Fourteenth Amendment intended to make at least some of the original Bill of Rights apply to the States. But, not surprisingly, the evidence is mixed.

We have two different doctrinal questions to ask about incorporation, both of which have already come up in our discussion of *Bolling v. Sharpe*:

- Which rights are incorporated? This includes a methodological question about the best approach to identifying incorporated rights.

- In what *manner* are those rights incorporated? That is, do they apply to the states just the same as they do to the Feds, with every little twist of the doctrine being interchangeable? Or should it make a difference which government is involved in any given case?

1.   Approaches to Incorporation—Which Rights?

There are three different theories of incorporation, which you can see developing in the separate opinions in *Adamson v. California*, 332 U.S. 46 (1947).

Mr. Adamson is convicted of Murder One in state court in CA and sentenced to die.

(What's the right that Adamson is asserting?)

The right not to have the prosecution comment upon his failure to testify at trial. This is part of the *federal* law under the Fifth Amendment's prohibition against self-incrimination.

(How does the Court approach the incorporation question in *Adamson*?)

a.   Fundamental Fairness

This approach to incorporation, which came to be associated with Justice Frankfurter, incorporates into the 14th Amendment's due process clause only those rights which are fundamental in a free society.

The Court uses lots of formulations: e.g., "principle[s] of justice so rooted in the tradition and conscience of our people as to be ranked as fundamental," or "of the very essence of a scheme of ordered liberty."

The essential question in the early cases is whether you can imagine a fair system of justice without this right. Later, it becomes whether *our* system could possibly operate fairly without this right. (You see that transition in the long footnote in *Duncan*.)

(What's Justice Black's criticism of this approach?)

It's too mushy. There's no fixed criterion for what rights are "in" and what rights are "out."

(Why is that bad?)

A couple of problems:

(1)   It transfers a lot of power to the judges in individual cases by giving them discretion.

(2)   It also makes it difficult to predict outcomes in advance.

(Why might we particularly care about predictability in these incorporation cases?)

Most of these cases are criminal procedure cases, and the incorporation of federal rights has profound consequences for how states setup their criminal justice systems. *Mapp* and *Miranda* are good examples.

Mapp holds that the exclusionary rule, which requires exclusion of evidence gained in a search that violates the 4th Amendment, binds the States. After *Mapp*, the States have to rewrite their criminal procedural rules to impose the exclusionary rule in a bunch of cases where state law might not have required it. That's pretty disruptive, and the states are much better off if they can tell in advance which federal rules they have to follow and which ones they don't.

Same thing with *Miranda*, which required the police to "read you your rights" when they arrest you. State and local police departments now have to reconfigure their interrogation practices and retrain their police officers to comply with a universal federal requirement.

(What's Black's position in *Adamson*?)

b.   Total Incorporation

Starting in *Adamson*, Justice Black took the position that the 14th Amendment simply incorporated the Bill of Rights - no more, no less.

(What's the primary advantage of this position?)

Although his position was based on his reading of the history, it's clear that the primary appeal of this position to Justice Black was it's bright-line rule quality - it did not leave it to the discretion of judges to pick and choose which rights they thought were fundamental.

The advantages of bright-line rules mirror the disadvantages of mushier tests, which are sometimes called "standards":

(1)   rules tend to constrain the decisionmaker more; and

(2)   rules also give more predictable results.

The most prominent present-day advocate of bright-line rules is Justice Scalia, who wrote a famous law review article entitled "The Rule of Law as a Law of Rules." In some ways, Justice Black was Justice Scalia before there *was* Justice Scalia. Although Justice Black demonstrates that you can be committed to bright-line rules and be a liberal on many issues.

(What are some disadvantages of bright-line rules?)

They tend to be over- and under-inclusive. That is, there's the rule and then there's the value that underlies it. A bright-line rule will always sweep in some cases that don't vindicate the underlying value, and usually leave out some cases that do.

(For example, do we really need to incorporate *all* of the Bill of Rights? How about the Third Amendment? Grand-jury indictment?)

If our underlying value is to protect *fundamental* rights, it's not at all clear these procedural details are important.

(What about *under*-inclusive? Do we think the first 10 (or 8) amendments should exhaust the meaning of "Due Process"?)

The Court has never taken this position. For instance, the reasonable doubt standard is not mentioned in the Bill of Rights, but has been incorporated as a requirement binding on the states. Not to mention rights like privacy.

There's a third position that emerges under the Warren Court:

c.   Selective Incorporation: *Duncan v. Louisiana*, 391 U.S. 145 (1968)

Justice Black's approach was never adopted by a majority of the Court. But the Warren Court - led by Justice Brennan -- used the language of fundamental fairness to incorporate almost all of the Bill of Rights.

This is classic Justice Brennan: He cares about theory, but he's pragmatic about finding a theory that will serve his broader goals *and* gather the support of a majority of the Court.

Justice White's majority opinion in *Duncan* is a good example of this approach. Duncan was convicted of "simple battery"—a misdemeanor punishable by up to 2 years' imprisonment and $300 fine under LA law. LA grants jury trials only in cases punishable by capital punishment or imprisonment at hard labor. So the legal question in the case is whether the 6th Am's right to trial by jury is incorporated against the States.

Note the particular facts, however: Duncan (who is black) intervenes in a confrontation between his two younger cousins and some white kids. Apparently the cousins had previously reported some racial incidents and tensions are high. Duncan allegedly slapped one of the white boys on the elbow, and he ends up prosecuted for battery.

(Why's the Warren Court interested in this case?)

A lot of the Warren Court's cases dealing with individual rights are in fact race cases, even when the claim on the merits doesn't have much to do with race discrimination. Here, we have overly zealous prosecution of a black defendant.

(Why would a jury trial be important in a case like this?)

Juries—especially if they mirror the community's actual racial makeup—tend to constrain abuses of prosecutorial power. And remember the Court had already held that you can't exclude black people from juries.

Lots of the criminal procedure cases fit this pattern: We're concerned that the criminal justice system in the South is run in a racist manner, and one remedy for that is to ratchet up procedural protections for defendants.

(What approach does the majority purport to apply in *Duncan*?)

They employ all the language of fundamental fairness, right? They talk about "fundamental principles," etc. But the *effect* is to incorporate a specific provision of the Bill of Rights. That's selective incorporation.

d. The Current State of Incorporation

The handout sets out the only provisions that have **not** yet been incorporated are:

- the 3rd amendment (no soldiers in your house)
- the 5th amendment's requirement of grand jury indictment
- the 7th amendment's guarantee of a jury trial in civil cases.

Note that *Adamson* itself has been overruled by the time we get to *Duncan*. And note also that the process is ongoing—the Court finally incorporated the 2nd Amendment's right to bear arms just a couple of years ago in the *McDonald* case,[24] which you have a little about in the Notes.

(You can see the bright-line advantages of using the Bill of Rights as a guide for what's "fundamental." But is it persuasive? Do you think every aspect of it is fundamental? How about grand jury indictment?)

Well, I think there's room for reasonable disagreement as to whether a lot of these requirements are the best system. One view – represented by Justice Harlan in a lot of these cases – is that such ambiguity necessarily means that it can't be a "fundamental" right.

You can see the alternative approach in Justice Stevens's *McDonald* dissent, where he tries to deny incorporation of the Second Amendment. *McDonald*'s an easy case under the total incorporation position: The right to bear arms is part of the Bill of Rights – Q.E.D.

---

[24] *McDonald v. City of Chicago*, 130 S. Ct. 3020 (2010).

Stevens argues, however, that *Heller's* individual right to bear arms shouldn't qualify as part of fundamental fairness. I've summarized his reasons in the Notes:

- Guns have an "ambivalent" relation to liberty (because they can be used to take others' liberty away);

- Gun rights are different in kind from other incorporated rights;

- Other countries don't recognize gun rights;

- The 2nd Amendment is really a federalism provision, so incorporation makes little sense; and

- The states have long regulated guns.

(Don't most of these reasons strike you as an effort to relitigate *Heller* itself?)

In any event, if fundamental fairness is flexible enough to support these kinds of distinctions, you can start to sympathize with Justice Black.

2.   Approaches to Incorporation—In What Manner?

Just because a particular provision "applies" doesn't mean it necessarily has to apply in the same *way.* Consider the Fourth Amendment and the Exclusionary Rule in *Mapp.* Prior to *Mapp,* the Court had already held that the Fourth Amendment bound the states. But you could think about this in two ways:

One position would be:

- Only the Core: Only the core meaning of a constitutional provision binds the states. Doctrinal wrinkles and remedial rules do not. *See, e.g., Wolf v. Colorado,* 338 U.S. 25 (1949) (states bound by Fourth Amendment, but not by exclusionary rule remedy).

Mapp, however, takes a different track:

- "Jot for Jot": Doctrine developed under a particular Bill of Rights provision applies to the States precisely as it does to the Federal Government. *See, e.g., Mapp v. Ohio,* 367 U.S. 643 (1961) (overruling *Wolf).*

You see the same thing in *Duncan:* The Court applies the federal test in determining which crimes require a jury trial; no variation by states is allowed. And this is pretty much the case across the board for incorporated rights. The result is that free speech cases involving the states and the federal government, for instance, are virtually interchangeable.

(Is this the best approach?)

Well, one could agree that the right to a *jury* ought to be incorporated without thinking it has to be 12 people, right?

And here's an anomaly it creates: The Fourteenth Amendment was pretty clearly intended to give Congress broad powers to promote racial equality. But the reverse, "jot-for-jot" incorporation of the Equal Protection Clause into the Fifth Amendment means that Congress has no greater leeway than the States to undertake "benign" discrimination – affirmative action – in service of racial equality. *See Adarand Constructors v. Pena*, 515 U.S. 200 (1995).

3.   Reverse Incorporation

Note that there is no Equal Protection Clause that applies to the *Federal* government. But the Equal Protection Clause of the 14th Amendment has been held to be incorporated against the Federal government through the due process clause of the *5th* amendment. See *Bolling v. Sharpe*.

Another (possible) example is the Contracts Clause, which is sometimes thought to impose some obligation on the federal government even though it's originally directed at the States. This remains extremely fuzzy, though, since there's not a whole lot of Contracts Clause enforcement going on anyway.

4.   Incorporation and Federalism

We've talked about Justice Black's objection to the fundamental rights theory of incorporation. One *defense* of that theory by Justice Frankfurter has to do with federalism.

(What's the argument?)

He's worried about preempting state experimentation and autonomy.

(What are the specific federalism concerns here?)

There are two primary worries:

(1)   The big concern at the time was that incorporation – especially in the area of criminal procedure – effectively *federalized* large areas of state law. As you'll learn if you take criminal procedure, the Fourth, Fifth, Sixth, and Eighth Amendments have been extrapolated into a pretty detailed code of criminal procedure which governs everything from how the police to their job to what evidence is admissible to how sentencing procedures have to be structured.

Because these rules are *constitutional* in nature, the States aren't free to deviate from them. This forecloses experimentation and accommodation of state rules to the particular circumstances in each state.[25]

(2)   The second worry is the enforcement power worry from *Slaughterhouse*. Every expansion of the rights protected by the 14th Amendment also expands Congress's enforcement power under Section 5. We'll read a case toward the end of the course – *City of Boerne v. Flores* – dealing with a federal statute enforcing the Free Exercise Clause of the First Amendment, which is enforceable by Congress only because it has been incorporated into the 14th.

I asked you to think about the Second Amendment and *Heller*. Incorporation is one of the big questions that will have to come up as soon as someone challenges gun control outside D.C.

(What's the best argument for non-incorporation?)

The 2nd Am is arguably a federalism provision. (You can make a similar argument about the Establishment Clause.)

(What's the best argument in favor?)

The Reconstruction history is pretty strong here. There may be a better case for incorporating the 2nd Am than for most other provisions of the Bill of Rights.

5.   Incorporation and Criminal Procedure

We've been talking about incorporation as a theoretical and structural phenomenon, but it's also important to understand its practical impact. That impact was most pronounced and most controversial in the particular

---

[25] Here's another example: The Boy Scouts case from a few years back, **Boy Scouts of America v. Dale**, 530 U.S. 640 (2000) held that the First Amendment right of free association overrides a state anti-discrimination statute protecting gays and lesbians. The prior law was that the federal anti-discrimination statute – passed as part of the 1964 Civil Rights Act – didn't cover gays but also didn't forbid the *states* from enacting their own laws which might be different. There's evidence that this made it possible for gays to vote with their feet – moving to places like New Jersey and Massachusetts where they were protected, and away from places like Colorado where they were not.

What the *Dale* case did, however, was to *constitutionalize* anti-discrimination law. Basically, it looks like the court will draw a line that the 1964 Civil Rights Act is constitutionally OK, but everyone that the statute doesn't protect *can't* be protected by the states without violating this new constitutional right of free association. This has the effect of imposing a single uniform rule throughout the country.

What does this have to do with incorporation? The First Amendment applied in *Dale* only because it has been held to be incorporated into the 14th.

field of criminal procedure. Cases like *Mapp* and *Miranda v. Arizona* came to symbolize the Warren Court's revolution in criminal procedure. They – not cases like *Griswold* – were the source of the "Impeach Earl Warren" signs that sprouted up all over the country in the 1960s.

Dolly Mapp is convicted for possessing dirty books that were discovered during a warrantless search of her home. Let's assume that violates the Fourth Amendment. The question is, what do we do about that?

(What would we do in *federal* court prosecutions?)

Exclude the evidence. That's *Weeks v. United States*, 232 U.S. 383 (1914).

(What's the problem here?)

The exclusionary rule only applies to federal prosecutions. That's the holding of *Wolf v. Colorado*, 338 U.S. 25 (1949).

(Does that mean the *Fourth Amendment* doesn't apply in state court?)

No. *Wolf* incorporated the Fourth Amendment's protection from unreasonable searches and seizures against the states. It simply refused to hold that that protection extends to imposing the federal *remedy* for a Fourth Amendment violation.

(Why?)

Because the *Wolf* court wanted to give the states freedom to select their own remedies.

(What are some problems with the exclusionary rule as a remedy?)

Two big ones:

- It's very costly in terms of letting the guilty go free; it tends to exclude very good, very reliable evidence.

- It has no impact if no evidence is found or no prosecution is brought.

- Its deterrent effect on the police is somewhat doubtful.

(What are some alternatives?)

Several:

- Civil suits for damages

- Internal disciplinary proceedings

(Why is the *Mapp* court uninterested in these alternatives?)

It says that the experience in the states is that they're not very effective. The states seem to be moving in the direction of adopting the exclusionary rule.

Note that the *Mapp* court seems to view the exclusionary rule as integral to the Fourth Amendment right; that position has considerably less support today. These days, the rule tends to be justified exclusively in terms of its deterrent effects, and exceptions crop up where that effect is particularly doubtful.

(What do you think of *Mapp*? Was the Court right to impose this remedy on the states?)

The other "signature" Warren Court crim pro case is *Miranda*. Note that *Miranda*, unlike *Mapp*, isn't really about incorporation at all. Instead, it's about the power of the Court to fashion prophylactic rules to protect constitutional rights.

(A final and more general question: I've used *Mapp* as the poster child for the Warren Court's criminal procedure "revolution." But is the Court really pioneering here?)

One thing to understand is that the Court isn't really innovating – it's just extending federal procedures to the states, and in many instances like *Gideon v. Wainwright*, imposing on the *South* procedures adopted already in the rest of the country. In this sense, it's not clear how counter-majoritarian any of this is.

Some other examples:

- *Gideon v. Wainwright*, **372 U.S. 335 (1963):** The Court holds that the Sixth Amendment requires states to provide counsel in all felony criminal cases.

- *Griffin v. California*, **380 U.S. 609 (1965):** The Court overrules *Adamson* and strikes down state rules allowing comment on the defendant's failure to testify.

- *Miranda v. Arizona*, **384 U.S. 436 (1966):** The Court holds that the before the police may interrogate criminal suspects, they must "read them their rights" – that is, alert them to their Fifth Amendment privilege against self-incrimination.

- *Furman v. Georgia*, **408 U.S. 238 (1972):** The Court holds that the procedures used to administer the death penalty in most states are unconstitutional.

Some of these decisions are extremely unpopular, and President Nixon runs for president in 1968 on a platform opposing them. He gets to appoint four justices pretty quickly; nonetheless, there's no wholesale rollback. See, e.g., *United States v. Dickerson*. The death penalty cases are the only ones the Court ever really retreated from, and even there it's not clear "retreat" is the right word. The Court has created exceptions to *Mapp* that some people might view as a retreat (such as a "good faith exception" to the exclusionary rule) but the general principle still stands forty years later.

6.   **Some More General Thoughts on the Warren Court**

My former colleague Professor Powe has offered both a summary of and a challenge to the conventional wisdom that the Warren Court was "revolutionary."

Several ways of thinking about the Court:

- Footnote Four (*Brown*, speech cases)

- Geography (Southerners and Catholics; rural vs urban)

- Reform by Experts (criminal justice)

If you look at what's stuck, it's things that the national, Protestant majority supported the Court on – e.g., race, speech, privacy, reapportionment.

So why "Impeach Earl Warren"? He was acting on behalf of most of us.

V.   **Chapter Seven – The Rebirth of Substantive Due Process**

This chapter returns to the "substantive" notion of due process raised in Dred Scott, *rejected in* Slaughterhouse, *revived in* Lochner, *then buried again in* West Coast Hotel. *Although the notion of a right to privacy seems different from freedom of contract in the earlier cases, students should be pressed on whether that distinction really holds up. These cases are also a fruitful ground for talking about divergent theories of constitutional interpretation. The materials use Robert Bork's famous critique of* Griswold *to introduce originalism, which Bork framed as an extension of Wechsler's idea of neutral principles.* Roe *then serves as an example of "living" or "unwritten" constitutionalism, as defended by Thomas Grey. And* Casey, *with its emphasis on* stare decisis, *demonstrates "common law constitutionalism". Finally,* Casey *also returns to some of the themes of the Court's role in the broader political system raised by the New Deal crisis and* Brown.

Today we begin to explore the implications of the "double standard" for substantive due process itself -- the Court's rejection of *economic* substantive due process, but its continued willingness to recognize unenumerated rights in other spheres.

Griswold is the first big case in the modern era to recognize a right to "privacy." In reading the *Griswold* case, we'll look at four different approaches to "privacy":

1.   "Penumbras" of specific constitutional provisions -- Justice Douglas, w/Clark

2.   The Ninth Amendment -- Justices Goldberg, w/Brennan & Warren

3.   Substantive Due Process -- Justices Harlan & White

4.   No Unenumerated Rights -- Justice Black & Stewart

The Court could have drawn either of two lines to limit the reach of *Griswold*: It could have said that the right of privacy is limited to the *marriage* relationship, or that only statutes which must be enforced by invading the home are invalid.

But neither of these limiting principles holds up in cases like *Eisenstadt v. Baird* and *Carey v. Population Services*.

The cases after *Griswold* pave the way for the leap from a right to use contraceptives to a right to have an abortion. We'll ask whether *Roe* can actually fit comfortably within the right defined in *Griswold*. I think you'll find that the joint opinion in *Casey* – which reaffirms *Roe* in 1992 – makes a better case for that than Justice Blackmun's opinion in *Roe* itself.

Finally, the *Casey* case gives us an opportunity to talk about two additional issues.

- How much weight should *precedent* get in constitutional adjudication? And should we treat precedent differently in particularly controversial cases?
- We also introduce another theory of constitutional interpretation – the *common law* theory – which arises out of a strong commitment to *stare decisis*. Under this theory, the constitution evolves slowly through judicial interpretation over time. *Griswold* and *Casey* may be the best example of this theory at work.

A.   The Right to Privacy

1.   Antecedents

a.   *Meyer v. Nebraska*, 262 U.S. 390 (1923)

In *Meyer*, the Court struck down a state law that forbade the teaching of foreign languages to young children. (This law is clearly passed as a reaction to WWI.) This is not a case of economic regulation, but note how it fits into the *Lochner* pattern:

- It's decided in 1923, in the heyday of the *Lochner* era.

- The majority opinion is by Justice McReynolds, one of the leaders of the "Four Horsemen," and Justice Holmes dissents.

- Justice McReynolds grounds the right that has been violated firmly in the same broad view of "liberty" under the due process clause that we saw in *Lochner*: Liberty, he says "denotes not merely freedom from bodily restraint but also the right of the individual to contract, to engage in any of the common occupations of life, to acquire useful knowledge, to marry, establish a home and bring up children, to worship God according to the dictates of his own conscience, and generally to enjoy those privileges long recognized at common law as essential to the orderly pursuit of happiness by free men.

Note that there's no double standard here: McReynolds' catalog includes both economic and non-economic rights.

The statute thus violated (1) the right of the teachers to teach, (2) the right of the students to learn, and (3) the right of the parents to control their kids' education.

Finally, note the reference to the *common law*, which becomes a common point of reference in both the economic and non-economic cases. For McReynolds, the common law serves as a point of reference for the traditional ways in which the government can and cannot intervene in private life. For instance, the right to privacy would be defined in party by a right against trespass in tort.

b.   *Pierce v. Society of Sisters*, 268 U.S. 510 (1925)

Pierce is similar to *Meyer*, although here we're dealing with an OR law requiring children to attend public schools. The Court strikes this down, finding that the due process clause protects parents' right to send their children to private or parochial schools.

c.   *Skinner v. Oklahoma*, 316 U.S. 535 (1942)

Skinner is most similar to *Griswold* and *Roe* on the facts, as it involves reproductive choice. The Court strikes down the Oklahoma Habitual Criminal Sterilization Act, which was basically a "three strikes and your sterilized" provision.

The big difference is that this is an equal protection case. The Court avoids the question of whether the government can sterilize you, period, by focusing on the discrimination that the statute imposes on different types of criminals. For three felonies involving "moral turpitude," you get sterilized. But the statute excludes crimes like embezzlement, for which you simply get jail time. The Court doesn't think this distinction makes any sense, so they can strike it down on equal protection grounds rather than ask whether it would be OK to sterilize everybody.

(Does everyone understand the difference between an equal protection theory and a due process theory here?)

Due process looks at the imposition on your rights in a vacuum; equal protection focuses on disparities in treatment.

Nevertheless, *Skinner* is very much *like* substantive due process in that it relies heavily on the conclusion that reproduction is a *fundamental right*. This is the first case in which we hear the term *strict scrutiny*, which means that the Court is going to look extra carefully at the rationale for the statute. The Court needs to make this distinction because *Skinner* is decided in 1942, at a time when the Court is backing off its scrutiny of most legislation. So the Court needs a story about why this case is different. It's a good early example of the double standard.

The Court distinguishes cases like *Lee Optical* by reasoning that where the government is dealing with fundamental rights – like reproduction – the Court must look extra carefully at the rationale for the law.

This case is thus important for the substantive due process cases that follow – especially *Griswold* – because it supports the notion that reproductive choice is entitled to special constitutional protection.

2.   *Griswold v. Connecticut*, 381 U.S. 479 (1965)

Connecticut outlawed use of contraceptives, even by married couples. The executive director of Planned Parenthood and a professor at Yale Medical School gave advice to married persons about how to use contraceptives. They were convicted of being accessories to a violation of the contraceptive ban.

The Court holds that CT's use restriction on contraceptives is unconstitutional.

a.   The "Penumbra Approach" (Douglas, J.)

(*Griswold* is usually thought of as a substantive due process decision. Does the majority embrace this theory explicitly?)

No – Justice Douglas identifies substantive due process with *Lochner*, and declines to rely on it.

(Why does the majority reject substantive due process?)

"We do not sit as a super-legislature to determine, wisdom, need, and propriety of laws that touch economic problems, business affairs, or social conditions."

(How does the majority distinguish this case from the *Lochner* doctrine?)

This case is different because the law at issue "operates directly on an intimate relation of husband and wife and their physician's role in one aspect of that relation."

(What are the majority's best precedents?)

Pierce and *Meyer*.

(But aren't those substantive due process cases?)

Justice Douglas characterizes them as First Amendment cases. *Meyer* and *Pierce* suggest that the right of free speech includes freedom to receive information, freedom of thought and freedom to teach.

This is pretty bogus – those cases don't rely on the First Amendment. They're substantive due process decisions, as Justice Black's dissent here points out.

(So is the majority relying on the First Amendment, then?)

Not really. The theory is that this case falls in the "penumbra" of several amendments that protect privacy interests.

Specific provisions of the Bill of Rights have "penumbras, formed by emanations from those guarantees that help give them life and substance. Various guarantees create zones of privacy," including the First, Third, Fourth, and Fifth amendments.

Also known as the "Alphabet Soup" theory: Take the "P" from "free Press," the "R" from "Religion," the "I" from grand jury "Indictment," . . . (you get the picture).

(But does the majority think that CT's law would be unconstitutional under *any* of these provisions?)

No. That's why Justice Stewart responds that while the Court refers to lots of amendments, it doesn't say *which* is actually infringed by the statute.

(Can someone make an argument based on these same specific rights provisions that contraception *shouldn't* be protected?)

(Why not infer from the Constitution's choice to protect "privacy" only in certain instances that all other instances were within the government's authority to regulate?)

(Why isn't economic substantive due process within the "penumbra" of the contract clause and the takings clause?)

In any event, the marital relationship lies within the zone of privacy created by these guarantees. Justice Douglas has some really nice prose here: "We deal with a right of privacy older than the Bill of Rights. [Marriage] is a coming together for better or for worse, hopefully enduring, and intimate to the degree of being sacred. It is an association that promotes a way of life, not causes; a harmony in living, not political faiths; a bilateral loyalty, not commercial or social projects. Yet it is an association for as noble a purpose as any involved in our prior decisions." (Douglas ought to know – he did it *four times*.)

b.   The Ninth Amendment (Goldberg, w/Warren & Brennan, JJ.)

(What constitutional theory does Justice Goldberg's concurring opinion rely on?)

He relies on the Ninth Amendment.

(What does the Ninth Amendment say?)

"The enumeration in the Constitution, of certain rights, shall not be construed to deny or disparage others retained by the people."

The point of the amendment was "to quiet expressed fears that a bill of specifically enumerated rights could not be sufficiently broad to cover all essential rights and that the specific mention of certain rights would be interpreted as a denial that others were protected."

You won't see many Ninth Amendment opinions – usually, the Court has said it's too vague to mean much. But Justice Goldberg says that the Ninth Amendment must mean *something*. What it means is that people have rights that aren't specifically set forth in the rest of the Constitution.

(How do we tell what those are?)

In determining what these rights are, judges can't simply rely on "their personal and private notions." Rather, they should look to the "traditions and [collective] conscience of our people" to determine whether a right is "fundamental."

(How does Justice Black respond to this argument?)

Justice Black has two answers here:

First, he says the 9th Amendment inquiry is completely open-ended, and will inevitably result in judges voting their own conscience. For that reason, he argues that the 9th Amendment creates no judicially enforceable rights.

(Is he right about that?)

Second, he argues that the 9th Amendment is a limit on *federal* power only – not *state* power. It hasn't been incorporated and thus can't apply here. The idea would be that it's up to the *states* to protect these other rights.

(How does Justice Goldberg answer that?)

He says he's not really applying the Ninth Amendment here; instead, he's just using the Ninth Amendment to show that "liberty" in the Due Process Clause shouldn't be limited to enumerated rights. So in the end, maybe this isn't much different from Justice Harlan's position.

(Are there other ways to think about the Ninth Amendment – that is, other than as a repository of unenumerated but fundamental and judicially-enforceable rights?)

Well, one alternative would be to think of it as an acknowledgement that many, if not most, rights may be protected by ordinary legislation at both the state and federal level. See, e.g., rights to housing, income security, employment, etc.

c.   Substantive Due Process (Harlan and White, JJ.)

The concurrences of both Justice Harlan and Justice White both rely directly on substantive due process, without any reference to "penumbras" or the Ninth Amendment. Justice White's opinion doesn't add much to Harlan's, except for his discussion of why this law fails strict scrutiny.

(Didn't we just see a Harlan dissent in *Lochner* itself in 1905? Isn't he getting pretty long in the tooth by the time *Griswold* rolls around in 1965?)

This is the second Justice Harlan – the first Harlan's grandson.

Justice Harlan says, I can't join this penumbra stuff. The question is whether the statute infringes the Due Process Clause of the 14th Amendment violating basic values "implicit in the concept of ordered liberty."

Note that this is the same question as the Court asked in the incorporation cases. For Harlan, the Due Process Clause incorporates both more and less than the Bill of Rights.

Note also that in *Griswold*, Harlan simply incorporates his prior dissent in *Poe v. Ullman*. What happened in *Poe* was that couples who wanted to use contraceptives sued the State of Connecticut for a declaratory judgment that the contraception law was unconstitutional. The majority of the Court held that the plaintiffs lacked standing to sue because they hadn't shown that the statute would likely be enforced against them. (That could also be expressed as a ripeness problem.) Justice Harlan dissented from the Court's refusal to reach the merits, and in that dissent he explained at length why he thought the statute was unconstitutional. And most of Harlan's reasoning in *Poe* gets explicitly adopted by the Court in *Casey*, 25 years later. We'll discuss it in more detail there.

But basically, he does a somewhat more persuasive verions of Justice Douglas's position: Harlan says that "[the] liberty guaranteed by the Due Process Clause . . . is not a series of isolated points pricked out [from the specific provisions of the Bill of Rights]. It is a rational continuum which, broadly speaking, includes a freedom from all substantial arbitrary impositions and purposeless restraints, . . . and which also recognizes . . . that certain interests require particularly careful scrutiny of the state needs asserted to justify their abridgment."

This is a lot like penumbras – both Douglas and Harlan are saying that the Bill of Rights just provides *examples* of liberty, but spreads its protection beyond it. But a better analogy might be to those awful math problems in high school where they give you a bunch of points on a graph, and you have to derive the equation of the line or curve that connects them all. Once you have derived the function, then it can tell you additional points on the same line.

d. Specific Enumeration (Black and Stewart, JJ., dissenting)

(How do the dissenters approach this case?)

They restrict the concept of "liberty" to those rights enumerated elsewhere in the Constitution. There's no constitutional provision recognizing a right to "privacy."

Justice Black says that "I like my privacy as well as the next one, but I am nevertheless compelled to admit that government has a right to invade it unless prohibited by some specific constitutional provision."

(What about keeping the Constitution in tune with contemporary mores?)

The only way to keep the Constitution "in tune with the times" is to amend it. Otherwise, judges will simply enforce their own subjective notions, and we will be back to *Lochner*.

(How does Justice Harlan answer these folks?)

He says the certainty that they derive from looking only at the text is an illusion: The text is often just as open-ended as these other modes of analysis – look at "equal protection." There's simply no escape from the need to exercise reasoned judgment.

(What provides the constraint on judges in Harlan's view?)

Basically some combination of intellectual integrity and the craft norms of individual lawyers. Now, Harlan was somebody who felt these norms very deeply, and it's not surprising he had a lot of confidence in them.

(Do *you* share that confidence?)

e. Applying the Standard: Means and Ends

Once the Court identifies that a fundamental aspect of liberty is at issue, it can't just rubber-stamp the legislature's judgment. So we're back to the familiar analysis of ends and means. Remember, you can attack both the ends pursued and the "fit" between those ends and the means adopted to pursue them.

Let's take ends first:

(Is the Court saying that this zone of privacy means that the State can't regulate activities that are essentially private, and that the State just wants to regulate out of a moral judgment that these things are immoral?)

No. Justice Douglas has no problem with laws against "adultery, homosexuality, fornication and incest." The problem is not that Connecticut's law represents a moral judgment. Courts should hesitate before supplanting a state's considered judgment on controversial moral question.

(Do you agree that the State should be able to make moral judgments?)

It's a recurrent question. But most laws are based on some kind of moral judgment. It's just that some are less controversial than others.

(Is the Court's position on these particular moral judgments consistent? Can he really draw a line between contraception and "adultery, homosexuality, fornication and incest"?)

Well, later cases show it's hard.

(What about the means? How does the Court approach them?)

The Court says a "governmental purpose to control or prevent activities constitutionally subject to state regulation may not be achieved by means which sweep unnecessarily broadly and thereby invade the area of protected freedoms."

So this is a form of heightened scrutiny – the Court is asking whether any legitimate interests that the State might have here can be realized through less intrusive means. We *don't* ask that question under rational basis review – there, the question is simply whether the state's means have some relationship to its ends, not whether the state's chosen means might be overbroad.

(What's the big problem with the means adopted?)

Potentially, this law could be enforced through the full rigor of the criminal law, inevitably involving an inquiry into private acts between married couples in their own homes. The Third and Fourth Amendments explicitly protect this privacy. Justice Douglas says, for instance, that a big part of the problem here is that the law might be enforced by "search[ing] the sacred precincts of marital bedrooms."

So for both Doublas and Harlan, this case stands at the intersection of two important lines of constitutional authority. On the one hand, we have judicial protection for family life and autonomy going back at least to *Meyer* and *Pierce*, and traditional notions of family privacy stretching back even further.

On the other, we have the Third and Fourth Amendment's protection of the privacy of the home. Here, both principles converge to require strict scrutiny in this case.

One last point. In *Poe v. Ullman*, Justice Harlan made a big deal out of the fact that no other state had criminalized the use of contraceptives.

(Why does that matter?)

Because substantive due process is employed – in Harlan's view – primarily to protect traditional freedoms against novel restrictions imposed by outlier states. If there were lots of these laws, it would be pretty good evidence that this right of marital privacy is *not* traditionally sacred.

But think about what that kind of analysis means for the role of the Court.

(Is the Court protecting minority rights, as Footnote 4 would urge?)

No – it's exercising a majoritarian function – bringing outlier regions into line with the rest of the country.

3.   Neutral Principles and Originalism

Griswold is one of the focuses of Judge Bork's article that I assigned in the packet.   He uses it as a starting point for his argument in favor of originalism as a theory of interpretation.

a.   Neutral Derivation of Principles

Bork puts together Bickel's idea of the counter-majoritarian difficulty with Wechsler's argument about neutral principles to make the following argument:

1. Judicial review is counter-majoritarian and can therefore be justified only if the court has a valid theory about when it may step in to protect minority rights.

2. A valid theory has to be neutral; the Court cannot be what Wechsler described as a "naked power organ."

(What does Bork add to Wechsler?)

He says Wechsler didn't take neutrality far enough.   Wechsler urged neutrality in the *application* of principle.

(Can we frame *Griswold* as a neutral *application* of principle?)

Well, it's worth noting how you can manipulate this requirement.   I've given you two different principles in the handout:

1. The government may not interfere with acts done in private.

2. The government may not prohibit the use of contraceptives by married couples.

(Does the first one pass Wechsler's test?)

No – There's all sorts of cases in which the Court wouldn't by willing to apply this principle: e.g., rape, incest, drug use.

(What about the second one?)

Sure.   But you can see what the Court has done – it has defined the principle so narrowly as to only include the cases it likes.

(What's Bork's response to this?)

He says we also have to be neutral in the *derivation* of principle. We have to have a neutral reason for why *this* is the principle rather than something else.

For him, originalism is the only neutral theory for the derivation of principles. But note that Bork doesn't think that his constitutional theory forecloses the result in *Brown*.

(This is the article that got Bork in so much trouble at his confirmation hearings. Is he saying anything so radical?)

b.   Originalism and Theories of Interpretation

You can also think of the argument as starting from a theory of judicial review similar to Hamilton's argument in Federalist 78. Remember he claimed that the judges exercise "judgment," not "will"; it's OK that judges aren't elected because they're simply enforcing the will of the People as expressed in the Constituion. This sort of theory puts a high premium on distinguishing between the sorts of choices that judges make – which are supposed to be just *applying* the law – and those that legislators make – which are *making* the law.

That means that we ought to focus on the capacity of the theory to constrain judges and keep them from just following their own whims. Different theories probably impose different degrees of constraint. Most originalists argue that originalism constrains more than the other theories. (This may or may not be the case.)

c.   Originalism and Theories of Obligation

(Remember we talked at the beginning about the relationship between one's theory of *interpretation* and one's theories of *obligation* and of *judicial review*. What sort of theories of obligation and judicial review is Judge Bork relying on here?)

I think it fits best with a *conventionalist* theory of judicial review. We want to be a government of laws, not of men -- so we need some kind of basic law. The Constitution is the only such law that commands common respect -- substituting an "improved" one would cause all kinds of disagreements. By agreeing to treat the basic structural issues as settled, we can move on to the pressing issues of the day.

We sometimes call this kind of theory *conventionalism* – that is, the Constitution is binding because it's a convention we can all agree on, much like the rules of a game that all the players agree to accept so that the game can go forward. The important thing about the Constitution is therefore not who wrote it or even what values it embodies, but simply that almost everyone in the country acknowledges the Constitution as authoritative.

(What would be the most important criterion for a theory of interpretation if you're a conventionalist?   What would you want your theory of interpretation to *do* for you?)

In interpreting the Constitution, you would want to interpret it in such a way as to facilitate this sort of social consensus.

(Can you make a *conventionalist* argument for originalism along these lines?)

Well, there's Justice Scalia's argument that "You can't beat somebody with nobody." In other words, if originalism has at least some intuitive appeal, and you can't get the critics to agree on an alternative theory, then we should stick with originalism.

A conventionalist might also care a great deal about making sure the principles you find in the Constitution are "neutral" ones – that is, principles that really come from the Constitution itself and not from the judges' preferences. You'll seek the idea of "neutral principles" developed in Prof. Wechsler's piece on *Brown*, and also in Judge Bork's defense of originalism (which we read in connection with *Griswold*).

Here's a different approach, grounded in a theory of obligation based on consent: You could view the Constitution as a classic social contract, and say that the authority of the Constitution – like that of the government itself – derives from the consent of the governed.

This might lead you to a theory that we frequently call "legal positivism" – that is, that law represents the command of some person or institution who has *authority*.

Here, if you think the Constitution's binding nature derives from the *authority* of its drafters or ratifiers – based on their claim to speak for the People as a whole – then it's logical in interpreting the constitution to focus on what the drafters or ratifies intended. This method is usually called *originalism*.

There are several problems with this approach:

- All those people are dead now. Why *should* the Constitution bind *us*? This is the "dead hand" problem.

- They didn't ask a lot of "us," even back then: women, black people, Indians. In fact, it might be even worse than that. We might think the Constitution is actually hostile to the rights and interests of those people – especially African- and Native-Americans – that weren't represented in 1789. We'll come back to that problem in connection with *Dred Scott*.

(Can you make a conventionalist argument *against* originalism? Can you argue that in some ways, originalism might make achieving a settled consensus more difficult?)

A conventionalist would pay particular attention to facilitating settled resolutions of disputes. Precedent, for instance, would play a big role in determining the Constitution's meaning. And precedent's a big problem for originalists, as Prof. Farber points out. That doesn't mean you can't *be* an originalist – it just means that respect for *stare decisis* is going to keep you from implementing your theory in a lot of cases.

d.   Criticisms of Originalism

As with all the theories of interpretation we'll discuss in this course, originalism has its critics. They tend to make two kinds of criticisms – first, that originalism is inappropriate *in principle*, and second, that originalism is unworkable *in practice*.

Let's take the "in principle" criticisms first:

- Intent of collective bodies: The Framers are a "they," not an "it"—that is, they're lots of different people making decisions in different settings at different moments, and it may be hard to distill one single "intent" or "understanding" of a given provision. Even if we focus on Philadelphia, the text represents compromises among different people with different views, and this problem becomes even more complex as we move out o the ratifying conventions.

- The "dead hand of the past" is, well, *dead*. Recall the problems with adhering to an old constitution at all, from the first day. Those problems intensify if we bar evolving understandings of the old text.

- One generation – no matter how brilliant – can't have all the answers. This is actually a conservative criticism: Classical conservatism (e.g., Edmund Burke) is skeptical of human reason, and it tends to correct for the deficiencies of particular individuals at one time and place by relying on evolving collective understandings over time. No matter how smart the Framers were (and they were *really* smart) they're not smart enough to have anticipated all the challenges that the Constitution would face down the line.

- Originalism is biased to "conservative" outcomes. I've quoted Senator Kennedy's statement about "Robert Bork's America" in the notes. It's pretty unfair. But a lot of critics think there's a grain of truth there, i.e., that originalism would rule out a lot of progressive changes that have made the world better.

(What do you think of these criticisms?)

There's also a more practical set of criticisms. With any theory of interpretation, we have to ask, Is the theory workable?

What are the theory's costs? There are two very basic kinds of costs:

- *Decision* Costs: How much in the way of resources does it take to arrive at a decision?

- *Error* Costs: What is the likelihood that judges applying the theory will make mistakes?

(What are the decision costs of originalism?)

They're fairly high, aren't they? You have to do all that historical research. When we come to the *Term Limits* case in Chapter Nine, you'll groan at having to read page after page of historical debate. But it's a good example of what it would entail to take originalism seriously.

(What about error costs? Do we have any reason to think that judges and lawyers will be good at historical research?)

It's a problem. There's lots of literature out there suggesting that the Supreme Court, for one, gets history wrong on a fairly regular basis.

You also get into even more difficult questions like, Do the accurate records we'd need to really get at the historical meaning of the Constitution even exist, or have they been lost? And is it possible to figure out the "intent" of the participants in 13 state ratifying conventions? What if they didn't think of the particular question at hand?

Still, I'm skeptical of any categorical conclusions that courts can't do history, for two reasons:

(1)   This problem may be inevitable. It would be a strange kind of law that never incorporated other disciplines. Can you imagine doing antitrust law without economics? Patent law without science? Criminal law without psychology? Unless law has no relation to reality, lawyers and judges will have to master fields for which they have no specialized training. There's no reason to believe they will be any less successful in history than in these other disciplines.

(2)   I'm not convinced that the historians are really that much better on a lot of these issues. I saw an op-ed piece on the history of the 11th Amendment by an eminent historian criticizing a recent Supreme Court opinion's historical analysis. I've done enough 11th Amendment history to know that this historian had no idea what she was talking about (and I reached this judgment notwithstanding that I agreed with her ultimate conclusion). That's just a single anecdote, but it makes you wonder.

B.   The Transformation of Marital Privacy

1.   Two Potential Limits on "Privacy"

The *Griswold* opinions emphasize two features of that case that could have served to limit the decision's reach:

- *Marital* Privacy: The opinions place a great deal of weight on the sanctity of the marriage relationship, suggesting that non-married persons shouldn't have similar rights.

  (Is this limit justified? Can the same arguments be made for a right of *non*-marital privacy?)

- *Use* vs. *Sale* Restrictions: The opinions also emphasize that Connecticut's law is unique in banning *use* of contraceptives as well as sale. The problem with *use* restrictions is that they might be enforced by actually coming in and searching the home.

  (How likely is this?)

  Not bloody likely. It's not what actually *happened* in *Griswold*. But in any event, the Court's reasoning suggests that sale restrictions might still be constitutional.

But neither of these lines is actually respected in later decisions.

2.   *Eisenstadt v. Baird*, 405 U.S. 438 (1972)

Massachusetts prohibited the distribution of contracep-tives to unmarried persons.

The Court holds (Brennan, J.) that the statute violates the Equal Protection Clause by discriminating between married and unmarried persons.

Purporting to apply rational basis review, the Court rejected the three interests put forward in support of the statute:

(a)   *deterrence of premarital sex*: The Court said that this couldn't be the purpose, because the statute was "riddled with exceptions," such as distribution of contraceptives to prevent disease. And it "would be plainly unreasonable to assume that Massachusetts has prescribed pregnancy and the birth of an unwanted child as punishment for fornication."

       (Isn't the latter point simply Justice Brennan imposing his own view of what's appropriate?)

(b)   *regulate potentially harmful articles*: The Court said that not all contraceptives are potentially dangerous, and this rationale doesn't distinguish between married and unmarried persons.

(c) *moral opposition to contraception*: The Court rejected this as inconsistent with *Griswold*. "[Whatever] the rights of the individual to access to contraceptives may be, the rights must be the same for the unmarried and the married alike. . . ."

Justice Brennan has alternate rationales for the last point, which is the heart of the opinion:

Recasting Privacy: "If the right of privacy means anything, it is the right of the *individual*, married or single, to be free from unwarranted governmental intrusion into matters so fundamentally affecting a person as the decision whether to bear or beget a child."

(Huh? Did Justice Brennan *read* the *Griswold* opinions?)

Equal Protection: "[I]f *Griswold* is no bar to a prohibition on the distribution of contraceptives, the State could not, consistently with the Equal Protection Clause, outlaw distribution to unmarried but not to married persons."

(Are unmarried and married people similarly situated? Doesn't *Griswold* hold that only married couples have a constitutional right at stake?)

[Chief Justice Burger, joined by 2 others, dissented.]

Due Process/Equal Protection Leveraging: *Eisenstadt's* method is to define a right using due process, then use the equal protection idea to require that the right be extended equally to everyone.

We'll see how this might operate when we talk about homosexuality and *Lawrence*. The question will be whether this sort of analysis might be a more persuasive basis than Substantive Due Process as a basis for a right to gay sex. It also might make a more persuasive case for gay *marriage*, given that the Court has recognized marriage as a fundamental right in *Loving v. Virginia*, 388 U.S. 1 (1967).

3. ***Carey v. Population Services International*, 431 U.S. 678 (1977)**

New York prohibited any person other than a licensed pharmacist from distributing contraceptives.

The Court holds (Brennan, J.) that the statute unconstitutionally burdens individual freedom to make decisions about contraception.

"*Griswold* may no longer be read as holding only that a State may not prohibit a married couple's use of contraceptives. Read in light of its progeny, the teaching of *Griswold* is that the Constitution protects individual decisions in matters of childbearing from unjustified intrusion by the State."

The statute is subject to strict scrutiny, and doesn't survive here.

(Where did strict scrutiny come from? Even *Eisenstadt* purported to apply rationality review.)

C.   **Abortion**

Note that all of you are now in trouble at your judicial confirmation hearings, because you can't say -- as some judicial nominees have tried to do -- that you haven't really thought about whether *Roe v. Wade* was rightly decided. If you try to do that, I'll crawl out from whatever rock I'm living under and testify against you.

I want to say at the outset that my own view is that the constitutionality of abortion regulations as a matter of law is ultimately inextricable from the moral issues. So it's perfectly appropriate to voice a moral viewpoint here. But you've got to ground your moral view in a *legal* argument.   Just because law and morality are related, they're not the *same*.

That raises a second point: Although the moral and legal issues are related, I do think it's possible to come to different conclusions on the two. I think you should worry a little bit if your legal conclusions always match your moral or policy views: Not every law that is bad for moral or policy reasons is unconstitutional.

Three Questions in *Roe*:

1)   Where does the abortion right come from?

2)   What countervailing interests does the State have in regulating abortion?

3)   What's with this trimester framework?

Two More Questions in *Casey*:

4)   Does the joint opinion do a better job of explaining the basis for the abortion right?

5)   If *Roe* was wrong as an initial matter, what role should *stare decisis* play in deciding whether to overrule it?

1.   *Roe v. Wade*, **410 U.S. 113 (1973)**

We have two different kinds of abortion statutes in *Roe* and its companion cases:

Texas criminalized abortions except for the purpose of saving the mother's life. This is the traditional form of anti-abortion law.

Georgia – whose law gets struck down in the companion case of *Doe v. Bolton* – had a more "modern" statute, based on the Model Penal Code. It made an exception for the life of the mother, birth defects, and

The Court, speaking through Justice Blackmun, holds that the law is unconstitutional.

Note the lineup – this case is 7 to 2. Only Justices White and Rehnquist dissent. Several of the more conservative justices, such as Burger, Stewart, and Powell, join this opinion. It's only later on that abortion become bitterly controversial on the Court.

a.   Derivation of the Right

(What does the Court base the abortion right upon? What source of legal authority?)

- **Tradition?**

Justice Blackmun's historical research – he spent the summer before *Roe* doing research at the Mayo Clinic – indicated that restrictive abortion laws in effect in most states in the early 1970s were a relatively recent development. They derived from the latter half of the 19th century. Prior to that, abortion performed before "quickening" (usually 16 to 18 weeks) was legal.

(Would that mean that history supports a *right* to an abortion?)

(Why isn't Justice Rehnquist right that the history belies any finding that abortion is a fundamental right?)

- **Precedent?**

This Court has recognized a right of personal privacy in cases dealing with marriage, procreation, contraception, family, and childrearing.

"This right of privacy . . . is broad enough to encompass a woman's decision whether or not to terminate her pregnancy."

Notice we're pretty much done futzing about with the 9th Amendment or "penumbras." *Casey* reaffirms that we're going with Harlan on the substantive due process rationale for privacy.

(Is abortion really within the holdings of the prior privacy cases?)

(As Justice Rehnquist asks, In what meaningful way is abortion "private"?)

It's the answer to this question—one which isn't really well developed in the majority opinion—that signals an important shift in privacy jurisprudence. *Griswold* is "private" in the sense of protecting activity that's ordinary undertaken away from the public eye. Abortion, on the other hand, is "private" in the sense of being the sort of *decision* that an individual expects to make autonomously, without interference from the state. It's not that the activity takes place "in private"—in fact, "private" back-alley abortions is one of the things the majority is trying to take us away from. Beginning with *Eisenstadt* but coming to fruition in *Roe*, we're moving from a seclusion model of privacy to an autonomy model.

- **Personal Autonomy?**

Justice Blackmun emphasizes that "[m]aternity, or additional offspring, may force upon the woman a distressful life and future. Psychological harm may be imminent. Mental and physical health may be taxed by child care. There is also the distress . . . associated with the unwanted child, and there is the problem of bringing a child into a family already unable, psychologically and otherwise, to care for it."

(This is surely all true. How can you make it count as a *constitutional* argument?)

(Is it better to think of *Roe* as a bodily integrity case? What does the Court say about that?)

The majority notes that some amici had argued for "an unlimited right to do with one's body as one pleases."

(What does the Court say about that?)

It's skeptical that the right of "privacy" in the earlier cases "bears a close relationship" to the bodily integrity idea.

(Are there any precedents on that?)

Yes – *Jacobson*, which upheld compulsory vaccination over an objection by Jehovah's Witnesses, and *Buck v. Bell*, which upheld compulsory sterilization for the mentally retarded.

(Do you think those cases are right?)

Maybe not – but it's clear that the *Roe* court doesn't disturb them. That doesn't mean that the Court hasn't recognized an important liberty interest in bodily integrity – just that it's not always fundamental.

- **Representation Reinforcement?**

(Does this case fit into the Footnote 4 framework? What would Prof. Ely say about it?)

It's hard to say that women are a discrete and insular minority. Easier, as Prof. Ely pointed in an article that was bitterly critical of *Roe*, to say the *unborn* are.

b.   The Other Side of the Scale

(Does the Court ban all regulation of abortion?)

No. The Court acknowledges that some regulation is appropriate, if it is narrowly drawn to further a compelling state interest.

3 possible justifications for restrictive abortion laws:

(1)   discourage illicit sex

(2)   protect women from hazardous procedures

(3)   protect prenatal life

One important feature of the "strict scrutiny" that comes with recognizing a right as fundamental is that some state interests just aren't good enough when it comes to restricting the right.

(Are any of these interests "compelling"?)

(2) and (3) are, at least in some circumstances. This is an important point: We noted in *Griswold* that morality standing alone is a *legitimate* government interest, but here the Court say's it's *not compelling*.

Take the health interest first.

(Why doesn't the health interest justify the law here?)

It doesn't justify a total ban. This is a least restrictive alternative argument.

(What would some less restrictive alternatives be?)

Well, you could regulate the procedure – require a qualified doctor, ban the more dangerous forms, do it in a hospital, etc.

Then there's the prenatal life interest.

(What difference does it make whether the fetus is a person?)

It might make two:

(1)   If the fetus is a person within the meaning of the 14th Amendment, then *it* has a right to life. A state that prohibited the murder of some persons, but not others, would be denying the "equal protection of the laws" in the classic sense.

(2)   The State has an interest in protecting the life of the fetus which grows as it approaches personhood.

(What does the Court say on the 14th Amendment issue?)

The fetus is not a "person" within the meaning of the 14th Amendment. The Constitution does not define "person," but uses it in a number of contexts in such a way as to indicate postnatal "persons."

(Is this a persuasive textual argument? Do any of these uses occur in contexts where a pre-natal "person" would be relevant?)

Why would we look at textual provisions like who can become a senator or what people count for purposes of apportioning votes, to tell when life *begins*? These provisions also aren't talking about *children*, right?

The Court also argues that 19th century abortion practices -- being less strict -- support the inference that the 14th Amendment doesn't cover the unborn.

(Is this an *originalist* position?)

Sure looks like it – which is too weird.

(Does the Court decide when human life begins?)

No – they duck that issue. "We need not resolve the difficult question of when life begins. When those trained [in] medicine, philosophy, and theology are unable to arrive at any consensus, the judiciary . . . is not in a position to speculate as to the answer." Texas, "by adopting one theory of life," may not "override the rights of the pregnant woman that are at stake."

(Can the Court really duck the "when life begins" question like this?)

(If it's a life, isn't the State clearly entitled to protect it? So isn't the Court actually taking a position here?)

(If there's no clear right answer to a question like this, is that a basis for judicial intervention? Or should the Court defer to the legislature?)

(Is there any way to argue that abortion restrictions are unconstitutional *even if* the fetus is a "life"?)

Maybe. Judith Jarvis Thomson, who was a philosopher at MIT, proposed a famous thought experiment involving an "unconscious violinist."[26] Basically, you wake up to find yourself strapped to a hospital bed and connected to an unconscious man in the next bed. It turns out that the man is a world famous violinist with a life-threatening condition, and the only way to save him is to connect him to a healthy person. You've been kidnapped by a band of music lovers and impressed into this service.

You can see the advantage of the hypo: There's no doubt that the violinist is a person, but it seems clear that you still have a moral right to pull the plug. The import is that no person has a moral person to keep another person alive by sacrificing their own autonomy.

There are some obvious problems:

- It works best for involuntary pregnancy – e.g., rape. In order to assimilate consensual sex, you have to make the more difficult point that women have a right to rely on the efficacy of contraception.

- There may be an important distinction between killing and letting die.

In any event, we've gone a long way beyond John Stuart Mill at that point. That's the key difference between *Griswold* and *Roe*—abortion is "other regarding" conduct in a way that contraception arguably isn't.

---

[26] Judith Jarvis Thomson, *A Defense of Abortion*, 1 Phil. & Public Affairs 47 (Autumn 1971).

c.   The Trimester Framework

The Court sets out the following framework for permissible abortion regulation:

- *First Trimester:* No regulation, period.

- *Second Trimester:* States may regulate abortion procedures in ways that are reasonably related to maternal health.

- *Third Trimester:* State may regulate or forbid abortion except when necessary to preserve the life or health of the mother.

(Where does this framework come from?)

The line between the first and second trimester reflects the point at which abortion may be more medically risky than childbirth.

The second line is supposed to be viability. The problem, though, is that viability is contingent on the state of medical technology, and the point gets earlier and earlier as the years go on after *Roe*. It's not surprising that the subsequent cases start to break down the framework on this point.

Why does the State's interest in *potential* life depend on viability? Suppose, for instance, we have a third trimester fetus who has some defect that means he's going to have to go on a respirator immediately after birth. He can't, in other words, survive outside the womb unassisted until a substantial time *after* birth.

(Does that mean he can be aborted in the third trimester?)

I doubt it. There is, by the way, a pretty good argument that my 16-year-old can't survive outside the womb without considerable assistance to this day. Hell, it's not clear *I* can.

(Let me ask a more general question: Doesn't this trimester scheme look more like a statute than like an interpretation of the due process clause? Isn't that a clue that the Court is legislating?)

Maybe. But let's suppose the Court did something more "restrained": It holds simply that abortion can't be outlawed whenever the woman's interest in controlling her body outweighs the state's interest in potential life.

(What's the problem with that?)

It would remain unclear when the right is controlling and when it's not. The Court is trying to provide guidance so both women and the government will know what they're entitled to do and when. The interest in predictability often requires the Court's *doctrine* to be considerably more specific than the constitutional text itself. It's not at all clear that's a bad thing, right? The *Miranda* warnings are another example.

d.   Some More General Questions

(What do you think of the *Roe* opinion as a matter of judicial craft? Is it a good performance?)

Here's what one respected law professor had to say:

"We might think of Justice Blackmun's opinion in *Roe* as an innovation akin to Joyce's [*Finnegan's Wake*] or Mailer's [*The Executioner's Song*]. It is the totally unreasoned judicial opinion. To say that it does not look like Justice Powell's decision in some other case is like saying that a Cubist 'portrait' does not look like its subject as a member of the Academy would paint it." Mark Tushnet, *Following the Rules Laid Down*, 96 Harv. L. Rev. 781, 821 (1983).

(What do you think? Is *Roe* an example of "Cubist judging"?)

(What would Professor Grey say about this case? Can the Court enforce *only* principles that you can find some textual warrant for in the Constitution?)

He says we do "non-interpretive" review all the time. This is probably the most helpful part of the Grey reading: He demonstrates that unenumerated or "unwritten" rights have a serious historical pedigree going back to the Founding.

Grey has, however, a very broad definition of "noninterpretive" review. He wants to say, for instance, that *Roe* is really the same as *Brown*.

(Is there really no difference between *Roe* and *Brown*?)

Well, pay attention to FN 46 on p. ___, where Grey distinguishes between three kinds of non-interpretive review:

(1)   cases where "the courts have created . . . independent constitutional rights with almost no textual guidance";

(2)   cases "where the courts have given general application to norms that the constitutional text explicitly applies in a more limited way" – like incorporation and reverse-incorporation; and

(3)   cases involving "the extension or broadening of principles stated in the Constitution beyond the normative content intended for them by the framers."

(Where would Grey put *Brown*?)

In class 3 – his claim is that the framers meant to protect equality, but didn't specifically mean to preclude segregation.

(Is there really no difference between (1), (2), and (3)?)

(Would it have been healthier to have left this question to the states? To have allowed different views to prevail in different parts of the country? To permit political compromise or subsequent legislative revision?)

This is a question the Court returns to in *Casey*.

2.   ***Planned Parenthood of Southeastern Pennsylvania v. Casey*, 505 U.S. 833 (1992)**

We're twenty years later now. Over that time, the Court has had a constant stream of abortion cases. None of them involve outright bans; instead, the states try to regulate the procedure in various ways. Some of these regulations seem like sensible medical regulation of a complicated and dangerous procedure; others seem like efforts to make it difficult to actually get an abortion.

In *Casey*, Planned Parenthood challenged five provisions of the Pennsylvania Abortion Control Act:

(1)   a woman seeking an abortion must give informed consent to the procedure, 24 hours after being provided with certain information;

(2)   minors may not obtain an abortion without informed consent of a parent, with a judicial bypass option available;

(3)   a married woman seeking an abortion must certify that she has notified her husband;

(4)   the preceding three requirements may be avoided only in the event of a "medical emergency"; and

(5)   facilities providing abortion services must report certain information to public authorities.

The joint opinion (O'Connor, Kennedy, & Souter, JJ.) does two things:

First, it reaffirms *Roe*'s "essential holding" that there is a constitutional right to an abortion.

The essential holding of *Roe* has three parts:

(a)   a recognition of the right of the woman to choose to have an abortion and to obtain it without undue interference from the State.

(b)   a confirmation of the State's power to restrict abortions after fetal viability, if the law contains exceptions for pregnancies which endanger a woman's life or health.

(c)   the principle that the State has legitimate interests from the outset of the pregnancy in protecting the health of the woman and the life of the fetus that may become a child.

Second, the Court upholds all the provisions of the PA law except for the spousal notification provision. It does this by adopting a new standard –

the "undue burden" standard – for evaluating restrictions on the right to an abortion. This standard is different, and more lenient than, the standard applied in the cases between *Roe* and *Casey*.

It's worth noting at the outset that *nobody* was all that happy with this decision. The pro-life people thought they'd been sold out by the three Republican appointees who seemed to have forgotten that they were put on the Court to overrule *Roe v. Wade*. ("No more David Souters!") The pro-choice people, on the other hand, thought that the undue burden standard was so lenient as to make the reaffirmation of *Roe* meaningless.

Uniform consternation may be a sign that the Court's gotten it right.

a.   Derivation of the Abortion Right

We won't spend much time here. Note primarily the Joint Opinion's heavy reliance on Justice Harlan's dissent in *Poe v. Ullman*.

(Do they do a persuasive job of bringing this case within that reasoning?)

(What's the best case you can make for that?)

I think it would go something like this:

- Cases like *Griswold, Pierce, Meyer* etc. are about control over family, childrearing. Abortion as a basic issue of reproductive choice fits within that tradition.

- It's true the earlier cases are about traditional families, and especially about married couples' choices. But *Eisenstadt* and similar cases require extension of this outside the traditional marital relationship.

(Is that persuasive?)

I don't know – it's a stretch. And the Court in any event also seems tempted to a much more general endorsement of a right of personal autonomy about basic life choices. The Court says abortion is unique, both because of its importance to the woman and its consequences for others. "Her suffering is too intimate and personal for the State to insist, without more, upon its own vision of the woman's role, however dominant that vision has been in the course of our history and our culture."

Justice Scalia isn't very nice about this: He says that the best the joint opinion can do is "rattle off a collection of adjectives that simply decorate a value judgment and conceal a political choice."

(Would the joint opinion be on stronger ground if they embraced the *Pierce*/*Meyer*/*Allgeyer* line—that is, a general right of self-determination in basic life decisions?)

(Is it possible to embrace those cases without embracing economic rights like freedom of contract?)

b.   Stare Decisis

(Do you think the Court really believes *Roe* was correct as an initial matter?)

Maybe not. The joint opinion says "the reservations any of us may have in reaffirming the central holding of *Roe* are outweighed by the explication of individual liberty we have given *combined* with the force of *stare decisis*."

The *stare decisis* inquiry involves four basic questions:

(a)   Whether *Roe*'s rule has proven "unworkable";

(b)   Whether people have significantly relied upon it;

(c)   Whether the law in the intervening years has evolved in such a way as to erode *Roe*'s doctrinal underpinnings; and

(d)   Whether time has overtaken *Roe*'s factual assumptions.

Justice Scalia points out that the joint opinion fails to mention one important factor: "how wrong was the decision on its face?" But I think it's fair to say that *stare decisis* analysis *begins* once we conclude that the prior decision was wrong.

(Why do we care about *stare decisis*?)

One might make a variety of arguments:

- Efficient compliance with the law requires that the law be reasonably settled. People rely on the current state of the law when they make choices and investments; abrupt changes disrupt these settled expectations.

- *Stare decisis* is a way of treating like cases alike over time.

- A strong doctrine of precedent is a way of recognizing that the current judges are beings of imperfect rationality and may not have all the answers. Precedent is, on this view, a repository of the accumulated wisdom of prior generations of decisionmakers.

- Some degree of *stare decisis* is practically necessary for the enterprise of law to go forward. We simply can't treat every single question as open in every single case. If we had to start from first principles every time, we'd never get anywhere.

(How strong a presumption should there be against overruling prior decisions? Should the strength of the presumption differ according to whether it's a constitutional case? In which direction?)

- **Workability**

(What do we mean by "workability"?)

Whether the rule of the prior case can be applied in a coherent and predictable manner.

(What does the Court say about this?)

"Although *Roe* has engendered opposition, it has in no sense proven 'unworkable.'" Judges can make the determinations required to say whether a law on abortion is constitutional or not.

It's worth noting, though, that the Court had had to develop a large, confusing jurisprudence about what restrictions were OK and what weren't.

- **Reliance**

(What does the Court mean by "reliance"?)

"The inquiry into reliance counts the costs of a rule's repudiation as it would fall on those who have relied reasonably on the rule's continued application."

(How do people rely on a right to abortion? Do they go out and have sex willy nilly, because they know they can abort the consequences?)

That seems doubtful. The Court admits that nobody "relies" on abortion in the customary sense: "Abortion is customarily chosen as an unplanned response to the consequence of unplanned activity or to the failure of conventional birth control."

But here there is reliance in a broader sense: "[F]or two decades of economic and social developments, people have organized intimate relationships and made choices that define their views of themselves and their places in society, in reliance on the availability of abortion in the event that contraception should fail. The ability of women to participate equally in the economic and social life of the Nation has been facilitated by their ability to control their reproductive lives."

(That sounds good but what does it mean? In what way do people "rely" on abortion to "organize their intimate relationships" or "define their views of themselves and their places in society"? Can someone give me an example?)

Note that the dissenters point out there is no *evidence* for this sort of reliance, other than "generalized assertions about the national psyche." On the other hand, it's hard to escape some general sense in that the expectation that abortion will be available has become pretty ingrained in many people's worldview.

- **Change of Law**

(Any relevant change in the law?)

"*Roe* stands at the intersection of two lines of decisions": the privacy cases, see *Griswold*, and the bodily integrity cases, see *Cruzan*. Both these lines of cases are still good law, and if anything have been strengthened since 1973.

But note that the Court had also tightened up on the right of privacy in *Bowers v. Hardwick*.

- **Change of Fact**

"[Time] has overtaken some of *Roe*'s factual assumptions: advances in maternal health care allow for abortions safe to the mother later in pregnancy than was true in 1973." And viability starts earlier, due to advances in keeping fetuses alive outside the mother.

But these changes go only to the validity of the trimester framework, not to *Roe*'s central holding.

(How do the dissenters respond to the *stare decisis* argument?)

They say that the Court has changed *Roe*'s holding too much to warrant a serious *stare decisis* argument. Justice Scalia says he's never heard of "this new, keep-what-you-want-and-throw-away-the-rest version" of *stare decisis*.

Of course, "keep what you want and throw away the rest is exactly what incremental, common law change is all about.

Note that this would ordinarily be it under conventional *stare decisis* analysis, but the Court adds another wrinkle here:

c.   ***Stare Decisis* in National Controversies**

"[T]he sustained and widespread debate *Roe* has provoked calls for some comparison between that case and others of comparable dimension that have responded to national controversies and taken on the impress of the controversies addressed." In other words, it's a good time to review where we've been in the course:

- *Lochner* and *Plessy*

Two other historical episodes are comparable: *West Coast Hotel*'s overruling of *Lochner*, and *Brown*'s overruling of *Plessy*. These are both, in the Court's view, epochal events in the history of the Court as an institution.

Lochner was overruled because "[t]he facts upon which [it] had premised a constitutional resolution of social controversy had proved to be untrue, and history's demonstration of their untruth not only justified but required the new choice of constitutional principle."

Likewise, *Plessy* was overruled because "[s]ociety's understanding of the facts upon which a constitutional ruling was sought in 1954 was . . .

fundamentally different from the basis claimed for the decision in 1896." (Although "we think *Plessy* was wrong the day it was decided.")

(Are either of these rulings really examples of "changed circumstances"?)

(Take *Lochner* first: Did *West Coast Hotel* really rely on "changed circumstances"?)

What about the institutional criticism of *Lochner* -- i.e., that courts shouldn't be imposing a particular economic theory?

Of course, it's true as a *practical* matter that the institutional pressure on the Court to uphold economic regulation was much greater in 1937 than it was in 1905.   But for the Court in *Casey*, public pressure seems to cut *against* change.

(What about *Plessy*?   Was *Plessy* wrong the day it was decided?)

I think it probably was, although I do think two things changed between 1896 and 1954:

- Segregation became more entrenched and vicious; and

- The Court discovered how hard it was to enforce "separate but equal as a coherent constitutional doctrine."

But this makes you wonder whether you need a *special* precedent inquiry in "big and important" cases; the problem with *Plessy* was that it proved unworkable, which is one of the standard criteria.

That may be true of *Lochner* as well, as the contrast with *Nebbia* shows.

- **Overruling and Legitimacy**

Overrulings based on changed circumstances are more defensible than ones based on a shift in composition of the Court, and therefore don't hurt the Court's legitimacy.

"In the present case, however, . . . the terrible price would be paid for overruling."

(How does overruling hurt the Court's legitimacy?)

Overruling can hurt the Court's legitimacy in two ways:

(i)   "frequent overruling would overtax the country's belief in the Court's good faith"; and

(ii)   overruling a watershed case that resolves a social controversy is particularly damaging.

The Court's decision in *Roe* thus has "the dimension present whenever the Court's interpretation of the Constitution calls the contending sides of a national controversy to end their national division by accepting a common mandate rooted in the Constitution."   This doesn't happen very often --

Brown and *Roe* are the only two cases in this lifetime. But under these circumstances, "[t]o overrule under fire in the absence of the most compelling reason to reexamine a watershed decision would subvert the Court's legitimacy beyond any serious question."

There are several issues here:

First, the Chief points out that it's odd for the Court to rely so heavily on *West Coast Hotel* and *Brown*, when those are cases where the Court *enhanced* it's stature by overruling its prior mistakes.

(Can we think of a case where the Court paid a "terrible price" for overruling?)

Frankly, it's hard. Most of the "big" overrules are praised today. There are a lot of examples in the Warren Court criminal procedure decisions as well (e.g., *Mapp v. Ohio* overruled *Wolf v. Colorado*), and they're well thought-of today.

Of course, this doesn't prove overruling is good: It may be that the ones we've had were successful precisely because they're rare. But the Court certainly hasn't *proven* that a terrible price will always follow.

Second, isn't Justice Scalia right that the Court's ego has gotten a little out of hand? Did *Brown* really "resolve" the controversy over Civil Rights? Another account would be that fight over civil rights in the 20ᵗʰ Century *started* with *Brown*, and was "resolved" – if it *was* resolved – only by the sacrifices made by the Civil Rights Movement and the action that Congress and the President took after 1964. That's certainly what Rosenberg's evidence suggests.

(Do you think that the Court is really describing the effect *Roe* actually had on the political debate over abortion?)

As Justice Scalia points out, another example of an attempt to "call the contending sides of a national controversy to end their national division by accepting a common mandate rooted in the Constitution" was the *Dred Scott* decision – which is arguably the *worst* mistake that the Supreme Court ever made. We know how that one turned out.

Scalia says the Court is behaving just like Chief Justice Taney, who thought he could resolve the slavery issue in *Dred Scott*. (Don't forget, though, that in *Dred Scott* the political branches were begging for a judicial resolution. Not so much true in the abortion context.)

On the other hand, I think it's fair to say that there are some very contentious issues the Court *has* managed to resolve:

• School prayer: A big *political* controversy almost throughout our history, but the Warren Court's resolution is pretty well accepted today. Interestingly, the Court's resolution isn't *quite* what schools actually do, but the general level of prayer even in non-complying schools has sharply declined and there's not all that much political controversy about it.

- Redistricting: There was serious political conflict between town and country over the balance of political power before *Baker v. Carr* and *Reynolds v. Sims*. But the Court's "one man, one vote" principle was widely and quickly accepted.

- *Bush v. Gore*: Legal academics are still mad about this, but it's not clear anyone else is (in fact, public opinion data strongly suggests they are *not*). Wouldn't you have to say that the public accepted the Court's resolution as legitimate?

Third, isn't the reference to public pressure sheer stubbornness? Is the Court saying, in effect, don't tell us what to do, because if you try we'll just do the opposite? As Justice Scalia says, "the notion that we would decide a case differently from the way we otherwise would have in order to show that we can stand firm against public disapproval is frightening."

Fourth, doesn't the idea of public pressure cut both ways? Isn't the Court *affirming* under fire? And aren't these three justices in particular *caving* to public pressure to ignore what they really thought the right answer is to this question?

Fifth, Justice Scalia says we should pay attention to the *reasons* for all the public pressure. The reason, he says, is that "the American people love democracy and the American people are not fools. As long as . . . the people though . . . that we Justices were doing essentially lawyers' work up here -- reading text and discerning our society's traditional understanding of that text -- the public pretty much left us alone. . . . But if in reality our process of constitutional adjudication consists primarily of making *value judgments* . . . [then] the people know that their value judgments are quite as good as those taught in any law school -- maybe better."

Of course, we've been wrestling since day one in this course with whether it's ever possible to avoid value judgments in constitutional law. Is *Casey* any different?

Sixth, is the Court making doctrine here? Would a future Court deciding whether or not to overrule, say, *Garcia* or *Morrison* have to determine whether those were "watershed" decisions requiring some special showing of necessity in order to overrule? Should a future court adhere to *Morrison* simply because there's a lot of public opinion opposed to the independent counsel? It's unclear.

Seventh, I've been a little critical but there's a sense in which I think *Casey* is the single best example that Justice Scalia is *wrong*—that is, that case outcomes aren't driven simply by the justices' moral or policy preferences. You can't always change doctrine simply by changing the composition of the Court. I don't think it's at all clear that O'Connor, Kennedy, and Souter would have joined the majority in *Roe*. But they stick to it here. There's something going on besides the justices personal political beliefs.

This also suggests that all the *sturm und drang* about abortion in judicial confirmation debates is misplaced. Do the math:

Casey is 5-4. Since then, one of the dissenters (White) has been replaced by a prominent advocate of choice (Ginsburg). That made it effectively 6-3 for most of the Rehnquist Court. Now we've had turnover that muddies the water a bit: Roberts for Rehnquist may be a wash, while Alito for O'Connor may shift us back to 5-4 – but still 5-4 in *favor* of *Roe*. More important: *Casey* makes clear there are two variables:

- What are the new justices' views on abortion? and

- Does *stare decisis* trump those views?

I've just suggested, with Alito replacing O'Connor, that it might be back to 5-4 on the first point. But *Casey* shows that the second point – *stare decisis* – is crucial. Two Republican Presidents, heavily focused on the abortion issue, appointed 5 justices between *Roe* and *Casey*. They guessed right about how those justices would vote in *Casey* only 40% of the time.

For Sotomayor and Kagan, the two factors cut the same way. But we don't know how Roberts and Alito would weigh *stare decisis*. Given the experience of the earlier Republican appointees, I submit that there's a good chance at least one of them adheres to *Roe* if the issue comes up again. So I think there's a good chance that even the current court is probably 6-3 in favor – still.

This means the real battlegrounds are things like federalism, the death penalty, and gay right, all of which tend to get short shrift in confirmation hearings.

d.   The Undue Burden Analysis

So now that the Court has reaffirmed the "central holding" of *Roe*, it still has to apply it. Many of the post-*Roe* cases had evaluated any restrictions on abortion under a strict scrutiny test, but the joint opinion says that test is inconsistent with *Roe*'s recognition of the State's legitimate interest. The proper standard is whether the regulation imposes an "undue burden" on the woman's decision. If it does, it's unconstitutional.

An undue burden exists if the law's purpose or effect is to place a substantial obstacle in the path of a woman seeking an abortion before the fetus attains viability.

(What does Justice Blackmun think of the undue burden test?)

He wants to stick with the old rule. All "non-de minimis" abortions regulations are subject to strict scrutiny. Under this standard, all the provisions of the PA statute are unconstitutional.

(So where do the votes come from to uphold four of the five provisions?)

From the people who want to overrule *Roe* altogether. They concur in the judgment that the four provisions are constitutional.

I'm not going to go through the specific statutory provisions. The point of having you read a little about them is to see that the undue burden standard seems to permit a fair amount of regulation, and that it's a pretty substantial break with prior precedent.

The statutory provisions:

• **Definition of "medical emergency"**

The Court of Appeals construed the exception to cover a number of conditions that might pose a "serious risk" of irreversible bodily harm. So construed, there is no undue burden.

• **Informed consent**

It's fine to require giving truthful, nonmisleading information about the nature of the procedure, the health risks of abortion and childbirth, and the gestational age of the fetus -- and to require 24 hours to think it over. To the extent that *Akron I* and *Thornburgh* struck down such requirements, they are overruled.

The fact that the waiting period makes it much more difficult for some women to obtain abortions isn't sufficient to create an undue burden.

• **Spousal notification**

Women in abusive families run major risks in notifying a spouse of an abortion. And the PA statute provides no exemption for those who haven't reported previous abuse. It therefore imposes an undue burden.

This statute perpetuates the view of women as property of their husbands. *See, e.g., Bradwell.* Simply because the husband has an interest in the potential life, the State may not empower him with "this troubling degree of authority over his wife." "A State may not give to a man the kind of dominion over his wife that parents exercise over their children."

(Does the statute really give the husband "dominion"? Or just a chance to try to talk his wife out of the abortion? Hasn't the Court again rested on an unstated assumption about when the fetus is a "child"? After all, if it's a child, the father has an *obligation* to try to protect it.)

(Isn't the Court also predicating its analysis on one view of what husbands are like? I.e., they're all batterers? Is the real problem that the statute doesn't have an adequate exemption for battered wives? Would a statute with a better exemption be constitutional?)

- **Parental consent**

The parental consent issue is largely governed by past decisions, and the PA statute is adequate here.

- **Recordkeeping**

These requirements are reasonably directed to preservation of maternal health. Collection of information about actual patients is vital to medical research.

e.   Alternative Theories

Both Justices Blackmun and Stevens think they can put *Roe* on firmer ground by grounding it in provisions of the Constitution other than due process.

- **Equal Protection (Blackmun, J.)**

(Should we think of this as a sex discrimination case?)

Justice Blackmun argues that we should. He says that abortion "also implicate[s] constitutional guarantees of gender equality. . . . By restricting the right to terminate pregnancies, the State conscripts women's bodies into its service. . . . This assumption -- that women can simply be forced to accept the 'natural' status and incidents of motherhood -- appears to rest upon a conception of women's role that has triggered the protection of the Equal Protection Clause."

It seems to me that this way of stating the argument has some big problems. Take the "conscription" argument first:

→   First, conscription happens to be constitutional for men.

→   Second, is it "conscription" when the State forces a man to pay child support? Is that a 13th amendment problem? Does this extreme language really get us anywhere?

There's also the notion of "outdated assumptions," which is an important trigger for heightened scrutiny in gender cases. But what outdated conceptions of women's role exactly are at issue here? It seems to me the only necessary "women's role" that the State is assuming is that women are still the only ones who can carry a fetus to term. Is that conception out of date? Does it violate the Equal Protection Clause?

I think a less contentious but more promising version of the Queal Protection argument would be that it's meaningless to say "neither women nor men can get an abortion" – the law is effectively imposing a burden on women (pregnancy and childbirth) that men are not required to bear.

This argument has some appeal – Justice Ginsburg is its most famous advocate. But it also has some problems:

→   Equal protection bars discrimination only where people are similarly situated. It's not at all clear men and women *are* similarly situated here.

→   Usually an equal protection claim requires a showing of discriminatory intent – not just a disparate impact on a protected group. Disparate impact is all we've got here, I think. The state's rationale – protection of unborn life – is not discriminatory in itself.

→   The current doctrine is that discrimination based on gender is subject only to intermediate scrutiny, i.e., the court asks whether the discriminatory law is closely related to an important state interest. Many abortion laws might pass that level of review.

But I think the real problem with the Equal Protection argument is this: It's just another way of getting to some kind of heightened scrutiny. As such, it may be more persuasive than substantive due process, which continues to carry some of the taint of *Lochner*. But what really makes abortion cases so intractable isn't the difficulty of identifying a fundamental right to get us to strict scrutiny; it's the presence of a very strong state interest (in the fetus) that may *pass* strict scrutiny. And whatever way you get to strict scrutiny, whether it's via Due Process or Equal Protection, you still have to address the significance of the fetus. No alternate theory is going to get you out of that.

- **Establishment of Religion (Stevens, J.)**

Justice Stevens thinks that abortion laws violate the Establishment Clause: "In order to be legitimate, the State's interest must be secular; consistent with the First Amendment the State may not promote a theological or sectarian interest."

Wait a second: Lots of laws implement moral views that have their basis in religion. For instance, laws against murder are, for many people, grounded in the Ten Commandments.

(Are they unconstitutional?)

Here's another problem: The Establishment Clause requires the state to be *neutral* on religious questions. If abortion is a religious question, then how could the State be neutral? After all, it's just as unconstitutional to endorse an *anti*-religious position as a religious one.

Fortunately, it's pretty well-established in Constitutional Law that the simple correspondence of religious teaching and law does *not* violate the Establishment Clause. Justice Stevens has always been *vox clamantis in deserto* on this one.

D.   Privacy after *Casey*

The notes in this section are sketchier than usual because I have rarely taught this portion of the materials—I generally end the unit with Casey *and then move on to Federalism.*

After *Casey*, the Court seems largely content to let the lower courts hash out the application of the undue burden standard. *Stenberg v. Carhart*, which struck down a Nebraska partial-birth ban, is the only case that makes it to the Court for a decade and a half. (We have a new partial birth case that the Court will hear next term.) Instead, the debate shifts to other aspects of privacy. We'll focus on the right to die and the question of gay rights.

I want you to know the basic doctrine in these two areas, but these cases are really here to illustrate two things:

1) How the Court goes about deciding whether to recognize a previously unrecognized "fundamental right". This is the primary issue.

   A perfectly fair exam question would be, for instance, to ask whether some *other* right – e.g., the right to clone yourself on the 2003 midterm exam – should be recognized as fundamental in light of these precedents.

2) The secondary issue is continuing debate about the basic framework for analyzing rights claims that we've been talking about for some time now.

That framework recognizes two main "tiers" of judicial scrutiny that the Court can apply when a government act is challenged:

- Strict scrutiny: Gov't action is upheld only if it's narrowly tailored to a compelling state interest. This is usually fatal in fact.

- Rational basis review: Gov't action is upheld if it's rationally related to a legitimate state interest. This is generally a rubber stamp.

Generally two things trigger strict scrutiny: Either government action burdens a fundamental right, or it discriminates against a suspect class, like racial or religious minorities. Everything else gets rational basis review.

The thing is, it's never been quite this simple. Justice Stevens, for instance, has always maintained that equal protection is a sliding scale with the intensity of judicial scrutiny varying inversely to the legitimacy of the sort of governmental discrimination at issue. In *Casey*, we saw the Court abandon strict scrutiny in abortion cases for the undue burden standard, which is a kind of intermediate scrutiny somewhere between strict scrutiny and rational basis review.

The cases in this section illustrate more slippage between the black-letter, hornbook model and the Court's actual practice. For instance, Justice Souter's separate opinion in *Glucksberg* rejects the two-tier framework entirely in favor of a more general arbitrariness standard. And the majority in *Lawrence* doesn't employ the strict scrutiny/rational basis framework either. I think it helps to understand the hornbook framework *first*, but then you need to take the additional step of knowing that the Court won't always analyze things this way.

1. **Physician-Assisted Suicide:** *Washington v. Glucksberg*, **521 U.S. 702 (1997)**

    a.   **The Legal Landscape pre-*Glucksberg***

- Longstanding Prohibition on Suicide: Although penalties have varied, the State has long prohibited suicide, and has also prohibited aiding and abetting a suicide.

- Common Law Right of "Informed Consent": A doctor commits a tort if she treats or operates upon a patient without explaining what she proposes to do and obtaining consent.

- Liberty Interest in Refusing Life-Saving Treatment: In *Cruzan v. Director, Missouri Dept. of Health*, 497 U.S. 261 (1990), the Court recognized a liberty interest in refusing treatment that would keep a patient alive under hopeless conditions—e.g., ventilators, feeding tubes. But the Court allowed the State to impose procedural safeguards (there, high burdens of proof) to ensure that only patients who really wished to refuse such treatment would be unplugged.

A liberty interest is different from a fundamental right! The Court refused to recognize the latter in either *Cruzan* or *Glucksberg*.

(Can you make the case for a fundamental right to physician-assisted suicide?)

(What would the big *practical* problem with such a right be?)

We *need* regulation of this practice.

    b.   **Two Approaches to Substantive Due Process in *Glucksberg***

- Fundamental Rights (Majority): Restrictions on fundamental rights are subject to "strict scrutiny"; such restrictions are unconstitutional unless "narrowly tailored to serve a compelling state interest."

Restriction on *non*-fundamental interests are subject only to rational basis review; such restrictions are OK if rationally related to a legitimate state interest.

- Arbitrariness Review (Souter): *Seems* to suggest a more flexible prohibition on "arbitrary impositions and purposeless restraints" involving balancing the competing state and individual interests.

  Justice Souter emphasizes the common law method as a constraint on judicial action.

(Which of these do you prefer?)

c.   Future Possibilities

- The Court could recognize a narrower right of particular individuals to treatment to mitigate severe pain at the end of life, even if such treatment might kill the patient.

- Social mores might evolve to the point that a fundamental right of assisted suicide might be recognized.

2.   Homosexuality: *Lawrence v. Texas*, 539 U.S. 558 (2003)

In *Lawrence*, someone reported a weapons disturbance at John Lawrence's apartment building. The police show up, enter the apartment, and discover Lawence and another man engaged in a sexual act. The cops bust both of them and hold them in jail overnight; ultimately, they're convicted of "deviate sexual intercourse" with a member of the same sex.

a.   Deriving the Right

(We've talked before about the two strands of privacy doctrine—the narrower traditionalist strand and the broader personal autonomy strand. Which do you think is more influential in *Lawrence*?)

The autonomy strand. Listen to Justice Kennedy in the first paragraph: "Freedom extends beyond spatial bounds. Liberty presumes an autonomy of self that includes freedom of thought, belief, expression, and certain intimate conduct. The instant case involves liberty of the person both in its spatial and more transcendent dimensions."

(Can you make a case for striking down sodomy laws on in terms of the more traditionalist strand of the doctrine?)

I think I can:

- The prior cases are all about sex—*Griswold* and *Roe* are essentially about the right to have sex *without* children. Gay sex is the "safest" kind in that regard, right? More seriously, if the prior cases are about sex, then this one fits.

- This case is also about the privacy of the home in a way that *Roe* and *Casey* were not. Prof. Tribe started out his oral argument in *Bowers* by saying, "This case is not about what Michael Hardwick was doing in his bedroom. It's about what the State of Georgia was doing in Michael

Hardwick's bedroom." So this case may be a better fit with *Griswold* than *Roe* was.

That, by the way, is what I think Justice Kennedy means by the "spatial" dimension of liberty – although it's an awfully grandiose way of saying it.

(What's the problem for this narrower account?)

Well, the big problem is *Bowers v. Hardwick*, 478 U.S. 186 (1986), in which the Court upheld GA's anti-sodomy law, refusing to recognize a fundamental right to engage in sodomy. We'll talk about the *stare decisis* effect of *Bowers* in a minute. But first, there's the evidence on which *Bowers* relied: the longstanding legal prohibition on sodomy going back to the founding of the Republic and beyond.

(Should that be conclusive?)

It should, I think, if you think the point of substantive due process is to protect *traditional* rights, as it arguably did in *Griswold*. Justice Kennedy evades it simply by arguing that *Bowers* misunderstood the right at stake—he defines it much more broadly.

(But let's think about that a minute. Let's define the right broadly—say, as the right to define yourself sexually. Is *that* right traditionally protected?)

I think I'd say no. The law has regulated who can have sex with whom and in what ways for centuries. Remember in *Griswold* everybody agrees that the State can regulate adultery and incest – as well as homosexuality. I think the only way the Court can make this work is to change the inquiry entirely, to a question of personal autonomy.

(What's the problem with personal autonomy?)

Well, it could cover all sorts of things:

- polygamy
- drug use
- adultery
- right to die

It seems to me there are then three possibilities:

1) The Court will endorse any halfway plausible autonomy claim;

2) The Court will pick and choose based on whether it approves of the conduct in question; or

3) The Court will try to evaluate a social *consensus*.

The first of these would upset a lot of traditional regulation and shift a good bit of power to courts. It would be hard to explain, for instance, why personal autonomy claims of an economic nature—e.g., the choice to be a lawyer as opposed to some other profession—shouldn't be included, and that would take us back in the direction of *Lochner*. It might also include, for example, the right to choose to be self-sufficient on matters of personal health (and not buy health insurance as required by the "individual mandate" of the Affordable Care Act.

The second is the position that Judge Bork was shooting at in his *Neutral Principles* piece.

(Are you more comfortable than Bork with courts making these kinds of judgments? How would you feel about Judge Bork making them?)

Finally, there are several problems with the last approach, which would rely on social consensus:

- How quickly does "consensus" evolve? Only 17 years pass between *Bowers* and *Lawrence*.

  (Should the Court have been so willing to overrule *Bowers*?)

  (Can you square *Lawrence* with *Casey*?)

- How good is the Court at identifying consensus? Polls indicate that support for gay rights drops after *Lawrence*.

- Should foreign law be considered in identifying consensus? See citations to the European Court of Human Rights by the majority, and Justice Scalia's response.

b.   The Foreign Law Debate

This issue is also covered in the next Part in connection with Printz v. United States. *You may prefer to save time and cover it there, although it may also be useful to compare use of foreign law in the context of individual rights with its use in interpreting constitutional structure.*

Lawrence is an early example of a practice which seemed to be becoming increasingly common for a while, although it's fallen off a bit lately. That is the practice of relying on "foreign law" as an aid to constitutional interpretation. Two kinds of foreign law are relevant: *international* law, which binds all states (subject to certain exceptions), and *domestic* law of foreign nations, such as the human rights law and practices of France or Germany.

(Who's right about foreign law? Is it relevant to interpreting the Due Process Clause?)

There was a big debate about this in the middle of the last decade both on the Court and in Congress, intensified by the Court's subsequent decision in *Roper v. Simmons* striking down the juvenile death penalty. If you're interested in something short on the subject, the November 2005 issue of the Harvard Law Review has three short (20pp) essays taking different positions – one of them by me.

I'll just make four points:

- There's a big difference between looking at foreign judicial decisions to see if they thought of any *arguments* you hadn't thought of (that's persuasive authority) and looking at the mere *fact* that foreign jurisdictions do or do not allow something. If that fact counts, without regard to the persuasiveness of the *reasons* that the foreign jurisdiction has for its practice, then you are treating the foreign law as *authoritative* in the strict jurisprudential sense. Note that *Lawrence* doesn't look at underlying reasons, but rather just the *fact* that the ECHR has come out a certain way.

- There's a lot of selectivity going on, along two dimensions:

    Which Countries? Notice the Court looks at how *Europe* deals with homosexuality—not the Muslim world. As our own society becomes more diverse, should the courts be more willing to broaden their focus? What effect would this have on rights?

    Which Issues? Advocates of using foreign law to interpret the Due Process Clause or the Eighth Amendment rarely suggest we should look at it to interpret the First Amendment (we are the only country in the world that makes it virtually impossible for a public figure to sue a newspaper for libel, and most other countries are much less protective of hate speech) or the Establishment Clause (most European countries have an established church). Most other countries also allow far more government surveillance than we do, and few are as generous in terms of procedural rights for criminal defendants. Should we narrow our constitutional protections in these areas?

- Remember our discussion of *decision costs* and *error costs* about using history in constitutional interpretation. Both kinds of costs are likely to be high when we're talking about unfamiliar materials usually not published in English.

- At the end of the day, you have to make a judgment about whether the foreign society is sufficiently similar to ours that its decisions are relevant to interpreting our own constitution. It seems to me that we have diverged fairly substantially from a lot of other countries on values questions, so comparisons may not be apt. On the other hand, this sort of judgment surely explains why the Court looks to Europe rather than Saudi Arabia on homosexuality.

c.   The End of Fundamental Rights Analysis?

The Court doesn't just change its approach to identifying rights; it changes the doctrinal means of analyzing restrictions on them.

(Does the Court say gay sex is a fundamental right?)

Not in so many words. "[Petitioners'] right to liberty under the Due Process Clause gives them the full right to engage in their conduct without intervention of the government." But the Court creates a lot of confusion by not using the traditional "fundamental rights" framework.

Under the old framework, if there's no fundamental right, then virtually any government interest would be good enough.

(What's the state's interest?)

Morality, right? They disapprove of the conduct.

(Is that good enough?)

No. "The Texas statute furthers no legitimate state interest which can justify its intrusion into the personal and private life of the individual."

I think most people see *Lawrence* as a heightened scrutiny case. But Justice Kennedy's refusal to work within the traditional analytical framework (or to explain why he's departing) is frustrating—especially for students trying to figure out what to put in their outline.

I think *Lawrence* is a sport in this respect. It will take more to convince me that we've abandoned tiers of scrutiny.

d.   Equal Protection as an Alternate Ground

Two possibilities:

* Narrow (O'Connor): This particular statute violates equal protection because it punishes sodomy by homosexuals but not by heterosexuals.

* Broad: The Due Process Clause protects sexual liberty for heterosexuals, and Equal Protection requires that the Constitution protect such liberty for homosexuals. This would be the *Eisenstadt* "leveraging" strategy we discussed earlier.

e.   Reach of the Decision

What does *Lawrence* portend for the constitutionality of prohibitions on gay marriage?

(What do you think? Will the Court mandate gay marriage?)

(*Should* it?)

3.   **Judge-Centered Theories of Constitutional Interpretation**

   a.   **Sager – Judges as "Partners"**

"Central to our constitutional practice is the partnership between the popular constitutional drafter who typically paints with broad strokes, and the judicial constitutional interpreter who is concerned with bringing rich content and close detail to the general principles announced in the text." "Judges are not merely or even primarily instruction-takers; their independent normative judgment is expected and welcomed."

   b.   **Young – Common Law Constitutionalism**

Constitutional meaning evolves over time through interpretation by judges. History counts in interpretation, but it is *all* of our history and not just the Founding. We adhere to judicial precedents not simply for purposes of stability, but because those precedents are part of what the Constitution means in the first place.

The Basic Idea: History and text are important, but judges should place a great deal of reliance on judicial precedent in determining constitutional meaning. And incremental judicial development of constitutional norms can, in some circumstances, elaborate upon and go beyond the plain text.

Grounding in a Theory of Obligation:

- Rational Traditionalism: The Constitution should be followed because its provisions reflect judgments that have been accepted by many generations in a variety of circumstances.

- Conventionalism: The Constitution is worth following because it reduces controversy by specifying ready-made solutions to problems that otherwise would be too costly to resolve.

Contrasts with Originalism:

- stronger reliance on precedent

- focus on the whole arc of our history, not just "snapshots" in 1789 or 1868

- acceptance of incremental change in the Constitution's meaning over time

Possible Objections:

- Judicial Restraint: Does common law constitutionalism constrain judges less than other methods?

- Democracy: Does common law constitutionalism transfer power from the constitutional founders and from contemporary legislators (both of which groups have a democratic pedigree) to unelected judges?

      c.   **Justice Scalia's Critique – Originalist Textualism**

A commitment to the original understanding of the text is the only way to constrain the discretion of the judge. Precedents do *not* change constitutional meaning; they are relevant only to the extent that (1) they aid determination of the original understanding, (2) they should be adhered to (even though wrong) for purposes of stability.

VI.   Chapter Eight – The Political Thicket

I have never taught this chapter, but I've always thought that the election law material would make a good end to the account of the history of judicial review in Part II of the book. These materials are included for two reasons: First, I think it is at least possible that when the history of the Rehnquist Court (and possibly the Roberts Court, too) is written after a few decades' distance, scholars will view its election law work as the most significant and distinctive contribution. The conventional wisdom is that the Rehnquist Court, at least, will be known for its federalism cases, but at the end of the day I doubt that those cases changed the landscape all that much. Second, focusing on election law allows Part II to end with Bush v. Gore, *which is certainly the most striking example of judicial review in the contemporary era. And by thinking about* Bush v. Gore *as a political question doctrine case, one can circle back to the themes of Part I.*

Having never taught this chapter, I cannot provide detailed class notes, except for a few notes on Bush v. Gore. *What follows simply outlines the principal issues that I see in the chapter and how I would approach them if the Curriculum Committee ever gave me another hour for the course.*

A.   Overview

This chapter raises five distinct sets of issues:

1. **Should the Court be involved in this area at all?** That question came up in *Baker v. Carr,* whichwe read in Part I on the "political question" doctrine. That doctrine applies to a wide variety of constitutional questions—not just in this area—but both *Baker* and *Bush v. Gore* at the end of this chapter put the question very starkly. You'll want to keep *Baker*'s holding in mind as we go through these materials and ask yourself again whether the Court was wise to venture into the political thicket.

2. **Apportionment and Gerrymanding:** *Baker* paved the way for an extensive jurisprudence requiring that legislative representation be apportioned on an equal population basis. You probably know that that question was probably *the* most hotly debated issue at the Constitutional Convention. I think it's fair to say that the one-man, one-vote jurisprudence has been fairly successful, but more recent cases have explored issues beyond *numerical* equality. *Shaw v. Reno* considered whether it was OK for governments to take race into

account in drawing voting districts, while more recent cases have struggled with political gerrymandering designed to benefit the incumbent political party. These latter cases revive *Baker's* debate about whether the political question doctrine should preclude judicial challenges.

3. **Political Parties:** The Court has also developed an extensive jurisprudence on the role of political parties—an issue that the Constitution doesn't speak to explicitly, because the Framers believed that political parties were "factions" and shouldn't have a role in government. *California Democratic Party v. Jones* illustrates the fundamental issue at the heart of this developing jurisprudence: are parties institutions of government or private associations with the same rights of speech and association as other individuals and groups?

4. ***Bush v. Gore:*** The most controversial issue of all, of course, is the Court's intervention to resolve the Presidential election in 2000. I want to talk about that case for its own sake, but also for what light it can shed on the whole enterprise of constitutional jurisprudence in the area of elections. Even more fundamentally, *Bush v. Gore* shows how far the Court's institutional role has come from the precarious days of *Marbury v. Madison.*

5. **Individual v. Group Rights:** Finally, I want to take up Professor Heather Gerken's question about whether it makes sense to view election cases through the prism of individual rights at all. That question serves as a bridge to the next unit, which focuses on constitutional structure.

B.   ***Bush v. Gore,* 531 U.S. 98 (2000)**

Unless want to make the instructor feel really old, you'll at least pretend to recall the basic facts: The 2000 presidential election in Florida is extraordinarily close. The initial results show Bush ahead; Al Gore requests recounts in four heavily democratic counties. The FL Secretary of State certifies Bush as the winner when the recounts don't get done within the seven day deadline prescribed under FL law; the Democrats sue arguing that state law required her to accept the recounted votes. Complicated proceedings ensue. Ultimately, the FL Supremes order a statewide manual recount, but they allow different counties to apply different standards in determining the intent of the voter in ambiguous cases—that is, cases in which the voter failed to properly mark the punch-card ballot. Complicated judgment calls are made regarding "hanging" chads, "dimpled" chads, and the like. The Bush people appeal the matter to the U.S. Supreme Court.

The Supreme Court – defying my prediction to my federal courts class that the Court would never take this case – reverses. There are two separate theories:

- Five justices join a *per curiam* opinion – almost surely written by Kennedy or O'Connor – holding that Florida's approach violates the Equal Protection Clause. Two of the dissenters seem to agree.

- The Chief writes a concurrence, joined by Scalia and Thomas, arguing that Florida is also violating Art. II by enforcing rules made by the state supreme court rather than by the legislature.

Four justices get really mad and dissent.

I think there are at least three issues worth talking about:

- Is the equal protection holding persuasive on the merits?

- If you accept that Florida was violating the Equal Protection clause, then what's the proper way of proceeding from there? What's the remedy for that violation?

- Should the Court have decided this case at all? Should it have been a nonjusticiable "political question" under *Baker*?

(First thing, how many people think the Court got this wrong?)

(OK, how many of you have a view about who should have won this case that's *different* from the way you would have voted in the 2000 election?)

One of the maddening things about *Bush v. Gore* is the extent to which people's views on the legal issues track how they voted in the election. It's important to try to keep the issues as separate as we can.

1. Issues on the Merits

Equal Protection (Per Curiam majority): The Florida Supreme Court's order permitted manual recounts to proceed under different standards for determining the intent of the voter in different counties, even where counties used the same voting equipment.

(How many justices think what the FL Supremes have done violates the Equal Protection Clause?)

Seven, right? Breyer's fuzzy, so maybe six. But Souter clearly thinks there's a violation. That ought to cast doubt on the claim that this result is purely political, yes?

Most academics don't take the EP claim seriously, though, for reasons I still don't quite understand. They're more interested in the other claim:

Article II (Rehnquist, Scalia, & Thomas): The Florida Supreme Court effectively changed the state's voting procedures specified by the state legislature, thereby violating Art. II's command that electors be chosen in the "manner directed" by the state legislature.

This is an interesting argument, but it has some serious problems:

- There's practically no precedent interpreting this aspect of Art. II, and it's not good to be making new doctrine in these very charged circumstances (although it's not clear how the issue could come up in circumstances that *weren't* charged).

- The FL Supremes purport to be following the FL election *statutes* as enacted by the legislature. And the FL Supreme Court is generally the last word on what FL law means. (That's why they call it the Florida *Supreme* Court.) So the concurring justices here have to be willing to say that the FL Supreme Court misinterpreted its own law *so badly* that we have to read their opinion as *changing* state law. That's a pretty tough row to hoe.

2.   The Issue of Remedy

The equal protection holding, in principle, permits two different ways of proceeding:

- Re-do the recount under uniform vote-counting standards, or

- Abandon the recount and go with the State's original certification of Bush as the winner.

The choice between these approaches is a question of state law, presumptively to be determined by the state courts in the first instance. But the Supreme Court majority orders the second without remanding first. This is pretty irregular, and the dissenters are understandably outraged. But you can also understand that the majority's trust level with the FL Supremes is not high at this point.

3.   Political Question? The Twelfth Amendment

The Twelfth Amendment contemplates that at least some election disputes will be resolved in the House of Representatives, where voting would be by state delegations (rather than by individual reps).

(Is that a textual commitment of Presidential election questions to the House?)

I don't think so. I think it commits one kind of dispute. But suppose that there's a dispute about *racial* discrimination – that black people were deterred from voting.

(Would the Court hear that?)

Surely yes. I think what that shows is that the key for the political question doctrine, as it exists after *Baker*, is the nature of the *challenge*, not the governmental activity *being challenged*. An equal protection claim is justiciable; a claim that the state certified the wrong slate of electors probably isn't.

(What about if Frankfurter had won in *Baker*?)

Then no way the Court hears this case.

C.   **Further Adventures in the Political Thicket**

The Pildes excerpt is there for the purpose of giving you a very brief overview of what the Court is up to in this area. It may be the "next big thing" in Constitutional Law.

1.   **The Legal Issues**

- **Racial Gerrymandering (*Shaw v. Reno*):** The Court has held that, although the Voting Rights Act requires drawing districts that increase minority representation, *too much* consideration of race will invalidate the district.

- **Partisan Gerrymandering (*Vieth v. Jubelirer, LULAC v. Perry*):** The Court has acknowledged that partisan gerrymanders may violate the constitution, but has held that there are no manageable standards to determine when.

These are both **vote *dilution*** claims: It's not that you don't get to vote, or that your vote counts for less. It's that it's less *effective.*

- **Campaign Finance (*McConnell v. FEC, Wisconsin Right to Life*):** The Court has held that campaign contributions are speech under the Free Speech Clause, but recently upheld broad regulation of campaign finance against First Amendment challenge.

- **Political Parties:** In a variety of cases, the Court has been willing to apply rigorous First Amendment scrutiny to state regulation of state political parties, e.g., by striking down open primary rules. *See California Democratic Party v. Jones.*

(How involved with all this should the Court be?)

2.   **The Theoretical Problem: Rights vs. Structure**

- Vote dilution is meaningful only with respect to identifiable groups.

- Regulation of political parties is all about rights of *association* for political purposes.

- Campaign finance pits an individual right (or the expressive rights of groups) against a government *interest* in structuring the political process in a way that makes it more open and less corrupt.

The problem is that *Marbury* says "[t]he province of the court is, solely, to decide on the rights of individuals."

(Should the Court look at these questions in a more structural way?)

(Can it do that without coming up with its own theory of how politics should work?)

Having ended up here, we have a brilliant segueway to the second part of the course, which is explicitly concerned with structural values.

PART THREE – THE STRUCTURAL CONSTITUTION

Part III of the book – which takes up roughly half my course – switches from a historical to a doctrinal account. With the preceding historical background in place, the remainder of the course offers a fairly detailed account of the doctrine governing federalism and separation of powers.

I. **Chapter Nine – The Federal Sytem**

A confession: Federalism is my primary area of scholarly interest, and there may be more in these materials (particularly in these notes) than most people want to cover in this area. It should be relatively easy to pick and choose, however. This introductory section invites students to step back and assess the Constituiton's overall political theory, particularly as described in the Federalist papers. It also considers the basic policy arguments for centralization and decentralization within a federal system. These arguments will be an important reference point in the more doctrinal sections to follow.

The first actual case, U.S. Term Limits, is exceptionally rich. I offer here a fairly long cut of it, for two reasons: First, it considers in depth the Framers' theory of political representation. Second, it affords a look at what it really means to take originalism seriously. One cannot evaluate a theory of interpretation without assessing (a) whether it poses a manageable task for courts, and (b) whether it can offer relatively determinate answers to constitutional questions. Reasonable people disagree about what lessons to take from Term Limits on both these points, but it does seem like a fair test.

The second case is Garcia, which poses the question of how much courts should enforce principles of federalism. Although the now-defunct doctrine of National League of Cities may strike current students as obscure, Garcia remains a critical reference point concerning the extent to which courts should defer to the "political safeguards of federalism" rather than enforce limits on national power directly.

The last section of the course puts aside our historical approach to focus on *doctrine* in two areas: federalism and separation of powers.

On the Federalism side, we'll be focusing on two questions:

1.   What functions does the Constitution allocate to the Federal Government, and what functions does it reserve to the State?

2.   What institution -- *i.e.*, Congress and the President, or the Judiciary -- is best suited for enforcing whatever limits on federal power exist?

But you should remember that there is always a third question lurking in the background:

3.   Where the federal government has power to act, should it nonetheless leave the issue to the States as a matter of policy?

This last question is probably the most important as a practical matter, because it is pretty well-settled that the Constitution allows the Federal Government a very broad scope.

The last couple of weeks will then shift to Separation of Powers.

A.   The Federal System and Dual Sovereignty

We start with Federalist political theory relating to both federalism and separation of powers. We want to talk about three different sets of theoretical issues:

- The political theory of the Federalist constitution;

- The political theory of federalism itself—that is, why we might want to divide power between national and state governments; and

- The extent to which a federal system requires a *judicial* referee to maintain.

Each of these theoretical questions has pretty practical implications.

1.   The Political Theory of the Federalist

I've assigned you two of the Federalist Papers – Federalist 10 and 51. These essays, both by Madison, set out the basic justifications the basic political theory behind the Constitution, and particularly behind the ideas of federalism and separation of powers.

a.   The Antifederalist Critique of the Constitution

The Antifederalists opposed the Constitution because they thought the government it created was too big, too far removed from the people, and too likely to be dominated by selfish interests or "factions."

Some of these criticisms may sound familiar – we still hear them today. How many times have you heard political candidates vowing to fight the "special interests"? That's the problem of faction.

In general, the Antifederalists preferred small communities because they thought that history showed that republican government – that is democratic government by a bunch of virtuous citizens making decisions together for the common good – could only flourish in small communities.

b.   The Federalist Response

The Federalists – the supporters of the Constitution – had to respond to these sorts of arguments in each state ratifying convention across the country. The Federalist Papers are a series of essays published in newspapers by James Madison, Alexander Hamilton, and John Jay in an attempt to influence the ratifying convention in the state of New York.

As we've already discussed, it's important to remember that you have to read The Federalist Papers on two levels:

- High political theory

- Political propaganda

Despite this caution, and despite the fact that not many people read them at the time they were published, the Federalist Papers are frequently used as a sort of "owner's manual" for the Constitution.

These essays are centrally concerned with the problem of faction raised by the Antifederalists. They reject the Antifederalist solution – which was that we should all live in small communities and not attempt to create a national government – and come up with an innovative solution: If you can't trust human nature – and you can't – then you have to come up with institutional safeguards that limit and offset people's selfish private interests.

This idea, and the specific applications of it developed both in the Constitution itself and in the Federalist Papers, is probably America's most original contribution to political theory.

c.   Federalist 10

As I've said, Madison is centrally preoccupied with the problem of faction. He starts out by observing that we can either try to remove the *causes* of factions, or try to control their *effects*.

(What are the causes of factions?)

Human nature. People are different; they have different backgrounds, beliefs, and preferences. They will never entirely agree.

(What's the most important difference?)

Inequalities of wealth.

(Does Madison think we can ultimately eradicate these inequalities enough to prevent the formation of factions?)

No. So we're stuck with controlling the effects.

Note that there are two different kinds of factions: Factions that make up only a minority of a political community, and factions that are in the majority.

(Is Madison worried about the minority factions?)

No – majority rule takes care of those.

This is where modern political science might differ from Madison. Much of the current literature in what's called "public choice theory" indicates that small, cohesive minority interest groups are frequently able to wield a disproportionate amount of power.

In any event, Madison's central concern is with majority factions – that is, the tyranny of the majority.

Now, the conventional wisdom among 18th century political theorists was that factions could only be controlled in small political communities – such as the city-states of Greece or the New England town meetings. This is the view that the Antifederalists adopted, and they were accordingly fearful of creating one giant nation where the common good would get lost.

(What's Madison's answer to this argument? This is the central point of the essay.)

He agrees that size does matter, but he flips the argument back on the Anti-Federalists. Bigger is better, he says.

(Why?)

Two reasons:

(1) In a larger community, it's harder for a faction to *become* a majority. They'll inevitably have to form coalitions with other groups, which tends to moderate their influence. The more people you have to *persuade*, the more reasonable you have to be.

(2) We can also expect to get better representatives in a larger community. Because it's a bigger pond, you have to be a more impressive person to become prominent. In other words, extending the sphere is a way to achieve elitism indirectly.

(What do you think of these arguments?)

Certainly there's some truth to them. The whole experience of slavery and racism looks like a case in which a local majority was able to oppress the minority, but that oppressive majority lacked power at the national level and was ultimately undone by that fact.

Similarly, the worst examples of corrupt machine politics have tended to occur at the local level – such as the Tammany Hall machine in New York or the Daley machine in Chicago.

(Can you think of any counter-examples?)

It's possible to quibble: The Civil Rights Movement, for instance, is an example of a cohesive minority group – a faction, although a *nice* one – which was able to get its preferences enacted into law at the *national* level but not the state level.

And we might question whether the qualities it takes to appeal to millions of voters – basically, an appealing façade and a ton of campaign money – are the ones we necessarily value the most. That's why, for instance, some people still value the New Hampshire primary, because it's still politics conducted one voter at a time.

(Let's step back for just a moment and think about the relation between Madison's concern about "faction" and the political parties that develop within the next decade after ratification. Is there anything in the Constitution about parties?)

No way.

(Why not?)

Because parties are exactly what Madison—and both the Federalist and Antifederalists—are worried about.

(In light of our experience, are parties as bad a thing as Madison thought?)

No – most political scientists think they're an essential part of the government structure.

(How are they beneficial?)

It's impossible for citizens to vote directly on every issue or monitor every action of their representatives. Having a party to aggregate positions on the issues solves a lot of informational problems for voters. I can evaluate whether I generally like the Republican or Democratic approach to things instead of analyzing each candidate's approach to every issue. This makes it much easier to hold politicians roughly accountable for their actions.

(So was Madison *wrong* about factions?)

I don't think so. In fact, you could think of our big national political parties as "extended spheres" in their own right. Neither the Republican nor the Democratic party is particularly coherent or homogeneous; they're each clusters of groups loosely allied. The same Federalist 10 dynamics of interest group cooperation have to take place within the parties. This is why our parties have generally been relatively moderate and non-ideological—at least compared with those in Europe.

d.   Federalist 51

In Federalist 10 the primary structural safeguard against tyranny is the sheer size of the country. Federalist 51 introduces the idea of specific institutional checks which prevent the accumulation of too much power in any one place.

Madison begins by talking about the separation of powers, which he's been talking about in the previous essays as well. The question is, How do we keep one branch from aggrandizing itself at the expense of the others.

(First of all, how would you describe Madison's basic view of human nature here?)

He's pretty pessimistic – people are selfish and ambitious, and they're always trying to increase their own power at the expense of others.

This is pretty similar to Madison's view of factions: some trouble is inevitable, and the trick is to contain its effects.

(How does Madison propose to do that here?)

By turning rival interests against one another, and by giving individual politicians an incentive to preserve the overall separation of powers through defending their own turf. He calls this the "policy of supplying, by opposite and rival interests, the defect of better motives."

Lots of examples of this: Congress has an incentive to try to keep the President from getting out of hand through Congress's power over legislation; the President uses his veto to check the power of Congress; Congress limits the jurisdiction of the federal courts to limit the power of the judiciary, etc.

The basic point is that the whole scheme is set up so that the very thing we're worried about – the inevitably selfish interests of politicians – is the primary tool for holding the government together.

(Are the checks and balances among the three branches of the national government the only example of this idea?)

No – there's also federalism. The second important point in Federalist 51 is the "double security." Separation of powers is one means of preventing too much power from accumulating in one place. Federalism – the division of authority between the national and state governments – is another. Madison's point is that when you put these two structures together, you have an even stronger safeguard:

"In the compound republic of America, the power surrendered by te people is first divided between two distinct governments, and then the portion allotted to each subdivided among distinct and separate departments. Hence a double security arises to the rights of the people. The different governments will control each other, at the same time that each will be controlled by itself."

e.   Two Concluding Thoughts

I want to step back and make two more general observations about all this:

- It's hard to get much done in this system. There are so many roadblocks to the exercise of power that this can't be an efficient way to run a railroad.

(How do you think Madison might respond to that criticism?)

I think he'd say, Fine – We've seen some "efficient" governments that were able to get a lot done, and they tended to run roughshod over the rights of individuals. In particular, some of the states had adopted constitutions in the period between 1776 and 1789 that had very effective legislatures, and they had done some bad things. So I think the Framers are more worried about government run amuck than the opposite problem. This builds in a certain conservative bias to the system. When we get to the New Deal, we see a shift in this view: Government impotence is also a problem, and we change the structure to deal with it.

I also want to suggest, though, that the difficulty of getting things done at the federal level may be a *feature* of the system, rather than a *bug*. Inefficiency may be a critical tool in maintaining the overall balance of the structure.

-      The second point has to do with constitutional rights and judicial review.

(How important are constitutional rights and judicial review in Federalist 10 & 51?)

They're not mentioned, right? Neither constitutional rights nor judicial review are prominent in this framework.

We know that Madison and Hamilton were expecting judicial review from Federalist 78, but it's equally clear that it's not the *primary* safeguard. Rather, they expect the political branches – the President and Congress – to check themselves.

As for the Bill of Rights, Madison thought it was unnecessary. If you get the structure right, then no one will have the wherewithal to govern in a way that oppresses individuals.

This view loses out almost immediately, as several states condition their consent to ratification on the promise that a Bill of Rights will be added right away. Nonetheless, it is important to understand that the structural design of the constitution was *itself* intended as a safeguard for individual liberty, and that it continues to play that role today.

We'll spend the next couple of weeks focusing on federalism—the division of authority between the Nation and the States.

2. The Values of Federalism

At the outset, it will help to get under our belt a basic toolbox of arguments about *why* we might want to allocate a particular government function to the national or to the state governments. These arguments may bear on the legal questions we'll be considering in a couple of ways:

- They may provide reasons to construe the constitutional grant of power to the national government broadly or narrowly; and

- They may also provide reasons that, within the vast range of matters on which the national and state governments enjoy *concurrent* authority, we should prefer that things should be taken up by Congress or, alternatively, left to the States.

We'll start with the states' side of the ledger:

a.   Reasons to Favor State Authority

- **Public Participation and Accountability:** State governments are closer to the people. It's easier to get involved on the state level, and your voice counts for more.

  But remember, some states are so big that this advantage may be fading.

- **Diversity:** State differences allow people to vote with their feet and find the jurisdiction that best matches their policy preferences. Moreover, it's not clear that the argument depends on people actually moving:

  Consider, for example, the current state of play on an issue like gay marriage. Let's imagine, further, that we don't have a strong view of who's right and who's wrong – we just want to make sure that as many people as possible get to live in a jurisdiction where the law reflects their own preference on the issue. Let's imagine we have a 50/50 split on the issue nationwide, but that the split is geographically skewed. If we adopt one national rule on the subject, half the people will be happy and half will be ticked off. But if Massachusetts and Texas can each adopt their own rule, you're much more likely to get significant majorities in each jurisdiction that are happy with the rule.

- **State Competition:** States have an incentive to constantly reform and improve in order to lure more citizens and businesses. This may keep state taxes down, for example, and it may provide an incentive to improve local schools.

- **State Experimentation:** Justice Brandeis called the states the "laboratories of democracy."

  Ex: States like Wisconsin have been experimenting with different forms of welfare reform, and the results of these experiments help in formulating federal policy.

  It's worth noting, moreover, that some states are sufficiently big and important in their own right that their "experiments" can have a global impact. CA's experiment with stricter air pollution standards for cars has had an impact on the worldwide auto industry, even without that experiment being "adopted" at the national level.

- **Administrative Efficiency:** States can tailor regulation to local conditions -- they don't have to use a one size fits all approach. It would make no sense, for example, to have one rule for allocating water rights for both the Northeast and the Southwest.

- **Diffusion of Power:** This may be the most important one. The Framers divided sovereignty precisely to keep any one part of the government from becoming too powerful. The existence of the States always provides some power base for resisting federal measures.

  But note that this includes resistance to *good* federal ideas as well as bad ones.

b.   Federalism vs. Decentralization

As the excerpt from the Rubin and Feeley article points out, it's important to distinguish between federalism and decentralization.

(What's the difference?)

The difference is that a centralized system may choose to decentralize certain programs, etc., as a matter of policy. But the sub-units don't have any authority to *resist* directives from the center that the center chooses to make. In a federal system, the sub-units do have their own governmental authority – their own *sovereignty*, if you will – and can sometimes oppose their own views to decisions made at the center.

(How many of the advantages we've talked about stem from decentralization, and how many would require actual federalism?)

I would argue that real decentralization depends on having viable sub-units that have proven governmental track records and the ability to command the loyalty of their citizens. You can't just replace "Texas" with "the Southwestern Administrative Unit" and expect the same sort of public support and respect.

Even Rubin & Feeley admit that diffusion of power depends on federalism, but they think the States don't really play that function because, unlike in the Founding period, no state is in a position to put up military resistance against national authority.

(Is that the only way states protect liberty?)

I don't think so. Here are three:

- Institutional clout: E.g., No Child Left Behind

- Rallying point for opposition: E.g., Patriot Act; Alien & Sedition Acts in the early Republic.

- Political circulation: Four out of the last five presidents were governors of their states when their party was out of power in Washington, D.C. Compare the plight of the British Tory party, which hasn't gotten to run *anything* since 1997.

The Rubin-Feeley position does concede one important function to federalism, as opposed to decentralization. Their view is that federalism is necessary only where you have a country that's divided between geographically-concentrated groups that share a strong cultural, ethnic, and/or religious identity.

Iraq would be an example: We encouraged a federal structure there to allow Sunni, Shia, and Kurdish regions to have some autonomy while still working together on national issues. And this may be at least partly why we have a federal structure in the U.S. The new states were a lot more ethnically and religiously distinctive in the late 18th century than they are now.

Rubin and Feeley doubt, however, that we need federalism for this purpose anymore. They think state identity is dead. There's a Starbucks on every corner, whether you're in Boston or Austin. So since we don't need federalism to accommodate strong state identities, they think we should simply junk it.

(What do you think? Is state identity dead? How many of you think of yourselves as "North Carolinians" or "Floridians" or "Californians"?)

It's important to note that the people who say state identity is dead are simply making assertions – it's a very difficult question to get a handle on empirically.

I want to make a more complicated point about identity, though. There are other reasons to want a strong federal system than to accommodate distinctive state identities – for instance, as part of our system of checks and balances. And as you'll see in this unit, the primary protection for federalism in the Constitution is *political*, not legal – that is, federalism tends to stay alive not so much because judges intervene to protect it as because political dynamics work to preserve it. But those dynamics are most likely to function strongly if people care about their states. Identity thus may be important as a means of protecting federalism, whether or not it still makes sense as an end for having a federal system.

c.   Reasons to Favor National Authority

Some of these are mirror images of the advantages of state authority:

- **Legal Uniformity:** Businesses that must operate in many states hate having to comply with 50 different sets of rules. For instance, imagine trying to regulate indecency on the Internet at the State level. Since it is available in every State, people posting things would have to know the law in every jurisdiction.

- **Externalities and Spillover Effects:** Decisions made in one state may have consequences in other states. Or residents of the state may not bear the full costs of activity carried on inside the state. In such cases, we can't count on the state's own political processes to adequately address the problem.

ex: Acid rain

- **Race to the Bottom:** Jurisdictional competition may be a harm as well as a help; failure to regulate in one jurisdiction may make it harder to regulate in another, due to the mobility of jobs and capital.

ex: Child labor laws

- **Administrative Efficiency and Concentration of Expertise:** Having multiple levels of government with authority over the same activity inevitably leads to jurisdictional disputes and delays.

For ex: Federal relief after Hurricane Andrew was significantly delayed because state officials had to request it through proper channels, and there were numerous failures of communication between state an national authorities.

- **Mitigation of Faction:** Madison's idea in Federalist 10 is that factions have a harder time taking control of a larger government.

Consider, for example, the likelihood of tough anti-tobacco legislation in North Carolina.

Remember, though, that many States are now themselves larger political communities than Madison could have dreamed of, and therefore may have some of the same virtues.

Moreover, modern political scientists argue that it's much easier for certain cohesive interests to influence the federal government than 50 different state governments.

- **Protection of Individual Rights:** The history is inescapable on this point: For much of our history, the most important way in which States struggled to be "different," and to resist federal encroachment on their power, was in preserving slavery and segregation.

Question: Is this simply an accident of history? Does federalism promote social diversity in both good and bad forms? Or is there some deeper connection between federalism and oppression.

Note: As a counterexample, many state constitutions are now being interpreted to provide broader protection for individual rights than the federal constitution. A number have explicit right to privacy clauses, for instance.

d.   The Argument from Fidelity

We might also argue for a particular balance between federal and state power not based on any judgment that federal or state power is a good thing, but rather on the view that the Constitution mandates a particular balance and we have an obligation to adhere to that balance until the Constitution is amended.

This view fits comfortably with a positivist or conventionalist view of constitutional obligation; it makes a lot less sense if we think the Constitution is binding only to the extent it's morally good or makes practical sense.

But even on those accounts, we might bolster the fidelity point by arguing that if we can ignore one important aspect of the original Constitution – like federalism – that inevitably undermines respect for other constitutional values – like individual rights.

e.   Institutional Alternatives

We aren't faced simply with a choice between state or federal regulation. There are a number of intermediate forms:

- **"Cooperative" Federalism:**   Federal and state regulators share authority over a particular field.   State regulators, for instance, may develop plans for implementing standards set at the federal level, and may receive substantial federal money for doing so.

  One important aspect of this structure is that, by relying on state regulators to implement federal law, the system necessarily gives state officials a significant say in how federal law turns out.   It also affords them opportunities to push back, through the bureaucratic process, against federal laws they don't like.   My co-clerk Heather Gerken has called this "uncooperative federalism."[27]

- **Interstate Compacts:**   The Constitution permits states to agree -- with Congressional approval -- to adopt certain rules or to establish certain common regulatory bodies.   The New York/New Jersey Port Authority is an example.

- **Uniform Laws:** Sometimes the States develop uniform rules that are then adopted individually by States that want to participate.   The Uniform Commercial Code is an example.

It may not be possible to generalize broadly about any of these arguments. Some may be true in some cases, but not in others. And some institutional forms may work well for some subjects, but not others.

---

[27] Jessica Bulman-Pozen & Heather K. Gerken, *Uncooperative Federalism*, 118 Yale L.J. 1256 (2009).

3.   Representation: *U.S. Term Limits, Inc. v. Thornton*, 514 U.S. 779 (1995)

So far we haven't talked much about an additional structural question, which is the issue of representation. That question, and the Federalists' view of it, is at the heart of the *Term Limits* case.

Arkansas voters passed an initiative ("Amendment 73") amending the state constitution to prohibit the name of otherwise eligible candidates for Congress from appearing on the general election ballot if they have already served three terms in the House or two terms in the Senate. The amendment also included term limits for state executives and legislators.

A group of citizens, as well as the League of Women Voters of Arkansas, sought a declaratory judgment that Amendment 73 was void as applied to federal legislators.

The Court (Stevens, J.) holds that Amendment 73 is unconstitutional.

(Does the Arkansas law actually limit the terms of members of Congress from Arkansas?)

No – It simply provides that if you've already served three terms in the House or two in the Senate, your name can't appear on the ballot in the next election.

So there are really two issues in the case:

(1)   whether States may add to or alter the qualifications for federal legislative office enumerated in the Constitution; and

(2)   if not, whether Amendment 73 is still valid as a ballot access restriction rather than as an outright disqualification.[28]

---

[28] In case anyone's interested in this question:

(What's the majority's position here?)

That the access restriction makes it impossible for incumbents to win, which is a *de facto* term limit.

(How does the dissent answer this?)

By arguing that the rule just "evens the playing field" – incumbents have huge advantages that the restriction simply offsets.

(Note the practical implications here: What kind of qualifications is the dissent worried that the States won't be able to enact?)

This decision appears to bar disqualification of mental incompetents, imprisoned felons, and people with past vote fraud convictions. The dissent is surely right about this.

We're only worried about the first question – the second is really just an election law question and doesn't implicate the basic federalism dispute.

a.   The Qualifications Clauses

(Do we have any constitutional text that bears on this question whether the states can change the qualifications for federal legislative office?)

We have the Qualifications Clauses, Art. I, § 2, cl. 2, and § 3, cl. 3. The House Qualifications Clause provides: "No Person shall be a Representative who shall not have attained to the Age of twenty five Years, and been seven Years a Citizen of the United States, and who shall not, when elected, be an Inhabitant of that State in which he shall be chosen."

The Senate version is similar, except you have to be 30 years old and a citizen for 9 years.

So in both cases, the Constitution imposes three requirements:

(1)   age

(2)   citizenship

(3)   residence

These clauses, incidentally, are why the Clintons had to buy that house in Westchester, NY before Mrs. Clinton could run for the Senate.

(Do these clauses say anything about how *long* you can serve?)

No.

(So what's the basic argument that they bar Arkansas's attempt to impose term limits?)

The plaintiffs claim that these qualifications are *exclusive* – that is, that the states can't add *additional* qualifications to this list.

(How does the dissent interpret the Qualifications Clauses?)

As setting only minimum requirements, which the States are free to add to if they like. Note that this is the same debate we had about the relationship between "liberty" and the Bill of Rights in *Griswold*.

In addressing this argument, the Court spends a lot of time on the Court's prior decision in *Powell v. McCormack*, 395 U.S. 486 (1969).

(What was the issue in *Powell*?)

Whether *Congress* could add other qualifications to those set forth in the Qualifications Clauses. Powell had been found to have engaged in certain corrupt practices while serving in the House, and the next time he was elected the House decided to prohibit him from taking his seat. So, as a practical matter, the House was adding a qualification to the constitutional list: You can't be a crook.

(Did the House have any textual support for its right to do this?)

They relied on Art. I, § 5, which gives each House of Congress the power to judge the "Qualifications of its own Members."

(And what did the Court say about this?)

That Congress can't do it – that Art. I, § 5 gives no such power, so the Qualifications Clauses are exclusive.

b.   Reserved Powers

(Why doesn't *Powell* just govern this case? The Qualifications Clauses are either exclusive or they're not, right?)

Powell doesn't answer the question whether the *States* might retain the power to alter or add qualifications.

Remember that this is a case where we have some text, but it doesn't say *much*. So one way to decide the case is to use a default rule – what do we do if the Constitution doesn't actually say anything about a question.

(What's the dissent's default rule?)

That the States presumptively have any powers that the Constitution doesn't explicitly take away from them.

(What text are the dissenters relying on?)

The 10th Amendment, which says that "The powers not delegated to the United States by the Constitution, nor prohibited by it to the States, are reserved to the States respectively, or to the people."

The dissent reads the 10th Amendment as establishing opposite default rules for the federal and state governments. For the Feds, the rule is enumerated powers: If the Constitution doesn't affirmatively give the Feds a particular power, they don't have it.

For the States, it's the reverse: If the Constitution doesn't affirmatively *take away* a power from the States, they retain it.

(Justice Stevens has a default rule, too, but it's different. What default rule is the majority using?)

If the Constitution doesn't affirmatively give the States the power to limit the terms of federal representatives, the States don't have that power.

(How does Justice Stevens square that rule with the 10th Amendment?)

The Tenth Amendment "reserves" only the States' original powers. The power to add qualifications is not within the "original powers" of the States, and is thus not reserved by the Tenth Amendment.

(Does that answer make any sense? Can someone argue the other way?)

The power to regulate cloning, or local telephone service, or registration of motor vehicles also weren't within the "original powers" of the States.

(Does that mean that the States can't regulate those subjects unless we amend the Constitution to say so?)

Obviously not. I think Stevens is putting a pretty implausible meaning on "reserved" – it doesn't have to be a function of time. I could give my first paycheck each year to my church and "reserve" the others for conspicuous consumption, even though I don't have that money yet. It seems more plausible (and more consistent with the rest of the 10th Amendment's text) to say that "reserved" simply means all powers (past, present, or future) not affirmatively delegated to the federal government.

You might make a narrower, more plausible argument for Justice Stevens's view. We might think the default rule should be different because here we're dealing with the internal composition of the federal government, which there's no presumptive reason to think should be subject to state control. But to say why that's true, you need a more basic argument about the relationship between the federal and state governments.

c.   Democratic Principles

One place you might look for support for that kind of argument is in the "democratic principles" that the majority derived from *Powell*.

(What are those two principles?)

(1)   egalitarianism – anybody ought to be able to run for Congress; and

(2)   freedom of choice – the people ought to be able to vote for whomever they choose.

(Why do those principles cut against state-imposed term limits?)

Justice Stevens seems to think that term limits are anti-egalitarian because mean that some people don't get to run.

(Anything weird about that argument?)

Well, the only people that are disqualified are the rich and powerful – the incumbents with huge war chests. The whole point is to give other people a shot. You may think that's a bad idea for any number of reasons – I do – but it's hardly anti-egalitarian.

The freedom of choice point is more serious.

(But isn't there a big difference between a limitation on the state electorate's choice imposed by Congress – as in *Powell* – and a limit that the people of Arkansas choose to impose on themselves? Isn't this just another instance of "tying oneself to the mast" – which is the whole idea behind constitutionalism itself?)

Well, yes. Probably the best argument is a third democratic principle that we *don't* find in *Powell*:

(3)   "the right to choose representatives belongs not to the States, but to the people."

(What in the world does the Court mean by that?)

It means that the relationship between the People and their federal representatives runs straight from the People to the representative – not through the state government as an intermediary. (See the nifty diagram on the handout.)

Justice Kennedy focuses on this point in his concurrence. He says:

"The Framers split the atom of sovereignty. . . . [O]ur citizens would have two political capacities, one state and one federal, each protected from incursion by the other." The result is "two orders of government, each with its own direct relationship, its own privity, its own set of mutual rights and obligations to the people who sustain it and are governed by it."

This is dual sovereignty again. Under this theory, the States cannot interfere with the relationship between the Federal government and the people.

(What's the dissent's view of sovereignty and the relationship between the People and their federal representatives?)

The dissent seems to be pushing the old "Compact Theory" – that the Constitution is a compact among sovereign states, and that federal representatives are essentially ambassadors from the states. If this is true, then it's up to the States to regulate the qualifications of their representatives. The states, in other words, are an essential party and intermediary to the relationship between a member of Congress and her constituents. (This is also on the nifty diagram in the handout.)

In fact, Justice Thomas denies that there is any such thing as "the People of the nation," as opposed to the people of individual statutes. He says that "[t]he ultimate source of the Constitution's authority is the consent of the people of each individual State, not the consent of the undifferentiated people of the Nation as a whole."

The Compact Theory was pretty clearly the design of the Articles of Confederation. The historical evidence indicates, however, that it is *not* the design of the Constitution of 1789. That document embodies a basic shift from state sovereignty to dual sovereignty.

(That's at least true of the House. What about the Senate?)

The Senate's originally designed on the Compact theory, right? Senators are elected not by the People but by the State legislators; they really *are* ambassadors to Washington from their States.

(But what happens?)

The 17th Amendment changes that by providing for direct election. So while the *original* understanding of representation may be mixed, the understanding that evolves over time seems more in accord with that of the *Term Limits* majority.

The dissent's refusal to recognize this highlights just how radical the four dissenters may be on federalism issues.

e.   Some Final Thoughts on *Term Limits*

- *We're all originalists now.* Note that there's not really a debate over interpretive method: Justice Stevens conspicuously doe *not* say that all this historical evidence proffered by the dissent is irrelevant and we should decide the case based on evolving notions of how the government should be structured. Instead, he rolls up his sleeve and wades into the historical debate.

- *Historical and structural debate occurs at different levels of generality.* A lot of the opinions – even more than you see, since a lot of this stuff is edited out – is taken up with very detailed debates about the history.

(Who do you think is winning that "line by line" debate?)

I'd have to say Justice Thomas. So many places, he's just one step more thorough than Stevens on this stuff. Here's an example:

Justice Stevens makes an argument that Congress's handling of the seating of Rep. McCreery in 1807 demonstrates that the early Congress thought the States had no power to limit the qualifications of federal representatives. But Justice Thomas has much more specific evidence on the meaning of that historical episode and demonstrates that Congress actually *rejected* a committee report that would have made this point. There are plenty of other examples.

But notice that there's also a much more "big picture" debate going on about the nature of the relationship between Congress and the People, and whether the States are themselves a party to that relationship. This is clearest in Justice Kennedy's concurrence. And it seems to me on this level Justice Thomas is clearly wrong.

So the point is that you can have very specific historic debates or very general ones that are really conducted at the level of political theory. And in order to ultimately be persuasive you have to keep track of all these levels.

- ***The persistence of foundational debate.*** It's striking in *Term Limits* how basic disputes that have been with us since 1789 – like the dispute between the Compact Theory and Dual Federalism – are very much alive and well. And these disputes are motivating much of the Court's revival of aggressive judicial review in the federalism area.

- ***The voting alignments.*** Note the line-up on the Court in *Term Limits*. There's a solid block of "nationalist" justices (who tend to be more liberal, although that label causes problems sometimes): Stevens, Souter, Ginsburg, and Breyer. There's also a pretty solid block of "states' rights" justices (who tend, with the same caveat, to be more conservative): Chief Justice Rehnquist, O'Connor, Scalia, and Thomas.

Justice Kennedy is in the middle, writing a separate concurrence. You'll see the same lineup in *Lopez* for next time, except that Justice Kennedy sides with the States this time. Again he writes a separate concurrence that sets out something of a more moderate ground. Then again in *Raich*, Kennedy flips – and takes Scalia with him.

These voting alignments are fairly consistent throughout the Rehnquist Court's federalism cases, with Justice Kennedy usually taking the states' rights view (but *not* signing on to the Compact Theory).

4.   The Political Safeguards of Federalism

Federalism is funny in that it's the only set of constitutional values where we see serious debate about whether courts should try to enforce them *at all*. The big reason usually given for rejecting *Lochner*'s freedom of contract, for instance, is that the due process clause simply doesn't protect that particular freedom. No one denies, on the other hand, that the Constitution protects federalism. People just want the Court not to enforce that principle.

That question has been fought out primarily in kind of a funny doctrinal context, and we'll need to get a handle on that first.

a.   Internal vs. External Limits

Except for *Term Limits*, the federalism cases so far have dealt with limits imposed on federal authority by the Commerce Clause itself; cases like *National League of Cities* and *Garcia* deal with a different sort of limit.

It may help to think in terms of two kinds of limits on national authority:

- *Internal Limits* derive from the power being exercised itself. So the internal limit on the Commerce Clause is that it only applies to interstate commerce. Internal limits are generally based on the idea of enumerated powers.

- *External Limits* may exist even when Congress is exercising a valid enumerated power.

248

Example: Suppose Congress decides to ban the interstate shipment of newspapers.

(Does Congress have enumerated authority to do this?)

Sure – It's a clear instance of regulating commerce between states.

(So is there any constitutional problem?)

Absolutely – It would violate the Free Press Clause of the First Amendment.

So in this situation, the Free Press Clause is an *external limit* on the Commerce Power. The important point is that the limit is *external* to – comes from outside – the provision that actually authorizes Congress's action.

National League of Cities recognizes an *external* limit on the Commerce Power that's derived from principles of federalism. You'll see different external limits in the anti-commandeering cases.

b.   *National League of Cities v. Usery*, 426 U.S. 833 (1976)

The Fair Labor Standards Act requires covered employers to pay employees a minimum hourly wage, and to pay one and one-half times regular wages for overtime above 40 hours per week.

The Supreme Court unanimously upheld the FLSA as a valid exercise of the commerce power in *United States v. Darby*, 312 U.S. 100 (1941).

The original FLSA passed in 1938 specifically excluded the States and their political subdivisions from its coverage. In 1966 amendments to the FLSA add state schools and hospitals, then in 1974 they extend the FLSA to apply the minimum wage and overtime provision to almost all public employees.

A couple of things to notice here:

- In cases like *Hammer v. Dagenhart* and *Jones & Laughlin*, we're talking about Congress's ability to regulate private entities like manufacturers.

  That's not the question here. *Darby* already upheld the FLSA as applied to private actors.

  Instead, the question is whether Congress can regulate the states *themselves*.

- There's also the question of *generally applicable laws*. The FLSA applies to *everybody*. So it regulates Texas and General Motors in exactly the same way.

  Some of the early cases suggest that when Congress regulates the states directly, it might make a difference whether they're also regulating private entities in the same way at the same time. *See, e.g., New York v. United States*, 326 U.S. 572 (1946).[29] We'll talk more in a bit about why that might be true.

So in *National League of Cities* we have a generally-applicable federal statute regulating state governments. The Court (Rehnquist, J.) says that the statute cannot constitutionally be applied to state employees performing traditional governmental functions.

Justice Stone had suggested in *United States v. California*, 297 U.S. 175 (1936), that, so long as Congress acts within its enumerated powers, the states are basically in the same shoes as private individuals. "The state can no more deny the power if its exercise has been authorized by Congress than can an individual." Justice Rehnquist says in *National League of Cities* that this statement is "simply wrong." The states *aren't* the same as individuals.

A lot of people read *National League of Cities* as relying on the Tenth Amendment, even though Justice Rehnquist only mentions the Tenth Amendment once.

It's hard to get any kind of external limit out of the text. The amendment says that "The powers not delegated to the United States by the Constitution, nor prohibited by it to the States, are reserved to the states respectively, or to the people."

That seems to me like an exhortation to take internal limits seriously – that is, to make sure a power really *is* delegated to Congress – rather than identifying any external limits.

We might also infer the limit from the overall structure. That is, we might say that the Constitution presupposes the independent existence of the states, and that they will remain "sovereign" in some meaningful sense. That implies that Congress can't do anything which would jeopardize their independence – like regulating them directly in an intrusive way.

(What do you think of this? Is it a "penumbra" just like *Griswold*?)

(Have we seen any other cases relying on this kind of inference from the nature of the structure itself?)

---

[29] In *New York*—not to be confused with another case of the same name decided in 1992—the Court upheld the application of a federal tax to bottled water sold by the State. Justice Frankfurter's plurality opinion says that "so long as Congress generally taps a source of revenue by whomsoever earned and not uniquely capable of being earned only by a State, the Constitution of the United States does not forbid it merely because its incidence falls also on a State."

Well, *Term Limits* relies on it pretty heavily. Another example would be the dormant Commerce Clause or foreign affairs preemption.

So here's the *National League of Cities* test, as stated in a subsequent decision:[30]

(a)   the challenged statute must regulate the States as States;

(b)   the federal regulation must address matters that are indisputably `attribute[s] of state sovereignty';

(c)   the States' compliance with the federal law must directly impair their ability `to structure integral operations in areas of traditional governmental functions'; and

(d)   there must not be any overriding federal interest advanced by the regulation.

Note that the Court is very divided: Justices Brennan, Marshall, White, and Stevens dissent. And the five-vote majority turns out to be pretty precarious. For the next 8 years, the Court doesn't manage to find any further instances in which the *National League of Cities* principle has been violated. And in many of these, the majority is the four *National League of Cities* dissenters plus Justice Blackmun.

The doctrine comes crashing down for good in *Garcia*:

>   c.   ***Garcia v. San Antonio Metro. Transit Auth.*, 469 U.S. 528 (1985)**

The FLSA amendments of 1974 apply wage and hour rules to public mass-transit systems. The Department of Labor concluded that transit operations are not constitutionally immune from the FLSA under *National League of Cities*.

The Court initially heard argument on whether mass transit was immune under the *National League of Cities* test, then asked for reargument on the question whether *National League of Cities* should be overruled.

The Court – Justice Blackmun writing, joined by the *National League of Cities* dissenters – overrules its prior precedent.

(Justice Blackmun joined the majority in *National League of Cities*. Why is he jumping ship now?)

The "traditional governmental functions" test is "unworkable."

Note that this is one of the key reasons to overrule prior precedent under *Casey*. *Garcia* is the example they give of an unworkable test.

---

[30] As stated in *Hodel v. Virginia Surface Mining & Reclamation Ass'n*, 452 U.S. 264, 287-88 & n. 29 (1981).

(How do we know *National League of Cities* was unworkable?)

Here, the evidence of unworkability is twofold:

- The lower courts had been all over the map as to what is a "traditional state function."

- The Court itself had decided four cases between *National League of Cities* and *Garcia*, and in none of those cases had a majority of the court been willing to apply the doctrine.

Now, it's not completely obvious to me that these intervening decisions prove the doctrine wasn't workable. It's possible to read them and conclude that the results in those cases pretty much make sense – that the doctrine itself is a good one but it simply didn't, and shouldn't have, applied in those cases.

The lower court mess was more serious, however. It's important to remember that a primary function of Supreme Court doctrine is to control the lower courts and get them to produce consistent results.

But the problem goes deeper than unworkability. The real problem is that you cannot limit the States by carving out areas of authority.

(Why is this so difficult?)

Justice Blackmun thinks that the doctrine is too indeterminate to constrain courts from following their policy preferences:

"Any rule of state immunity that looks to the `traditional,' `integral,' or `necessary' nature of governmental functions inevitably invites an unelected federal judiciary to make decisions about which state policies it favors and which ones it dislikes."

This is the Frankfurter Constraint again, right? The idea is that a doctrine that is indeterminate is also illegitimate.

(Is there any protection for federalism left?)

The real measure of state sovereignty lies in the structure of the Federal Government itself, which is designed to protect the States.

This argument raises a much broader set of questions:

d.   The Political Safeguards Debate

There are several different versions of the political safeguards theory. I want to start by considering what these safeguards *are*, and then ask what conclusions we should draw from their existence.

Professor Wechsler's Argument: We start with Prof. Wechsler's position, which was first developed in a famous law review article. *See* Herbert Wechsler, *The Political Safeguards of Federalism*, 54 COLUM. L. REV. 543 (1954).

Wechsler highlights two kinds of "political safeguards":

- **Political Culture:** Wechsler relies heavily on a consensus that national action is "exceptional in our polity, an intrusion to be justified by some necessity, the special rather than the ordinary case."

(Did anybody catch when Wechsler was writing this?)

1954.

(Do you think we have the same political culture today?)

It seems unlikely that federal lawmakers feel any such hesitation today. Even Republicans, who are supposed to be ideologically committed to federalism, tend to prescribe a federal solution to any problem they actually care about.

Some examples: Republicans have pressed for No Child Left Behind; national legislation banning assisted suicides; restricting securities fraud class action suits, even when they're brought under state law; federalizing the gay marriage question.

- **Composition and Selection of the National Government:** Wechsler stresses four aspects of this, but the most important one is State-by-State Representation in Congress. The States are directly represented in Congress, and can look after their own interests.

Justice Powell's Critique: The primary point in Justice Powell's dissent is an attack on the "political safeguards" theory offered by the majority.

(What are his arguments?)

The central criticisms are:

- **The political safeguards theory puts the fox in charge of the henhouse.**

How compelling an argument this is depends on how far you take the *Garcia / Wechsler* position in terms of denying a role for courts (a question we'll come back to).

(Can you see an answer, though?)

Well, if we reject the majority, then the Court is judging the extent of its own power vis a vis Congress, right?

(Is there any answer back?)

That objection can be made to any form of judicial review, and it's subject to the usual answers—e.g., outside control of appointments, jurisdiction, etc.

The Court is more of a neutral referee than Congress is, and its biases are probably toward a broad view of federal authority.

253

- ## The majority's theory of representation is wrong.

(Do you think federal representatives represent state governments, or simply the people of their State? Do you see why the question matters?)

Garcia's fundamental assumption is that federal representatives represent the interests and prerogatives of state *governments* – not just the people who happen to live in their states.

Protecting state interests isn't good enough, because a state government with no power can't serve as a check on the federal government.

(Do you understand the difference?)

There's no question but that a congressman is going to represent the people of his district – they're the ones who have to re-elect him. The question is whether he cares about the institutional autonomy of the state government itself. That turns out to be a tougher question.

Moreover, national representatives are increasingly beholden to national interests. The New York senate race when Hillary Clinton first ran, for instance, drew funding from all over the country on both sides.

Sometimes, moreover, the influence runs the other way: National actors control positions taken in state government. Ex: The Texas redistricting mess a few years ago, in which the Democratic legislators famously fled to Oklahoma and New Mexico to stop the Republicans' redistricting proposal from going through, was controlled by the White House and GOP leadership in Congress. It probably wasn't particularly good for the GOP *in the state*—who had other fish to fry—but they deferred to the wishes of national politicians.

One question I want to flag for you is this: Wechsler seems to be envisioning congressmen as *ambassadors* for their State governments.

(Is this consistent with the view that the majority takes in *Term Limits*?)

I think it directly contradicts *Term Limits*. *Garcia* views congressmen as basically ambassadors from their state governments. But *Term Limits* rejected that idea as fundamentally inconsistent with the Founders' vision. *Term Limits* makes clear that the state governments aren't a party to the relationship between federal representatives and their constituents. So why would we expect federal representatives to care particularly about the state government as an institution? But no one pointed this out in the case.[31]

---

[31] Three other institutional safeguards:

Term Limits shows the problem with *Garcia* in theory; the same problem has a very practical side, which is that federal representatives *compete* with state politicians.

Let's say the most important issue to the State of North Carolina today is the quality of public education. Let's say that there's also a debate about whether that question should be handled at the state level. You're the governor of North Carolina, you're facing re-election in two years and you've got a plan to deal with education that you think will work and get you a lot of votes.

(How do you feel about the proposal to transfer power over education to Washington?)

You hate it, of course.

Now suppose you're the junior senator from North Carolina. You know education is incredibly important to your constituents, and you have your own ideas about how to fix it.

(Are you inclined to defend the state government's primary control over education policy?)

- **State Control over the Federal Electorate:** Art. I, § 2 and the 17th Amendment provide that who can vote in federal elections for Congress is a function of state law.

  But this power can be exercised only indirectly by limiting the *state* electorate, and what little control there was has been eradicated by constitutional amendments (14, 15, 19, 24, and 26), federal voting rights legislation, and equal protection decisions.

  Term Limits would be a good example of how limited this power is.

- **The Electoral College:** Wechsler concedes that the President is really a *national* figure who is supposed to transcend narrow interests of individual states. But he says even here, the States play a role because they are the units – through the electoral college – by which the President is selected.

  But formalization of the process -- the popular canvass and winner-take-all rules – seem to have eliminated any leeway that would make the College a meaningful protection for federalism.

- **The Senate:** This check may have been the most important to the Framers, who provided that Senators *would* be direct representatives of state governments.

  But this pretty much went away with the passage of the Seventeenth Amendment, providing for direct election of Senators. Now Senators function precisely the same as representatives.

No way – You want a chance to pursue *your* ideas and get the credit for success in a field that matters to your constituents. It doesn't help *you* get re-elected if the governor gets to fix education on the state level and gets all the credit, right? So you'll favor federalizing the issue and won't give a hoot for the institutional prerogatives of the state government.

The *Lopez* case – which you'll read for next time – is an example from real life: The case involves the federal Gun Free School Zones Act, enacted in response to a lot of horrible incidents involving shootings in schools. Even though many States had already passed laws, *federal* legislators wanted credit for banning guns in schools.

Now, the education example can also show us why even *state* officials won't always stick up for state prerogatives. Suppose you're the governor again, and you think the education problem is simply intractable – it can't be fixed, and whoever tries is just going to look bad. But you also know that as things stand, most people perceive education as a *state* responsibility.

(How do you feel now about that proposal to federalize the problem?)

You love it, right? That way when the program fails, it won't be your fault! So state officials are often happy to shift responsibilities to the Feds if it's in their immediate political interests to do so.

(Is this necessarily good for the *people* of the state?)

No – It might be more efficient to handle the problem on the state level than in Washington. State officials are pursuing their *own* interests in abdicating, not the *public* interest. In that instance, we might want a court to hold the state officials' feet to the fire by refusing to permit Congress to federalize the issue.

Vertical vs. Horizontal Threats: Another problem is that the sort of political safeguards that Professor Wechsler talks about only guard against certain kinds of threats to state autonomy.

Vertical Aggrandizement is when the national government attempts to increase its own power at the expense of all the states. E.g., federalization of crime. The Feds take over various aspects of criminal law because they think political rewards can be gained or because they simply want to concentrate power at the federal level.

We might expect political safeguards to slow this down to the extent that federal representatives really do represent the interests of their home state governments.

Horizontal Aggrandizement is when some states seek to use the national government as a tool to impose their preferences on other states that may disagree. Consider, e.g., the fugitive slave law. The fugitive slave law was a successful effort by a politically powerful group of states – the South – to impose their preferences on northern abolitionist states that wanted to at least give some due process to people accused of being escaped slaves.

Other examples: polygamy, gay marriage, assisted suicide bans.

Wechsler's political safeguards can't possibly do anything about horizontal aggrandizement; in fact, those safeguards are the *mechanism* by which horizontal aggrandizement occurs. Wechsler's argument is that federal representatives are responsive to voices at the state level – but that's exactly why federal representatives will vote to impose the preferences of some states on other states. The more responsive Congress is to the states, the bigger problem this is.

The only way to guard against horizontal encroachment is simply to make it hard to act at the federal level.

- **The modern national legislative process is so complex in other ways – the role of administrative agencies, congressional staff, national interest groups, the national media – that the "political safeguards" view is anachronistic.**

This last argument, however, may actually pave the way for rehabilitating Wechsler:

The *New* Political Safeguards: Although Wechsler's institutional arguments might seem a little dated, other commentators have proposed different political safeguards that play similar roles. Probably the most important figure here is Larry Kramer,[32] who highlights two institutional factors that Wechsler doesn't mention.

Political Parties: Parties "broker state/federal relations" by "linking the fortunes of officeholders at state and federal levels, fostering a mutual dependency that protects state institutions by inducing federal lawmakers to take account of (at least some) desires of state officials."[33]

This works in two ways:

- "first, parties offer tangible aid to help candidates get elected;"

- "second, parties provide a fraternal connection among officials that helps expedite the day-to-day affairs of governing." *Id.* at 1528.

These factors protect federalism because they work *across* levels of government.

---

[32] *See* Larry D. Kramer, *Putting the Politics Back into the Political Safeguards of Federalism*, 100 COLUM. L. REV. 215 (2000); Larry D. Kramer, *Understanding Federalism*, 47 VAND. L. REV. 1485 (1994).

[33] Kramer, 47 Vand. L. Rev. at 1523.

But remember the TX redistricting story, in which state politicians undermined their own popularity and goals by acting to further the interests of their party at the national level. And think also about No Child Left Behind – a law that many Republicans in Congress .

Administrative Bureaucracy: Much of federal law is administered by state officials—such as law enforcement, environmental law, housing, welfare benefits, and health care. To this extent, *state* officials exercise the administrative influence on the national legislature that would otherwise go to federal bureaucrats.

It would be hard for the federal government to get rid of state administration for many of these programs. Moreover, private interests develop working relationships with state bureaucrats, and become willing to help protect those relationships.

> e.   **The Relevance of Political Safeguards to Judicial Review**

If we accept that the States have some influence in the federal political process, we still have to ask what that means in terms of the role of the Court.

Professor Wechsler drew a fairly modest conclusion: He says that "[t]his is not to say that the Court can decline to measure national enactments by the Constitution when it is called upon to face the question in the course of ordinary litigation."

He's simply saying the Court should be deferential to Congress in federalism cases. "[T]he Court is on weakest ground when it opposes its interpretation of the Constitution to that of Congress in the interest of the states, whose representatives control the legislative process and, by hypothesis, have broadly acquiesced in sanctioning the challenged Act of Congress."

Dean Choper, in an influential book,[34] went further than Wechsler. He argued that federalism issues should simply be nonjusticiable – the Court shouldn't decide them at all. That's because the political process is an adequate protection for federalism, and the Court should be saving its political capital so that it can use it to protect individual rights.

(What do you think of this argument? Should there be no judicial review?)

You could attack it on two levels:

---

[34] *See* JESSE H. CHOPER, JUDICIAL REVIEW AND THE NATIONAL POLITICAL PROCESS: A FUNCTIONAL RECONSIDERATION OF THE ROLE OF THE SUPREME COURT (1980).

(1)   the political process might *not* be an adequate safeguard – that's the argument we've already developed and will talk about more.

(2)   you might also question Choper's assumptions about political capital. The Court's political capital might be more like muscles than money – it grows the more it's exercised. I'm not saying this is true – just that it's possible. It's an empirical question, but very difficult to measure.

(What does Justice Powell say about this point?)

The judiciary has a responsibility to enforce *all* of the Constitution, not just part of it. We wouldn't, for instance, think that the Court should just stop enforcing Separation of Powers, even though the same political arguments could be made there.

This goes back to our discussions about the double standard: Is it OK for the judiciary to just decide that some parts of the Constitution just don't need enforcing?

f.   A Partial Defense: The *Procedural* Safeguards of Federalism

Given all these problems, I have to say that I think that Wechsler's "political safeguards" argument works better in practice than it has any right to in theory. There are at least two reasons:

- Federal representatives aren't *completely indifferent* to the interests of state governmental officials. One reason is that there's probably some advantage in federal re-election campaigns from having the support of the state political establishment. At least in situations where they aren't competing, federal reps are willing to occasionally do nice things for state governments.

  Example: The Unfunded Mandates Reform Act.

- The much more important point, though, is that it's simply hard for Congress to make law. That's because the Article I process is arduous, and there's lots of points – committees, two houses, presidential veto, etc. – where things can go wrong. Any time the federal government *can't* act, that leaves the subject open for *state* policy decisions.

  So the federal political process *does* protect the states, but not so much because the states are represented there as because the process is simply cumbersome. What this means is that separation of powers becomes very important to federalism. In particular, SOP doctrines are very important to the extent that they require *Congress* to act rather than some other national actor – like the President – that can act more easily.

g.   Antecedents – Madison's Federalist 45 & 46

The roots of Wechsler's and Choper's argument are in Federalist 45 & 46, where Madison rebuts the critical charge against the proposed Constitution -- that it confers too much power on the national government. These essays put a somewhat different spin on the whole political safeguards argument.

Madison starts by recognizing that federalism basically involves a competition between the state and federal governments for the loyalty of the People.

(Who does Madison expect to generally win this competition?)

The States.

(Why?)

He thinks the states will win this competition, for two central reasons:

(1)   One reason is the one Wechsler and Choper pick up – that is, that the federal government depends on the States for its composition and selection.   And Madison cites much the same institutional safeguards – especially the Senate.

(2)   Probably the more important reason, though, is his expectation that the States will retain their primary role in providing beneficial regulation, services, and benefits to their citizens.

We might break this second argument down into two kinds of benefits:

(a)   government jobs, offices, and subsidies

(b)   beneficial regulation

(Why does Madison expect the States to dominate this competition in regulation and services?)

He sees the national government as basically distant and involved in affairs that, while important, don't come up that often – like wars.   The states are dominant in the areas that matter most to people's everyday lives: States build schools, prosecute criminals, enforce contracts.

Because of this fact, Madison expects people to look to the States to satisfy their most basic needs, with the result that people will continue to feel a primary *loyalty* to the state governments. That means that in any test of strength between the federal and state governments, the states should come out on top due to their support from the people themselves.

Madison's basic analysis is basically consistent with a lot contemporary political science, which suggests that people trade their political support – both their votes and their campaign contributions – to politicians in exchange for government benefits and beneficial regulation.

(Think about it: Let's say you have $1000 budgeted for campaign contributions. How are you going to decide whom to give it to?)

I think you're going to decide what issues are most important to you, then give it to the candidate most likely to advance your views on those issues.

Part of that decision will involve figuring out what *level* of government is most likely to be responsible for those issues that matter most to you.

(Do you think Madison's expectation of how these things will shake out is still a fair description of the way things are? When society perceives the existence of a new problem, do we tend to look for a federal or state solution?)

I think it's fair to say we look much more frequently for federal solutions now. The New Deal and the Great Society changed our baseline expectations about who does what. And for much of the 20th and 21st centuries we've lived in a state of "perpetual war"—that is, a period in which meaningful security threats were everpresent and the role of the national government in countering them continued to seem very important.

Unlike Choper and Wechsler, Madison is not focusing on when judicial review would or would not be appropriate to protect federalism. But his view has implications for that question.

(If Choper's view of political safeguards would lead courts not to intervene at all, and Wechsler's view would lead courts to intervene only to fix process defects, when would a Madisonian view justify intervention?)

The important thing for Madison is the opportunity to provide beneficial regulation and services to the citizens, because citizens tend to repay those benefits with political loyalty. So the key is ensuring that the States retain the opportunity to provide those benefits and services. That would justify judicial intervention when the federal government attempts to usurp that role.

That said, it's important to recognize a second strand to Madison's argument:

(What happens if the People shift their loyalty to the Feds?)

Madison's second answer to the Antifederalists' criticism is that if a strong national government is what it takes to make the People happy and safe, they are entitled to their choice. The States are just a means to the public welfare, not ends in themselves.

So if I'm right that we've shifted our primary *expectations* of government from the states to the federal government as a result of historical experience suggesting the Feds do a better job, Madison might very well say that this is perfectly appropriate.

(Is there any limit on this reasoning?)

On the other hand, Madison says this in the context of a competition with certain rules: If, acting within those rules, the Feds win out then so be it. But one of the rules is the doctrine of enumerated powers – that is, the Feds can compete only by exercising the powers allotted to them. Nothing in Federalist 45 or 46 suggests that its OK for Congress to unilaterally exceed those enumerated powers. So he shouldn't be read as ruling out judicial review to enforce those limits.

5.   After *Garcia*

Having explored the political safeguards argument, I want to turn back to a couple of final aspects of the *Garcia* opinion.

a.   The Dissents – A Portent, or just Judicial Trash Talk?

The dissents are important here not only for the arguments they make but also because they set the stage for the later federalism cases. Justices O'Connor and Rehnquist make an important prediction/promise: That the Court will in time return to enforcing constitutional limits on national power. That promise is fulfilled in *New York*, in *Lopez*, and in the 11th Amendment cases starting with *Seminole Tribe*.

Note that this is basically judicial trash-talk – and it's unclear how appropriate it is. These Justices are promising to change the law simply by getting more conservative votes on the Court. You see the same kind of thing in the sovereign immunity cases, where the liberals offer the same kind of trash-talking.

The interesting thing will be to see the extent to which the *Garcia* dissenters follow up on their promise.

b.   What's Left after *Garcia*?

The majority suggests two things:

- **Interference with the "political safeguards" of federalism may warrant judicial intervention.**

This is the beginning of what we call "process federalism." Here's what Justice Blackmun says:

"[W]e are convinced that the fundamental limitation that the constitutional scheme imposes on the Commerce Clause to protect the 'States as States' is one of process rather than one of result. Any substantive restraint on the exercise of Commerce Clause powers must find its justification in the procedural nature of this basic limitation, and it must be tailored to compensate for possible failings in the national political process rather than to dictate a 'sacred province of state autonomy.'"

The Court doesn't elaborate on what these "process" limits might be, but it *could* suggest a sort of John Hart Ely, *Democracy and Distrust* sort of argument: Courts would step in when the political process is failing to protect States. T§he Court begins to develop that idea in *Gregory*. I'll have a bit more to say about this after we do that case.

- **Congress can't destroy the States' "independent existence."**

With respect to the latter limit, consider the following statement from Professor Tribe:

"Of course, no one expects Congress to obliterate the states, at least in one fell swoop. If there is any danger, it lies in the tyranny of small decisions -- in the prospect that Congress will nibble away at state sovereignty, bit by bit, until someday essentially nothing is left but a gutted shell. The real question, therefore, is this: short of its prohibition of Armageddon, does the Constitution grant the states any judicially enforceable protection from Congress?" Tribe, American Constitutional Law § 5-20, at 381 (2d ed. 1988).

6.   Three Models of Federalism Doctrine

A few years later, in *Gregory v. Ashcroft*, the Court returns to the issue of generally applicable federal laws that regulate the states. *Gregory* would have been a good case to overrule *Garcia*: It raises the same issue (whether a state can be subjected to generally applicable laws), it involves what is clearly a core state function (the selection and retention of state judges), and Justice O'Connor seems to have picked up a fifth vote (although Souter switches sides later on).

But they don't do it. I think it's for a couple of reasons;

- *National League of Cities* was never such a great doctrine. It was really amorphous. (For that reason, I'm not sure Justice Scalia would have had any great enthusiasm for reviving it.)

- The more important reason is that in *Gregory* the Court starts to realize that the process federalism approach adopted by *Garcia* doesn't have to mean a surrender to national power. In fact, it has some real potential to generate doctrines like *Gregory*'s clear statement rule that really protect state autonomy.

This makes it worthwhile to talk about three quite different judicial approaches to protecting federalism.

a.   Power Federalism

Power federalism tries to impose substantive limits on what the federal government can do.

Examples:

- Cases like *Hammer v. Dagenhart* and *United States v. Lopez* put substantive limits on the reach of the Commerce Power.

- *City of Boerne v. Flores* puts a similar limit on the reach of the Section Five power.

b.   Process Federalism

Process federalism is designed to rely upon – and possibly also to maximize – the extent to which states are protected by the federal political process.

Examples:

- Clear statement rules of statutory construction. *E.g., Gregory*; the presumption against preemption.

- Enforcement of various separation of powers rules that require *Congress* to make federal law and therefore ensure state representation. *E.g.*, limits on delegation of lawmaking authority to federal administrative agencies; limits on federal common lawmaking by courts.

- Enforcement of rules that require the federal government to internalize its costs. *E.g.*, anti-commandeering.

- Heightened suspicion for federal regulation of state entities where the regulation is *not* generally applicable. *E.g., Condon v. Reno*.

c.   Immunity Federalism

Immunity federalism relieves the states of their obligations to conform to federal norms, or at least makes those norms hard to enforce against the states.

Examples:

- 11th Amendment decisions holding states can't be sued for money damages under federal law.

- Habeas corpus decisions making it harder for federal courts to overturn state criminal convictions for failing to comply with federal procedural rights.

Unfortunately, you don't really get this model until you take Federal Courts as a 2L or 3L, but it's really important in practice.

Areas of Overlap: These models are not perfectly exclusive; some sorts of federalism doctrines may combine elements of two or more models.

For example, *National League of Cities* is in some ways a doctrine of power federalism – it tries to put a substantive limit on the reach of Congress's regulatory authority.

But the *National League of Cities* didn't say Congress can't make a law about X or Y subject – it simply said that states couldn't be subject to some federal laws. So in that sense it's a doctrine of immunity federalism.

Choosing a Model: These models are not necessarily created equal. We need to think about several issues:

- **Which sorts of federalism doctrines are most likely to protect the aspects of values of federalism that we care about?**

For instance, if we buy Madison's argument that "political safeguards" depend on the loyalty of citizens, and that this loyalty depends on the states having something meaningful to do, then we might conclude that process federalism is incomplete without *some* substantive limit on national power.

On the other hand, we might also conclude that *immunity* federalism is less important because it does nothing to protect state regulatory authority – it just exempts state governmental institutions from compliance with federal law.

- **Which sorts of federalism doctrines are easiest for courts to implement?**

Here, the experience of the *Lochner* period suggests that courts have a problem developing coherent and enforceable power federalism doctrines. Dual federalism – which is the classic form of power federalism, in that it sought to confine both the state and national governments to well-defined and separate spheres – didn't work out very well.

Process federalism doctrines, on the other hand, generally involve courts putting up roadblocks to federal action but leaving the ultimate decision to Congress. That's comparatively easy for courts to handle.

You'll see examples of each of these models as we go forward, but hopefully this overview will give you some perspective for evaluating them and keeping them straight.

II.   Chapter Ten – The Powers of Congress

Aside from structuring the national political process to represent the States (at least to some extent), the Framers' other primary strategy for maintaining the federal balance was to limit and enumerate the powers of the national government, while making clear (in the Tenth Amendment) that all powers not delegated to the national government were reserved to the States. That strategy arguably has not worked very well; as many of the cases in our historical survey showed, it turned out to be quite difficult to determine the precise location of the enumerated line between national and state authority, and after 1937 the Court largely seemed to give up trying. Recent years have seen a revival of sorts, however, with a series of landmark cases reaffirming the principle that Congress's powers are, in fact, enumerated—even if those cases seem to leave an extremely broad scope to national power. This chapter considers the three most important powers—the commerce and spending powers in Article I, as well as Congress's authority to enforce the Reconstruction amendments.

One continual concern in these materials concerns the Court's ability to frame doctrine to enforce structural principles in a determinate and sustainable way. Especially with the Commerce Clause, the Court has tried to draw the line between state and national authority in a variety of ways, but has had to abandon each formulation (e.g., direct vs. indirect effects on commerce) after it produced results that seemed arbitrary and unpredictable. The question in cases like Lopez *is whether the Court has finally found a workable formula. The spectre that haunts this effort, of course, is* Lochner—*see especially Justice Souter's dissent in* Lopez. *So don't forget to tie this section in with the earlier chapter on the* Lochner *period.*

A.   The Commerce Power

1.   *United States v. Lopez*, 514 U.S. 549 (1995)

The Gun-Free School Zones Act of 1990, 18 U.S.C. § 922(q)(1)(A) makes it a federal offense "for any individual knowingly to possess a firearm at a place that the individual knows, or has reasonable cause to believe, is a school zone." These zones extend for 1000 feet from any school.

Lopez is a high school senior arrested for carrying a .38 caliber handgun at Edison High School in San Antonio, Texas on March 10, 1992. He was initially charged with firearm possession on school premises under Texas law, *see* Tex. Penal Code Ann. § 46.03(a)(1), but the state charges were dismissed after federal agents charged Lopez with violating the federal Act. Lopez was found guilty and sentenced to 6 months imprisonment and 2 years supervised release. The Court of Appeals reversed on the ground that the Act exceeded Congress's commerce power.

The Court holds (Rehnquist, CJ) that statute exceeds Congress's power under the Commerce Clause.

Note the line-up here: Rehnquist, O'Connor, Scalia, Kennedy, and Thomas. With the exception of *Term Limits*, this majority has been pretty solid through the federalism cases of the last five years. Again, Kennedy concurs with a somewhat more moderate concurrence – just like in *Term Limits*.

a.   A Sharp Break?

We've just gone through the New Deal Court cases after 1937 – *Jones & Laughlin*, *Wickard*, and *Darby* – that all define the Commerce Power very broadly.

(Does the Court overrule these cases in *Lopez*?)

No – the Court purports to work within the framework established by *Jones & Laughlin* and the cases that come after.

The Chief identifies three areas that, under the modern cases, Congress can regulate.

1) Congress may regulate the use of the *channels* of interstate commerce.

2) Congress may regulate and protect the *instrumentalities* of interstate commerce, or *persons or things in interstate commerce*.

It's not clear these two are distinct. The classic examples -- railroads, interstate highways and businesses catering to travelers -- seem to fall under each.

3) Congress may regulate activity having a *substantial relation* to interstate commerce, i.e., activities with *substantial effects* on interstate commerce.

This case doesn't involve "channels" or "instrumentalities" of commerce.

(What about "substantial effects"? Does the government have to show that Alfonso Lopez bringing a gun to school substantially affected the national economy?)

No. We have what is called the "aggregation principle," which the Court derives from *Wickard v. Filburn*. So the question is whether *all* guns brought to school might substantially affect interstate commerce.

(Is this question up to the Court in the first instance? Or is it first and foremost Congress's call?)

Congress's. Remember, the other branches have their own obligations to determine whether their own actions conform to the Constitution. That's why FDR's advice to the Congressman to leave the constitutionality of proposed legislation up to the Courts – advice which dealt with this very issue of the scope of the Commerce Power – was so bad.

(So if Congress makes the "substantial effects" call in the first instance, does the Court just accept that judgment?)

No – it still has to review that determination.

(What's the standard of review?)

Rational basis – that is, the Court has to accept Congress's judgment if there was any rational basis for it. This is a very deferential standard.

(Why so deferential? After all, this is the fox guarding the henhouse – that is, Congress making judgments about the extent of its own power.)

Justice Breyer has the best explanation for why Congress should get some deference on its judgment about substantial effects. Two reasons:

(a)   the Constitution delegates the commerce power directly to Congress. (But *all* governmental powers delegated directly to the branch that gets them, so this can't be doing much work.)

(b)   Congress has a better capacity to make difficult empirical judgments about economic effects.

We've already talked about the institutional capacity advantages that Congress may have, through its ability to hold hearings, question experts, etc. I've always found these arguments a bit underwhelming, given that you can do a lot of the same stuff at a judicial trial.

(What's the big advantage that Congress has, though?)

Well, we can vote them out of office if we think they get it wrong. So the ultimate advantage Congress has may be *accountability* rather than expertise. I don't mean to say I don't buy the expertise argument *at all* – I think there's something to it. I just don't think Congress's expertise advantage is all that clear.

In any event, note the agreement among all justices that this rational basis test is the right standard (although Justice Thomas says the Court should reexamine it in an appropriate case). They disagree rather radically about how to apply it.

b.   The Impact on Commerce

(Does the Court think Congress could rationally have concluded that guns in schools substantially affect interstate commerce?)

No.

(What's the best argument against the Court on this point?)

Justice Breyer's primary argument is that, in reality, the problem of guns in schools has a huge effect on interstate commerce. The argument goes as follows:

Step 1: Guns in schools make everyone feel insecure; they may even deter some people from coming.

Step 2: This sense of insecurity keeps kids from learning. Johnny won't learn to read if he gets a gun pulled on him at recess every day – it's distracting.

Step 3: If Johnny doesn't learn to read, he's less likely to get a good job. More generally, the quality of education has a major effect on the economic prospects of both local communities.

Step 4: These economic effects ripple through the state and the national economy – they may even effect international competitiveness.

Justice Breyer supports these inferences with an extended appendix citing various social science research, etc.

(Does the majority think that Justice Breyer is wrong as an empirical matter?)

No – He's gotta be right.

(Then why doesn't the majority accept this chain of causation?)

The simple answer is that it proves too much – there's simply nothing that wouldn't be covered if Breyer's view were the law.

(Can anyone give me an example of something that *wouldn't* affect interstate commerce?)

Well, all the Justices – even the dissenters – seem to agree that the Federal Government can't regulate family law.

(Can someone make a Breyer-like argument that foster-care rules, for instance, substantially affect interstate commerce?)

It's easy. Upbringing affects earning prospects, just like education.

So the critical problem is to figure out limiting principles that create some meaningful limits on Congress's powers.

At oral argument, Justice O'Connor asks the Solicitor General of the United States the following question: "If Congress can reach [this case] under the interstate commerce power, what would be an example of a case which you couldn't reach?"

His answer is "Well, your Honor, I'm not prepared to speculate generally." In other words, he can't think of one.

This is "Game Over," right? O'Connor might as well have a big "5" tattooed on her forehead when she asks this question, and the SG has got to know that the Court's looking for *some* limiting principle. They're not prepared to hold that the Commerce Clause is meaningless as a constraint on national power. So it's the SG's job to be able to point to *something* that wouldn't be upheld under the government's theory.

This is a general point about law practice, and it's important in all areas of the law. It's *always* better—and generally essential—to have a limiting principle for your argument. This allows you to tell the Court that it can hold in your favor without committing itself to really extreme results in the cases that come along in the future. If you don't have that kind of principle – and more particularly if you can't think of any cases that would fall on the other side of the line you're trying to draw – you're probably in big trouble.

c.   The Majority's Analysis

The SG's failure leaves the question, of course, whether the majority can do any better coming up with a limiting principle. The Chief makes three main points in explaining why the Gun-Free School Zones Act doesn't pass the "substantial relation" test.

1)   **The statute doesn't regulate commercial activity.** Nor is it an integral part of a larger scheme governing commercial activity.

2)   **There is no jurisdictional element** which would limit the statute's reach through case-by-case adjudication.

3)   **There are no legislative findings.** These are not required, but they would make it easier to conclude that the implicit judgment in the statute was correct.

Take these in reverse order – findings first: Congress enacted a statute in response to the Court's decision in *Lopez*. It has a bunch of findings to the effect that

- Gun crime is a national problem;

- Guns move in interstate commerce all the time;

- Violent crime in school zones hurts the quality of education;

- The decline in education hurts the economy; and

- States have trouble dealing with this problem on their own.

(Should the Court uphold the statute now, as amended?)

(Why should legislative findings make a difference?)

Two reasons we might care about findings:

- Expertise: If we're going to justify deference to Congress based on Congress's expertise, we want to make sure they've actually *applied* their expertise.

It's important to recognize how unusual this is – the Court is kind of treating Congress like an administrative agency. But note that all justices agree in the end that the presence or absence of findings can't be dispositive.

- Political Safeguards of Federalism: You could think of findings as designed to force Congress to deliberate about the federalism question when it passes a statute. That ensures some level of state representation; it also adds another procedural hurdle.

(What about the jurisdictional element? Many statutes do, in fact, have a jurisdictional element. Why should that matter?)

It effectively puts off the 'affecting commerce' question until someone is actually tried under the case. Then they can litigate that question and the jury can decide it.

We might characterize the legislative findings idea as a *wholesale* determination by Congress that commerce is affected by the activity at issue, while the jurisdictional element is a *retail* determination of the same issue by the trial court in every individual case.

(What about the first point – the statute doesn't regulate commercial activity. Didn't Justice Breyer prove that wrong?)

No – the question is whether the activity that the statute actually regulates directly is *itself* commercial in nature. Only then do we ask whether that activity – and it can be wholly *intra*state and small in magnitude – affects interstate commerce in the aggregate.

(Does this analysis remind you of anything in the prior case law?)

It's a lot like the direct/indirect effects test in the *Lochner* period. That's a problem. And we'll talk more about whether the commercial vs. non-commercial distinction is workable when we do *Morrison*.

d.   Other Approaches

So these are the three factors that are explicit in the opinion. I think that there are two other more general tests that are possible, however:

4)   Congress may regulate only where there is some good reason to prefer federal action over state action – e.g., spillover effects, race to the bottom concerns, etc.

There's a version of this sort of test suggested in the quotation from Prof. Regan in the notes. He says courts should ask, "Is there some reason the federal government must be able to do this, some reason why we cannot leave the matter to the states?"[35]

European law contains a similar principle, which they call "subsidiarity": The EU regulates only those subjects that can't be efficiently handled by the Member States individually.

(Is there any good reason for federal action here?)

In fact, lots of states had already regulated the problem of guns in school zones. There's no obvious reason it's a problem that can't be handled at the federal level. In fact, what this really looks like is federal officials trying to take credit for something the states had already been doing.

---

[35] Don Regan, *How to Think About the Federal Commerce Power and Incidentally Rewrite* United States v. Lopez, 94 MICH. L. REV. 554, 557 (1995).

(Is there any problem with approaching the Commerce Clause question this way?)

Well, it seems like you're asking for a policy judgment from the Court. Why would they be better at telling the need for federal action than Congress is?

One more possibility:

5) **The statute fails simply because it is impossible to come up with any principled rationale for excluding *anything* from Congress's power if this law is OK.**

This gets back to the SG's dilemma at oral argument that I mentioned earlier. Maybe the Court's back is just to the wall here.

e. Souter's Dissent: The Judicial Role

(How is Justice Souter's critique of the majority different from Justice Breyer's? What does he mean by saying that the majority's opinion is a "backward glance"?)

He focuses on the idea of judicial restraint. Justice Souter compares the majority's position to the Court's decisions during the *Lochner* era, when the Court was widely viewed as striking down economic regulation based on the Justice's own preference for *laissez faire* economics, rather than on any legitimate legal basis. That's what he means by the "backward glance"

(What's the best answer you can make for the majority?)

The majority's implicit answer is that it is following precedent, not simply imposing its preferences as under *Lochner*.

(Is this an accurate description? Is *Lopez* consistent with the post-New Deal cases?)

(Is it fair to accuse the majority of imposing its own policy preferences in *this* case? Is the majority in *favor* of guns in schools?)

(What does Justice Kennedy say in response to this charge?)

Justice Kennedy's concurrence argues that the judiciary cannot simply abdicate its responsibility to enforce federalism. The Courts enforce other structural elements: checks and balances, separation of powers. Given the centrality of federalism to the Framers' thought, it would be strange to abandon enforcement of that principle.

f. Thomas's Concurrence: Taking Original Intent Seriously

(What does Justice Thomas have to say about all this?)

Justice Thomas says the case law "has drifted far from the original understanding of the Commerce Clause." In an appropriate case, the Court should reconsider those precedents.

(Why not reconsider them in *this* case?)

Because the case comes out the same way under the modern doctrine, so in a sense a re-evaluation of the case law is unnecessary to the decision.

(What's Justice Thomas's view of "commerce"?)

The Framers understood "commerce" in a much more limited sense, as distinct from "manufacturing" or "agriculture." We should stick to that narrow reading.

(What would be the effect of adopting Justice Thomas's view? What about the doctrine of *stare decisis*?)

It may be that it's simply too late in the day to go back to the narrower definition, no matter how right Justice Thomas is about the history. This is frequently a constraint on originalism – it often comes into conflict with the doctrine of precedent.

g. Where Do We Go From Here? Implications of *Lopez*

(How many people think the majority is right? The dissenters? How many people would go even further along with Justice Thomas? Why?)

(Is this case a big deal? Or is it just an anomaly that will not reverse the trend toward broad federal power?)

You could read *Lopez* as a "shot across the bow" designed to "cue" Congress to pay more attention to the need to leave some sphere of power to the States.

It becomes clearer what *Lopez* means in *Morrison*:

2. *Lopez* to *Raich*

Just a few quick words about developments in the 10 years between *Lopez* and *Raich*:

a. *United States v. Morrison*, 529 U.S. 598 (2000)

Congress enacted the Violence Against Women Act, 42 U.S.C. § 13981, in order to address crimes of gender-motivated violence.

We've got a particularly nasty crime here: Christy Brzonkala's a Virginia Tech student raped by two football players. She sues under a provision of the VAWA, which provides a federal cause of action against anyone who commits such a crime.

The Court holds (5-4, usual suspects) that this particular provision of the VAWA is unconstitutional. Three important things you need to know about *Morrison*:

- It makes clear the Court is at least somewhat serious about putting limits on the Commerce Clause. *Lopez* isn't just a "sport."

- It clarifies the relationship among the different "factors" noted in *Lopez*. In particular, there is a mountain of findings in *Morrison* – Congress held two years' worth of hearings and developed a big record about the impact of violence against women on interstate commerce. The Court says that doesn't matter.

  They also say that the jurisdictional element thing isn't a big deal, so it's clear that the crucial question is whether the regulated activity is "commercial" or not.

- Justice Souter's dissent takes the flat-out Choper/Wechsler line: He says the Court shouldn't be deciding these questions because "the Constitution remits them to politics." That's a more extreme position than he took in *Lopez*. It amounts to a wholesale abdication, and it raises the question why Courts are competent to develop substantive due process doctrine, but not federalism.

b.   The Lower Courts

After *Lopez* and especially after *Morrison*, a lot of observers predicted that the lower courts would start striking down federal statutes willy nilly under the Commerce Clause. That didn't happen – indeed, people who did empirical studies of the lower court reaction found almost willful disregard of *Lopez* and *Morrison*.

This highlights the fact that it's not easy for the Supremes to control how the lower courts deal with their precedents.

c.   Statutory Construction as an Alternative

The other thing that happens is you see a number of cases construing federal statutes narrowly in order to avoid Commerce Clause concerns. This starts well before *Lopez*:

- *United States v. Bass*, 404 U.S. 336 (1971): The Court narrowly construes a federal criminal statute because a broad reading would push the limits of the Commerce Clause.

But it accelerates after 1995:

- *Jones v. United States*, 529 U.S. 848 (2000): A unanimous Court construes the federal arson statute to reach only *commercial* buildings.

- *Solid Waste Agency of Northern Cook County v. United States Army Corps of Engineers*, 531 U.S. 159 (2001): The Court invalidates an administrative regulation promulgated by the corps that prohibited developing any wetland inhabited by migratory birds. If federal power were to extend into such a problematic area, *Congress* – not the agency – would have to make the decision.

You can even put the recent Oregon right-to-die case in this bunch, which suggests that *Raich* won't stop the trend. We'll read these cases, which are important in their own right, in our section on clear statement rules. But they also give a picture of the Court's views on the Commerce Clause itself.

3. The End of the Line? *Gonzales v. Raich*, 545 U.S. 1 (2005)

The Court (Stevens, J) upholds Congress's authority to regulate the medicinal use of homegrown marijuana under the Controlled Substances Act.

I want to focus on three questions here:

- Does the result in *Raich* prove that the Court's federalism cases are "political"?

- How does/should the doctrine play out in *Raich*?

- What does *Raich* portend for the future? How do the new appointees to the Court affect that picture?

a. Politics

A lot of people thought the decision in *Raich* would turn on political grounds, and a lot of people think the way it came out is good evidence that politics determine results at the Supreme Court. (The pundit Dahlia Lithwick wrote a piece after the oral argument entitled "Dude, Where's My Integrity?") I actually think *Raich* is good evidence for the opposite position.

(What's the Conservative position here? The liberal position?)

(Do these labels fit cases like *Lopez*?)

(What was the liberal position in *Lopez*? How do you know?)

(What's a "political" preference? Is a preference for federalism political?)

A lot of the political scientists who run empirical "studies" claiming the court follows its political preferences will classify a "preference" for limiting national power as a "political" preference. But how is that so? Isn't that a belief about what the law requires? I'm not saying there's nothing political about it, but that's true of all law. The point is there's no easy distinction between politics and law.

Let's talk about how the justices actually voted. The Court rules 6-3 in favor of the Feds on this one.

(What's the argument that's a political result?)

Compare it to *Lopez*: When national power helps a liberal cause (gun control) the conservative court strikes it down. When national power helps a conservative cause (war on drugs), the conservative court upholds it.

(But now let's disaggregate "the Court" and think about individual justices: How many judges did a political about-face like that?)

Only two, right? The four liberals were nationalist in both cases; three conservatives voted for the states in both cases. So this glass of principle is seven-ninths full, right? (One could answer Ms. Lithwick, "Dude, there's your integrity.")

And are Kennedy and Scalia being political, or do they simply hold a moderate view of federalism? Suppose their view is the Feds can regulate just about anything, but not everything. That's not a crazy position, and it would explain both votes. Having voted the way they did in *Lopez*, are they really hypocritical if they don't vote to strike down every other federal statute that gets challenged on their watch?

b.   Doctrine

Raich is a hard case, doctrinally speaking.

The first question is How to Characterize the Regulated Activity: Is the activity *only* "medicinal use of homegrown marijuana" or is it "marijuana consumption in general"?

This is a *level of generality* problem: The more generally we define the activity, the more plausible it is that Congress can regulate it. This kind of problem crops up in lots of areas in constitutional law, and it's worth taking note of these general kinds of doctrinal dilemmas. Think for a minute about substantive due process:

(What's the most specific way you could characterize the right at issue in *Griswold v. Connecticut*?)

It's about the right to use contraception in the home by married couples.

(What are some more general ways?)

I can think of several:

- Right to decide whether or not to beget a child;

- Right of sexual intimacy;

- Right to make decisions basic to one's personal autonomy.

Think about the implications of characterizing the right in each of these ways:

- The first one gets you *Roe v. Wade*.

- The second gets you the right to gay sex in *Lawrence v. Texas*.

- The third gets you the right to die.

The problem is that courts often confront a choice about how to characterize the rights or activities at issue in a case. What we worry about is that this choice is manipulable by the court.

The trick in *Raich* is to find a way to let somebody outside the Court choose the appropriate level of generality. That way the court can't manipulate it and will be behaving in a principled manner. There are a couple of ways to approach it:

Facial vs. As-Applied Challenges: Can people challenge a federal regulatory scheme as it applies to particular circumstances that may not implicate interstate commerce? Or must they challenge the scheme as a whole?

As-applied challenges are the norm.

(Can you see why?)

Because they involve the facts actually before the court, and because they're sufficient to decide the case. Facial challenges ask the court to speculate about circumstances not before them, and they stretch the judicial power beyond what's necessary to resolve a particular dispute. But if you allow as-applied challenges here, you're likely to get a lot of "carve outs" for unusual subclasses of activity that can ordinarily be regulated.

The majority responds by allowing Congress to effectively determine the level of generality:

Comprehensive Scheme: The CSA regulates *all* marijuana use, so Congress has effectively chosen the higher level. The court essentially defers to this choice. The fact that a subset of the regulated activity may be somewhat distinct doesn't matter. This is based on language in *Lopez* that suggested that Congress may regulate non-commercial activity as "an essential part of a larger regulation of economic activity."

(But here's a question: Has Congress really chosen the higher level of generality? Does the CSA lump together medicinal and non-medicinal uses for drugs?)

No – it distinguishes them. But the Feds think there is not a medical use for marijuana. I'd say that conclusion is irrelevant; the issue here is whether these are distinct classes of activity.

In any event, the Court's comprehensive scheme notion obviously creates perverse incentives for Congress to regulate broadly; on the other hand, there are also strong countervailing forces.

One possibility would be to acknowledge a "comprehensive scheme" principle but *review* whether a particular piece of it was really connected to the rest.

(Should courts do that?)

I think you can see why the Court would be reluctant to do that. But imagine:

(Suppose Congress says they're banning gay marriage as part of the comprehensive scheme of federal pension regulation under the ERISA statute? Is that really a part of that regulatory regime? Or is it the equivalent of a "rider"?)

Necessary and Proper: The other way to think about the case is Justice Scalia's concurrence. He concedes that medical marijuana is non-commercial, but says that Congress can regulate *non*-commercial as a necessary and proper means of regulating commercial activity.

(Why's it necessary?)

I think the best example is problems of proof. The possibility that some marijuana is *legal* makes it necessary to prove that any given defendant's was *not* – and that has to be proven beyond a reasonable doubt.

(Could someone please spin out an identical argument to uphold the statute in *Lopez*?)

I think it's easy. Federal law regulates the market for guns. It's hard to catch people in the act of selling, so we need to regulate possession as well. And if we want to prevent sales to minors, then regulating possession at places they congregate – i.e., schools – makes some sense.

(What then, if any, are the limits on this power? How would you answer Justice O'Connor's question in *Lopez*?)

I think you could limit it in two ways:

- **Clear Statement:** Make *Congress* make the determination of necessity. This would be a process federalism strategy.

- **Review the Necessity Finding:** Obviously this will be quite difficult for courts for all the reasons *Lochner* went awry. And it would require you to revisit *McCulloch*'s deferential test for necessity.

State Regulation: The last question is, Is it relevant to the question of national power that a *state* regulatory scheme is already in place?

It should be easy to see why we might *want* it to matter: The values of federalism in promoting experimentation, participation, etc., are much more pronounced where the State is doing something *different* from the Feds.

(Should it matter?)

It's hard to make it matter, given the structure of Art. I and the Supremacy Clause.

But here's how it might matter: The "necessity" argument is a very practical one; it relies on facts in the world, not abstract allocations of power. So the presence of state regulation is a fact in the world that ought to be taken into account. Consider the problem of proof argument again, but with CA's regulatory regime taken into account. The CA identification card goes a long way toward solving the problem of proof, doesn't it?

c. Reading the Tea Leaves

Two questions about the future of the Commerce Clause after *Raich*:

- **How much is left?**

    I think the doctrine's likely to stay where they left it in *Morrison* and *Lopez* – there's some limit, but not much, and it's not going to get any more restrictive in the future.

- **What are the new justices likely to do?**

    I'm skeptical that either Roberts or Alito cares that much about protecting states. There are three different reasons Conservatives care about federalism:

    → they actually love States as vital political communities

    → they want to reduce government power

    → they bridle at the idea that certain constitutional principles can simply be abandoned

    Justice O'Connor was a good example of (1), and probably agreed with (2) and (3) as well.

    But I don't think there's anybody like that left on the Court. We may occasionally see some support for (2)—particularly in the healthcare case, if it goes against the Government. But a lot of conservatives with a libertarian bent have figured out that leaving things to the States often results in *more* regulation rather than less. I do think all the conservatives on the Court believe in (3), but *Raich* is a good example of how that argument only gets you so far. It supports *Lopez*—that's why the SG needed a better answer to Justice O'Connor's question at argument—but not *real* serious restrictions on national power.

B. Congress's Power to Enforce the Reconstruction Amendments

These cases implicate not only the line between national and state power but also separation of powers concerns about the allocation of authority to interpret the

Constitution between Congress and the Courts (see Cooper v. Aaron *earlier in the course). It seems likely that SOP concerns drove the Court's analysis in* Boerne.

These cases deal with Congress's power to enforce the Reconstruction Amendments: No. 13 (abolishing slavery); No. 14 (requiring states to provide due process and equal protection, among other things); and No. 15 (barring racial discrimination in voting). We sometimes call the power to enforce these provisions the "Section Five" power, because we're usually talking about the power to enforce the 14th amendment rather than the other two. But it's important to remember that there are similar enforcement provisions attached to 13 and 15.

These powers are important for at least two reasons:

First, they confer power on Congress to act in at least some areas where there is no other enumerated power. For instance, in *City of Boerne*, the Government doesn't make much of an argument that the Religious Freedom Restoration Act can be supported under the Commerce Clause.

Second, the Section Five power is often thought to be *stronger* in some sense than the powers in Article I. For instance, Congress can't use its Commerce Power to override the sovereign immunity of the states from being sued for money damages. But it *can* use its Section Five power to override the States' immunity.

The reason usually given for this is that the Reconstruction Amendments – unlike other parts of the Constitution, which are generally directed at limiting either the Federal Government or *both* the Federal Government and the States – are specifically directed at limiting state sovereignty. And they come as the direct result of a bloody Civil War which is about, in many ways, limiting the sovereignty of the States.

The result is that we have a lot of situations in which both the Section Five power and some other power – usually Commerce – are potentially available when Congress wants to regulate something. In those cases, the issue usually isn't whether Congress can regulate *at all*, but rather whether it can use the stronger Section Five power rather than the Commerce Power. For instance, we have a bunch of cases – like *Florida Prepaid*, *Kimel*, and *Garrett* – where Congress wants to override state sovereign immunity from suit, and it can only do that if the federal statute involved can be justified under the Section Five power. When the government loses those cases, it doesn't mean that the statutes are unconstitutional – just that they have to be justified under the Commerce Clause instead. That has certain consequences, since the Commerce Power is in some sense a weaker power.

1.   Text and History

Each one of these amendments has a virtually identical provision at the end (it's § 5 in the 14th Amendment; § 2 in the other two) that provides: "The Congress shall have power to enforce, by appropriate legislation, the provisions of this article."

All of these amendments are proposed and ratified during Reconstruction – that's the part in Gone with the Wind when the mean Yankees come down and threaten to take over Tara. No. 13 is ratified in 1865, immediately at the close of the War. No. 14 follows in 1868, and No. 15 comes in 1870.

Two aspects of this history are important:

First, the Civil War and the Amendments that result from it are all about diminishing state sovereignty. Some people think that this means you should interpret the text more broadly than, say, the Art. I powers, which were a result of compromise between Federalists and Anti-Federalists.

The problem with this view is that the Reconstruction Amendments are also compromises, as the discussion of the drafting history in *City of Boerne* makes clear. And it's not clear how much the Reconstruction generation wanted to change the federal system overall, as opposed to simply giving the Federal Government broader responsibility for enforcing basic human rights.

Second, it is absolutely clear that the Reconstruction Congress that drafted these amendments had had it with the courts. It's true they enacted provisions in each of the Amendments, such as the Due Process and Equal Protection Clauses, that were *self-executing* in the sense that courts could enforce them directly by striking down state laws that violated them.

But it's equally clear that the Reconstruction Congress didn't count on this mechanism: The federal courts were the people that brought us *Dred Scott*. They viewed *themselves* as the branch of government that was actually going to make the aspirations for justice embodied in the amendments come true. That's why they give themselves a new enumerated power in each amendment to enforce its provisions. For example, the 14th Amendment was pretty clearly designed to give Congress the power to enact the 1868 Civil Rights Act, which tried to do a lot of the same things that the 1964 Act did a century later.

2.   *Katzenbach v. Morgan*, 384 U.S. 641 (1966), and the Voting Rights Act Cases

The key question in all these cases is the extent to which Congress's power to enforce the Reconstruction Amendment goes beyond simply doing by statute what a court might do by judicial decision. In *Morgan*, Congress has enacted a provision in the Voting Rights Act of 1965 that bans literacy tests aimed at Puerto Ricans. This is the leading case before *Boerne* on what the § 5 power means. To see the various possibilities, I want to start by distinguishing between Congress's power to *remedy* 14th amendment violations and Congress's power to *interpret* the 14th Amendment in the first place.

a.   Remedial Powers

Everyone agrees that Congress may devise remedies for racial discrimination and other constitutional violations that go further than what a court would ordinarily prescribe. For example:

- **Complex Remedies:** Courts generally just strike down the offending provision. Congress can prescribe much more intricate remedial mechanisms

  Example: The Voting Rights Act of 1965 is designed to enforce the 15th Amendment's ban on racial discrimination in voting. But the statute does much more than just say, "no racial discrimination in voting." Instead, § 5 of the Act has requirements designed to ensure that southern states can't set up their political systems in ways that will disadvantage racial minorities. For instance, whenever a southern jurisdiction wants to make a substantial change in its election procedures, it has to "pre-clear" that change with the Justice Department. This is very intrusive and complex; it's hard to see a court requiring it via an injunction. *See South Carolina v. Katzenbach*, 383 U.S. 301 (1966).

- **Preventive Remedies:** Ripeness doctrine generally prevents courts from acting in advance, but Congress may judge some actions necessary to prevent constitutional violations in the future.

  You see this in *Morgan* when the Court says that guaranteeing Puerto Ricans the right to *vote* is a way to prevent them from being unconstitutionally discriminated against in the future. *See also Oregon v. Mitchell*, 400 U.S. 112 (1970) (upholding the nationwide ban on literacy tests in the Voting Rights Act as reasonably necessary to prevent future use of such tests to discriminate).

b.   Interpretive Powers

The scope of Congress's interpretive powers are much more controversial. Two different theories in *Morgan*:

- **Factual:** Sometimes courts may be reluctant to find certain factual predicates to a constitutional violation, such as discriminatory intent. But *Congress* can find such facts and legislate against the constitutional violations they create.

  Ex: Literacy tests

  (What had the Court said about literacy tests in the past?)

It upheld them in the *Lassiter* case. The argument against literacy tests is that they have a disparate impact on racial minorities. The Court refuses to strike them down in *Lassiter*, however, because ordinarily it requires evidence of discriminatory intent before finding an equal protection violation.

(What difference should it make when Congress legislates?)

It might make a difference for the following reason: In some areas of constitutional law, the substantive doctrine is shaped by a view about the institutional competence of courts to do certain kinds of things and enforce certain kinds of rules. For instance, there is a rule that only *intentional* discrimination based on race is subject to strict scrutiny under the Equal Protection Clause; other kinds of government action that may have a *disparate impact* on racial minorities is *not* subject to strict scrutiny. *See Washington v. Davis*. A related rule is that you have to have pretty clean evidence of purposeful discrimination to get strict scrutiny.

Now, its probably true that lots of government policies that have a disparate impact on racial minorities are, in fact, motivated by discriminatory purpose or at least have the same sorts of irrationalities associated with them that motivate the general ban on purposeful discrimination. In that sense, those forms of disparate impact discrimination *ought* to be held unconstitutional. But we *don't* apply strict scrutiny because we doubt the institutional capacity of courts to either identify covert discriminatory purposes or separate the problematic types of disparate impacts from the unproblematic ones.

Professor Sager wrote a famous article in which he called this situation the "underenforcement" of constitutional norms. What it means is because of the practical limits on what courts can do and find out, we don't enforce certain constitutional principles – like equal protection – as far as might be justified in an ideal world.

Now one version of the Section Five power would say that just because institutional limits on *courts* keep them from enforcing equal protection all the way to the hilt, *Congress* shouldn't be bound by the same limits. Because it has investigative resources that the courts don't, Congress may be in a better position to make a judgment that some practices that have disparate impacts are, in fact, motivated by discriminatory purpose. Here, it's made that judgment about literacy tests. So it's not that Congress takes a different view of what the Constitution means from what the courts thought, but rather that Congress is able to apply the same legal rule to a different factual record than was available to the Court. The Court then defers to Congress's factual finding when the law banning literacy tests comes up for review.

- **Substantive:** Some language in *Morgan* suggests that when reasonable minds differ as to what the Constitution *itself* means, the Court should defer to Congress.

(Should we apply rational basis review to questions of law?)

Certainly some of these cases are cases in which reasonable minds could differ about the underlying law. Suppose we're not sure the equal protection clause should be limited to purposeful discrimination – certainly the text doesn't explicitly put that limit on it. We might think an interpretation by Congress that equal protection bars more than that would be plausible or reasonable.

(Should the Court defer?)

(What's Justice Harlan worried about if it does?)

He's worried that if we defer to Congress when it interprets rights more broadly, courts will also have to defer to Congress when it interprets rights more narrowly.

(What's Justice Brennan's answer?)

He says there's a "one-way ratchet" – Congress's power is only to broaden, not narrow.

(Do you agree?)

It seems like a brute force argument. There's no principled reason that would be true. And there are some logical problems:

- Sometimes rights trade off with one another;

- Rights trade off with other constitutional values, like federalism, SOP, and the rights of victims in criminal cases.

So in many cases you can't "err on the side of more rights" without restricting other constitutional values.

It's important to emphasize that *Morgan* can stand just on the *factual* deference ground, and that's generally how it's been interpreted. But more generally it stands for a pretty broad § 5 power. We come up on an important limit, however, in *Boerne*.

3.   *City of Boerne v. Flores*, 521 U.S. 507 (1997)

City of Boerne arises out of Congress's response to the Supreme Court's earlier decision in *Employment Division v. Smith*, 494 U.S. 872 (1990). Smith is a case about Free Exercise of Religion under the First

Amendment. Smith was penalized[36] for using drugs in violation of an Oregon statute that simply banned the use of all narcotics. Smith claimed that he was entitled to an exemption because the drug in question – a hallucinogen called peyote – was used as part of a religious ritual of the Native American Church.

The Court held that Smith was not entitled to an exemption. In particular, it rejected Smith's claim that because the Oregon statute burdened his free exercise of religion, it was subject to strict scrutiny. The Court said that strict scrutiny should apply only when the laws *discriminate against* or *single out* religious observance for unfavorable treatment. Here, the law was *generally applicable* – it applied to *all* narcotics, not just peyote, whether they were used for religious purposes or not.

Smith's holding was pretty broad and controversial. It would mean, for instance, that Catholics in a dry county would not necessarily be able to claim an exemption for sacramental wine. There are lots of laws that are generally applicable but happen to impose incidental burdens on religious exercise.

Congress decided that *Smith* had left too little protection for free exercise and proposed to put some of that protection back by statute. So it enacted the Religious Freedom Restoration Act of 1993 by huge bipartisan majorities§. As the Court points out, the purpose of the RFRA is to "restore the compelling interest test as set forth in [Sherbert]" – the case that *Smith* effectively overruled – "and to guarantee its application in all cases where free exercise of religion is substantially burdened."

In keeping with that purpose, the RFRA prohibits both the federal and state governments from "substantially burdening" a person's exercise of religion – even if the law in question is generally applicable – unless the law can pass strict scrutiny.

This case arises when the RFRA is applied to a land use dispute outside of San Antonio. (When you think about *Garcia*, *Lopez*, and *Boerne* – not to mention *Roe v. Wade* – you realize we could pretty much teach this course *only* using Texas cases.) A church wants to tear down its sanctuary and build a much larger one to meet the needs of its growing congregation. It applies for a building permit, which the City's zoning board denies on the ground that the church is a historical landmark and can't be altered.

---

[36] *Smith* did not involve a criminal prosecution; instead, Smith was denied unemployment benefits when he lost his job on the ground that he had lost the job for illegal conduct.

So the landmark law is a *generally applicable* law – it applies to religious and non-religious properties alike. But it happens in this case to burden the church's free exercise of religion by making it hard for the church to grow and use its facilities in the way that it wants.

(How would the rule of *Smith* apply to this case?)

The zoning rule would be subject only to rational basis review, since there's no evidence that the zoning rule is *singling out* the religious practice or discriminating against the church.

(What about the RFRA?)

RFRA would instead require strict scrutiny.

(What does that mean?)

The City would have to defend its landmark rule by showing that it was the least restrictive means of furthering a compelling governmental interest.

The Court (Kennedy, J.) holds that the RFRA exceeds the scope of Congress's power under Section Five.

One sidelight: This holding means that the RFRA is unconstitutional insofar as it regulates the activities of *state* governments. The RFRA also regulates the *federal* government, and to that extent it's simply a rule of federal self-restraint. You don't need an enumerated power for that, so the RFRA is still constitutional as applied to *federal* activities.

a.   Plenary vs. Remedial Authority

(What does Justice Kennedy mean when he says Congress has *remedial* rather than *plenary* authority?)

He means that Congress doesn't have any substantive power to define what the Constitution means, but it does have the power to *prevent or remedy* a constitutional violation. So, for instance, if we think segregated schools are unconstitutional, Congress can pass a law banning them.

This is a pretty substantial power: We've already discussed the Voting Rights Act cases, where legislative remedies go considerably beyond what a court itself might order. The obvious question is whether Congress can do anything that a *court* wouldn't do on its own, perhaps by issuing an injunction. The answer is "yes" in at least two ways: Congress can enact more preventive or complex remedies than a court could do.

What the Court *rejects* is the idea that Congress has some ability to interpret the Constitution in a way that *disagrees* with the Supreme Court. According to the Court, Congress may legislate under § 5 only if:

(1)   the legislation is designed to prevent or remedy an actual constitutional violation by a State government; and

(2)   the legislation is proportional, in terms of its scope and duration, to the constitutional violation identified.

There's a lot of disagreement about how this test should be applied; that gets played out in a series of cases afterwards that we cover in Federal Courts but not here.

In announcing this rule, the Court's worried about both federalism and separation of powers.

b.   The Federalism Problem

Remember that § 5 is basically a tool for regulating the states. That's because, under the *Civil Rights Cases*, it only extends to state action. But we need to consider, what is the *range* of state policy that § 5 would allow Congress to supersede.

Take a case like *Lee Optical*. Remember that the claim was twofold: The discrimination was irrational under both the DP clause and the EP clause.

Now suppose *Congress* can enforce those aspects of DP and/or EP.

(Is there any limit on state policies that Congress could preempt?)

I don't think there is, if the Court has to defer to Congress's view of what's irrational.

c.   The Separation of Powers Problem

The more fundamental point, though, is about SOP – hence all the somewhat pompous citations to *Marbury*. This is a fundamental debate about who has the final authority to interpret the Constitution. Is Congress final? Or the Court?

A bit of review: We talked about 3 positions in *Cooper v. Aaron*.

- **Legislative Supremacy:** Congress could *always* have the last word, but this seems to have been ruled out in *Marbury*.

- **Judicial Supremacy:** In *Cooper v. Aaron*, 358 U.S. 1 (1958), the Court unanimously announced "the basic principle that the federal judiciary is supreme in the exposition of the law of the Constitution," and "[i]t follows that the interpretation of the Fourteenth Amendment enunciated by this Court in the *Brown* case is the supreme law of the land."

- **Departmentalism:** Consider, for instance, President Andrew Jackson's veto of the bill to recharter the Bank of the U.S. Jackson thought the Bank was unconstitutional, but people argued that he couldn't veto the bill on that ground because the Court had upheld the Bank in *McCulloch*.

(Let's go back to a question we played around with earlier when we did *Cooper v. Aaron*: If we accept departmentalism, does that mean that in a case like *Boerne*, the Court should accept Congress's judgment on the meaning of the Free Exercise Clause?)

I think these cases show how the distinction between judicial supremacy and departmentalism can ultimately collapse. The point is that once somebody sues in *Boerne*, the Court has to exercise *its* judgment to do *its* job. This doesn't mean that departmentalism doesn't work great most of the time.

d.   Prophylactic Remedies

There is one very important qualification on the principle that the Court has that last word, which is that the Court leaves the door open for "prophylactic remedies." This idea corresponds pretty well to the principle of *factual* deference in *Morgan*.

Congress finds that *most* literacy tests are motivated by racial bias and the desire to exclude minority voters. This isn't *always* the case: If some county up in Maine that hasn't seen a black person for years enacts a literacy test for elections, there's probably not a racial motive.

What we mean by prophylactic remedies is that Congress is allowed to be somewhat overinclusive when it legislates to enforce rights. So if it finds that 95% of literacy tests are motivated by an unconstitutional purpose, it can ban them *all* in order to avoid the expense and effort – and risk of error – that would be involved if we tried to identify the motive in each case. In other words, a statute enforcing the constitution is allowed to sweep a little more broadly than the Constitution itself, just to be sure of catching all the unconstitutional state conduct.

What's harder is to determine *how much further*. Take a case called *Trustees of the Univ. of Alabama v. Garrett*, 531 U.S. 356 (2001), in which the Court held that provisions of the Americans with Disabilities Act barring discrimination against the disabled were not valid Section 5 legislation. The disabled are not a suspect class; that means that that only truly irrational discrimination against them is unconstitutional. Most gov't discrimination against the disabled will survive rational basis review. But the statute barred basically *all* discrimination against them. So the statute swept a *lot* more broadly than the Constitution did.

This comparison is what the "congruence and proportionality" test is all about. Does the statute prohibit a lot more state conduct than the constitution itself? Or does it just sweep a little more broadly for prophylactic reasons?

The Court's later cases suggest that the Section 5 power is a lot easier to use in areas where the state action in question is subject to some form of heightened scrutiny. If a statute bans a form of discrimination – e.g., against the disabled in *Garrett* – and the Constitution itself only subjects it to rational basis review, the statute will not be congruent and proportional. You're much more likely to satisfy that test if the Constitution imposes a higher degree of scrutiny, such as for gender discrimination. Recently, the Court has upheld several Section 5 statutes that implicated a higher degree of scrutiny.[37]

e. Loose Ends

The Legislative Record: There's a lot of talk about the legislative record in *Boerne*. Some think this is like the findings requirement in *Lopez*. I think that's wrong. A record just helps the court figure out the proportionality inquiry.

The Structure of the Statute: Finally, there's some stuff about the statute's geographic and time limitations. These are just factors that demonstrate Congress isn't trying to legislate more broadly than is necessary to reach actually unconstitutional conduct.

Aftermath of *Boerne*: So what happened to the RFRA? Two things:

- It remains applicable to *federal* action. The national government doesn't need an enumerated power to regulate *itself*. There's a constitutional argument against RFRA as it applies to the Feds, but it's under the Establishment Clause, and the Court has unanimously rejected it.[38]

- Congress tried to re-enact RFRA in a way that would satisfy *Boerne*— by relying on the Commerce Clause in some areas, the Spending Clause in others, making better findings, etc. But the political coalition fell apart. In the end, all that could get through was protection for churches from zoning laws and protection for prison inmates (not usually an incredibly powerful lobby). That's the Religious Land Use and Institutionalized Persons Act (RLUIPA), which relies on commerce for zoning and spending for prisons.

3. *United States v. Morrison*, 529 U.S. 598 (2000)

You have a little bit in the notes about *U.S. v. Morrison*—the VAWA case—which also had a section 5 component. Recall that the VAWA

---

[37] *See, e.g., Nevada Dept. of Human Resources v. Hibbs*, 538 U.S. 721 (2003) (upholding provisions of the Family Medical Leave Act, which were designed to prevent or remedy gender discrimination); *Tennessee v. Lane*, 541 U.S. 509 (2004) (upholding provisions of the Americans with Disabilities Act insofar as they protected disabled persons' access to courts, which is a fundamental right).§

[38] *See Gonzales v. O Centro Espirita Beneficente Uniao do Vegetal*, 546 U.S. 418 (2006).

provided women who had been the victims of gender-motivated violence with a federal right to bring civil suit against their attackers in federal court. The *Morrison* court held that this exceeded the Section 5 power because the defendants in such suits are not state actors. In this sense, *Morrison* was a re-run of the *Civil Rights Cases*.

(Is that the only way to think about the Section 5 issue? Is there no relevant state action in *Morrison*?)

What about Virginia Tech University—a state school—that didn't adequately pursue penalties against Christy Brzonkala's attackers? What about the State of Virginia itself, which like nearly all states arguably doesn't do enough to ensure that rape and spousal abuse cases are given a high priority?

The argument would be that by not adequately pursuing and punishing the perpetrators of gender-motivated violence, the States are not providing women with "the equal protection of the laws." That seems like a more sound argument, but the Court didn't really address it.

The problem with that sort of argument, though, is that it relies on a wide range of state activities—the discretionary decisions of juries, judges, and prosecutors, the presence of outdated laws on the books, like spousal privilege rules, that protect perpetrators of violence against women, etc. Some of these things may be unconstitutional, and some may not. The main point is that it's easier to apply *Boerne*'s analysis to a discrete and specific constitutional violation rather than to these sorts of general inequitable tendencies in the enforcement of the law.

4. The Section 5 Power vs. the Commerce Clause

Finally, I want to emphasize that most things Congress might regulate under the Section 5 power, it could also regulate under the Commerce Power. That raises the question whether there's anything "wrong" with relying on commerce. Consider the 1964 Civil Rights Act, which banned private discrimination in employment and public accommodations. Congress couldn't use the Section 5 power because of the *Civil Rights Cases*, but by 1964 the Commerce Power was a lot broader than in the 1880s, so Congress *could* rely on that.

(Some people thought that reducing these basic issues of racial justice to "commerce" somehow cheapened what Congress was trying to do. What do you think?)

I don't agree at all. Consider the two critical cases, which I cite in the Notes: *Heart of Atlanta Motel, Inc. v. United States*, 379 U.S. 241 (1964), upheld title II of the 1964 Act as applied to accommodations at a hotel in, well, the heart of Atlanta, GA. And *Katzenbach v. Mcclung*, 379 U.S. 294

(1964), upheld the same provisions as applied to Ollie's Barbecue in Birmingham, AL.

Now, put aside that the latter case involves one of the most fundamental American liberties – the right to barbecue. These cases were supposedly hard under the Commerce Clause because they involved small transactions in the middle of their states. But Congress had heard volumes' worth of testimony that black people basically couldn't travel interstate because they couldn't stop to eat at a restaurant or stay overnight in a hotel. I think the testimony really brought home two things:

- Segregation was a massive impediment to interstate commerce; and

- Excluding a whole race of people from the ordinary economic life of the nation is actually one of the most oppressive things you can do.

That's why I think the Commerce Power is an extremely appropriate vehicle for a civil rights statute. These cases show that economic integration and economic equality are terribly important forms of civil rights, and in a capitalist society they may be the foundation or at least the entry point for everything else.

C. The Spending Power

These cases raise two issues that transcend the Spending Power itself. The first is Congress's ability to use conditional spending as an end-run around other limits on its authority. It could, for instance, overcome Lopez by conditioning federal education funds on each state banning guns in schools. Does the Court need to tighten the spending power constraints in order to protect its other federalism rulings? The second is the "unconstitutional conditions" doctrine, which is a pervasive problem in constitutional law—especially on the individual rights side. No one has yet come up with a satisfactory resolution to the unconstitutional conditions conundrum—a fact that should lower expectations about the Court's willingness to try and constrain the spending power.

The last congressional power we'll consider is the Spending Power. The Court has construed that power very broadly. That creates a risk that Congress can end-run other limits on its power by throwing its financial weight around.

1. Textual Basis

It's worth noting that there's some disagreement about the proper source of the spending power.

a. The Taxing and Spending Clause:

Art. I, § 8, cl. 1: "The Congress shall have Power To lay and collect Taxes, Duties, Imposts and Excises, to pay the Debts and provide for the common

Defence and general Welfare of the United States; but all Duties, Imposts and Excises shall be uniform throughout the United States."

b.   The Property Clause:

Art. IV, § 3, cl. 2: "The Congress shall have Power to dispose of and make all needful Rules and Regulations respecting the Territory or other Property belonging to the United States; and nothing in this Constitution shall be so construed as to Prejudice any Claims of the United States, or of any particular State."

It's not clear why the source would make any difference. If it's the Art. I, § 8 provision, then you've got the "general welfare" requirement as a limit on the scope of spending, but that hasn't ever been interpreted as much of a limit, anyway. Just don't be shocked if you see the Property Clause cited as a basis for the spending power sometimes.

2.   Hamilton and Madison on the Spending Power

In the early Republic, Madison and Hamilton squared off over the proper interpretation of the spending power.§

Madison: Madison's view was that the Spending Clause "amounted to no more than a reference to the other powers enumerated in the subsequent clauses of the same section; that, as the United States is a government of limited and enumerated powers, the grant of power to tax and spend for the general national welfare must be confined to the enumerated legislative fields committed to the Congress." *United States v. Butler*, 297 U.S. 1, 65 (1936).

In other words, Congress can use the enumerated means -- spending -- only for enumerated ends.

Hamilton: Hamilton maintained that "the power of Congress to authorize expenditure of public moneys for public purposes is not limited by the direct grants of legislative power found in the Constitution"; rather, "its confines are set in the clause which confers it. . . ." Alexander Hamilton, Report on Manufactures to the House of Representatives, 3 Works of Alexander Hamilton 372 (Lodge ed. 1885).

In other words, the only limit on the purposes for which Congress may spend money are that they have to implicate the common defense or the general welfare.

Implications of the Hamiltonian View: It is Hamilton that gives us the general relation between ends and means that we talked about earlier:

- **Principle of Unenumerated Means:** When Congress legislates in furtherance of an enumerated end -- *i.e.*, regulation of interstate commerce -- it may use any necessary and proper means.

- **Principle of Unenumerated Ends:** When Congress employs and enumerated *power*, it may do so for any purpose whether or not it is an enumerated end.

In other words, as long as *either* the goal that Congress is pursuing or the *means* Congress is using is specifically set forth in the Constitution, the law will be constitutional. (This is subject, as always, to the proviso that no *affirmative* constitutional limitation is implicated.)

Don't forget the two corollaries.

- **Corollary #1:** Congress's necessary and proper authority doesn't extend to unenumerated ends. In other words, if the goal isn't in the Constitution, Congress is stuck with the limited means that the Constitution explicitly gives it.

- **Corollary #2:** Unenumerated *ends* do not themselves have the force of federal *law* -- i.e., they have no preemptive effect. States are free to legislate in pursuit of contradictory goals.

  For instance, Congress can bar interstate shipments of lottery tickets because it thinks lotteries are immoral, but it can't keep a state from holding a lottery.

And note one additional point: Some things are both means and ends. Example: Regulation of Interstate Commerce. Sometimes Congress has a commercial purpose; other times, Congress uses regulation of commerce to reach some other goal.

3. *South Dakota v. Dole*, 483 U.S. 203 (1987)

Congress conditioned 5% of federal highway grants on states' raising their drinking age to 21. South Dakota's drinking age, as to some forms of beer, was 19. The State sued in federal court for a declaratory judgment that the statute exceeded the spending power and violated the Twenty-First Amendment. The District Court rejected these claims, and CA8 affirmed.

The Court holds (Rehnquist, CJ), that the condition is constitutional.

(Why isn't this just an easy case under the Commerce Clause? Couldn't Congress just mandate a national drinking age if it wanted to?)

No. The Twenty-First Amendment repeals the Eighteenth Amendment (empowering Congress to enforce Prohibition) and provides that "[t]he transportation or importation into any State, Territory, or possession of the United States for delivery or use therein of intoxicating liquors, in violation of the laws thereof, is hereby prohibited."

This has been construed to grant the States "virtually complete control over whether to permit importation or sale of liquor and how to structure the liquor distribution system."

The Court assumes in *South Dakota v. Dole* -- without deciding the issue -- that Congress could *not* impose a national drinking age directly. So the question is whether Congress can do it *indirectly* through conditions on federal highway funds.

The Court reaffirms the Hamiltonian view that spending power is not limited by Art. I's direct grants of legislative power.

(*Are* there any limits on the spending power?)

Federal spending is constitutional if it:

(1)   is in pursuit of the general welfare;

(2)   conditions are stated unambiguously;

(3)   is related to the federal interest in particular national projects or programs; and

(4)   does not violate any other constitutional provisions.

(How meaningful is the first prong of this?)

Not very; the Court says that in evaluating the public purpose of spending, the Court should defer to Congress's judgment.

The second prong is important – it's effectively a clear statement rule. The States aren't bound by conditions unless they're clearly stated. The idea here is one of contract – you want to know there was a meeting of the minds on the terms of the deal. *See Pennhurst State School & Hospital v. Halderman,* 451 U.S. 1 (1981).

The rule has also been justified as a way of making sure that there is a *political* check on federal power to impose conditions. By requiring Congress to speak clearly, we make sure that the States' own representatives there have actually considered and deliberately chosen to impose the condition.

The Court says there's no problem here with (1) or (2).

(What about the third prong?)

This is the familiar sort of means/ends scrutiny that we've seen in other contexts. The big question, of course, is how close the relationship has to be. Here, the Court says that the state has never argued (3), and the cases don't say how germane spending has to be. But it is clear that the relationship between highway safety and underage drinking is close enough.

(What does the Court mean by the fourth requirement – the independent constitutional bar?)

The "independent constitutional bar" limit "is not . . . a prohibition on the indirect achievement of objectives which Congress is not empowered to achieve directly." It means simply that the spending power "may not be used to induce the States to engage in activities that would themselves be unconstitutional."

Those are the four prongs of the test that they list when they say, "This is the test." But later in the opinion it sounds like there's a fifth issue: It is possible that spending may be unconstitutional if it is unduly coercive, but that is not true here. This is only 5% of highway funds.

(Does Justice O'Connor disagree with the legal rules for conditional spending as stated by the majority?)

No. The Court basically gets the law right: Congress's spending is not limited to the Art. I powers, and the four-part test is correct.

(So what's the problem?)

But the Court misapplies the germaneness requirement. A minimum drinking age is both over- and under-inclusive with respect to highway safety. Teenagers are only a small part of the drunken driving problem, and the drinking age applies far beyond driving.

(How does Justice O'Connor define the appropriate germaneness limits on a spending condition?)

Congress is limited to putting conditions on the actual use of the highway funds at issue. "Congress has no power under the Spending Clause to impose requirements on a grant that go beyond specifying how the money should be spent."

Despite what Justice O'Connor says, this *is* a fairly significant disagreement about the nature of the relevant legal rules.

(Why do we need a stricter limit?)

If the Spending Clause is limited only by Congress's notion of the general welfare, Congress can subvert the States entirely.

(Why do you think Justice Brennan joined Justice O'Connor's dissent? I'll give you a hint – it isn't because he gives a flip about federalism.)

Because he cares a lot about the doctrine of unconstitutional conditions in *individual rights* cases. And he understands that those cases are structurally similar to this one.§

4.   **Unconstitutional Conditions as a Limit on the Spending Power**

South Dakota v. Dole is our introduction to the unconstitutional conditions doctrine, which holds that the Constitution limits the Government's ability to condition a benefit on the relinquishment of a constitutional right. The classic example is *McAuliffe v. Mayor of New Bedford*, (1892), where they restrict the free speech rights of police officers. Justice Holmes says, you "may have a constitutional right to talk politics, but [you have] no constitutional rights to be a policeman."

Here, the States are being asked to relinquish their authority to set the drinking age (a constitutional state right under the 21st Amendment) in exchange for federal money. But the unconstitutional conditions doctrine is most frequently seen in situations where people are being asked to give up *individual* rights in order to get something from the government:

- denial of family planning funds to people seeking abortions;

- denial of federal money to people or groups engaging in certain forms of expression -- for instance, denial of grants from the National Endowment for the Arts to artists whose work is arguably indecent;

- conditioning development permits on landowners' agreement to use their land in ways that the Taking Clause would bar the Government from requiring directly.

It's all these individual rights applications that have Justice Brennan worried. Similarly, it's probably these cases that Justice Rehnquist is thinking about when he votes against the states in *Dole*. He knows that if he recognizes an unconstitutional conditions doctrine for states, it will be that much harder to deny it in individual rights cases.

You can approach the unconstitutional conditions idea in a number of ways:

- Clear Statement: No substantive limit, but any condition must be stated clearly.

- Germaneness: The condition must be tied somehow to the purpose of the funds.

Germaneness is not necessarily inconsistent with the principle of unenumerated ends. It just requires that the condition be related to the enumerated *means*, *i.e.*, the federal spending requirement itself.

One advantage of germaneness is that is helps a State to make a rational decision about whether to accept the grant. Such decisions would be skewed if, for example, highway funds were tied to completely unrelated areas, such as abortion laws.

A difficulty, however, is that what is germane may be pretty subjective.

- **Coercion:** The Chief suggests there may be a coercion limit, but doesn't elaborate what it is. This seems even more subjective than germaneness.

There are others, but they all have their problems. It's probably fair to say that unconstitutional conditions is one of the most messed up parts of constitutional law.

5.   The Next Big Battleground?

The excerpts from Prof. Baker's article are intended to give you a sense of just how important these conditional spending questions are. As she points out, decisions like *Lopez* and *Printz* may be relatively meaningless if Congress can always evade any limitations on its power through the conditional spending tool.

For example, Prof. Baker notes that right after *Lopez* was decided, President Clinton proposed to avoid the impact of the decision by structuring the next federal guns in schools law as a condition on the grant of federal funds.

This means that the next important round of federalism cases may come in the conditional spending area. I'm skeptical, though, that the current court will do much to tighten up the rules. The unconstitutional conditions problem is highly intractable.

Professor Baker proposes a two step analysis:

a) Presume that conditions on spending are unconstitutional, *unless*

b) The Government can rebut the presumption by showing that the spending is simply "reimbursement spending."

She illustrates with a hypothetical on p. ___:

A. Federal "safe school funds" are conditioned on enacting a gun free school zones act, and limited to the amount of prosecuting offenders under that act.

B. Any state getting *education* funds generally must have a gun free school zones act; the funds are simply $100 per student.

(Are either of these constitutional under Baker's approach?)

Sure. The first one is pure reimbursement spending, the second is not. The point of the test is to keep the Government from leveraging money it's spending on some general need into state compliance with some particular goal. The idea is to rein in "regulatory spending."

III.   Chapter Eleven – External Limits on National Power

By external limits, I mean limits on national power that do not stem from the terms of the Constitution's enumerated power grants themselves. The National League of Cities *doctrine, considered earlier, would be an example. This chapter considers the anti-commandeering doctrine and the various pro-federalism "clear statement" rules of statutory construction. The anti-commandeering doctrine (especially* Printz) *lends itself to a discussion of the various sources of constitutional meaning, as well as the contrast between rule-like and standard-*

like constitutional doctrines. The clear statement cases, on the other hand, serve as an excellent introduction to general issues of statutory construction, especially the problem of canons of construction.

We shift now from talking about the extent of the national government's powers and the internal limits on those powers to *external* limits on national power. By that we mean situations in which a particular policy or program may fall within one of Congress's enumerated powers, but that power is nonetheless limited by some external principle of federalism. We've already encountered one such limit—the *National League of Cities* principle that Congress can't regulate state governmental institutions performing traditional governmental functions.

Two more external limits here:

- clear statement rules

- the anti-commandeering doctrine

One thing you should be asking yourself as we work through this material is whether these external limits are a more promising approach to limiting national power than, say, simply construing the Commerce Clause more narrowly.

A.   Clear Statement Rules

Clear statement rules are principles of statutory construction—that is, rules for construing what Congress *has done*, not hard constitutional limits on what Congress *can do*. For that reason, lots of people don't even consider these rules to be part of constitutional law at all. I think they are a crucial part, for reasons we'll discuss in a few minutes. First, we need to talk a bit about statutory construction in a more general way.

1.   An Introduction to Statutory Construction

Agency Theory: The dominant paradigm of American statutory construction is that judges are to be "faithful agents" of the Congress that enacted the statute.

The Basic Problem: Statutes are inevitably ambiguous. Human language is limited in its ability to convey determinate meanings; legislative foresight is limited in its ability to anticipate cases that may arise; political supporters of a statute may not be able to agree on all conceivable applications and hence "fudge" on those questions.

Consider, for instance, a famous example from the British jurisprude H.L.A. Hart: A local ordinance says "No vehicles in the park." That probably has *some* clear applications – you can't drive your Humvee through the park. But what about tricycles? Or suppose you think it means no *motorized* vehicles: What about a truck or a tank that's incorporated as part of a war memorial?

You can see how cases will always find some ambiguity in the statutory text.

A Solution—Default Rules or "Canons" of Statutory Construction: Some examples:

- Expressio Unius est Exclusio Alterius: "Inclusion of one thing indicates exclusion of the other."

- Avoid Surplusage: Every word in the statute should be construed so as not to be superfluous.

- Repeals by Implication are Disfavored: Statuts should be read, where possible, to be consistent with prior law.

- The Rule of Lenity: Penal statutes should be narrowly construed.

Two Kinds of Canons

- Descriptive: Rules of thumb meant to approximate the most likely intent of the legislature in the unprovided-for case.

    Ex: You should read every word in the statute to have some meaning and avoid surplusage.

- Normative: Default rules designed (usually by courts) to promote certain values whether the legislature cared about them or not.

    Ex: Rule of lenity.

Two important rules that are relevant to these cases:

The Canon of Constitutional Avoidance: "Where an otherwise acceptable construction of a statute would raise serious constitutional problems, the Court will construe the statute to avoid such problems unless such construction is plainly contrary to the intent of Congress." *Edward J. DeBartolo Corp. v. Florida Gulf Coast Bldg. & Constr. Trades Council*, 485 U.S. 568, 575 (1988).

The *Chevron* Doctrine: Courts must defer to reasonable constructions of an ambiguous statute by the agency that administers the statute. *Chevron U.S.A. Inc. v. NRDC*, 467 U.S. 837 (1984).

Two Step Analysis

    Step 1: Is the statutory language ambiguous?

    Step 2: Is the agency's construction reasonable?

Justifications

- The agency has expertise concerning the subject matter and intent of the statute.

- Ambiguous language may signal a delegation of lawmaking authority by Congress to the agency.

- The agency is more democratically accountable than unelected judges.

Chevron has gotten a *lot* more confident than this, but this is enough introduction for our purposes.

2.   Federalism "Clear Statement" Rules

I've given you three cases as examples of the "clear statement" principle at work in federalism cases: *Jones*, *Gregory*, and *Solid Waste*.

a.   *Jones v. United States*, 529 U.S. 848 (2000)

It is a federal crime to damage or destroy "by means of fire or an explosive, any . . . property used in interstate or foreign commerce or in any activity affecting interstate or foreign commerce." 18 U.S.C. § 844(i). Mr. Jones tossed a Molotov cocktail through the window of his cousin's home in Fort Wayne, IN. The Court holds that the statute does not cover arson of a private residence.

(What's the ambiguity in the statutory text that the Court has to wrestle with?)

Whether a private residence is property "used in interstate or foreign commerce or in any activity affecting interstate or foreign commerce."

This language is a good example of a jurisdictional element.

(Is it enough under the statute that arson "affects" interstate commerce?)

No – the statutory language is narrower than that. It has to be "used in . . . any activity affecting . . . commerce."

(What's the Government's argument that this property is covered?)

They have three:

- The residence was used to obtain a mortgage from an OK lender;

- The residence was used to obtain a fire insurance policy from a WI insurer; and

- The residence was used to obtain natural gas from outside IN.

(Let's take the last one first: What would *not* be reachable under this argument?)

Only buildings not connected to the electric, gas, phone, and cable grids.

(What about the first two: Does anything with respect to the crime turn on the mortgage or insurance coming from out of state?)

I don't think so. The point is it was used to obtain a mortgage, and mortgage lending is an activity affecting interstate commerce.

You see the point, right? The Government's reading of the statute would cover *all* arson.

(Let's put the actual language of the statute aside for a moment. Would it be unconstitutional to write an arson statute that covered private residences?)

Maybe not. Constructing buildings is a commercial activity, and protecting those buildings from fire is arguably a regulation designed to protect that activity. It's at least not clear that's unconstitutional. I do think it's a stretch.

Perhaps the stronger argument would be that regulating arson is necessary and proper to regulating the mortgate market (we've seen the "substantial effects" of that market lately), the insurance market, or the interstate power and communications grids. Again, that seems thin to me, but not inconceivable.

(If we *don't* think a *general* federal arson statute would be unconstitutional, can the Court's approach here be justified?)

I think so – the point is that, within the broad constitutional bounds, the clear statement rule protects the states by erring on the side of construing what Congress has actually done narrowly.

The justification for this would be based in part on the idea that the Commerce Clause limit is *under-enforced*.

(Is the clear statement rule a normative or a descriptive canon?)

You can argue either way, but I think it's best described as normative.

b.   *Gregory v. Ashcroft*, 501 U.S. 452 (1991)

Article V, § 26 of the Missouri Constitution provides that "[a]ll judges other than municipal judges shall retire at the age of seventy years." This case is about two state judges in Missouri who want to challenge the MO state constitution's mandatory retirement provision, which requires most judges to retire at 70. (By way of comparison, Justice Holmes served on the U.S. Supremes until he was 91!) They argue that the MO provision violates the ADEA.

A group of Missouri state judges brought suit alleging that sec. 26's mandatory retirement provision violated the Age Discrimination in Employment Act (ADEA) and the Equal Protection Clause. The ADEA makes it unlawful for an "employer" "to discharge any individual" who is at least 40 years old "because of such individual's age." 29 U. S. C. §§ 623(a), 631(a). The term "employer" is defined to include "a State or political subdivision of a State." § 630(b)(2).

The ADEA says, however, that "the term 'employee' shall not include any person elected to public office in any State or political subdivision of any State by the qualified voters thereof, or any person chosen by such officer to be on such officer's personal staff, or an appointee on the policymaking level or an immediate adviser with respect to the exercise of the constitutional or legal powers of the office." 29 U. S. C. § 630(f).

The district court granted the State's motion to dismiss, finding that the judges were "appointees . . . on a policymaking level" and therefore within an exception to the ADEA.[39]

The Court holds (O'Connor, J) that the ADEA doesn't cover judges, because they are policymaking level appointees.

(Is the Court applying the ordinary rules of statutory construction here?)

No – the Court creates a special rule of statutory construction. Congress's intent to cover state judges must be "unmistakably clear in the language of the statute."[40]

(What's the basis for this plain statement rule?)

The Court relies in part on the canon of statutory construction that statutes should be construed to avoid a constitutional difficulty.

(What would the constitutional objection to this statute be?)

It's *National League of Cities*, right? But I thought that was overruled. Maybe the Court is suggesting that whether *Garcia* should be overruled is a "problem" to be avoided. (Remember, Justice O'Connor promised to revisit the issue when she had the votes.) But here the Court acknowledges that *Garcia* constrains the Court's ability "to consider the limits that the state-federal balance places on Congress' powers under the Commerce Clause."

The clear statement rule seems instead grounded in a concern for state sovereignty straight up. Missouri's constitutional provision establishing qualifications for state judges "is a decision of the most fundamental sort for a sovereign entity." Congressional interference "would upset the usual constitutional balance of federal and state powers."

---

[39] The judges might also be exempt as elected officials. Missouri state judges are appointed by the governor, then retained in office by means of unopposed retention elections which are subject only to a "yes" or "no" vote. The Supreme Court doesn't reach this question.

[40] Quoting *Atascadero State Hospital v. Scanlon*, 473 U.S. 234, 242 (1985); *Will v. Michigan Dept. of State police*, 491 U.S. 58, 65 (1989).

The Court replaces the *National League of Cities* test for unconstitutionality with a presumptive rule of statutory construction: Where Congress legislates in a way that arguably alters the federal/state balance, Congress's intent must be "unmistakably clear in the language of the statute."

(Is there any textual basis for the rule?)

The Court invokes the 10th Amendment. This case involves "a power reserved to the States under the Tenth Amendment and guaranteed them by that provision of the Constitution under which the United States `guarantee[s] to every State in this Union a Republican Form of Government."

(What about *Garcia*'s rejection of the 10th Amendment?)

In fact, *Garcia* actually *supports* this process-based approach:

More importantly, "inasmuch as this Court in *Garcia* has left primarily to the political process the protection of the States against intrusive exercises of Congress' Commerce Clause powers, we must be absolutely certain that Congress intended such an exercise."

(Is it any easier to figure out when *Gregory's* rule should apply than it was to apply *National League of Cities*?)

Maybe not. But since Congress can always override a statutory construction result, maybe that's not so much of a problem.

(Can we justify this is if we assume *Garcia* is good law?)

I think so. The Court says, "inasmuch as this Court in *Garcia* has left primarily to the political process the protection of the States against intrusive exercises of Congress' *Commerce Clause* powers, we must be absolutely certain that Congress intended such an exercise. 'To give the state-displacing weight of federal law to mere congressional *ambiguity* would evade the very procedure for lawmaking on which *Garcia* relied to protect states' interests.'"

(How does the clear statement rule protect the process values emphasized in *Garcia*?)

Two ways:

- It gives notice to political defenders of state prerogatives; and

- It adds yet another hoop to the difficult federal lawmaking procedures.

> c.   ***Solid Waste Auth. of Northern Cook Cty. v. U.S. Army Corps of Engineers*, 531 U.S. 159 (2001)**

The Statute: Section 404(a) of the Clean Water Act , 33 U.S.C. § 1344(a), regulates the discharge of dredged or fill material into "navigable waters."

The term "navigable waters" is defined as "the waters of the United States, including the territorial seas." § 1362(7).

Corps Definition of Waters of the U.S.: Corps regulations define these waters to include ""waters such as intrastate lakes, rivers, streams (including intermittent streams), mudflats, sandflats, wetlands, sloughs, prairie potholes, wet meadows, playa lakes, or natural ponds, the use, degradation or destruction of which could affect interstate or foreign commerce . . . ." 33 CFR § 328.3(a)(3).

The Migratory Bird Rule: Subsequent regulations clarify that "waters of the U.S." extends to all waters

> "a. Which are or would be used as habitat by birds protected by Migratory Bird Treaties; or
>
> "b. Which are or would be used as habitat by other migratory birds which cross state lines; or
>
> "c. Which are or would be used as habitat for endangered species; or
>
> "d. Used to irrigate crops sold in interstate commerce." *51 Fed. Reg. 41217.*

(What would a court ordinarily do with a regulation like this?)

Defer under *Chevron.*

The Clear Statement Rule: The Court refuses to defer to the Corps under *Chevron* because the regulation is at or near the limits of Congress's commerce power.

(Do you think the Migratory Bird Rule is really unconstitutional?)

(Why is it important not to defer here?)

3.   Other Federalism Clear Statement Rules

* **Presumption Against Preemption:** Congress must clearly state its intent to preempt state law, especially in areas of traditional state regulation.

* **Conditional Spending:** Conditions on grants of federal monies to the States must be clearly stated.

* **Use of Section Five Power:** Congress must clearly state its intent to proceed under Section Five of the Fourteenth Amendment rather than under the Commerce Clause. (This is at the end of *Gregory.*)

(What do you think? Is this a good way for courts to protect federalism?)

I think it is, for three reasons:

- We've already seen that the Commerce Clause is going to be construed very, very broadly. This means that state and national power are almost always **concurrent**. In that sort of world, the real boundary between state and national authority is going to be set by the terms of federal statutes; the question is how much of the field Congress actually has chosen to occupy—not how much it *could* occupy if it wanted to. This is part of the "constitution outside the constitution" idea—statutes set the "constitutional" boundary, and so it's important to take constitutional values into account when construing those boundaries.

- As a practical matter, default rules of statutory construction matter a great deal. There are lots of ambiguous statutes, and default rules tell courts which side to err upon in cases of ambiguity. So it turns out that, by applying clear statement rules designed to protect federalism, courts can actually make a fair amount of progress in limiting national power.

- Statutory construction rules are also well-suited to judicial enforcement because they're ultimately defeasible by Congress.

B.   The Anti-Commandeering Doctrine

The "anti-commandeering" principle limits Congress's ability to require State governments to participate in federal regulatory programs.

One important question is, "Where does the anti-commandeering principle come from?"

Note Justice Stevens' statement in *Printz* that "[t]here is not a clause, sentence, or paragraph in the entire text of the Constitution" that supports such a principle.

As in *McCulloch*, it's important to pay attention to the *kinds* of constitutional argument going on in these cases.

1.   *New York v. United States*, 505 U.S. 144 (1992)

The Low-Level Radioactive Waste Policy Amendments Act of 1985 makes each State responsible, in cooperation with other States, for disposal of low-level radioactive waste generated within the State. The States are authorized to enter into interstate compacts to provide for regional disposal facilities.

The Act creates three types of incentives:

(a)   *Monetary incentives:* One quarter of the surcharges collected by sited states are transferred to an escrow account held by the Secretary of Energy, then distributed to each State that complies with a series of deadlines toward developing a disposal plan and joining a sited compact, etc.

(b)   *Access incentives:* States failing to meet deadlines can be charged double surcharges for a brief period, then denied access to disposal facilities thereafter.

(c)   *The Take Title requirement:* States failing to provide for waste generated within the State by 1996 must, upon request of a waste generator, take title to and possession of the waste, and are liable for all damages directly or indirectly incurred by the generator or owner as a result of the State's failure to take possession.

Within 7 years of passage, 42 states joined nine regional compacts. The six unsited compacts and four of the unaffiliated states met the first three statutory deadlines.

New York failed to join a regional compact, and had trouble siting a disposal facility in the State. It sued for a declaratory judgment that the Act violated the Tenth Amendments, the Due Process Clause of the Fifth Amendment, and the Guarantee Clause.

The Court (O'Connor, J.) holds that the monetary and access incentives are OK, but the take title provision is unconstitutional.

a.   The Basic Principle

(What does the Court mean by "commandeering the legislative processes of the States"?)

The Court says that "Congress may not simply 'commandee[r] the legislative processes of the States by directly compelling them to enact and enforce a federal regulatory program."

(Why not?)

The critical shift in moving from the Articles of Confederation to the Federal Constitution was from a government that acted on the States to a government that acted on the people directly.

(How did the Articles work?)

If Congress wanted to make policy, it had to request that the States act to pass and enforce the relevant laws.

It's very clear that the federal Constitution wanted the national government to be able to act on individuals directly, rather than having to go through the States.

(Is that alone sufficient to establish the anti-commandeering principle?)

No – there's still the question whether this new authority to act on individuals directly was supposed to be *exclusive*, or whether the 1789 Constitution envisioned making *both* means available to Congress.

(Why does the majority reject the argument that *both* means should be available?)

Two reasons:

(a)   *Historical experience* was that regulating the States didn't work very well and caused friction.

        (What does Justice White think of this historical analysis?)

        The dissent calls the majority's historical analysis "elaborate window dressing": The rule isn't *compelled* by history, and the Civil War and New Deal changed history anyway. It would be better to defer to Congress where there's no textual support for the rule.

        This is the last serious methodological dispute I can think of in the federalism cases. It raises a number of interesting and important issues, which I can only flag for you:

        - Should history should ever be dispositive in the absence of pretty clear support in the text of the Constitution itself?

        - When we look at history, should we read the Civil War and the New Deal as having profoundly changed the constitutional order.

(b)   Regulating through the states blurs lines of *political accountability*. People need to be able to see clearly which government is imposing something on them -- especially something unpopular. Here, it looks like the States are regulating when the Federal Government is really pulling the strings.

(Is the anti-commandeering principle an *internal* or an *external* limit on federal power?)

The anti-commandeering principle applies even where Congress would otherwise be legislating within its Commerce Clause powers. It's an *external* limit in the sense that it does not rely on any textual limitation in the Art. I powers and applies even within the normal extent of those powers. In other words, a *Lopez* analysis will not answer the anti-commandeering question.

b.   The Statutory Provisions

The anti-commandeering rule still leaves three ways that the Federal Government can achieve its ends:

(a)   *Direct Regulation*: Congress can always simply regulate on its own.

(b)   *Conditional Spending*: Congress can put conditions on federal funds, so long as fairly loose constraints are observed. *See South Dakota v. Dole.*

(c)   *Conditional Preemption*:   Congress can give States a choice of regulating according to federal standards or accepting federal direct regulation of the same subject matter.

So maybe the most difficult part of *New York* is figuring out which sort of regulation the statute undertakes.

(Does each provision present a commandeering problem?)

No.

(How would you classify the monetary incentives?)

The monetary incentives are simply a tax with a conditional grant-back to the States.

(What about the access incentives?)

They're an example of conditional preemption. The access incentives are optional -- a conditional decision to allow states to discriminate against other states if the States meet certain requirements.

(What about the take title provisions?)

They're conditional, too – states have a choice of either regulating radioactive wastes or taking title to them. It's a conditional preemption of state liability law.

(So what's the problem?)

These conditions are OK only if they're non-coercive -- i.e., only if the alternative to regulating according to federal standards is a viable one. Here, the alternative is the "take title" option, which is simply punishment for not meeting Congress's requirements.

So the Court treats the take title provisions as the equivalent of a direct order to regulate in a particular way.

c.   **Justice White's Dissent**

(What's Justice White's best answer to all this?)

Justice White's dissent argues that Congress is simply facilitating resolution of an interstate dispute here -- the States overwhelmingly wanted an agreement, but needed some sort of enforcement to prevent free-riding. And New York agreed to be bound by the agreement.

(What's the majority's answer? Why shouldn't New York be held to its agreement?)

The Court says States can't waive their sovereignty, which is held for the benefit of individual liberty. In fact, State officials might have an interest in avoiding or blurring political responsibility for politically unpopular but necessary policies.

(Does Justice White think that the anti-commandeering doctrine really protects the States' interests?)

No. He argues that "the Court gives Congress fewer incentives to defer to the wishes of state officials in achieving local solutions to local problems."

(What's the alternative to commandeering for Congress?)

Justice White argues that the alternative is more direct federal regulation, which would leave the States' *worse* off. Remember, there's a certain degree of power bound up with implementing federal law.

2.   Branch by Branch

The Court has approached the anti-commandeering problem separately for each branch of state government that might be commandeered:

- **Legislative:** In *New York v. United States*, the Court holds that Congress *can't* commandeer the state legislature by requiring to pass laws implementing a federal program.

New York discusses an older case, which is about courts:

- **Judicial:** In *Testa v. Katt*, 330 U.S. 386 (1947), the Court held that Congress can give state courts jurisdiction over federal claims, and that state courts can't refuse to hear such claims -- at least when comparable claims under state law would be heard.

  To put this in context, think about what you've learned about federal jurisdiction in Civil Procedure. Federal question jurisdiction—that is, jurisdiction over suits based on violations of federal law—is not exclusive. And for much of our history, it didn't exist—the primary use of the federal courts was for *diversity* suits between people from different states. So the expectation was that most federal question cases would be brought in *state* court. The question in *Testa* is whether the states can refuse to hear them.

  Here, the federal Emergency Price Control Act provides that a buyer of goods above the prescribed ceiling price may sue the seller "in any court of competent jurisdiction." Federal courts have jurisdiction "concurrently with State and Territorial courts."

  Testa purchased a car for a price in excess of the ceiling, and successfully sued the dealer, Katt, in state court in Rhode Island. On appeal, the State Supreme Court reversed on the ground that a state need not enforce the penal laws of a government which is "foreign in the international sense," and that the federal statute was both penal and foreign for those purposes.

The Court held (Black, J., for a unanimous court) that State courts have to hear federal causes of action, at least where a comparable claim arising under state law would be heard.

The Supremacy Clause binds state courts, and it forbids an individual state to refuse to enforce federal law on grounds that it contradicts local policy.

- **Executive:** In *Printz*, the Court extends *New York*'s prohibition to attempts by Congress to commandeer state executive officials by requiring them to enforce federal law.

3. *Printz v. United States*, 521 U.S. 898 (1997)

The Brady Act provides for a national instant background check system for handgun sales. In the interim before the system is operational, the Act requires local "chief law enforcement officers" (CLEOs) to perform certain duties: (1) on receipt of notice from a firearms dealer, to "make a reasonable effort" to ascertain whether the purchaser may legally buy a gun; (2) to provide a written statement of reasons if the CLEO notifies the dealer that the purchaser is ineligible; and (3) to destroy any records if the CLEO finds no basis for objecting to the sale.

Two CLEOs challenged the interim provisions. The Court holds (Scalia, J.) that the interim provisions impermissibly commandeer state executive officials.

The most interesting thing about the case is the method by which the opinions get to their conclusions, since everyone agrees there is no binding text on this issue.

One possibility is that we should just stop there – that is, if there's no binding text that says otherwise, the default rule is that the law is constitutional. That was Justice White's view in *New York*. But no one seems to take that position here.

a. Sources of Authority

(What kinds of authority does the majority rely on?)

- **Precedent**

(The best case for the majority is obviously *New York*. Does it necessarily govern this case?)

No – remember, *New York* deals only with commandeering of state *legislatures*.

(The question, though, is why that distinction should make a difference. Why does the Government think it should?)

The Government has two arguments here:

(a)   The Court should draw the line between "making law" and "enforcing" it.

(Would that distinction support a bright line between the state legislative and executive branch?)

No – Administrative agencies frequently make law as a practical matter, not only at the federal level but also at the state level.

(So what's the line that the Government proposes to draw?)

That the Court should limit the anti-commandeering doctrine to situations in which state officers are being asked to make *policy*.

(What does the Court say about this?)

It's an unmanageable distinction (remember *Gregory*) and this case involves policymaking.

(b)   There is no political accountability problem here.

(Is that right?)

Justice Scalia says that you blame the official enforcing a policy.

(What's the best precedent for the Government?)

Testa v. Katt, which held that state courts generally have to hear federal law claims.

(How does the Court distinguish *Testa*?)

The Supremacy Clause specifically mandates that "state judges" are bound by federal law. But aren't state legislatures also bound by federal law, whether or not the Supremacy Clause says so?

Probably the best way to make sense of this is to note that courts frequently apply the law of sovereigns – for instance, a state court might also have to apply *foreign* law in some situations, depending on the relevant choice of law rules. But no one thinks the state court is *commandeered* in that situation.

(There's another case that the Court *could* cite, but doesn't. Anybody know what it is?)

Prigg v. PA, where the Court holds you can't make state officials enforce the fugitive slave law.

(What other sources of authority do the opinions rely on?)

- **History**

(What kinds of historical evidence?)

Two kinds of evidence here:

(a)   congressional practice

(b)   statements in the federalist

(c)   general historical ideas about constitutional structure

(Why do we care about congressional practice?)

Because it's evidence of the original understanding of the Constitution.

(Who's got the better of this argument? Why?)

It seems fairly inconclusive to me.

(What do you think about all the back and forth over particular passages of the Federalist? Is the Federalist binding?)

This also strikes me as a bit excessive.

- **Structure**

State Sovereignty: Justice Scalia reiterates and expands Justice O'Connor's discussion in *New York* concerning the Framers' rejection of federal authority to act on States, as opposed to the citizens directly.

The Necessary and Proper Clause: Justice Stevens says the Necessary and Proper Clause gives textual support for a commandeering power.

(What's the Court's answer to this?)

"Proper" may be an internal limit on the Clause, even though the Clause as a whole expands Congress's power. Justice Stevens doesn't address this possibility.

b.   "Bright-Line" Rules

(What about some good old fashioned policy arguments? Doesn't the Court care how important the Brady Act is? What's the Court's answer to the important federal interest here?)

That this isn't a balancing test – it's a bright line rule.

This is an example to the rules/standards debate. Rules categorically ban certain approaches; standards allow for balancing of interests or consideration of particular circumstances (like a "reasonable person" test).

Rules are criticized as being inflexible or over- and under-inclusive.

Standards are criticized as too indeterminate to constrain judges' political judgments or to provide predictability to others.

(So what's Justice Scalia's argument for why you need a rule here?)

That it's the only way to safeguard the structure from erosion.

c.   The Political Safeguards of Federalism

(Justice Stevens argues that *Garcia* should govern this case. Is the anti-commandeering rule consistent with *Garcia*?)

Yes and no. It's a judicially-enforced rule, so it's not a reliance on the pure political safeguards.

But the Court does identify ways in which commandeering can skew the political process, so that States' interests may not be adequately represented.

The best way to put this is that a key "political safeguard" is the requirement that the Federal government internalize its costs, so that Congress can only regulate if it's willing to bear the financial pain of doing so. Commandeering allows the federal government to *avoid* internalizing regulatory costs. (You have an excerpt from me explaining this in the notes.)

Two kinds of costs:

- Political costs

- Financial costs

The existence of these costs is one of the more effective "political safeguards".

d.   International Comparisons

(What is the relevance of Justice Breyer's discussion of other countries?)

He says other countries have demonstrated that states may be *better* off with commandeering, because they get to have a say in the implementation of law made at a higher level.

Justice Scalia's response is that the Federalist papers explicitly consider European systems which had a commandeering-type structure, that is, the central government gave directives which the sub-units carried out. And it is specifically in *rejecting* those systems that the Framers articulated their hostility to the idea of one government giving orders to another.

This seems pretty devastating to me.

e.   The Unitary Executive Argument

(What does separation of powers have to do with this case?)

The Unitary Executive idea is one we'll be seeing over and over. The idea is that the Framers intended that the Executive branch should be united, and that a unitary executive is better able to implement policy and maintain a balance of power vis a vis Congress.

(How does commandeering allow Congress to get around the separation of powers?)

Ordinarily, when Congress legislates, it depends on the Executive for enforcement. This dependence is an integral part of checks and balances.

But if Congress can use *state* officers, then it's not dependent on the federal Executive any more.

4.   **Summing Up**

- The Anti-Commandeering Doctrine means the federal government cannot *force* the states to serve as instruments of regulation of third parties. In other words, Congress can't make the state legislatures pass state law according to some federal recipe, and can't force state executive officials to enforce federal law.

- It applies to state legislatures and executive officials, but not to state courts in most instances.

- It's based on two primary rationales:

    (a)   History of Dual Sovereignty: The Framers meant to replace the Articles of Confederation's reliance on the states as instruments of regulation with federal power to regulate individuals directly.

    (b)   Political Accountability: Using the States as instr§§uments of federal regulation skews political accountability by making it unclear to citizens who is actually responsible for particular governmental actions. Best version of this puts it in terms of *internalizing costs*.

We probably haven't seen the last case here. Imagine some of the War on Terror scenarios that Justice Stevens anticipates in *Printz*. Say we have to inoculate for smallpox *right away*, and need state officials to help.

(Should the States really not have to help?)

(Do we think there's any risk they wouldn't volunteer to help?)

(If not, what happened to political safeguards?)

IV.   **Chapter Twelve – Limits on State Power**

This chapter covers the dormant Commerce Clause, the Privileges and Immunities Clause of Article IV, the application of Equal Protection doctrine to discrimination against out-of-staters, and the doctrine of preemption. Unlike many of the doctrines covered so far, these principles come up all the time in real life. And because we have several different doctrines that all serve similar purposes, this unit affords an opportunity for students to think about litigation strategy in framing a complaint challenging a state law that impacts interstate commerce. Dormant commerce clause, privileges and immunities, and equal protection theories each have certain advantages and disadvantages from a litigation standpoint, and it is useful to get students used to thinking about doctrines as elements of strategy rather than simply as constitutional rules.

The preemption cases continue the opportunity, begun with the clear statement cases, to address issues of statutory construction. One can make the case that preemption is the most practically significant issue in federalism doctrine, because it (a) comes up all the time, and (b) directly implicates the states' ability to develop their own regulatory policies. Finally, the critical issue of preemption by federal actors other than Congress offers a preview of some of the separation of powers issues in the next unit. (Also, don't forget to connect the issue of judicial preemption through federal common law with Erie R.R. v. Tompkins, *which your students are hopefully reading in Civil Procedure.)*

We're shifting gears now to consider the limits that federalism places not on the actions of the Federal government, but on the actions of the States. Not surprisingly, the federal courts have been considerably more aggressive about limiting *state* power than federal power.

We've already discussed these matters as part of our historical survey. This time we're focused on current doctrine, as this is a part of constitutional lawyers that real lawyers in private practice actually tend to come into contact with.

A.   Four Kinds of Limits on State Authority

We'll be discussing three different kinds of limits:

- **The Dormant Commerce Clause:** We'll spend by far the most time on what is usually called the "dormant" Commerce Clause – that is, the negative implication of Congress's power over interstate commerce that limits the States' corresponding authority over that commerce.

  We first saw this idea in *Gibbons v. Ogden* and *Willson v. Black Bird Creek*, and we'll talk more about *Gibbons* in a few minutes.

We'll briefly touch on the effect of two other constitutional provisions which impose similar limits on State regulation of interstate commerce:

- The **Privileges and Immunities Clause of Art. IV**, § 2, which restricts the ability of states to confer some "privileges or immunities" on their own citizens – like the right to work in the state – without granting similar privileges to out-of-staters.

- The **Equal Protection Clause** of the 14th Amendment, which forbids states in some circumstances from discriminating against out-of-staters in favor of in-staters.

Finally, there's

- **The Preemptive Effect of Federal Law:** Finally, we'll look at the impact on state regulatory authority when Congress *does* exercise its own legislative power – in other words, the preemptive effect of federal statutes under the Supremacy Clause.

As federal regulation becomes more and more pervasive in many important areas, this may become the most important aspect of these materials. My own view is that the issue of preemption, and the rules that should govern it, dwarfs all the other aspects of federalism doctrine in importance.

B. The Dormant Commerce Clause

1. A Review of the History

Constitutional Text: Remember that all Art. I, § 8 actually *says* on the subject of commerce is that Congress shall have power "[t]o regulate Commerce with foreign Nations, and among the several States, and with the Indian Tribes." Nothing in the text explicitly limits state regulatory authority.

Constitutional History: There is, however, strong historical evidence that the power over commerce – and indeed the Constitution generally – may have been designed to end interstate trade wars and achieve some level of uniformity of commercial regulation.

Against this background, the Commerce Clause is usually viewed as an attempt to promote two kinds of unity:

• Economic Unity: The Framers aimed to achieve economic prosperity by creating a national market free of internal trade barriers.

• Political Unity: The Framers also thought that economic barriers went hand in hand with political barriers, and that interstate trade wars would lead inevitably to political conflict that might threaten the Union.

Doctrinal Adventures: We've already talked through some of the early cases. Prior to 1937, Congress's power over interstate commerce and the States' power over in-state and noncommercial activities were thought to be mutually exclusive. But it was really hard to draw the lines:

• The Marshall Court tried to distinguish between commerce and "police" regulation. That's *Gibbons* and *Willson v. Black Bird Creek*.

• The Taney Court, starting with *Cooley v. Board of Wardens*, 12 How. (53 U.S.) 299 (1851), tried to distinguish between inherently national and inherently local activities.

• Later on, the Court used the same direct/indirect effects test that it used in the affirmative Commerce Clause cases like *E.C. Knight*.

None of this worked out very well, leading the Court to adopt a much different framework after 1937. One often over-looked fact is that just as the Court freed up the *national* government to regulate under the

Commerce Clause after the "switch in time", it also freed up the states by rolling back the stricter dormant Commerce Clause tests.

2.　　The Modern Framework

Modern doctrine is dominated by two distinct tests:

- **The Anti-Discrimination Rule:**　Where states discriminate against interstate commerce, such statutes are virtually *per se* invalid.

  Note that the cases distinguish to a limited degree between statutes that are *facially* discriminatory – which are the easiest ones to invalidate – and laws that have a protectionist or discriminatory purpose or effect.　But both are ultimately subject to the same high burden of justification.

- **The Balancing Test:**　Non-discriminatory laws that incidentally burden interstate commerce are subject to a balancing test that weighs the legitimate local interests against the impact on interstate commerce.

Congress's Power to Consent or Preempt:　Remember that the dormant Commerce Clause principle extends from the existence of Congress's power to regulate interstate commerce.　That means the rules that the judiciary is willing to impose in the *absence* of Congressional action are always subject to Congress's own power.

- Consent:　Congress is free to exercise its power by *permitting* state laws that would otherwise violate the dormant Commerce Clause.　One example is the McFadden Act, which allows states to keep out-of-state banks from opening branches within the State.

  There is a limit on the consent principle:　Congress must express itself clearly before courts will hold that it has conferred permission to discriminate against or burden interstate commerce.

- Preemption:　Even where a state law doesn't fall within the relatively narrow categories of laws that courts are willing to strike down, Congress can still determine that it undermines national interests.　Congress retains the power to *preempt* state laws by passing federal laws that either explicitly trump the state law or regulate in a way that conflicts with state requirements.

The Importance of Inertia:　One reason that judicial review is more aggressive in this area is the possibility that Congress can override judicial decisions that it doesn't like.　Judges are more willing to strike down laws when they know that the people's elected representatives can correct their mistakes.

Don't underestimate the importance of inertia, however.　It's hard to get a law passed, and the effect of the dormant Commerce Clause is to place the burden of overcoming legislative inertia on States that wish to discriminate against or burden interstate commerce. In effect, the dormant Commerce Clause establishes a *default rule*.

A Key Defense – the Market Participant Rule: States are not subject to dormant Commerce Clause constraints when they are operating as *participants* in a market rather than *regulators* of the market. We'll talk about this in detail in the next assignment.

3. **Discrimination Against Interstate Commerce—***Philadelphia v. New Jersey*, **437 U.S. 617 (1978)**

The most important thing is the basic rule against discrimination, illustrated in *Philadelphia v. New Jersey*. New Jersey law prohibits importation of most waste that originated outside the state. Private landfill operators challenged the law.

(Why might New Jersey want to ban outside waste?)

The New Jersey legislature found that New Jersey had a big waste problem, that land fill space was limited and decreasing, and that disposal of wastes from outside the state was exacerbating the problem.

The Court holds (Stewart, J.), that NJ's law is unconstitutional.

The Court gets rid of two preliminary issues first: There's no federal statute that preempts NJ's law, and interstate movement of waste is "commerce."

The Court then lays out the basic rule forbidding discrimination against interstate commerce: Where a state engages in "simple economic protectionism," "a virtually *per se* rule of invalidity has been erected." A law blocking the flow of interstate commerce at a State's border is the clearest example of such a law.

On the other hand, "[w]here the statute regulates evenhandedly to effectuate a legitimate local public interest, and its effects on interstate commerce are only incidental, it will be upheld unless the burden imposed on such commerce is clearly excessive in relation to the putative local benefits." *Pike.*

(How do we tell whether there's discrimination? Does the Court look at legislative motive here?)

No – The Court says it doesn't have to decide that, because whatever the State's purpose, "it may not be accomplished by discriminating against articles of commerce from outside the State unless there is some reason, apart from their origin, to treat them differently."

(But why shouldn't NJ be able to give preference to its own waste in the State's own landfills?)

"[I]t imposes on out-of-state commercial interests the full burden of conserving the state's remaining landfill space." The statute thus runs afoul of prior decisions holding "that a State may not accord its own inhabitants a preferred right of access over consumers in other States to natural resources located within its borders."

"What is crucial is the attempt by one State to isolate itself from a problem common to many by erecting a barrier against the movement of interstate trade."

(What's the alternative, if NJ doesn't want to become the nation's waste dump?)

(Could NJ just ban all dumping within the State?)

Sure – that wouldn't discriminate.

(And what would happen then?)

All the waste generated in NJ would have to go somewhere else.

Now, I think, you can see Justice Rehnquist's point – that NJ ought to have an intermediate alternative. It's responsible for NJ to take care of its own waste, but it shouldn't have to become a trash haven.

(What about the quarantine cases, which allow states to quarantine sick cows and other stuff coming in from out of state?)

There is no claim here that out-of-state waste is somehow *more* harmful -- for instance that it can only be safely disposed of close to its point of origin.

(Should that make a difference?)

It may help to think more generally about *why* we're so stringently prohibiting discriminatory regulation:

Political and Economic Unity: The Framers believed that economic unity was a precondition to political unity, and they were worried about beggar-thy-neighbor policies in the States. We see the same story in Europe today – we begin with economic union as a hedge against wars, and political unity grows out of that.

Social Welfare: Protectionism undermines efficiency by distorting the natural workings of the market. Trade barriers encourage goods to be produced within a state, for instance, even though another state could produce them more efficiently. And many protectionist laws are designed to *externalize costs* by exporting them to other states.

But note how complex these arguments can be:

(Who bears the costs of the New Jersey law? Who benefits?)

The costs are borne by out-of-state producers and in-state landfill operators; striking the law down, on the other hand, harms out-of-state landfill operators and in-state producers.

Representation Reinforcement: It's hard for courts to make good determinations about efficiency. So instead we rely on parties adversely affected by a law to oppose it, since they have the best information. Where costs are exported outside the jurisdiction, however, the affected parties don't have the necessary opportunity to participate in the political process.

But note some cautions here, as well.

(Does anyone in the picture in *Philly v. NJ* have an incentive to protect the interests of out-of-state waste generators?)

Virtual representation often means that out-of-state interests will be represented by in-state parties with similar interests, like the landfill operators in *Philadelphia v. New Jersey*.

4.   Surviving Strict Scrutiny – *Maine v. Taylor*, 477 U.S. 131 (1986)

Strict scrutiny is sometimes described as **"strict in theory, fatal in fact."** But *Maine v. Taylor* is the one example I know where a state law that discriminated on its face survived review.

Maine prohibited the importation of live baitfish. Evidence at trial indicated that out-of-state baitfish had parasites not found in Maine baitfish, and that those parasites could damage Maine's population of wild fish. The trial court also found that there was no satisfactory way to inspect imported baitfish for parasites or commingled species.

The Court holds (Blackmun, J.), that this is constitutional. The statute discriminates, and is therefore subject to strict scrutiny. But Maine's interest in guarding its ecosystem against risks is legitimate, and there was no evidence that nondiscriminatory alternatives were available. There was also no evidence of protectionist intent.

Note that *Maine v. Taylor* is the only state law that I know of to ever have survived strict scrutiny (at least in the Supreme Court).

5.   Facially-Neutral Laws with Discriminatory Purposes or Effects

Not all discriminatory state laws are discriminatory *on their face*, and the Court has sometimes accorded strict scrutiny to state laws that have the purpose and/or effect of discriminating against out-of-staters, even if those laws are facially neutral. I have you the example of *Hunt v. Washington State Apple Advertising Comm'n*, 432 U.S. 333 (1977), in the notes. North Carolina grows apples, but the big dog in the apple business is Washington State. One big advantage WA has is its brand name, which is based in part on its really rigorous inspection and grading system under WA state law. There's also a *federal* inspection and grading system, but nobody thinks it's as good. So what NC does is to ban labeling with any grade *other than* the federal one – e.g., it bans the WA state label. The Court says that's unconstitutional, because the NC law has a discriminatory purpose and effect.

The case law's a mess however. Professor Chemerinsky offers four factors that are likely to persuade courts to find a law to be discriminatory where it imposes a disparate impact on out-of-staters:

- "[A] law is likely to be found discriminatory if its effect is to exclude virtually all out-of-staters from a particular state market, but not if it only excludes one group of out-of-staters."

- "[A] law is likely to be found discriminatory if it imposes costs on out-of-staters that in-staters would not have to bear."

- "[T]he Court is more likely to find discrimination if it believes that a law is motivated by a protectionist purpose, helping in-staters at the expense of out-of-staters."[41]

I want to stress, though, that these are tendencies rather than rules, and the caselaw in this area does not follow a particularly determinate pattern.

6.   Incidental Burdens on Interstate Commerce and the Balancing Test

Where there's no facial or de facto discrimination against interstate commerce, the Court applies a considerably more lenient test. The classic formulation is in *Pike v. Bruce Church, Inc.*, 397 U.S. 137 (1970):

"Where the statute regulates even-handedly to effectuate a legitimate local public interest, and its effects on interstate commerce are only incidental, it will be upheld unless the burden imposed on such commerce is clearly excessive in relation to the putative local benefits."

The Court makes clear that this is necessarily a question of degree – more of a burden on interstate commerce will be tolerated if the local interest is really important.

This all sounds sensible in theory but it's very hard to do in practice, mostly because the values on the different side of the scale may be incommensurable. Suppose, for example, that you have a state safety regulation that imposes $10 million in costs each year on interstate commerce, but saves 5 lives per year.

---

[41] ERWIN CHEMERINSKY, CONSTITUTIONAL LAW: PRINCIPLES AND POLICIES § 5.3.4, at 436 (3rd ed. 2006).

(How do you weigh that?)

Remember Justice Scalia's comment – that it's a lot like asking whether a line is longer than a rock is heavy. The two values don't use the same metric, so it's hard to weigh one against another.

So the subtext in a lot of these cases is the Court groping for ways to avoid having to actually balance the values involved. In *Pike*, the Court mentions one: The Court asks not only how important the State's interests are, but also "whether it could be promoted as well with a lesser impact on interstate activities." In other words, is there a less burdensome alternative. If there is, then maybe we can discount the state's interest in terms of justifying the more restrictive law.

7.   *Kassel v. Consolidated Freightways Corp.*, 450 U.S. 662 (1981)

An Iowa statute prohibited the use of 65 ft. double-trailer trucks on its highways. Doubles, trucks carrying vehicles or livestock, and mobile homes could be 60 feet, while most other trucks were limited to 55 feet. No other state in the West or Midwest imposed these restrictions.

The statute permitted cities abutting the state line to adopt the length limitations of the adjoining state by local ordinance. Iowa truck manufactures could also ship trucks as large as 70 feet, and oversized mobile homes could be moved from a point within Iowa or delivered to an Iowa resident.

A trucking company wishing to use larger trucks challenged the law.

The Court says Iowa's law is unconstitutional.

(How does the state defend the statute? What interest is the state trying to promote here?)

The state says it's a safety provision.

(What's the primary interest on the other side?)

Money -- Iowa's law added about $12.6 million each year to the costs of trucking companies.

(Why's it so expensive?)

Because companies using these trucks have to either uncouple their doubles, load their cargo into smaller trucks to pass through Iowa, or go around.

(Does the Court really want to weigh lives saved against financial costs?)

No. The Court says that "if safety justifications are not illusory, the Court will not second-guess legislative judgment about their importance in comparison with related burdens on interstate commerce."

(So what's the problem here? Why doesn't the Court accept the legislature's rationale?)

The Court says you can't just invoke safety -- the actual extent to which the state law furthers safety must be weighed in light of the burden on interstate commerce.

(How do we tell if the safety benefits are illusory?)

We have a trial. The state brings in its experts, and the plaintiffs bring in theirs. Note that the plurality gives no deference to the state on these empirical safety questions.

(What did the evidence on safety say?)

Three points:

- No good evidence that the 65-foot doubles are more dangerous than the 55-foot singles in terms of braking, turning, & maneuvering;

- The double may be safer in terms of "off-tracking" (whatever that is), splashing, and vulnerability to wind; and

- The effect of Iowa's law is to divert much trucking around Iowa, therefore increasing miles traveled in other states and, in all likelihood, the number of accidents there.

So if anything, safety cuts *against* Iowa's law.

Note how the Court has avoided the need to actually balance interests here by deciding that there's *nothing* on the state's side of the scale. This makes things a lot easier.

(How does Justice Rehnquist evaluate the safety arguments?)

The question is simply whether the safety rationale is pretextual -- not whether it "outweighs" burdens on commerce.

Iowa's safety justification is rational. All states regulate truck length, and most limits are between 55 and 65 feet. 65 foot doubles are prohibited in 17 states in New England and the Southeast.

(What's the problem with the majority's analysis of the safety issue?)

It doesn't help to compare trucks slightly over the length limit with those at the length limit. The state has to draw lines somewhere, and you can always show that a slight increment might not make much difference. The only question is whether the line chosen is a rational one.

(What's the effect of the majority's holding on state regulation? What does Iowa have to do to avoid burdening interstate commerce?)

Any state safety regulation more stringent than that of the state's neighbors incidentally deflects interstate commerce to the neighboring

States. The Court effectively compels Iowa to bow to the policy choices of neighboring states. But only Congress has the authority to preempt state decisions in this way.

Note – You might think of the majority's position as a race to the bottom argument, cast in a *good* light.

(Does the majority give any other reason to discount the State's safety interest?)

The state law also contains exemptions "that weaken the deference traditionally accorded to a state safety regulation."

(Why should we worry about the exemptions?)

The normal deference to state determinations is partly attributable to our confidence that state political processes will ordinarily air all the relevant arguments. But here, the burdens fall disproportionately on out-of-staters; exemptions ease the burden on in-staters. Less deference is therefore warranted.

Iowa basically is seeking to keep trucks out of Iowa. But States can't cut safe vehicles off from their own highways.

(Brennan and Marshall concur in the judgment. What's the difference between the plurality's approach and Justice Brennan's?)

He doesn't think that the Court should be second-guessing the legislature on empirical judgments.

(Why not?)

Because these judgments really are committed to the political branches.

(How do we check up on the legislature, then?)

We hold them to their *actual* purpose – not the purpose dreamed up by their lawyers after the fact. *Compare Lee Optical*, in which the court was willing to just make up rationales, or at least allow the State's lawyers to make them up *post hoc*.

(What was the actual purpose here?)

The legislature simply sought to keep trucks out of Iowa.

(Is that a legitimate purpose?)

No. Iowa acknowledges that it is seeking to export safety problems to other states -- such behavior should be virtually per se invalid.

(What does Justice Rehnquist say about this? Who's right?)

He says that the Court has consistently rejected this argument. For one thing, it's impossible to determine a single "actual" purpose in the context of a multi-member body. What happens if the legislators have different purposes in mind? The question is whether the legislature's determination that the statute would meet its actual purposes was wholly irrational in light of the evidence available to it.

Avoiding the Weighing of Values: The more balancing test cases you read, the more you'll be struck at how often the Court seeks to avoid a straight-up comparison of values. There are several ways to do this:

(a)   Apply a presumption or "thumb on the scale." This will decide the close cases.

(b)   Limit the interests considered – either by focusing on *actual* purpose or excluding *illegitimate* purposes.

(c)   Flip the interests on one side – like when the plurality in *Kassel* says that safety actually cuts *against* the State.

(d)   Discount the interests on one side because they can be served by less restrictive or burdensome alternatives.

8.   **The Market Participant Doctrine–*South-Central Timber Dev., Inc. v. Wunnicke*, 467 U.S. 82 (1984)**

Alaska proposed to sell timber that it owned, but only to buyers that would process the timber before it was shipped out of Alaska.

(Why would Alaska want to do this?)

The stated purpose of the restriction was to protect existing timber-processing industries, promote new industries, and derive revenue from the sale.

A potential buyer who wished to ship the timber elsewhere before processing sued for an injunction against the local processing requirement.

The Court of Appeals held that Congress had implicitly authorized the restriction.

The Court holds (White, J., for a plurality) that Alaska's policy violates the dormant Commerce Clause.

There are really two issues in this case:

(a)   Did Congress authorize Alaska's policy by statute? and

(b)   Does Alaska's policy fall within the "market participant" exception to the dormant Commerce Clause?

On the first point, the Court holds that the policy was not authorized. This is actually an important point, because the Court articulates a clear statement rule: Congressional intent to authorize state action that would otherwise violate the dormant Commerce Clause must be "unmistakably clear." We'll talk more about Congressional "consent" in the next assignment.

Note that on this point, Justice White's opinion attracts a majority of seven justices. The rest of his opinion, however, is only a plurality.

The Market Participant Issue: Alaska's restriction is not shielded by the market participant doctrine.

(What *is* the market participant doctrine, anyway?)

"[I]f a State is acting as a market participant, rather than as a market regulator, the dormant Commerce Clause places no limitation on its activities."

One reason you have *South-Central Timber* in the packet is that it provides a pretty good account of the preceding caselaw.

The first case recognizing the doctrine was *Hughes v. Alexandria Scrap Corp.*, 426 U.S. 794 (1976), which held that States may confer subsidies on local interests when acting as a market participant.[42]

Note that *Alexandria Scrap* was decided on the same day as *National League of Cities*. Both are designed to protect the operations of state government. Note also that the plurality in *Wunnicke* were all in dissent in *National League of Cities*, and in the *Garcia* majority.

(Why isn't this case governed by *Alexandria Scrap*?)

Here, Alaska is a participant in the timber sales market -- not the timber *processing* market. This is therefore a *downstream restriction*. *Alexandria Scrap* doesn't apply.

Note that this is a lot like antitrust law's prohibition on tying – Alaska is trying to tie purchase of the lumber to purchase of the processing services. This is what Microsoft got into trouble for.

What about *Reeves, Inc. v. Stake*, 447 U.S. 429 (1980), which held that States may choose with whom they will or will not deal when acting as market participants.[43]

(How does Justice White distinguish *Reeves*? Isn't Alaska just saying it won't deal with buyers who don't process within the state?)

---

[42] In *Alexandria Scrap*, Maryland offered a "bounty" on Maryland-licensed junk cars. Out-of-state scrap processors had to meet more stringent documentation requirements than in-state processors. The Court said this was constitutional. Maryland was participating in the market for scrap processing, and could legitimately favor its own citizens.

[43] In *Reeves*, South Dakota restricted sales of cement from a state-owned plant to South Dakota residents. The Court held that the Commerce Clause does not limit a State's refusal to deal with particular parties when it is participating in the interstate market in goods.

Reeves is likewise distinguishable, because here we have (a) a restriction on foreign commerce (b) concerning a natural resource, and (c) a restriction on resale.

"The limit of the market-participant doctrine must be that it allows a State to impose burdens on commerce within the market in which it is a participant, but allows it to go no further. The State may not impose conditions . . . that have a substantial regulatory effect outside of that particular market."

The key to this "regulatory effect" seems to be the restriction on resale. But what about the *White* case?

White v. Massachusetts Council of Construction Employers, Inc., 460 U.S. 204 (1983) held that States can impose restrictions on their dealings as market participants beyond the limits of formal privity – in other words, the state can affect transactions beyond its immediate dealings.[44]

(How does the Court avoid the implication of *White* that it's fine for states to reach beyond their own contracts?)

The Court says that *White* does not *eliminate* the significance of privity. There, the Court found that the restricted contractor's employees were effectively "working for the city."

Alaska's restriction is invalid because it regulates what purchasers do with the timber after the State no longer has an interest in the wood. States have a greater interest as "private traders" in their own immediate transactions, and downstream restrictions have a greater regulatory effect than do limitations on the immediate transaction.

Finally, this restriction is particularly pernicious because it regulates *foreign* commerce. "[S]tate restrictions burdening foreign commerce are subjected to a more rigorous and searching scrutiny. It is crucial to the efficient execution of the Nation's foreign policy that 'the Federal Government . . . speak with one voice when regulating commercial relations with foreign governments.'"

(Is this broad preemption for foreign commerce practical? Couldn't we say that virtually *all* commerce is now potentially foreign?)

I think it makes no sense – everything's potentially foreign, just like everything's potentially interstate.

---

[44] In *White*, Boston required all construction projects funded in whole or in part by city funds to be performed by a work force of at least 50% city residents. The Court said that although there are some limits on restrictions that reach beyond the immediate parties dealing with the government, everyone in this case was -- at least informally -- "working for the city."

Finally, note Justice Rehnquist's point that the State could validly reach the same result in a number of ways:

(a)   it could sell only to companies maintaining processing plants in-state, *Reeves*;

(b)   it could directly subsidize the Alaska processing industry, *Alexandria Scrap*; or

(c)   it could pay to process the logs in Alaska and *then* sell only processed logs.

Justice Rehnquist says it's silly to strike down this particular method, when all these others would be OK.

But this point just highlights the fact that the Court has had to draw some fine lines in this area, and that the *form* that a state program or policy takes may make a big difference. This is why it's important for lawyers that may have to *counsel* state or local governments to understand this area, because there's frequently freedom to achieve the result you want if you structure the program correctly.

C.   The Privileges and Immunities Clause of Article IV

1.   Text and History

Article IV, § 2, cl. 1 provides that "The Citizens of each State shall be entitled to all Privileges and Immunities of Citizens in the several States."

The leading case defining the privileges and immunities of state citizenship is still Justice Bushrod Washington's opinion in *Corfield v. Coryell*, Fed. Cas. No. 3,20 (C.C.E.D.Pa. 1823), which said that the clause protects interests "which are fundamental; which belong, of right, to the citizens of all free governments. [These] may [all be] comprehended under the following general heads: Protection by the government, the enjoyment of life and liberty, with the right to acquire and possess property of every kind, and to pursue and obtain happiness and safety; subject nevertheless to such restraints as the government may prescribe for the general good of the whole."

Note that there is also a Privileges and Immunities Clause in the Fourteenth Amendment, which has been read somewhat differently. It's important to keep them straight.

2.   *United Bldg & Constr. Trades Council v. Camden*, **465 U.S. 208 (1984)**

A Camden ordinance required at least 40% of the employees of contractors and subcontractors on city projects to be Camden residents.

The NJ Supreme Court had held that the Privileges and Immunities Clause didn't apply. The Court says it does apply, and reverses and remands.

(Why isn't this a dormant Commerce Clause case?)

Because the market participant exception applies. After this case is filed, the Court decided the *White* case, rejecting the dormant commerce clause argument on very similar facts.

So the first point about the Privileges and Immunities Clause is that certain defenses – the market participant defense and also the Congressional consent defense – aren't available to the State.

It's important to evaluate these doctrines from a litigation strategy viewpoint – be thinking about when you'd want to plead which doctrine and why.

(The first question the Court considers is whether the Privileges and Immunities Clause even applies to laws passed by a municipality. How does the Court answer that?)

The Privileges and Immunities Clause applies to municipal ordinances as well as to state laws. Municipalities are merely political subdivisions of the State, and derive all their authority from the State.

The next problem is whether discrimination on the basis of *municipal* citizenship – rather than *state* citizenship – implicates the Clause.

(What does the Court say about that?)

This ordinance is not immune from Privileges and Immunities attack simply because it discriminates solely on the basis of *municipal* residence -- not *state* residence. After all, any municipal residence requirement will *a fortiori* bar all out-of-staters.

(Is there a representation problem here? How does Justice Blackmun answer the majority's argument?)

He says the in-staters excluded by the law will virtually represent the out-of-staters who are also affected.

(How does the Court respond?)

The Court's answer to the argument that New Jersey residents from outside Camden will represent the interests of out-of-staters is that New Jersey has delegated authority to localities on this issue. The dissent has some answers, but the important point is simply that we're talking about the same kind of representation issues that we saw in *Philadelphia v. New Jersey*.

With these questions out of the way, we can now ask whether the ordinance denies privileges and immunities under Art. IV. Privileges and Immunities scrutiny involves a two-step inquiry:

(a)   Does the law burden a right sufficiently fundamental to the promotion of interstate harmony to be protected by the Clause?

(b)   Is there a "substantial reason" for the difference in treatment? And does the degree of discrimination "bear a close relation" to that reason?

(Is this standard of review higher or lower than under the Commerce Clause?)

This looks like some kind of intermediate scrutiny.

(So what about the first question – is this a fundamental right? First of all, what's the specific right at issue?)

Here, "the pursuit of a common calling is one of the most fundamental of those privileges protected by the Clause." The question is whether *public* employment is also such a right. There is no such right for purposes of the Equal Protection Clause, and no such right in a case like this under the dormant Commerce Clause. *See White.*

The fact that the city is acting as a market participant is not dispositive under the Privileges and Immunities Clause. That Clause has different purposes and sets different standards than the Commerce Clause. The Commerce Clause is a restraint on state *regulatory* authority, and has no application to non-regulatory activity. The Privileges and Immunities Clause is a direct restraint on all state action in the interests of comity. It therefore cuts across the market participant/market regulator distinction.

The fact that Camden is spending its own money is relevant, but not dispositive here. So the right is protected, and the question is whether Camden's law passes under step two.

(What's the step two question, again?)

Whether there's a substantial reason for the discrimination, and whether the law bears a close relation to that reason.

(What's Camden's reason here?)

Here, Camden's hiring preference is designed to increase employment in the city and stop middle class flight.

(Does the Court resolve whether that's good enough?)

No. The New Jersey courts never reached that issue, and without a trial, it is impossible to evaluate Camden's justifications for the law. We therefore remand to the New Jersey Supreme Court.

3.   Other Examples

- **The Right to Practice Law:** In *Supreme Court of New Hampshire v. Piper*, 470 U.S. 274 (1985), the Court struck down a New Hampshire law that restricted bar admission to local residents. It held that practicing law is a "privilege" because of the lawyer's role in the national economy and the noncommercial role in representing persons with unpopular federal claims.

- **The Right to Travel:** *Camden* and *Piper* are both about the right to work; the other important area of privileges and immunities is in the right to travel cases. These cases are frequently decided on equal protection grounds, but in the *Edwards* case some concurring justices suggested that privileges and immunities might be a sounder basis. But note the merging of Fourteenth Amendment privileges and immunities concerns with Article IV privileges and immunities.

4.   Final Notes on Privileges and Immunities

To sum up:

(What would the advantages of a P&I theory be to an out-of-state plaintiff looking to strike down a state law?)

- exception to the market participant doctrine.

(What are the *dis*advantages?)

- low standard of review (compared to DCC)

- *corporations* are not citizens for purposes of the Privileges and Immunities Clause.

The question of corporate rights is one you'll want to pay attention to under each constitutional provision.

D.   The Equal Protection Clause

It's important to recognize that the Equal Protection Clause also puts some limits on the ability of states to discriminate against out-of-staters.

1.   *Metropolitan Life Ins. Co. v. Ward*, 470 U.S. 869 (1985)

In *Ward*, Alabama taxed the gross receipts of in-state insurance companies at 1%, while taxing out-of-state insurance companies at 3 to 4%. Out-of-state companies could lower this by 1% if they invested substantially in Alabama.

(Why are the plaintiffs proceeding under the Equal Protection Clause rather than the Commerce Clause?)

The federal McCarran-Ferguson Act said that the States can regulate and tax insurance companies. This had been seen as an exemption from dormant Commerce Clause scrutiny.

The McCarran-Ferguson Act is irrelevant to equal protection analysis. Equal protection protects persons from unconstitu-tional discrimination, and is not subject to congressional waiver. (In this respect, it's just like Privileges and Immunities.)

The Court says this is unconstitutional.

(What's the standard of review here?)

Rational basis review applies: Discrimination is OK if it is a rational means to accomplish a legitimate state purpose.

This is an extremely lenient standard.

(Why doesn't the AL law pass it, then?)

Alabama's purpose of "encouraging the formation of new insurance companies in Alabama" was an impermissible one.

But note that a direct subsidy to in-state companies – which the Court has said is clearly OK in a number of cases – would have precisely the same purpose.

Note that *Metropolitan Life* is the *only* case in which the Court has used the Equal Protection Clause to strike down a discriminatory restriction on interstate commerce. It's possible that the Court might not follow it today.

2.   Picking a Theory

(What are the advantages of using Equal Protection instead of the Commerce Clause in this context?)

No market participant or congressional authorization defense.

(What are the advantages of using Equal Protection over the Privileges and Immunities Clause?)

Equal Protection applies to corporations, but Privileges and Immunities doesn't.

(What are the disadvantages of Equal Protection as a legal theory?)

It's a much more lenient standard of review.

(Would an Equal Protection challenge have succeeded in *Philadelphia v. New Jersey*?)

Probably not – the State had a health and safety rationale which was at least rational.

E.   Summing Up: Is Limiting State Regulation Worth the Trouble?

Justice Scalia has said, in a series of concurrences and dissents, that "to the extent that we have gone beyond guarding against rank discrimination against citizens of other states . . . the Court for over a century has engaged in an enterprise that it has been unable to justify by textual support or even coherent nontextual theory, that it was almost certainly not intended to undertake, and that it has not undertaken very well."[45]

(Is he right? Could the same be said even of the prohibition on "rank discrimination"?)

(Is there any reason to think that the Court is better at this than Congress? Should we just leave it to the political branches?)

One argument the other way is that Congress shouldn't have to specifically preempt every little state law that burdens interstate commerce. The costs of overcoming legislative inertia are just too great.

(Is this a bigger mess than in other areas we've considered?)

Maybe not. There's an irony that the conservatives – Thomas and Scalia – want to get rid of the dormant commerce clause doctrines because they're unworkable, but then want to pursue the affirmative commerce clause and commandeering doctrines. The liberals take the opposite tack on both sorts of issues.

My own view is that this is all a little bit messy, but that this shouldn't be dispositive.

On the other hand, it's worth returning to the basic question: Where is the constitutional support for this area of doctrine? Two big reasons have been given in support of the DCC:

- Congress's power is exclusive; or

- Congress's silence should be read as implicit preemption.

(Does either one of these make sense?)

Not really. We know that Congress's power isn't exclusive, because we've junked the whole dual federalism, separate spheres thing. And if we think that states *can* regulate interstate commerce, then it makes little sense to read congressional silence as a prohibition. There's no evidence Congress actually intends that.

The other problem is that this jurisprudence, even on the discrimination side, requires the judges to make too many policy judgments.

(Do you agree?)

I have a lot of sympathy. Doesn't seem like the *national* government needs all this judicial assistance to limit state power. And it's ironic to see judicial restraint on the affirmative commerce side, but not on the made up dormant side.

---

[45] *Tyler Pipe Indus. v. Washington St. Dept. of Revenue*, 483 U.S. 232, 265 (1987) (Scalia, J., concurring in part and dissenting in part).

On the other hand, don't forget that creating a free trade area was one of the founding purposes of American federalism. You can see that clearly by comparison with the much-newer European Union. What's the first thing the Europeans did? They created a free trade area. Every other aspect of integration – regulation, human rights protection, an attempt at a common foreign policy – came after that. They have very specific restrictions on protectionist legislation by Member States. What we have is the dormant Commerce Clause. You can argue that the DCC thus plays an absolutely fundamental role in the federal system.

A lot depends on what you think the alternatives are. Justice Thomas thinks that the Import/Export Clause can do a lot of the same work, but we'd have to overrule some case law saying it only applies to *foreign* trade. The other big possibility is affirmative preemption of bad state laws by federal statutes.

F.   Preemption of State Law

Preemption is terribly important for three reasons:

First, preemption is the classic problem of *concurrent power* -- it arises only in areas in which everyone agrees *both* the federal and state governments have authority to enact their own laws. If it's true that we really do live in a world where there are no longer enclaves of purely state authority, then how we handle cases of overlap between federal and state regulation becomes the critical question.

Second, recall Madison's version of the political safeguards of federalism from the Federalist Papers: The States will always retain their place in the Constitutional scheme because they will command the primary loyalties of the People. And the reason that will be so is that the States are the governments that regulate the bread-and-butter aspects of everyday life.

Preemption strikes at the heart of that idea, by eliminating State lawmaking power directly. (Compare *National League of Cities* or *New York* and *Printz*, none of which really implicate this problem at all.)

Third, preemption is the single most common constitutional claim -- especially in the commercial litigation contexts where many of you will spend most of your professional lives. It's so common we forget it's a constitutional claim at all, arising under the Supremacy Clause.

To understand the development of preemption law, it's useful to begin with the modern framework:

1.   Three Kinds of Preemption

These are described in the *Pacific Gas & Electric* case.

(1)   ***Express*** preemption in the statutory text.

(2)   *Field* preemption where the scheme of federal regulation is so pervasive that we infer Congress intended no state supplementation.

(3)   *Conflict* preemption where compliance with both federal and state regulations is a "physical impossibility," or where state law "stands as an obstacle to the accomplishment and execution of the full purposes and objectives of Congress.

There may also be a fourth kind:

(4)   *Frustration* preemption occurs where state law does not conflict directly with a federal statute, but it would unduly frustrate the purposes of that statute to permit concurrent state regulation. This may simply be a form of conflict preemption.

It is absolutely critical to remember that under modern doctrine, these different categories are simply aids in answering the critical question: Did Congress *intend* to preempt state law?

2.   Historical Development

There are basically four historical stages of preemption doctrine:

Early Cases: The Court held that federal law was supreme in the event of a conflict, but did not recognize any doctrine that the existence of federal legislation precluded the States from passing their own laws, at least where no conflict occurred.

Late 19th Century: The Court begins to suggest that when Congress legislates, it ousts the States of their authority in that area. But the cases are inconsistent and no state laws are actually struck down.

Early 20th Century: The first Supreme Court case actually decided on preemption grounds is *Southern Railway Co. v. Reid*, 222 U.S. 424 (1912). There, a North Carolina statute required railroad companies to transport tendered freight. The Court found that Congress, through the Interstate Commerce Act, had "taken possession of the field" of railroad rate regulation, and therefore the state had no concurrent power to regulate.

The rule in this period is automatic field preemption whenever Congress acts. Many statutes are struck down during this period.

The New Deal and After: Beginning in the 1930s, the Court shifts away from the automatic field preemption rule. Instead, it focuses on whether or not Congress intended to preempt state law. And it develops a "presumption against preemption" which is fairly protective of state law. The leading case in this period is *Rice v. Santa Fe Elevator Co.*, 331 U.S. 218 (1947).

(Do you think this is an anomaly in the general New Deal shift toward *expanded* federal power?)

No -- it's necessary to permit that expansion. If Congress's powers expand significantly *and* that power preempts every field it touches, the results would be intolerable. It's also part of a trend toward more regulation generally -- field preemption often creates a regulatory vacuum.

As I said, an important feature of the modern doctrine is the "presumption against preemption" – that is, a rule of statutory construction that resolves ambiguities in federal law against preemption of state authority. The canonical cite is *Rice v. Santa Fe Elevator Corp.*, 331 U.S. 218 (1947), so the rule is sometimes called "the *Rice* presumption."

This presumption fits into the category of clear statement rules we've talked about before – it furthers the idea that the states are primarily protected by the political process in Congress by ensuring that Congress has focused on the question of preemption before finding that state authority has been superseded.

You should recognize that the presumption is not consistently applied. Some preemption cases it seems dispositive; in others it is not even mentioned. The Court sorely needs to be more consistent on this.

3.   *Pacific Gas & Elec. Co. v. State Energy Resources Conservation & Development Comm'n*, 461 U.S. 190 (1983)

CA law imposed a moratorium on the certification of nuclear energy plants until a state agency finds that a safe means of disposal for high-level nuclear waste has been developed and approved by the federal government.

A utility company – presumably one that wants to build a nuclear power plant in CA – challenges the state law.

(What's PG&E's claim?)

That the state law is preempted by the federal Atomic Energy Act.

(Is this a *constitutional* challenge?)

Yes – the argument is that the state law violates the Supremacy Clause of Art. VI because it's inconsistent with federal law.

(But what do we actually have to interpret in order to resolve this challenge? Are we arguing about what the Supremacy Clause itself means?)

No – We have to interpret the federal and state laws. This is the case in almost all preemption litigation – the focus is on statutory interpretation, rather than *constitutional* interpretation.

That's why, even though preemption is such an important part of federalism doctrine, it's hard to develop any focused "preemption doctrine" – because the cases themselves focus exclusively on the various statutory schemes involved.

The Court (White, J.) holds that the state regulations are not preempted.

Remember we have these four forms of preemption:

(a)   express

(b)   field

(c)   conflict

(d)   frustration

(Is PG&E arguing for *express* preemption here?)

No. PG&E has three different arguments, which fit into the "field," "conflict," and "frustration" categories, respectively.

Field Preemption

(What's the field preemption argument?)

That the state law is an attempt to regulate the *safety* of nuclear plants, and that the federal Act preempts the field of safety regulation.

(How do we know if field preemption has occurred?)

Basically, you look at the federal regulatory scheme and see if it looks *comprehensive* – that is, like Congress didn't intend to the states to supplement the federal rules.

(Does the AEA create this kind of comprehensive regulatory scheme?)

The Court agrees with PG&E's basic characterization of what the federal Act does – it divides up responsibility for regulation of nuclear power, so that the federal government sets uniform safety standards but gives the states authority to decide the economic issues about when power plants should be built.

Note that the Court invokes the presumption against preemption here, because regulation of public utilities – like electrical generating plants – has historically been a function of state governments.

This is an important point: In a number of cases, the Court has suggested that the *Rice* presumption should only apply in fields of traditional state regulation. One example is United States v. Locke, 529 U.S. 89 (2000), which I've summarized for you in the notes. That case involved oil tanker regulation in Washington State.[46]

(Is that a traditional state field or a federal field?)

Well, maritime law is traditionally federal, and in fact there are federal statutes and even international treaties on oil tanker safety.

On the other hand, this is safety regulation, as well as regulation of a vital aspect of WA's environment and economy: an oil spill in Puget Sound will pretty much shut down the state.

The Court unanimously says in *Locke* that there's no presumption against preemption, because this is not a traditional state area. But I'm skeptical of limiting the presumption to fields of traditional state activity – that's exactly the idea that the Court found so hard to define in applying *National League of Cities*, and we've seen over and over again that these categories overlap.

(What about *PG&E*? Is that a traditional state or federal field?)

Well, if it's nuclear power, then it's federal. But if it's public utility regulation, it's state. See the problem?

The last point about field preemption is that we still have to construe the *state* law, to see if it ventures into the preempted field. Here, the Court says it doesn't – that the state is regulating the economic decision when to build a reactor. The state has simply made a judgment that atomic power plants aren't economically viable without a viable means of waste disposal.

Conflict Preemption

(What's the conflict preemption argument?)

PG&E says, look, the NRC has decided that it's OK to go ahead and license new reactors despite the waste disposal problem, and that CA's decision is in direct conflict with that.

The first question we ask is whether it's physically possible to comply with both the state and federal mandate.

(Is it?)

---

[46] WA enacted safety regulations that went over and beyond federal requirements. These included:

- Training requirements
- English language proficiency requirements
- Navigation watch requirements
- Reporting requirements for accidents

Sure – the NRC isn't *making* anyone build a nuclear plant. So you can still comply with the state denial of a permit.

(What about the argument that the state decision is an obstacle to the NRC's decision?)

It's no obstacle, because the NRC was only thinking about safety – it was still leaving the economical-ness decision up to the states. That means the states are free to say no for economic reasons.

Frustration Preemption: The last argument is that the AEA's general purpose is to promote the commercial use of nuclear power.

(How does the Court answer this argument?)

It *isn't* the AEA's purpose to promote nuclear power *at all costs*. That means the State is free to say here that the costs are too high.

This is a recurring problem in preemption law: What do we do when a statute arguably has multiple purposes? If federal law only has one purpose—to promote nuclear power—then the state law should be preempted. But the Court says the law has *multiple* purposes, or at least allows room for additional *state* purposes.

The problem is in a slightly weird posture in *PG&E*; let me give you a more typical example: The federal environmental laws regulate pollution up to a certain point. One purpose is clearly to reduce pollution. So state laws that regulate pollution even more strictly are surely consistent with that purpose.

But pollution is always costly. So what if we consider an additional federal purpose as minimizing the *costs* of pollution control? Now the federal purpose is more like striking a balance. And while stricter state pollution laws might further one federal purpose, they undermine the purpose to reduce costs. So *any* departure by state law in either direction would arguably conflict with the purposes of federal law.

You can see how interpreting federal law as striking a balance between competing purposes will preempt just about everything, right? I wish I could tell you that the Court always does it one way or the other, but they don't. It really varies by how clearly the federal statute in question looks like it's trying to promote one primary purpose or rather to strike a balance. It's not surprising the cases turn out differently, because they involve different statutes.

4.   *Lorillard Tobacco Co. v. Reilly*, 533 U.S. 525 (2001)

I asked you to read a final preemption case, *Lorillard*, in order to see where preemption fits into the broader jurisprudence of federalism developed by the Rehnquist Court.

Federal law requires that cigarette companies print a warning that smoking is dangerous both on the package and along with their print advertising, and it bans radio and TV advertising. The question in this case is whether MA can impose additional requirements designed to protect kids – for instance, they ban outdoor advertising within 1000 feet of a park or school, and they ban in-store ads lower than five feet off the ground if the store is near a school.

(Does the federal law say anything about preemption?)

Yes. There are two aspects to the preemption provision:

(a) Additional statements. "No statement relating to smoking and health, other than the statement required by section 1333 of this title, shall be required on any cigarette package."

(b) State regulations. "No requirement or prohibition based on smoking and health shall be imposed under State law with respect to the advertising or promotion of any cigarettes the packages of which are labeled in conformity with the provisions of this chapter."

(What's the best argument that this doesn't prohibit the MA law?)

Well, Stevens says that the purpose of the federal law was to make sure that there wouldn't be 50 different warning requirements for labeling – this would be extremely costly for the industry. But there's no indication Congress cared about *location* regulations, which are easy to comply with on a state-by-state basis.

(How does the majority answer this?)

They basically say that the content/location distinction isn't in the text of the statute.

(Do they faithfully apply the presumption against preemption?)

Hard to say. It's even hard to say if the statute is really ambiguous.

I want to focus, though, on FN 8 in Justice Stevens' dissent, where he notes the irony of comparing this case w/*Lopez*. Stevens basically says, "Gee, if there's anywhere I'd have thought the State would get to win, it would be within 1000 feet of a school."

(How does the majority answer that?)

They don't get the joke. That was a commerce clause case, this is a preemption case.

(*Should* we consider the two lines of cases related?)

(Why would the conservatives be pro-states in Commerce Clause and commandeering cases, but anti-states in preemption cases?)

Make no mistake, the pattern that *Lorillard* illustrates is a general one. The lineup of justices in preemption cases is a little less rigid and predictable than in Commerce Clause cases, but by and large the conservatives have pretty consistently favored preemption and the liberals have pretty consistently opposed it. The emerging exception is Justice Thomas, who is working out a general theory of preemption that is, on balance, considerably more friendly to the States.

I think there are several possible explanations, some more admirable than others:

- Views about regulation: Preemption is almost always *deregulatory*— that is, preemption claims get brought when federal law is less strict than state law. So if you're pro-business and anti-regulation, then you love preemption. Significantly, groups like the American Enterprise Institute are generally in favor of limiting national power, but pro preemption. So maybe that's why a conservative court is pro-preemption. It's one kind of conservatism (the economic kind) trumping another (the federalist kind).

But you should consider two other possibilities that I'm pretty sure are also part of the mix:

- Views about statutory construction and agencies: The justices have pretty firm views about method and about the relationship of the courts to other institutional actors. Justice Scalia, for instance, tends to think texts are clear, so he has comparatively less use for canons of construction like the presumption against preemption. Not surprisingly, that makes him more pro-preemption.

  And both Scalia and Breyer love administrative agencies – they're old Admin Law profs, after all. So they tend to defer to agencies, and agencies preempt a lot of state law.

- Views about federalism strategy: I care about limiting preemption because I don't think there's any other realistic prospect for limiting national power under the Constitution; this whole Commerce Clause thing, in my view, isn't going anywhere and anti-commandeering doesn't mean much unless you also tighten up on the Spending Clause, which I doubt will happen. But if you think that we can actually limit the enumerated powers, then you'd have comparatively less use for strict rules on preemption. That's the position my friend Professor Dinh takes in the notes.

  On the Court, it may be that people like Roberts and Alito (and O'Connor and Rehnquist before them) simply have decided to put their chips on the Commerce Clause cases rather than limiting preemption.

The converse point is important: The liberal justices don't hate federalism. They just don't believe in limiting the enumerated powers, probably mostly because of the Court's pre-1937 experience. That, at least, was Justice Souter's view. And so they *do* tend to invest in limiting preemption. *See, e.g.*, the great quote from Justice Breyer in *Egelhoff* in the notes, where he says the "true test of federalist principle" is in preemption case. The best justice for the States in preemption cases—*by far*—was Justice Stevens. I miss that guy. Ironically, as I've suggested, his replacement may be Justice Thomas.

5. Preemption by Actors other than Congress

One last point: Most preemption cases so far have involved the preemptive effect of federal statutes. It's important to recognize, however, that the actions of the Executive and Judicial branches may sometimes have preemptive effect. And the newer preemption cases always seem to have an agency involved.

- **Administrative Preemption:** "Pre-emption may result not only from action taken by Congress itself; a federal agency acting within the scope of its congressionally delegated authority may pre-empt state regulation." *Louisiana PSC v. FCC*, 476 U.S. 355 (1986).

This is awfully important, since administrative agencies have rulemaking authority and actually make considerably more federal law than Congress does.

My own view is that administrative preemption may be unconstitutional, except when the agency is following guidelines prescribed pretty narrowly by Congress. For one thing, if we're serious about this political safeguards thing, then it should matter that the States have no representation at, say, the FCC. But most people think I'm crazy on this.

It may help to break out two distinct sets of situations, as I have in the notes:

The **first** is when a *statute* is ambiguous as to whether it preempts state law, but a federal agency is interpreting it to do so. In these cases, we have a clash between the *Rice* presumption (which says no preemption) and the *Chevron* doctrine (which says defer to the agency if the agency's interpretation is reasonable). There's no definitive answer to this question, but the courts have often hesitated to defer to the agency.

The **second** situation is when the relevant statute simply delegates rulemaking or adjudicatory authority to an agency, and the *agency* takes action that preempts state law. It's not clear that Congress should be able to delegate its authority to preempt state law for the reasons I've just mentioned, but the Court has never held that. On the other hand, the Court has sometimes found that the relevant agency action was unauthorized by the underlying statute, and in so doing it has sometimes refused to accord the agency *Chevron* deference. The *Solid Waste* case is an example of this.

- **Judicial Preemption:** Preemption may also occur through *judicial* action. Federal courts sometimes make federal common law in various areas, such as admiralty cases or cases where the U.S. is a party. This law is generally held to have preemptive effect.

  This raises the same kind of political safeguards problems as administrative preemption, and may be unconstitutional for the same reasons. But here again, most people think I'm crazy. In any event, the primary limit on federal *judicial* lawmaking is the Court's 1938 decision in *Erie Railroad v. Tompkins*, which you'll read in Civil Procedure (in a just world). They won't tell you this in that class, but *Erie* is the single most important federalism decision of the 20th century. It's not fair that it's in that class rather than this one.

We'll talk a bit more about administrative preemption when we consider agencies in the separation of powers unit.

V.   Chapter Thirteen – The Separation of Powers

It's helpful to consider separation of powers, not as a whole new topic, but as an extension of the same structural themes addressed in the units on federalism. These include the Framers' central concern with faction, the role of structure in protecting rights, tensions between "formalism" and "realism" or "functionalism," the ways in which judicial review interacts with and augments "political safeguards," the importance of a "constitution outside the constitution," the role of "clear statement" rules of statutory construction in protecting constitutional values, and the ever-present anxiety that a two-centuries-old constitutional structure may not be ideal for meeting the challenges of our modern world.

In a sense, we've already been talking about separation of powers – the *vertical* separation between national and state governments. This last unit has to do with *horizontal* separation among the Legislative, Executive, and Judicial branches of the national government. All state governments likewise have a horizontal separation among the branches of their own governments, although the details vary from state to state. The terms of that separation are governed by state constitutions. Our study will focus on the national level.

A.   Theory, Values, History, and Text

Separation of powers grows out of 17th and 18th century liberal political theory, with the primary influence on the Framers being Montesquieu's *Spirit of the Laws*. The basic idea was that the same people who make the laws should not execute them – as Madison summed it up, the accumulation of executive, legislative, and judicial power in the same hands is "the very definition of tyranny."

There was a debate, however, over exactly what this meant.

1.   Two Principles: Separated Powers vs. Checks and Balances

Separated Powers: Some argued that the goals of separation of powers could only be realized if government were divided into distinct departments with sharp boundaries between them – no mixing. The proposed Constitution was thus criticized for giving each branch a little piece of the powers of the other branches.

Madison is concerned with refuting this view in Federalist Nos. 47 and 48. He's defending a second principle:

Checks and Balances: According to Madison, defining the powers of the three branches as distinct raises only "parchment barriers" to encroachment by rival branches. Instead, you have to give each branch weapons that it can use in self-defense. So you make it impossible for any branch to live without the others.

For example:

- Congress can't legislate without opportunity for the President to veto.

- The President can't make treaties or appoint officers without Senate confirmation.

- The courts can't function without judge appointed by the President and confirmed by the Senate.

Note that these ideas are in tension: checks and balances necessarily involves some blurring of the lines the separate the legislative, executive, and judicial powers. Depending on which principle you emphasize, you might argue for two different theoretical approaches to separation of powers cases:

2.   Two Theories: Formalism vs. Functionalism

Formalism emphasizes the idea of separated powers. The key is to draw bright lines between the functions of each branch. To do that, we ask two questions:

- What sort of power is being exercised – legislative, executive, or judicial?

- Who is exercising that power? If it's the wrong branch, strike it down. Sometimes we ask instead, Is a branch exercising power in a way different from the way formally set forth in the text? For instance, is the legislature acting but without bicameralism and presentment?

Departures from separated powers are thus confined strictly to those authorized in the constitutional text itself.

Functionalism puts greater emphasis on the idea of checks and balances. It's OK for one branch to have its fingers in another branch's function. The critical question is simply whether a particular governmental arrangement undermines the independence and core functions of one of the other branches.

We might identify three kinds of functionalist problems:

- *Aggrandizement*: A particular measure *increases* the power of one branch vis a vis the others.

  Ex: Allowing President Truman to seize the steel mills would *aggrandize* the power of the Presidency at the expense of Congress.

- *Encroachment*: A particular measure *decreases* the power or autonomy of one branch vis a vis the others.

  Ex: The independent counsel law arguably *encroaches* on the autonomy of the Executive by allowing executive officers to be investigated by a person not subject to the President's control.

- *Dilution*: Conferring a power or function on one branch renders that branch less able to do the job it's supposed to do.

  Ex: The federal sentencing commission conferred quasi-legislative powers on judges, which arguably undermined their appearance of impartiality when they're called upon to apply those guidelines in individual cases.

This judgment whether one of these problems exists depends largely on the particular situation at issue. The two theories – formalist and functionalist – thus track the distinction we've talked about between bright-line rules and flexible standards.

Another thing to understand is that the tendency of the functionalist approach is almost always to uphold innovative governmental arrangements, while a formalist approach will frequently strike them down.

(Any idea why that would be true?)

I think it's because the innovations being challenged generally have strong practical arguments in their favor—like Truman's argument that he needed to seize the steel mills to avert a military disaster.

(Are those arguments relevant to a formalist?)

Generally not. But a functionalist will have to take them into account, and that will often carry the day. *Youngstown* is one of the few cases where even the functionalists strike the law down.

The Court has oscillated back and forth between functionalism and formalism. One question to keep in mind is whether you can explain *why* is applies one sort of approach in one set of cases but the other approach in other cases.

3.   **Values**

The historical record makes fairly clear that the primary value underlying the separation of powers is

- ***Preserving Individual Liberty:***   Keeping the powers to make, interpret, and enforce the laws separate keeps any one individual or institution from exercising arbitrary power.   And it decreases the net amount of government regulation by simply making it difficult to get anything done.

There's also the related purpose of

- ***Mitigating the Problem of Faction:***   We already saw in Federalist No. 51 that separation of powers and federalism together form a "double security" to prevent any particular interest group from dominating the government and imposing its will on others.

There's a third purposes which seems to me a little more dubious:

- ***Efficiency in Government:***   The Framers thought they could promote efficiency through division of labor.   In particular, the point was to create an executive branch that was more independent and powerful than anything we had had before, which would allow the Nation to respond better to crises.

Finally, you should be aware of the shifting historical emphasis in this area. A lot of what the Framers were *for* was a function of what they were reacting *against*:

4.   **Historical Orientations**

The Declaration of Independence reflects a preoccupation with the abuse of executive power by George III.

After the Revolution, you find the first wave of State constitutions sharply limiting executive authority and placing virtually all the power in the legislature. Madison says in Federalist No. 48 that the legislatures turned out to be almost as bad in terms of abusing their power as George had been.   In effect, he says the state constitutions are still fighting the last war.

The experience under the Articles of Confederation also showed, at the national level, that we couldn't get along without a relatively strong executive. So the Constitution of 1789 reflects a concern with restoring a strong executive and checking the power of the legislature.

In the 20th Century the power of the Presidency has expanded to the point that we may be back – or maybe we *should* be back – to a primary preoccupation with executive power.

That concern seemed to fade a bit after Watergate, and we had a succession of less threatening presidents. But concern about executive power may be reviving with the War on Terror.

Before we go any further, it's worth stopping to ask: Where does all this show up in the Constitution?

5.   Constitutional Text

In the handout you have some examples of what the text *could have* looked like, as well as the text we *do* have.

Some states have specific separation of powers provisions in their state constitutions. You have the Indiana provision in the handout, which provides:

Indiana Constitution, Art. 3, § 1: Three departments.

"The powers of the Government are divided into three separate departments; the Legislative, the Executive including the Administrative, and the Judicial; and no person, charged with official duties under one of these departments, shall exercise any of the functions of another, except as in this Constitution expressly provided."

Madison proposed a similar provision for the federal Constitution at the time that the Bill of Rights was under consideration. You also have that in the handout. It would have provided:

"The powers delegated by this constitution, are appropriated to the departments to which they are respectively distributed: so that the legislative department shall never exercise the powers vested in the executive or judicial; nor the executive exercise the powers vested in the legislative or judicial; nor the judicial exercise the powers vested in the legislative or executive departments."

This provision was approved in the House but rejected by the Senate, for reasons that are unclear.

So we're left with the "vesting" clauses of the Constitution, which vest "legislative" power in Congress, "executive" power in the President, and "judicial" power in the Courts. Defining what these terms mean is notoriously difficult, however, and a specific constitutional separation of powers provision probably wouldn't have avoided this problem.

There are also specific provisions charging the different branches with particular responsibilities, such as the "Take Care" clause and the Commander in Chief clause.

The interpretation of the vesting clauses, the "Take Care" clause, and the Commander in Chief clause is central in the *Steel Seizure Case.*

B.   *Youngstown Sheet & Tube Co. v. Sawyer*, 343 U.S. 579 (1952)

In December 1952, the steelworkers threatened to strike for a wage increase.   President Truman persuaded the union to await a recommendation by the Wage Stabilization Board, made up of representatives of producers, workers, and the public, which ultimately recommended certain wage increases. The industry, however, rejected the recommendation and the unions set a strike date for April 1952.

President Truman feared that a steel strike would undermine the war effort.   In order to prevent this, he issued an executive order transferring control of the steel industry to the government, to be run by the Secretary of Commerce.

The industry sued the Secretary of Commerce for an injunction against his seizure and possession of their steel plants.

1.   **The President's Options**

Before diving into the opinions, I think it will be helpful to think about the situation from the *President*'s perspective.

- **Wage Stabilization Board Proceedings:**   Three-way negotiations between the administration, labor, and management, leading to recommendations on wage and price increases by the Wage Stabilization Board.

This is the President's first choice. The obvious drawback is that it doesn't ultimately *bind* the parties to accept the WSB's recommendation. After the industry rejects that recommendation, he's back at square one.

- **Taft Hartley Injunction:** Where a strike imperils national health or safety, the President can appoint a board of inquiry to report on the underlying facts; if the report doesn't induce agreement, the Attorney general may seek an injunction barring a strike for 80 days. At the end of 80 days, the President reports to Congress with recommendations.

(Why not go this route?)

The injunction's only good for 80 days. And there's some sense it's an *alternative* to the WSB procedure. But the big problem is that it enjoins the *strike*—it leaves the mill owners still able to pay the low wages, without helping the unions out at all.

- **Seizure under the Selective Service Act:** When producers fail to fill orders for goods required by the armed forces, the President may seize the facilities subject to an obligation to pay compensation.

(What's the drawback?)

It's not clear it applies – the problem isn't that the mills aren't filling military orders (at least not yet).

- **Condemnation under the Defense Production Act:** The President may seize property when necessary for national defense, provided that the Government pays 75% of compensation up front.

(Why not do this?)

Tough to figure out appropriate compensation and it's a lot of money to pay up front.

- **Submit the Problem to Congress**

(Why not just do this?)

It will take time for Congress to act, and it may not act in a way consistent with the President's wishes.

- **Seize the Mills under the President's own Executive Power**

That, of course, is the option that Truman ultimately decides to pursue.

It's important to be clear about the stakes. The Government has *two* distinct interests here:

- Guaranteeing steel supply, *and*

- Doing so in a way that won't be inflationary.

(Let's say we only care about the first. Is there a way to accomplish that?)

Sure. Just give the owners their price increase.

(What's the problem?)

That would be inflationary and – in the administration's view – unwarranted. It would also really tick off the unions that helped elect Truman president.

2.   Majority Opinion (Black, J.)

The seizure was unconstitutional, because the President lacks any such power.

The Government's argument is that this seizure power should be implied from the Take Care clause and the Commander in Chief clause.

Now, we've already talked about why the Government is relying on the President's inherent constitutional powers – it's not just that the statutes are too cumbersome to use in an emergency. They have other drawbacks too.

But the important thing is that the President is resting on either general or implied powers here.

The Commander in Chief Clause

(Why does the majority say the Commander in Chief clause doesn't confer this power?)

It is clear that the Commander in Chief clause doesn't cover this case -- the link to the war here is too attenuated, and the Commander in Chief power can't cover *anything* that has an effect on military efforts. The idea is that we have to reject any theory that doesn't come with a limiting principle attached.

Justice Jackson adds two important points here. One is that it would be really dangerous if the President could expand his own *domestic* powers by committing our troops to foreign ventures, especially where he doesn't get a declaration of war from Congress.

The other has is that the President "has no monopoly of 'war powers.'"

(Is the Commander in Chief power the power most obviously relevant to supplying the armed forces?)

No—*Congress* has primary authority for supplying the armed forces: Art. I gives Congress power "to raise and support Armies" and "to provide and maintain a navy." And Congress alone can raise the necessary revenues. We'll come back to the allocation of military authority at the end of the unit.

The Take Care Clause

Article II gives the President the authority—and obligation—to "take care that the laws be faithfully executed."

(Why does the majority reject the "Take Care" argument?)

The power to execute the laws doesn't include the power to be a lawmaker. All legislative power is instead vested in Congress. Here, the President is *making* policy -- not executing a congressional policy.

(Which approach -- formal or functional -- does the majority's approach fall into?)

Formal. It starts by classifying what the government is doing as either legislative or executive, then asks whether the right branch is exercising the right power.

Note the related argument by the Government that the vesting clause of Article II "constitutes a grant of all the executive powers of which the Government is capable." Justice Jackson explicitly rejects "the view that this clause is a grant in bulk of all conceivable executive power"; instead, the clause must be "an allocation to the presidential office of the generic powers thereafter stated."

So Justice Black is clearly adopting the view that presidential powers have to be enumerated in Art. II.

350

(Do Justices Frankfurter and Jackson pursue the same formalist approach?)

No way.

3.   A Functional Approach: Looking to the Relationship of Executive and Congressional Action

Justices Frankfurter and Jackson both agree that the constitutional text doesn't end the matter.   Justice Frankfurter says we can't define the powers of the respective branches through "abstract analysis" -- we can't restrict ourselves to the words of the Constitution and "disregard the gloss which life has written upon them."

Justice Jackson goes on to reject the formalist separated powers idea. He says the "[w]hile the Constitution diffuses power the better to secure liberty, it also contemplates that practice will integrate the dispersed powers into a workable government.   It enjoins upon its branches separateness but interdependence, autonomy but reciprocity."

The key idea for both Jackson and Frankfurter is that presidential powers are a function in part of whether or not *Congress* has already acted in the area at issue.

Justice Jackson's concurrence is one of the single most influential separation of powers opinions.   For Justice Jackson, focusing on the relationship between congressional and executive action on a given subject creates three categories of cases:

(1)   ***Presidential Action with Congressional Authorization:*** When the President acts pursuant to an express or implied authorization of Congress, his authority is at its maximum, for it includes all that he possesses in his own right plus all that Congress can delegate. In these circumstances, and in these only, may he be said . . . to personify the federal sovereignty. If his act is held unconstitutional under these circumstances, it usually means that the Federal Government as an undivided whole lacks power."   Presidential actions in this class are "supported by the strongest of presumptions and the widest latitude of judicial interpretation, and the burden of persuasion would rest heavily upon any who might attack it."

(2)   ***Presidential Action/Congressional Silence:***   "When the President acts in absence of either a congressional grant or denial of authority, he can only rely upon his own independent powers, but there is a zone of twilight in which he and Congress may have concurrent authority, or in which its distribution is uncertain. . . . In this area, any actual test of power is likely to depend on the imperatives of events and contemporary imponderables rather than on abstract theories of law."

(3)   *Presidential Action Contrary to Congressional Action*: "When the President takes measures incompatible with the expressed or implied will of Congress, his power is at its lowest ebb, for then he can rely only upon his own constitutional powers minus any constitutional powers of Congress over the matter. Courts can sustain exclusive presidential control in such a case only by disabling the Congress from acting upon the subject. Presidential claim to a power at once so conclusive and preclusive must be scrutinized with caution . . ."

(Which category does this case fit into?)

This case fits into category (3), because Congress has acted in ways that are inconsistent with this seizure.

(What have they done?)

Justice Frankfurter points out that Congress has specifically provided for executive seizures at least 16 times, but it always qualifies this grant of power with limitations and safeguards. This is pretty good evidence that congress didn't intend the President to have an unlimited seizure power. Moreover, Congress clearly and emphatically withheld the authority the President used here in the Taft-Hartley Act of 1947.

In light of Congress's actions, the Court would have to hold Congress acted beyond *its* authority in order to sustain the President's action here.

Note the importance of executive practice here. As I've said, these issues tend to be only very rarely litigated, so most of the precedents come from the past practice of the political branches. Justice Frankfurter points out that the other branches have a duty to interpret and follow the constitution, too, so their judgments -- as reflected in their actual practice -- are entitled to respect.

Here, there are really only three isolated precedents (setting aside cases where war had been declared); these "do not add up, either in number, scope, duration or contemporaneous legal justification, to the necessary kind of executive construction of the Constitution."

4.   "Emergency" Powers

(What's the dissent's big objection to all this?)

That the President *has* to be able to respond to an emergency like this. This is in part an argument from historical executive practice, but also part pure necessity.

Note that David McCullough's recent biography of Harry Truman points out that Chief Justice Vinson had confidentially advised Truman that he could go ahead and seize the steel mills. It seems pretty clear from

McCullough's account that the Court's ultimate ruling came as a pretty big shock to the President.

(How do the other justices answer the necessity argument?)

The majority's answer to the dissent is that "[t]he Founders of this Nation entrusted the lawmaking power to the Congress alone in both good and bad times."

And Justice Jackson adds than an emergency can't justify making up presidential powers. The Framers "knew that emergencies were, knew the pressures they engender for authoritative action, knew, too, how they afford a ready pretext for usurpation. We may also suspect that they suspected that emergency powers would tend to kindle emergencies."

(Does the Constitution talk about emergency powers at all?)

Yes, but there's only one express "emergency" provision -- the provision for suspension of the writ of habeas corpus in times of rebellion or invasion, or when public safety requires.

Justice Jackson adds that Congress can easily grant -- and *has* granted -- emergency powers when they are really needed.

Truman's response to the Court's ruling in his memoirs basically says that the President "must always act in a national emergency," regardless of what the Court thinks. This echoes Teddy Roosevelt's view that "it was not only [the President's] right but his duty to do anything that the needs of the Nation demanded unless such action was *forbidden* by the Constitution or by the laws." But it may go further; Truman may have been saying the President can *violate* the law in an Emergency. That would be more similar to Lincoln's position during the Civil War.

(What do you think of that view?)

It's worth remembering, regardless, that the stakes may not really have been this high. Congress had conferred emergency power to act, just not in the way Truman preferred. But the critical question remains -- would the President have power to act in an emergency if no such alternative were available?

5.   **The Slippery Slope**

(In rejecting emergency powers, are Justices Frankfurter and Jackson really focused on the impact of this particular seizure? Or are they worried about what happens down the line?)

There's a real sense that Truman is one of the good guys. After all, these justices are all New Dealers -- Roosevelt and Truman appointees.

So Frankfurter says that "[i]t is absurd to see a dictator in a representative product of the sturdy democratic traditions of the Mississippi Valley. The accretion of dangerous power does not come in a day. It does come, however slowly, from the generative force of unchecked disregard of the restrictions that fence in even the most disinterested assertion of authority."

And Douglas makes a similar point when he says that "[t]oday a kindly President uses the seizure power to effect a wage increase and to keep the steel furnaces in production," but tomorrow a mean president might use the same power to thwart progressive goals.

(Here's a question, though: Why do these New Deal justices buy the slippery slope argument when it comes to separation of powers, but *not* when it comes to federalism?)

After all, in the Commerce Clause cases these same justices were completely unwilling to foreclose incremental encroachments on state sovereignty. Jackson, for instance, is the author of *Wickard*.

One possible explanation for the discrepancy is the experience of World War II. Both Frankfurter and Jackson draw a link between the history of the Founding period, where the Framers had reacted against the arbitrary powers exercised by George III, and the totalitarian dictators of the 20th Century. (Remember Jackson was the U.S. prosecutor at Nuremburg.) It's not clear this is a good distinction: There's evidence, for instance, that the Nazis' dismantling of German federalism contributed to the erosion of checks on their authority.

6.   "Political Safeguards" Again?

(Justice Jackson says we shouldn't worry so much about over-limiting the President's implied powers here, because practically speaking he has other important powers. What are those?)

Jackson says there is a huge gap "between the President's paper powers and his real powers." The modern presidency has greatly expended its power. He has all kinds of leverage as "the focus of public hopes and expectation," and his capacity to monopolize the national attention. This gives him influence over Congress, which out to check him. The party system also expands presidential influence.

One might expand on this point by noting institutional advantages deriving from:

- the unity of the office;

- its capacity for secrecy and dispatch;

- its superior sources of information;

- easy access to the media;

- the President's role as head of his political party; and

- the fact the President is always in session.

Note also Justice Jackson' point that the political branches are not only *able* to look out for their own interests, but that they will lose their power if they don't do their job. The Court can't preserve Congress's power "if it is not wise and timely in meeting its problems."

7.   The Problem of Efficiency

(Remember the Framers thought that separation of powers might actually enhance government efficiency. Do we still think this is true?)

Note Justice Jackson's frank acknowledgment that the separation of powers may actually undermine governmental efficiency: "With all its defects, delays and inconveniences, men have discovered no technique for long preserving free government except that the Executive be under the law, and that the law be made by parliamentary deliberations. Such institutions may be destined to pass away. But it is the duty of the court to be last, not first, to give them up."

This statement reflects the period, when communism seemed to be making a credible claim to be a superior system for meeting the needs of society. There's a certain self-conscious defensiveness about the drawbacks of our own system here, and an attempt to justify them in terms of higher values.

VI.   Chapter Fourteen – Structure of the Political Branches

These materials spend a great deal more time on delegation than most casebooks. Although the nondelegation doctrine is largely moribund in the courts (except possibly in its incarnation as a rule of statutory construction), the problem *of delegation remains a central concern of the administrative state. Wave after wave of law and scholarship in administrative law can be understood as an effort to address this central dilemma. My aim is to give students a sense not only of the old doctrine that used to be but of the complex structure of administrative law that took its place.   I hope both to inspire my students to take the course in Administrative Law, as well as to give some sense of its contours to the large number of students that will skip that course. After all, it would give a serious misimpression simply to say that nondelegation is dead, without exploring to some extent the elaborate edifice that has arisen to take its place.*

The second set of materials deal with more recent efforts to restructure the legislative process—in particular, the legislative and line-item vetoes. These materials sharply illustrate the formalist/functionalist divide in separation of powers law, and they sharply pose the question whether we ought to allow ourselves to depart from the original separation of powers in order to protect the goal of an effective and accountable government. As an aside, you may wish to consider showing the classic Schoolhouse Record video, "I'm Just a Bill," in conjunction with Chadha. *It's readily available on DVD and on the Web and may be a more coherent account of the Court's rationale than the majority opinion.*

Finally, the book contains a unit on Executive Privileges and Immunities. I have never managed to fit that unit into my course; hence the absence of notes on that subject.

The next two assignments spring directly out of the concern that the constitutional system of separated powers is inefficient. These concerns loom particularly large in the area of lawmaking, and Congress has often acted to alter the legislative process. It has been largely successful in winning the right to *delegate* lawmaking authority to administrative agencies. Its efforts to restructure its own participation in the lawmaking process—through the legislative and line-item vetoes—have been less successful.

A.   The Problem of Delegation

1.   Overview

Delegation is a bit of a puzzle. In Federalist 51, Madison's bedrock assumption is that no one ever willingly gives up their power. So why is Congress so eager to give it away? At least 3 possible answers:

- **Expertise:** Especially in technical areas such as environmental protection or telecommunications, administrative agencies are seen as having the expertise necessary to determine the details of government policy.

- **Flexibility:** Conditions in many regulated areas may change over time -- sometimes very quickly. And it's sometimes difficult to enact a new law because of legislative inertia. Delegation allows an agency to adapt the original law to changed conditions.

- **Avoiding Political Costs:** In many cases, there may be broad political consensus in favor of some goal, but bitter disputes over how to pursue it. Congress can take credit for pursuing the general goal -- like air quality -- without taking the blame for deciding whose ox will be gored.

As the last point makes clear, delegation has some downsides. And so we have—at least in theory—a constitutional principle limiting delegation. The nondelegation doctrine protects several important values:

- **Separated Powers:** Delegation allows Congress to transfer the legislative power to the executive branch. The Framers thought that combination of lawmaking and enforcement functions in one place would lead to tyranny.

- **Accountability:** Congress should not be able to avoid responsibility for difficult policy choices. If they can, then elections don't matter because *agency* officials are the ones making the real decisions.

- **Predictability:** The flip-side of regulatory flexibility is that it's easier to predict what the law governing your activity will be if it's written in a statute, rather than subject to changing agency interpretations.

- **Cabin Administrative Discretion:** Agency officials are not directly accountable to the people, so its important to cabin their discretion in order to prevent arbitrary or capricious decisions.

These values have not diminished in importance, even though the nondelegation doctrine itself has mostly gone away. A central problem in this unit is to figure out how to protect these underlying values through a different set of doctrinal and institutional mechanisms.

The core of the classical doctrine has three components, the first of which is by far the most important:

- **The Intelligible Principle Doctrine:** Congress can't delegate its authority without providing an "intelligible principle" that limits agency discretion. *Schechter.*

- **Private Delegations:** Delegations of lawmaking authority to *private* entities is particularly problematic. *Carter Coal.*

- **Independent Constitutional Authority:** Delegations are less problematic where the executive branch already has a certain degree of inherent authority over an area. *Loving; Curtiss-Wright.*

As you'll see, however, the classical doctrine hasn't held up very well. Several key questions:

- **Is there Anything Left?** There may not be. The nondelegation doctrine is frequently described as a dead letter. *American Trucking* is our guide on this.

- **Was it *Lochner*?** Nondelegation is identified with economic substantive due process (*Lochner*) as well as restrictive pre-New Deal interpretations of the Commerce Clause (*E.C. Knight, Hammer v. Dagenhart*). Is the nondelegation doctrine equally illegitimate?

- **Statutory Construction:** Courts may still construe statutory delegations narrowly in order to avoid a nondelegation question. One might compare this point to the federalism clear-statement rules: doctrines that it's hard for the Court to enforce outright (like *Nat'l League of Cities*) sometimes come back as clear statement rules.

2.   *A.L.A. Schechter Poultry Corp. v. United States*, 295 U.S. 495 (1935)

The National Industrial Recovery Act authorized the President to approve or promulgate "codes of fair competition" for different industries, provided such codes will further the purposes of the Act.

Note that we've already seen this case once before, in connection with the Court's holding that Congress had exceeded the limits of the Commerce Clause.

(What's the separation of powers claim?)

That the NIRA works an unconstitutional delegation of legislative power.

The Court (Hughes, CJ) holds this unconstitutional on both federalism and SOP grounds.

The Government's first argument is, Look – there's a depression on. But the Court doesn't buy that; the economic "emergency" doesn't justify this law. "Extraordinary conditions do not create or enlarge constitutional power."

(Does the Court condemn *all* delegations of authority to administrative agencies?)

No. The Court says that the Constitution does not preclude Congress from laying down policies and standards while delegating authority to make "subordinate rules" and determine facts. This gives Congress the flexibility it needs to make regulation practical.

(What's the test?)

The question is whether Congress "has established the standards of legal obligation."

So Chief Justice Hughes's opinion is effectively a canvass of all the different possible ways that Congress could have limited administrative discretion.

(What are the possibilities?)

- **The term "fair competition":** Here, the Act does not define "fair competition." That term might provide a limit if it were a term of legal art with a meaning developed through case law, but it's clear that the NIRA envisions more than the common law meaning of the word.

- **Case-by-case adjudication:** The FTC Act, for example, leaves "unfair methods of competition" to be defined through case-by-case determinations in an administrative adjudication procedure with lots of procedural safeguards. That option isn't followed here.

- **The NIRA's "Declaration of Policy":** (Have someone read it -- it's on pp. 982-83.)

  NIRA declares the "policy of Congress . . . to remove obstructions to the free flow of interstate and foreign commerce which tend to diminish the amount thereof; and to provide for the general welfare by promoting the organization of industry for the purpose of cooperative action among trade groups, to induce and maintain united action of labor and management under adequate governmental sanctions and supervision, to eliminate unfair competitive practices, to promote the fullest possible utilization of the present productive capacity of industries, to avoid undue restriction of production (except as may be temporarily required), to increase the consumption of industrial and agricultural products by increasing purchasing power, to reduce and relieve unemployment, to improve standards of labor, and otherwise to rehabilitate industry and to conserve natural resources."

(Do these goals limit the President's discretion?)

These goals are so broad that they don't constrain at all.

- **Industry Standards:** The Government argues that the codes are constrained by the judgments of the people in each industry, who make the codes. These people, after all, know their industry best.

(How does the Court respond to this?)

The Court emphatically rejects this idea: "Such a delegation of legislative power is unknown to our law and is utterly inconsistent with the constitutional prerogatives and duties of Congress." This is the private delegation point.

- **Presidential findings:** In order to approve a code, the President has to find that (a) the trade groups don't restrict their membership, (b) the code is not designed to promote monopolies, and (c) that the code will further the policies of the Act.

(What does the Court say about these?)

(a) just goes to who can make the code, not what it says;

(b) doesn't meaningfully restrict policy choice either; and

(c) is just a repeat of (3) above.

- **Other cases:** The cases that the Court distinguishes suggest other ways that Congress could adequately constrain administrative discretion.

    (a) Background statutory rules: The Interstate Commerce Act permits issuance of certificates to common carriers when they are "in the public interest." But the public interest is defined against a variety of statutory rules in the code governing common carriers.

    (b) Nature of the industry: The Radio Act similarly allows licensing by the Federal Radio Commission (now the FCC) based on the "public convenience, interest or necessity." But this is defined against "the nature of radio communications, and . . . the scope, character and quality of the services to be rendered and the relative advantages to be derived through distribution of facilities."

The NIRA has none of these constraints, and it is therefore unconstitutional.

(Is this *Lochner*? Is the Court just striking down this key New Deal program in an effort to protect *laissez faire* economic policy?)

Note that *Schechter* includes both the nondelegation holding and a very restrictive construction of Congress's power under the Commerce Clause. The only laws invalidated on nondelegation grounds are also during the same period when the Court is striking down laws on grounds that they violate freedom of contract, etc.

(Should we reject the nondelegation doctrine as another example of bad judicial activism?)

3.   *Whitman v. American Trucking Ass'ns*, 531 U.S. 457 (2001)

Note that *Schechter* and *Panama Refining* are the only *public* delegation cases in which the Court has ever struck down a law under the nondelegation doctrine. People are fond of saying that the delegation doctrine had two good years and 218 very bad ones.

A case called *Amalgamated Meat Cutters* provides a good modern example of what passes these days: There, a lower court upheld a statute allowing the President to impose wage and price controls limited only by *implicit* standards of "broad fairness and avoidance of gross inequity."

Many thought *American Trucking* might be the *Lopez* of the delegation doctrine; it wasn't.

It's a complicated case. The Clean Air Act delegates a bunch of authority to the EPA to promulgate "national ambient air quality standards." There are two delegation issues:

- Whether the delegation is standardless and therefore unconstitutional; and

- Whether an agency can "cure" an unconstitutional delegation by *self-constraint*—that is, by promulgating rules setting out more definite standards, even though the standards don't come from Congress.

The Court rejects this second idea, which the D.C. Circuit had adopted, as not what delegation is really about. So then they have to consider the first issue. On that, the Court adheres to the intelligible principle requirement, but finds that the relevant Clean Air Act provisions provide one.

One formula that the modern intelligible principle cases take is to ask whether Congress has narrowed the discretion of the agency sufficiently to give a *court* a basis for judicial review of agency action. In other words, if the court can't tell from the statute whether a particular agency action is legal or not, that's an indication that too much discretion has been delegated to the agency.

(What's the constraint on the agency's discretion?)

The Court reads the statute to require that "for a discrete set of pollutants and based on published air quality criteria that reflect the latest scientific knowledge, the EPA must establish uniform national standards at a level that is requisite to protect public health from the adverse effects of the pollutant." And they define "requisite" pretty narrowly as "not more than necessary."

Now, there might still be a tough question if the EPA had to balance costs and benefits – weighing health against cost, for instance, seems fairly legislative.

(Do they have to do that?)

No – the Court interprets the CAA as forbidding them to consider costs.

(So what do you think of the scope of the delegation, then? Is it too broad? Broad as *Schechter*?)

It doesn't strike me as anywhere near as broad as *Schechter*. So I don't think the Court's back is against the wall here as it was in *Lopez*. It's not true that if you uphold this law, you can't imagine *anything* you'd strike down.

That's one reason to think the nondelegation doctrine isn't necessarily dead. Here's a second: After rejecting the delegation argument, the Court nonetheless rejects the agency's construction of the underlying statute as unreasonable – thereby exercising meaningful judicial review of the *exercise* of delegated authority.

3.   Remaining Checks on Delegation

a.   Statutory Construction

Courts may still construe statutory delegations narrowly in order to avoid a nondelegation question.

- Scope of Delegations: The broader a delegation is argued to be, the more clear Congress has to be in granting that broad authority. Ambiguous delegations are construed narrowly.

- Delegations Impinging on Constitutional Values: Where an agency asserts delegated authority to act in a way that impinges on some other constitutional principle—an individual right like free speech, or a structural value like federalism—then the courts will tend to construe the delegation narrowly. *See, e.g., Solid Waste.*

b.   Congressional Oversight of Agency Action

Congress has many mechanisms to control what agencies *do* with their broad delegated authority:

- **Legislative Vetoes:** Congress can nullify legislative action after the fact (struck down in *Chadha*, but survives in practice).

- **Oversight Hearings:** Congress can call executive officials before it to explain their actions publicly.

- **Confirmation of Officers:** Congress can often exercise a check and extract concessions when confirming nominees to executive departments.

- **Budgetary Controls:** Congress can use control of funding for agencies to control agency action.

These sorts of mechanisms don't address the argument that it's simply unconstitutional to transfer legislative authority from the legislative to the executive branch.   But they do help to maintain some overall balance between Congress and the Executive, and to preserve some of the underlying values of accountability in the administrative process.

c.   Judicial Review of Agency Action:

The abandonment of constitutional limits on delegation has been offset by the rapid growth of judicial review of agency action for conformity to statutory purposes.   Most of this review takes place under the Administrative Procedure Act (APA) and is the subject matter of the course in Administrative Law (which everyone should take).

- **Substantive Review – Law:** Courts review whether actions taken and regulations issued are substantively consistent with the terms of the underlying statutes delegating authority to the agency.

- **Substantive Review – Fact & Policy:** Very deferential here. "Arbitrary and capricious" standard.

- **Procedural Review:**   Courts also review whether agency decisionmaking satisfies procedural requirements in the APA, such as "notice and comment" for certain forms of rulemaking.

An important limit on judicial review of agency action:

- **The *Chevron* Doctrine:** If a statute is ambiguous, then a court will defer to an interpretation offered by the agency tasked with enforcing that statute so long as the agency's interpretation is reasonable.

The second half of the *American Trucking* opinion illustrates this issue of statutory review.

This is a complicated question of statutory construction about the way that you do with ozone regulation in "nonattainment" areas. There are two sets of implementation provisions, and the parties are fighting about which one applies. The important point is that ordinarily, courts defer to agency interpretations of law under the *Chevron* doctrine.

(Is the statute ambiguous here?)

Yes – it's not clear that Subpart 1 or Subpart 2 applies, because there are certain gaps that applying Subpart 2 would entail.

(So what would the Court ordinarily do?)

Defer defer defer.

(Do they?)

No, because they find the agency's interpretation unreasonable. That's because it would wholly dispense with Subpart 2.

Historically, the Court has almost *never* second-guessed the agency's interpretation of a statute it finds to be ambiguous. But here they do. And they've done the same thing in a couple of other cases lately. This has the effect of cutting back on the scope of delegated power.

American Trucking's pretty scary because the statutory issue is so intricate and obscure. Here's what you need to know about that part:

- Statutory review limits the discretion of the agency by holding them to the bounds of what Congress has actually delegated.

- *Chevron* is an important liberating force here – it expands the bounds of delegated authority by allowing the agency to effectively set its own bounds through interpretation.

- But *Chevron* isn't absolute. Statutes must be ambiguous, and the agency's interpretation must be reasonable.

- *American Trucking*'s a good example of a) the Court's willingness to say an interpretation's unreasonable, and b) what makes such an interpretation unreasonable (rendering part of the statute meaningless).

Statutory review of administrative action is yet another example of how non-constitutional law—here the Administrative Procedure Act and the attendant structure of judicial enforcement of statutory limits on agency discretion—takes over a job which had once been performed by constitutional doctrine (nondelegation). It's the same story as in federalism, where once Congress's Commerce Power becomes very broad, the real boundaries between national and state power are determined by statutory construction in preemption cases. So don't get the idea that just because the delegation doctrine is largely defunct, the constitutional *value* that Congress is the primary legislator has gone away. It's just protected in a different way, by way of the "Constitution Outside the Constitution." Concerns about excessive delegations of legislative power continue to shape the law in a wide variety of areas.

B.   **Altering the Lawmaking Process**

We're talking today and next time about broad structural statutes that rearrange the functions of the government. These are all "delegation" problems in a broad sense, because they involve assignment of a particular power of one branch to an official in another branch. Or, in the case of the legislative veto, the question is Congress's ability to still hold something back when it delegates.

These structural statute cases involve five principal sorts of separation of powers claims:

- **Nondelegation Claims:**   Pay particular attention to how the nondelegation doctrine can creep back in, even when it is disavowed. For instance, it seems to do so in the majority opinion in *Clinton v. NY* and Justice Scalia's dissent in *Mistretta*.

- **"Same Branch Limits" or *Chadha* Claims:** These are claims that a branch has sought to evade the constitutional limits on its own actions. Art. I claims -- as in *Chadha* -- are the classic example, but the standing cases (which we'll do at the end of the semester) raise the same sorts of issues for courts under Art. III.

- **"Mixing" Claims:**   These are claims that one branch is improperly exercising powers that belong to a different branch. A more extreme form of this claim is that Congress has created a hybrid "fourth branch" -- *see, e.g.*, Justice Scalia's dissent in *Mistretta*.

- **"Aggrandizement" "Encroachment," or "Dilution" Claims:** These are the functionalist concerns -- has something upset the balance of power among the branches. Once this is defined to be the question, the statute is almost always upheld.

  Although most cases speak in terms of "aggrandizement" or "encroachment," there is also a third subcategory of claims where the concern is that a particular function will undermine the authority of a branch. For example, Mistretta claimed that participation of judges in the Sentencing Commission undermined the judiciary's appearance of impartiality.

- **Appointments Clause or Unitary Executive Claims:**   These questions revolve around whether an officer is subject to removal by the President. The key question is locating the line between *Myers* and *Humphrey's Executor*.

1.   *INS v. Chadha*, 462 U.S. 919 (1983)

Chadha was ordered deported for having overstayed his visa.   The immigration rules allow a deportation to be suspended if the alien meets certain conditions, and the immigration judge granted a suspension.

These suspension determinations were subject to a one-house legislative veto, however.   The House passed -- without debate or recorded vote -- a resolution opposing the suspension of six deportations, including Chadha's. Chadha was then ordered deported.

The Court holds (Burger, CJ) that the legislative veto is unconstitutional.

(The Court notes that there have been roughly 300 legislative veto provisions in various statutes.   Why would Congress want to put a legislative veto provision in a statute?)

To control the exercise of delegated power.

(Does the Court care that this is a useful legislative device?)

"[The] fact that a given law or procedure is efficient, convenient, and useful in facilitating functions of the government, standing alone, will not save it if it is contrary to the Constitution. Convenience and efficiency are not the primary objectives -- or the hallmarks -- of democratic government . . . ."

(What constitutional provisions is the Court relying on here?)

Bicameralism -- Art. I, § 1 provides that legislative power is vested in a Senate *and* a House of Representatives.

Presentment -- Art. I, § 7 provides that every bill passing Congress shall be presented to the president, and must be approved by him before taking effect (unless the veto is overridden).

The Framers felt strongly about this procedure and required that it be strictly adhered to.

(How do we tell when these procedures must be complied with?   For instance, does the House have to comply with this rule when it hires a Sergeant at Arms? When it sets ethics rules for Members?)

The question is thus whether the House has exercised legislative power; if so, its action must satisfy bicameralism and presentment. The stated test is that the House's action was legislative if it had "the purpose and effect of altering the legal rights, duties and relations of persons . . . outside the legislative branch."

(Is the House's veto over Chadha's case "legislative"?)

We know it's legislative because, absent the legislative veto provision, it would have taken a statute to do what the House did here.   Congress's disagreement with the Attorney General here is over questions of policy, and Congress can implement its view only through a full-fledged statute.

(Doesn't agency rulemaking fit this description? How does the Court distinguish it? Does the Court's reasoning assume a non-defunct nondelegation doctrine?)

(What about Justice Powell's argument? What kind of power does he think the House has exercised?)

He says the action is *judicial* in nature. It is, after all, not a *general* rule that Congress has implemented.

(Would Justice Powell's argument make *all* legislative vetoes unconstitutional?)

No -- only those that adjudicated the rights of particular individuals.

(How does the Court answer that?)

This isn't judicial because no justiciable case or controversy concerning Chadha was presented by the Attorney General's suspension of the deportation. Who would appeal? And the AG's decision on these issues is unreviewable.

Is this the dumbest argument ever or what? The question is whether this is more like what a court does than like what a legislature does. The fact is, this is like a bill of attainder -- it's a legislative judgment of unfitness to remain. But it's probably not *punishment*, since Chadha has no *right* to remain. So it wouldn't be unconstitutional under the Bill of Attainder clause.

You can see, in any event, the difficulty of fitting a real-world action into a legislative or judical (or executive) box.

The Constitution contains only four situations in which a single House can take real action: House initiation of impeachment, Senate impeachment trials, confirmation of appointments, and ratification of treaties.

(Is the Court's approach here formalist or functionalist?)

Formalist – the Court categorizes the exercise of power, then applies a bright line rule that determines whether the exercise is permissible.

But note that we might have three sorts of formalist claims:

(1)   nondelegation

(2)   same-branch limits

(3)   mixing

(What sort of argument does Justice White advance in dissent? Formalist or functionalist?)

Functionalist – Separation of powers is about accommodation and practicality -- the Constitution doesn't require *total* separation. Legislative vetoes are common and useful, and striking them all down is a terrible idea.

(What's so great about them?)

The legislative veto is a central means by which Congress makes agencies accountable. Without it, Congress must either try to write detailed laws itself or abdicate its lawmaking function altogether.

The legislative veto is a means of self-defense for Congress, not aggrandizement.

The Constitution doesn't authorize *or* prohibit the legislative veto. The question should be whether it is broadly consistent with Art. I and the purposes of separation of powers.

(How does he answer the presentment and bicameralism arguments?)

Presentment and bicameralism don't answer this question, because Congress is not making new law when it vetoes. The Art. I clauses are concerned with *new* legislation.

Lots of "legislative" action circumvents Art. I, because it involves the exercise of delegated authority. Agency rulemaking is clearly lawmaking -- in fact, it is *most* lawmaking. Here, all Congress has done is delegated some authority to a subset of itself.

In any event, departures from the status quo happen only when the President and both Houses concur.

There is no invasion of executive or judicial authority here. If there were, there might be a problem.

Finally, he makes an important big-picture point: "Today's decision strikes down in one fell swoop provisions in more laws enacted by Congress than the Court has cumulatively invalidated in its history." So this is a case where political-branch precedent doesn't count for very much at all.

2. After *Chadha*

Limiting Principles: After *Chadha*, the Court could have limited the reach of the decision by drawing three possible lines, but it didn't:

- The Court could have followed Justice Powell's lead and limited its holding to cases where adjudication-like decisions are being made by Congress. But in *Process Gas* and *U.S. Senate v. FTC* the Court summarily affirmed lower court decisions striking down legislative vetoes over agency rulemaking.

  (Does everyone understand the difference between administrative adjudication and rulemaking?)

367

- The Court could have drawn a line between legislative vetoes of agencies that are under the President's direct control and "independent" agencies like the FTC or FCC. But both these summary affirmances involved independent agencies.

- The Court could have drawn the line between one-house vetoes, like in *Chadha*, and two-house vetoes. But the *Senate v. FTC* case involved a two-house veto.

It seems to me that the majority's reasoning has to extend to all these cases. Only Justice Powell's approach would have allowed a distinction.

Alternative Mechanisms: Congress can still achieve the same ends through other means:

- *Report and Wait*: Congress can require that rules be submitted to Congress and become effective only after a period of, say, 60 days. This would give Congress time to pass a statutory restriction if it really wanted to.

- *Sunset Provisions*: Congress can provide that agency authority lapses after a few years, requiring renewal through a new statute. (Note that it does this with some laws, like the Independent Counsel statute.)

- *Joint Resolutions*: Congress can provide that agency action becomes effective only if approved by both Houses of Congress through a joint resolution, which can be vetoed by the President. Note that you could require a joint resolution of *approval* or *disapproval*. The former is *more* strict than the original legislative veto because it places the burden on the Executive branch to overcome legislative inertia.

- *Informal Agreements*: Congress can refuse to grant agency authority to act unless the agency informally agrees not to do certain things without the approval of, say, its supervising committee. These aren't legally binding, but the committee is in a position to punish the agency -- for instance, by cutting its funds -- if it reneges.

- *Appropriations Rules*: Congress can provide, by internal rule, that appropriations for a particular action will not be approved by the appropriations committee without a resolution by the authorizing committee approving the action.

Note that one separation of powers scholar asserts that there have been over 400 legislative vetoes enacted *since Chadha*.

3.   The Line-Item Veto: *Clinton v. New York*, 524 U.S. 417 (1998)

The Line Item Veto Act of 1996 authorized the President to cancel any items of new spending or any limited tax benefit. Cancellation prevents the item "from having legal force or effect." Canceled funds go into a "lockbox" provision to be applied to deficit reduction.

(Why enact a line-item veto? Why would Congress be willing to give away this kind of power?)

In identifying items for cancellation, the President must consider the legislative history, purposes, and other relevant information concerning the items. He must then determine that each cancellation will

(i)　　　　reduce the Federal budget deficit;

(ii)　　　not impair any essential Government functions; and

(iii)　　　not harm the national interest.

He must notify Congress of any cancellation within five days after enactment of the canceled provision.

Cancellation takes effect upon Congress's receipt of the cancellation message. But Congress may enact a "disapproval bill" by majority vote, subject to a Presidential veto.

Plaintiffs who stood to benefit from canceled items sued to invalidate the law.

The Court (Stevens, J) holds that the law is unconstitutional.

The line-up here is frightening: You have both Scalia and Breyer in dissent – the smartest formalist, and one of the smartest functionalists, both agreeing that the majority has gotten it wrong.

(What's the majority's rationale for striking down the statute?)

a.　　　The Article I Claim

The Act permits the President to amend acts of Congress by repealing a portion of them. Repeal and amendment must comply with the Art. I process -- here, there is no such compliance.

(What's the dissenters' answer to this?)

The dissenters say that this isn't an Art. I case at all -- Congress has simply delegated authority to cancel spending in the course of implementing the budget act. This is no different than discretionary spending.

(What do you think of Justice Breyer's hypothetical at p. 1149? I've tried to illustrate it in the handout. Can we distinguish among the three cases?)

Justice Breyer's Hypothetical:

Case 1:　　　§ 101. Hospitals meeting certain qualifications in New York shall be exempt from federal taxes. The President may prevent this provision from having legal force or effect if he determines that so doing will (i) reduce the federal budget deficit; (ii) not impair any essential government functions; and (iii) not harm the national interest.

Case 2:   § 101. Hospitals meeting certain qualifications in New York shall be exempt from federal taxes.*

§ 102. Gas stations selling ethanol shall receive a federal tax credit on all such sales.*

§ 103. The federal government shall spend $50 million to build a new dam in Idaho.*

---

* The President may prevent this provision from having legal force or effect if he determines that so doing will (i) reduce the federal budget deficit; (ii) not impair any essential government functions; and (iii) not harm the national interest.

Case 3:   *1996 Statute:* The President may prevent any tax or spending provision in a federal law from having legal force or effect if he determines that so doing will (i) reduce the federal budget deficit; (ii) not impair any essential government functions; and (iii) not harm the national interest.

1999 Statute: Hospitals meeting certain qualifications in New York shall be exempt from federal taxes.

(What's the difference between these three cases?)

There may be important differences in terms of the weight and placement of the burden of overcoming legislative inertia.

The best case the dissenters have for their position is a case called *Field v. Clark*, 143 U.S. 649 (1892). In *Field*, a federal statute created certain exemptions from the tariff on imports, but also allowed the President to suspend those exemptions – that is, subject the countries in question to the tariff – if those countries were imposing duties on American products. So, in effect, the statute authorized the President to suspend the effect of a federal law.

Field upheld the law on the ground that all the President was really doing was finding whether certain factual conditions were met -- like whether other countries are trading with us on reasonable terms.

(How does Justice Stevens deal with *Field*?)

b.   The Nondelegation Claim

The majority rejects the *Field v. Clark* argument on the ground that here, the President is not merely finding facts. Rather, the President gets to make a discretionary decision in light of facts that also existed when

Congress acted. Moreover, the *Field*-type statutes were all dealing with foreign affairs, where the President has inherent authority.

(What kind of argument is this? What do we call a claim that the President has been given an excessive degree of discretion?)

This looks like a nondelegation argument, so it implicitly concedes that more is going on than a mere Art. I, § 7 violation. So for the dissenters, the critical question is the delegation claim. The dissenters reject nondelegation, basically on the ground that broad delegations are par for the course.

(What constraints does Justice Breyer identify on the President's discretion?)

There are three kinds of constraints:

(a)   Procedural -- President must consider legislative history, purposes of the laws, etc.

(b)   Purposive -- President is supposed to focus on eliminating wasteful spending and promoting fiscal accountability.

(c)   Substantive -- President must determine that cancellation will reduce the deficit, not impair essential government functions, and not harm the national interests.

(Are these enough?)

c.   The "Mixing" Claim

(What kind of power does the Court think the President is exercising here?)

The Court doesn't clearly say, but it seems to think it's legislative. You might also characterize the majority's argument as saying that the President is exercising his executive authority outside the constitutional procedure.

Breyer and Scalia says it's executive, so there's no mixing problem. After all, the Executive usually doesn't *have* to spend money that Congress appropriates.

(What's the majority's best argument for distinguishing this case from the ordinary executive power over discretionary spending?)

This is not simply discretionary spending -- no prior law has given the President authority to change the text of statutes.

(Should that matter? Is this distinction too formal?)

I think this is actually a close question. Remember the criticism of formalism is always that it's over and under-inclusive in terms of the values you're protecting. On the other hand, though, it's frequently true that more standard-like principles are more difficult to enforce. By enforcing a formal set of rules, we may establish *some* limits on the powers of the branches, and may end up approximating where we want to be.

(Note that Justice Scalia says that the cancellation power is just like the budget sequestration power in *Bowsher*, which the Court says is *executive*.)

d.   The "Encroachment" Claim

This seems at least implicit in the Court's Art. I discussion -- the President is horning in on Congress's power of the purse.

(What's Justice Breyer's argument here?)

He says the increase in the President's power is limited to the budget, and it's not as big as some other delegations upheld in the past.

(Isn't Breyer avoiding the practicalities of the situation? What effect is the Act likely to have on the relationship between Congress and the President in this area?)

I think it's a pretty big change – it fundamentally alters the bargaining relationship between the President and Congress. No more take-it-or-leave-it, package deals.

(Is it worth it? What about Justice Kennedy's point that "A nation cannot plunder its own treasury without putting its Constitution and its survival in peril"?)

C.   Executive Privileges and Immunities

I have always skipped this part, simply for reasons of time. Some of the same issues of presidential accountability can be raised in connection with Morrison *and the independent counsel law. You may want to at least mention* Nixon *as a reference point in earlier discussions about the role of the Court vis-à-vis the political branches.*

D.   Appointments and the Unitary Executive

In *Chadha* and *Clinton v. New York*, we dealt with efforts to restructure the legislative process; in *Morrison*, Congress has tried to restructure the Executive Branch.

It is important to keep straight the various challenges to the independent counsel statute in *Morrison*. The executive officials challenging the law argued that

- the independent counsel was improperly appointed by someone *other than the President*;

- even if Congress could vest authority to appoint the independent counsel in another official, it could not vest that authority in *another branch* of government;

- the statute improperly restricted the President's power to *remove* the independent counsel;

- more generally, the independent counsel exercised executive authority but was *not subject to the control of the President*; and

- the independent counsel statute *altered the balance of power* between Congress and the Executive.

Several of these claims can be argued in both formalist and functionalist ways. For instance, Justice Scalia proposes a formalist test for who's an inferior officer, and the majority responds with a functionalist test instead.

The Court ultimately decides, 8-1, that the statute is OK, but Justice Scalia's lone dissent has been looking pretty good in light of the whole Monica Lewinsky/Ken Starr fiasco.

(Ask someone how old they were in 1997 when the Monica scandal broke.)

1.   *Morrison v. Olson*, 487 U.S. 654 (1988)

The Ethics in Government Act of 1978 allows the appointment of an "independent counsel" to investigate and prosecute certain high-ranking government officials for violations of the federal criminal laws. "Covered" officials include the President and Vice President, Cabinet-level officials, certain high-ranking officials in the Executive Office of the President and Justice Department, and others.

Upon receipt of information that the Attorney General determines "is sufficient to constitute grounds to investigate whether any [covered] person may have violated any Federal criminal law," the Attorney General must conduct a preliminary investigation. Within 90 days, the Attorney General must report to a special court, the "Special Division," whether there are reasonable grounds for further investigation. If such grounds exist, the Attorney General must apply to the Special Division for appointment of an independent counsel. The Special Division then appoints an independent counsel and defines the counsel's jurisdiction.

An independent counsel can be removed only by impeachment or by personal action of the Attorney General for good cause, physical disability, mental incapacity, or "any other condition that substantially impairs the performance of such independent counsel's duties." The Special Division may also terminate the independent counsel if it finds that investigation of all matters within the independent counsel's jurisdiction have been completed or so substantially completed that the Department of Justice can take over.

The Court holds (Rehnquist, C.J.) that the independent counsel provisions are constitutional.

There are three issues in the majority opinion:

(1)   Appointments Clause: Does the appointment of the independent counsel by the Special Division, rather than the President, violate the appointments clause?

(2)   Article III: Does the power of the Special Division to appoint the independent counsel and define her jurisdiction violate Article III?

(3)   Separation of Powers: Finally, does the "independence" of the independent counsel violate more general separation of powers principles?

a.   Appointments Clause[47]

(What's the *rule* under the Appointments Clause?   When does an officer have to be appointed by the President himself?)

The President must appoint "principal" officers, but Congress has the power to vest appointment of "inferior" officers in "Heads of Departments" or "Courts of Law."

(How does the majority go about telling the difference between a principal and an inferior officer?)

The majority admits that the line between "inferior" and "principal" officers is unclear, and it says you have to look at a variety of factors.

(What are the key variables here?)

• She can be removed by the Attorney General,

• she is authorized to perform only certain limited duties, and

• her office is limited in jurisdiction and tenure.

(How does Justice Scalia define "inferior" officer?)

The independent counsel is a principal officer, because she is not *subordinate* to any other officer in the Executive Branch.   Principal officers have generally been removable at will.

(What's the primary virtue of Scalia's approach?)

---

[47] Art. II, § 2, cl. 2 provides: "[The President] shall nominate, and by and with the Advice and Consent of the Senate, shall appoint Ambassadors, other public Ministers and Consuls, Judges of the supreme Court, and all other Officers of the United States, whose Appointments are not herein otherwise provided for, and which shall be established by Law: but the Congress may by Law vest the Appointment of such inferior Officers, as they think proper, in the President alone, in the Courts of Law, or in the Heads of Departments."

It's a fairly bright-line rule. It's not quite perfect – lots of principal officers *do* have superiors, but one could still say that anyone with *no* superior must be a principal.

The Majority's conclusion leaves the question whether Congress may authorize an "interbranch" appointment, i.e., whether it may give a *court* the power to appoint an "inferior" executive officer.

(What's the answer here?)

Here, the text of the Appointments Clause is clear: It allows Congress to vest the appointment "in the President alone, in the courts of Law, or in the Heads of Departments." The "as they think proper" language indicates that Congress is supposed to have a lot of discretion.

Two potential limits on interbranch appointments remain: Such an appointment might be unconstitutional if

- it impaired the constitutional function assigned to a branch, or

- if there were some "incongruity" between the power to appoint and the functions normally performed by the appointing branch.

These possible problems take us into the Article III claim

b.   Article III or Mixing

(What does the majority say about the incompatibility issue?)

There is no incongruity in having judges appoint prosecutors -- they have experience with prosecutors all the time. And the Act avoids any conflicts of interest by disqualifying judges of the Special Division from participating in any matter relating to the independent counsel they appointed.

(Note that the historical evidence indicates that courts frequently appointed prosecutors earlier in the country's history. Until very recently, for example, the Connecticut attorney general was appointed by the State supreme court.)

The powers granted to the Special Division are not incompatible with Art. III because they are mostly "passive" or "ministerial." The termination provision is more troubling, but this is construed as simply allowing removal of an independent counsel who's done but is unwilling to acknowledge that fact.

(Is this argument about the removal power persuasive?)

(Isn't the decision when a prosecutor should give up the hunt pretty critical?)

After all, that's a primary criticism of Ken Starr. It seems like the better argument would be that it's not unconstitutional to ask judges to wear other "hats" – for example, some judges serve on various Rules Committees that write the rules of procedure, not to mention the federal Sentencing Commission. Here the conflict of interest reasons not to put the discretionary "you're done" termination power in the executive branch are sufficiently persuasive to justify giving that power to the Special Division.

c.   Removal

There are two issues:

- whether the "good cause" removal limitation is itself sufficient to interfere with the President's constitutional functions, and

- whether the act as a whole impermissibly interferes with those functions.

The first of these is the true unitary executive argument. That's a formalist claim. The other is the more functionalist approach to the same question: Does the independent counsel encroach or otherwise interfere with Executive functions.

We have two primary precedents on the removal issue: *Myers v. U.S.*[48] and *Humphrey's Executor v. U.S.*[49] *Myers* held that it was unconstitutional for Congress to try to limit the President's authority to remove federal postmasters. *Humphrey's Executor* held that Congress *can* limit the removal power over commissioners of the Federal Trade Commission.

(So is the independent counsel more like a postmaster or an FTC commissioner? How do we choose between these two precedents?)

There's two possible dividing lines – the old one and the new one.

(What's the old one?)

(What's the new one?)

Unlike *Bowsher* or *Myers*, Congress is not trying to gain a role in the removal process for *itself*. The executive branch keeps the power -- it's just limited. This case is therefore closer to *Humphrey's Executor*.

Humphrey's Executor and *Wiener* did characterize the functions of independent agency officials as "quasi-legislative" or "quasi-judicial," but that's not the key to whether Congress can limit presidential removal to "good cause." Rather, the question is whether Congress has interfered with the President's duty to take care that the laws be faithfully executed.

The removal limitation does not itself cause such interference here. The Attorney General retains a lot of authority over the independent counsel;

---

[48] 272 U.S. 52 (1926).

[49] 295 U.S. 602 (1935).

the legislative history, for example, makes clear that she can be removed for "misconduct."

Nor does the Act as a whole upset the separation of powers. The three branches don't have to operate "with absolute independence." Here, there is no aggrandizement by Congress or the judiciary. Nor does the Act prevent the Executive from performing its functions.

d.   Justice Scalia's Dissent

This case has what I consider to be the greatest Scalia line ever: "Frequently an issue of this sort will come before the Court clad, so to speak, in sheep's clothing; the potential of the asserted principle to effect important change in the equilibrium of power is not immediately evident, and must be discerned by a careful and perceptive analysis. *But this wolf comes as a wolf.*"

Justice Scalia says that the Court is wrong to take the Appointments Clause first. The requirements of that clause are a function of the larger separation of powers concerns.

(What's Justice Scalia's central argument?)

The strong unitary executive position. *All* of the executive power is vested in the President. That means that the statute is unconstitutional if:

(a)   prosecution involves a purely executive function, and

(b)   the statute deprives the President of exclusive control over the exercise of that power.

(Does the statute do both these things?)

The Court concedes that both these things are true. Executive power has to be defined "by reference to what has always and everywhere -- if conducted by Government at all -- been conducted never by the legislature, never by the courts, and always by the executive." The independent counsel's functions clearly meet that description. (Note that Scalia appears to be wrong about this as an historical matter.)

The whole point of the statute is to deprive the President of control over the independent counsel's prosecutorial function. And the Court exaggerates the degree of control that the Attorney General does have. The Constitution requires that the President have *all* control. We wouldn't tolerate Congress or the judiciary giving up "just a tiny bit" of their exclusive functions.

(What's the obvious problem with this argument?)

It makes the President unaccountable to anyone else.

(How does Justice Scalia answer this problem?)

It is no less unthinkable that the President should be able to control the independent prosecutor than that Congress should have exclusive power to exempt itself from laws or that the Court should have exclusive power to pronounce final decisions, even in cases concerning the Court.

(Is that answer good enough?)

One problem is that "Congress" is a "they, not an it." Individual congressmen aren't nearly as powerful as the President, so it's less problematic to have less checks in some ways.

(Justice Scalia also has a methodological problem with the Court's approach. What is it?)

The Court replaces clear rules in this area with a "balancing test," but gives no standards "to determine how the balance is to be struck, that is, how much removal of presidential power is too much?" And the Court doesn't explain how it reaches the result it does.

Scalia says that the Court is engaged here in an "ad hoc approach to constitutional adjudication" -- reaching the result they *want* by ignoring the strict rules of the Constitution.

(Is that a fair criticism? Do you think the Chief Justice is deciding this case based on ideology?)

That seems unlikely. Rehnquist was head of the Office of Legal Counsel – the President's legal advisers – before he became a Justice. He's not exactly hostile to presidential power.

(What's the practical impact of the statute?)

The independent counsel weakens the President by

(a) reducing the zeal of his staff, and

(b) eroding his public support.

The statute guarantees "massive and lengthy investigations" based on very little showing of legal violations.

Note that Scalia links these practical concerns to the basic purpose of separation of powers, which is "not merely to assure effective government but to preserve individual freedom."

(How does the independent counsel threaten liberty?)

The independent counsel laws undermines the liberty of people subject to such investigations.

The primary check on prosecutorial abuse is political. Here, however, the prosecutor is cut off from any such checks. "What if [the judges of the Special Division] are politically partisan, as judges have been known to be, and select a prosecutor antagonistic to the administration?"

One advantage of the unitary executive is that is assures a uniform application of the law. But "[t]he mini-Executive that is the independent counsel, however, . . . is intentionally cut off from the unifying influence of the Justice Department, and from the perspective that multiple responsibilities provide. What would normally be regarded as a technical violation . . . may in her small world assume the proportions of an indictable offense."

(This is surely prescient. But would the "unitary executive" provide any better guarantee of uniformity?)

(Isn't the fear that the President will discriminate, too -- but in his own favor? Isn't that the lesson of the campaign finance scandal?)

e.   Some More General Questions

(Is *Morrison* consistent with *Chadha*?) (What's the tension?)

(What does our experience with the Independent Counsel Act since *Morrison* tell us? Was Scalia right?)

(Is the primary objection to Starr structural? Or is it simply an objection to the choices he's made (or perhaps to the power that *any* prosecutor has)? Are these issues related?)

They are, in the sense that Scalia says the primary check on prosecutorial discretion is ordinarily political.

(The Act sunset a couple years ago. What should Congress have done? Should it have renewed the act, tried something different, or given up entirely?)

f.   Institutional Alternatives

- *No Statute:* After all, we got an independent counsel in Watergate without a statute. A lot of people say that the system worked there. But there were some special circumstances: Attorney General Elliott Richardson was confirmed after the scandal had begun to break, and the Senate was able to extract a promise to appoint a special prosecutor at his confirmation hearings.

  Now, the special prosecutor actually *wasn't* impossible to fire – after all, Archibald Cox got fired in the "Saturday Night Massacre." But it's unclear which way that example cuts.

  In any event, if the political effect is to make the special prosecutor impossible to remove, don't Justice Scalia's problems sneak back in?

- *Congressional Investigation:* Congressional committees can investigate anyone they like, including the President. Such investigations were launched concerning both Whitewater and the Campaign Finance scandal.

379

What does that experience tell us? Would this option be as effective? Even more political?

- *Civil Service:* Prof. Tom Merrill at Columbia has proposed that independent counsel-type investigations should be conducted by a special division of the Justice Department composed of only civil service people -- no political appointees. The office would have a limited budget, so it would have to set priorities. And it would be subject to supervision by the Attorney General, except that she would recuse herself if she, the President, or the Vice-President were being investigated.

Is this a better solution?

2. *Free Enterprise Fund v. Public Company Accounting Oversight Board*, 130 S. Ct. 3138 (2010)

The Court recently revisited this aea in a case arising out of the Sarbanes-Oxley Act, which Congress enacted in response to the Enron scandal and several other high-profile accounting disasters. That case focused largely on the removal issue, but it suggested a somewhat more formal approach than did *Morrison*. The PCAOB was a quasi-private, quasi-public entity with authority to regulate accounting standards. Members of the Board could be removed only on narrow grounds, and the power to remove them was vested in the Securities Exchange Commission—an agency that was itself insulated from *presidential* removal under *Humphrey's Executor*. The *Free Enterprise* Court decided one level of removal-protection was enough; nesting *two* layers of such protection pushed the incursion on the President's authority too far. Given that many regulatory entities have this structure, the case may call into question a number of federal instrumentalities. More generally, it may suggest a trend back toward formalism in this area.

VII.   Chapter Fifteen – Military and Foreign Affairs Powers

This chapter covers a lot, and if you're doing the book in order, it comes at a point in the semester when time grows short. Doing all the subjects justice can be challenging. On the other hand, students seem to enjoy this chapter, and it probably illustrates better than any other unit the crucial importance of the Constitution outside the courts. After all, many of these issues—particularly war powers—are unlikely ever to be definitively resolved through litigation. I have tried to provide a somewhat broader selection of non-judicial materials for this reason.

On the other hand, one crucial lesson of the War on Terror materials is that the Court remains "on the case" and willing to intervene in order to enforce constitutional limitations, even in national security cases. In a sense, Hamdan may be the best conclusion to our unit on the "History of Judicial Review," since it shows a Supreme Court intervening in an area where John Marshall would likely have feared to tread (and where Abraham Lincoln did not tolerate intervention), in order to protect individual liberty and the separation of powers.

A.   Presidential Power in Foreign Affairs

It's frequently said that the President holds the "foreign affairs" power. But there's no "foreign affairs" power in the Constitution. And the specific *powers* dealing with foreign affairs in the text are divided between the Executive and Legislative branches.

I want to proceed in two stages here:

- First, I want to think about the nature of power over foreign affairs generally, without focusing on which branch of the national government holds it. The key question is whether foreign affairs powers are of the "limited and enumerated" kind, or whether they are "inherent in sovereignty."

- Second, we focus on *allocation* of foreign affairs power between Congress and the President. That will depend, however, on whether we see foreign affairs power as enumerated or inherent.

So we'll start the question where the national government's foreign affairs powers come from, then move to the allocation issue.

1.   Enumerated or Inherent Powers?

A key question in this section is whether the United States government has only the foreign affairs powers listed in the Constitutional text. Professor Louis Henkin has offered a list of "missing" powers. Some of the high points:

- recognition of foreign governments

- setting up consulates and maintaining the whole apparatus of foreign policy

- establishment of "doctrines" to guide U.S. foreign and defense policy, like the Monroe Doctrine or the recent doctrine of preemption

- termination of treaties, as opposed to making them

- a lot of powers to deal with immigration

Some of these, maybe, can be inferred from textual provisions that *are* there; for instance, the recognition power is often inferred from the President's textual power in Article II to "receive Ambassadors"; I guess you can refuse to recognize a foreign country by not receiving their ambassador.

A lot of them seem "necessary and proper" to other powers; setting up consulates, for instance, would be necessary and proper to the textual power to appoint Ambassadors.

But the point remains that the textual powers granted to the United States are fairly limited, and there are lots of things that the government might want to do in foreign affairs that don't have a clear constitutional basis. The issue is whether that means the government can't do it, or whether there are basic powers just inherent in being a sovereign nation.

That question in turn implicates a larger issue that we talked about briefly with respect to the dormant *foreign* commerce clause – that is, whether or not the "ordinary" rules of constitutional law apply in the context of foreign affairs.

2.   The Neutrality Controversy and the "Vesting Clause" Theory

The Neutrality Controversy arises out of the war between France and Britain following shortly after the French Revolution in 1789.

Right at the end of the Revolutionary War, we made various treaties with France. These treaties obligated us to do things like help protect French colonies in the Americas and indirectly support French naval activities by allowing French warships to bring ships they had captured into U.S. ports.

After the French Revolution sets off war with Britain, the French start asking us to do more. They want, for instance, to recruit American ships and sailors to be "privateers" – that is, private navy vessels that would be rewarded by the French for preying on British shipping.

There's a lot of Americans willing to do this, because the French Revolution is extremely popular in America at the time. We regarded them as having thrown off monarchy in the same way we had; we didn't realize that they were about to set up the guillotine and start cutting eveyone's heads off.

So the French send a new ambassador – Edmond Charles Genet, who is kind of a flamboyant character – to America to try to stir up support. The Washington Administration is terrified that Genet is going to help drag the U.S. into the war between France and Britain, which would probably result in our getting crushed like a bug.

Washington issues a proclamation on April 22, 1793, basically purporting to make it a federal crime for any American citizen to aid either side in this war.

a.   Who Can Proclaim Neutrality?

Once the Neutrality Proclamation goes out, Hamilton and Madison get into a spat over whether President Washington really had the authority to do it. Each of them does what any good law professor would do if he really wanted to make a difference in the world: They write op-ed pieces for the local newspapers. Probably because they don't want to publicly air the Administration's dirty laundry, they come up with catchy Latin pseudonyms: Pacificus is Hamilton; Helvidius in Madison.

(What's Pacificus's argument for why the Neutrality Proclamation was OK?)

His primary argument goes like this:

1. Making a proclamation of neutrality is an Executive function.

2. The Constitution vests all "executive power" in the President.

Therefore, the President has the power to make the proclamation.

(Why does Hamilton think this is an executive function?)

Several reasons:

- It involves dealing with other countries, which Congress isn't in a position to do directly.

- It involves interpreting the laws in force.

(I thought the judiciary "interpreted" the laws?)

Hamilton says the judiciary interprets in cases where they are competent to do so. Hamilton's point is that there will be a whole range of circumstances in which interpretation is required outside the context of a litigated case. In those instances, interpretation is an *executive* function.

I'm not sure it makes sense to suggest, as Hamilton does, that interpretation is *exclusively* an executive function. Consider this hypothetical: Suppose we think that France has violated their treaty with us, and Congress is thinking about declaring war on the basis of that. In that instance, isn't Congress going to have to interpret the treaty for themselves?

I think Hamilton's stronger argument is that the Neutrality instance goes beyond interpretation to *execution* of the laws.

- It's an instance of the Executive's responsibility to "take care that the laws are faithfully executed."

(But wait a second: What "laws" is Washington executing?)

Hamilton says he's executing the treaties themselves. But he goes further than this to say that the President has power to execute *international* law in general. "The Executive is charged with the execution of all laws, the laws of Nations as well as the Municipal law."

That question – the extent to which the Laws of Nations are really "part of our law" – is something we'll talk a lot about later on.

Madison's answer to all this is twofold: He says that the proclamation is most closely related to the power to declare war and make treaties, and that these both *legislative* functions and therefore reserved to Congress.

Take the war power first. Madison's argument is that declaring that we're *not* going to war is just the flip side of declaring war.

(How does Hamilton answer this?)

By saying it's the Executive's job to keep the peace until Congress declares war, by making sure that the nation obeys all its treaty obligations.

Last point: Madison thought Hamilton was using the British monarchy as a model, since the King had the power to make treaties and declare war. The Jeffersonians always suspected Hamilton of having monarchist sympathies. But this charge implicates a much broader debate about whether the Executive – or sometimes the national government in general – should be presumed to have all the powers that other governments have in foreign affairs, whether or not the Constitution specifically grants them.

b. The Modern Vesting Clause Theory

The Prakash & Ramsey piece tries to stake out a modern version of Hamilton, based on a textualist and originalist reading of Article I. That position has four elements:

- **The "executive power" vested in the President in the first section of Article II includes a *general* power over foreign affairs.** We know this because the "executive power" in 18th century political theory and British practice was understood to include such a power.

- **The executive foreign affairs power is *residual* in that it includes only those foreign affairs powers not allocated elsewhere in the text.** We've already talked about how the Framers were suspicious of broad executive power, and the text explicitly takes away several things – like the power to declare war – that were included in the "executive power" as understood in England.

- **The general executive power doesn't include things that *wouldn't* have been understood to have been included in "executive" functions in 18th century England.** This is a hard core originalist component, but I'm not sure it's essential. All their examples – e.g., appropriating money or making laws – are also things that the *text* allocates elsewhere.

- ***Congress* has only its enumerated powers in foreign affairs, but these include a "necessary and proper" power to legislate in furtherance of the President's powers.** That means, for instance, that *Fong Yue Ting* is out – there are no "powers inherent in sovereignty." But if the President has a general authority to send diplomats abroad, Congress would have power to build embassies for them and regulate their conduct.

There's an additional principle that they don't state quite so clearly up front but emerges from their discussion later on: The general executive power includes a power to *do* things – for instance, to state what the foreign policy of the United States is on a particular issue. But it's *not* a power to *legislate* – that is, to take actions that operate with the force of law on private individuals. Prakash & Ramsey give the example of Washington's Neutrality Proclamation. They say that he clearly had the power to *make* it, but that as an executive act it wasn't the sort of "law" one could prosecute someone for violating.

(What do you think of this theory?)

I have to say I like it a lot:

- It seems to explain much of what the Government actually *does* better than its competitors; and

- It has a rigor to it, being based in the text and history, that the others tend to lack. (Incidentally, I think it's a great example of how an originalist approach will sometimes be better adapted to current needs than more loosey-goosey methods.)

(Is this approach formalist or functionalist in character?)

(What's the biggest drawback to this approach?)

It puts a high premium on being able to distinguish which acts are "executive" in character. We'll see that becoming somewhat difficult in a lot of these cases.

3.   United States v. Curtiss-Wright Export Corp., 299 U.S. 304 (1936)

Congress, by joint resolution, authorized the President to prohibit the sale of arms to persons in South America if he found that such a prohibition would contribute to the establishment of peace in the region. The President exercised this authority, and Curtiss-Wright was indicted for selling machine guns to Bolivia.

(What's the constitutional claim here?)

The lower court held that the joint resolution was an unconstitutional delegation of legislative power to the President.

Remember that this is the old, pre-New Deal Court, prior to the 1937 "switch-in-time." As we've seen, the Court is doing the same thing during this period on the federalism and due process fronts, enforcing strict limits on the ability of Congress and the state governments to regulate the economy. And it's just decided *Schechter* and *Panama Refining* a year earlier, enforcing the delegation doctrine as a check on the administrative state.

The picture is very different in foreign affairs, however. The Court holds (Sutherland, J.) that the delegation is constitutional. Note that this is the same justice that wrote *Carter Coal*, and it's just six months after the decision in that case.

Justice Sutherland says that it's not necessary to decide whether the resolution would be constitutional if it involved solely internal affairs. Assuming that it would *not*, the question is whether it is constitutional as respects *external* affairs.

a.   The Nature of Federal Power in Foreign Affairs

Sutherland thinks that the idea of limited and enumerated powers is really true only with respect to internal affairs.

(Why would that be true?)

Federal powers over domestic and foreign affairs are different in origin and nature. The point of the Constitution was to carve federal powers out of the preexisting legislative powers possessed by the States.

The States never had their own international powers, so the external powers of the federal government came not from the States but from Great Britain, which had previously exercised all powers of external sovereignty.

Note the explicit invocation of the doctrine of unitary sovereignty here, which we talked about last time: "[Rulers] come and go; governments end and forms of government change; but sovereignty survives. A political society cannot endure without a supreme will somewhere."

The result is that federal power over external affairs "did not depend upon the affirmative grants of the Constitution. The powers to declare and wage war, to conclude peace, to make treaties, to maintain diplomatic relations with other sovereignties, if they had never been mentioned in the Constitution, would have vested in the federal government as necessary concomitants of nationality."

(What do you think of this argument?)

This is nutty on several fronts:

First, it's wrong as a matter of history. Sovereignty passed not from Great Britain directly to the federal government created by the Constitution of 1789, but rather to the Continental Congress created by the Articles of Confederation. It's not at all clear that the Articles foreclosed all exercises of sovereign power by the States over external affairs. The first substantive article said that "each state retains its sovereignty, freedom, and independence," and the Articles gave Congress only "the sole and exclusive right of determining on peace and war," which is narrower than external affairs generally.

Second, it's wrong as a matter of political theory. The Framers viewed sovereignty as moving from the States to the *People*, not simply to the Federal Government. Then the People allocated the delegation of their sovereign powers between the federal and state governments, according to the terms of the federal Constitution.

Third, and maybe most important, it doesn't have anything to do with anything. *Curtiss-Wright* is about the allocation of power over external affairs between the President and Congress, not between the Federal Government and the States. So it's very odd to have this long disquisition about how powerless the *states* are in foreign affairs cases, since this isn't a case about federalism. The delegation challenge to the statute is about separation of powers, that is, the allocation of power between Congress and the President.

If anything, Justice Sutherland's little excursion into political theory cuts the wrong way on the separation of powers question, because if British sovereignty over foreign affairs passed to the central government under the Articles of Confederation, it could only have passed to *Congress* -- there was no Executive at all at the time.

There's a method to Justice Sutherland's madness, however, and it has to do with the aspects of the inherent powers doctrine that Prof. Cleveland notes. One key aspect of these extra-constitutional powers is that they are basically off-limits to judicial review. That helps explain why the Court is going to be so willing to defer to the President and reject the delegation challenge to his authority.

b.   The Allocation of Foreign Affairs Power Among the Branches

(What's Sutherland's argument for why it's Executive rather than Legislative power?)

"In this vast external realm, with its important, complicated, delicate and manifold problems, the President alone has the power to speak or listen as a representative of the nation." Quoting Justice Marshall, Sutherland says that "[t]he President is the sole organ of the nation in its external relations, and its sole representative with foreign nations."

There's a couple of problems with this part, too:

First, Sutherland is taking Marshall out of context. Marshall's speech went to the question of who implements foreign policy once it is made. It doesn't speak to who has the authority to *make* foreign policy.

Second, it misreads the constitutional text. Congress is granted all kinds of direct power over foreign affairs; most importantly, Congress declares war and regulates international commerce.

Sutherland has some more pragmatic arguments for presidential authority, too:

(What institutional characteristics of the presidency does Sutherland emphasize?)

He talks about the practical necessity of wide Presidential discretion to deal with quickly evolving situations, the President's unique access to information regarding conditions abroad, the need for secrecy in foreign affairs, etc.

Note that these are the grounds upon which *Curtiss-Wright*'s strong view of Presidential authority is usually defended.

The upshot is that because the President has his own broad authority over foreign affairs, Congress may delegate more discretion to him than might be constitutional in purely domestic affairs.

This still leaves a question, though. You could get to the same place simply by saying that Congress has broad leeway in delegating authority to executive officials; in fact, that's what all the cases since *Carter Coal* in fact *have* said. But that's no departure from the theory of enumerated powers.

(Why not do it that way?)

Because the Court – in 1936 at least – wants to preserve strict limits in the *domestic* context without imposing them in foreign affairs. If it interprets Art. I to permit broad delegations, that holding will apply in both contexts. The powers inherent in sovereignty argument, though, can be confined to foreign affairs.

4.   Summing Up

One thing you'll realize about this course is that almost nothing is ever definitively resolved. But at least we can review the bidding.

Two Broad Approaches to Foreign Affairs Powers

- The *ordinary rules apply* approach requires that governmental activity in foreign affairs be grounded in an enumerated powers, and subject to affirmative limitation by the Bill of Rights and similar safeguards.

- The *powers inherent in sovereignty* approach grounds foreign affairs powers not in the Constitution but in the nature of nationhood and international law. Government action need not be based on enumerated power grants; it is generally not subject to much judicial review by courts; and it is often not restricted by affirmative constitutional guarantees.

Problems with Powers Inherent in Sovereignty

- It flies in the face of our commitment to the constitutional text and its notion of a government of limited and enumerated powers.

- It's grounded in some pretty repellent aspects of American history, including imperialism, racism, and xenophobia. The whole point is a sense that the Constitution is something that was meant to apply only to white, Anglo-Saxons; the government needed power to treat less worthy people differently. Moreover, the government needed the power to acquire colonies and govern them extra-constitutionally, just like the other imperial powers.

  None of this is a very worthy legacy today.

- It also depends on a strong distinction between foreign and domestic affairs. To the extent that that line is harder to draw today, it's a far less workable theory.

So where do we stand today with respect to powers inherent in sovereignty?

- Doctrinally, the underlying doctrines such as plenary power over immigration are still at least nominally intact, but they're under pressure. The Court has chipped away, and at least before September 11, 2001, there was a real question how much longer plenary power would last. Not surprisingly, we've seen some retrenchment in light of the war on terror – but not as much as you might think. We'll talk about this more when we get to the terrorism cases.

- *Curtiss-Wright* itself is still good law. It has a somewhat odd citation pattern: Advocates of unlimited presidential powers cite it over and over again – it figures prominently in the DOJ's infamous "torture memo," for instance. But advocates of international law also cite it for the proposition that American states – which internationalists typically see as annoying and unnecessary – can't do anything in foreign affairs. So if you're trying to preempt Texas's death penalty with an argument based on customary international law, you may well cite *Curtiss-Wright*.

5.   *Dames & Moore v. Regan*, 453 U.S. 654 (1981)

Dames & Moore gives us a picture of where things stand in the modern era. Note that this case is the law clerk's dream come true: Rehnquist clerked for Jackson the term *Youngstown* was decided. Here, he gets to apply his old boss's framework, and also putter around with it a little.

Following the seizure of the American Embassy in Tehran in 1979, President Carter -- acting pursuant to the International Emergency Economic Powers Act (IEEPA) -- froze Iranian assets in the United States. Dames & Moore sued Iran in federal district court in December of 1979 for failure to pay $3.5 million owed in connection with an atomic power plant. The district court issued orders attaching Iranian property to secure any judgment that might result.

The hostages were related in 1981, following an Executive Agreement providing for submission of all claims regarding Iranian assets to the Iran-U.S. Claims Tribunal.

Pursuant to the agreement, President Carter issued a series of Executive Orders suspending all litigation in U.S. courts concerning Iranian assets. Also pursuant to the agreement, the order nullified all existing attachments of Iranian assets and transferred them to a security account held by the Bank of England the Algerian central bank. After taking office, President Reagan issued an Executive Order "ratifying" Carter's orders and suspending all federal litigation claims that could be presented to the claims tribunal.

Dames & Moore challenged the suspension of its claims.

The Court (Rehnquist, J.) upholds the President's actions. Justice Rehnquist begins by saying that Justice Jackson's analysis in *Youngstown* is useful, but instead of three pigeonholes there is probably more of a continuous spectrum.

The first question is whether § 203 of IEEPA authorized the President's actions.

§ 203 provides: "The President may [nullify,] void, prevent or prohibit, any acquisition, holding, withholding, use, transfer, withdrawal, transportation, importation or exportation of, or dealing in, or exercising any right, power, or privilege with respect to, or transactions involving, any property in which any foreign country or a national thereof has any interest; by any person, or with respect to any property, subject to the jurisdiction of the United States."

The Court breaks the President's action down into two parts:

- nullification or the district court's attachment of Iranian property, and

- suspension of Dames & Moore's claims in federal court.

(Which of Justice Jackson's categories does the nullification fit into?)

§ 203 authorized nullification of the attachments; that part falls within Jackson first category, and is presumptively constitutional. The Court is not prepared to say that the Government as a whole lacked power to nullify the attachments.

(Which category does the suspension fall into?)

But § 203 doesn't say anything about authority to suspend claims pending in American courts. Neither does the Hostage Act.

(Does this make the statutes irrelevant?)

But both IEEPA and the Hostage Act are "highly relevant in the looser sense of indicating congressional acceptance of a broad scope for executive action" in situations like this. That is relevant in the 'gray area," since we can't expect Congress to anticipate and authorize everything that might become necessary.

Moreover, there is a history of Congressional acquiescence in these kinds of suspension. This puts the President over the top. *See Youngstown* (Frankfurter, J., concurring). And Congress hasn't disapproved the action taken here, although it has held hearings on the Iranian Agreement. In fact, Congress has said that the Tribunal "is of vital importance to the United States."

And additional point is that the Court says its conclusion is "buttressed" by the fact that the President' means afford Dames & Moore an alternative forum for its claims.

(Why is this relevant?)

Remember, Separation of Powers is meant to protect individual rights. Therefore it can't be entirely irrelevant that the actual individual rights most directly at issue are protected here.

Note that the standing of the President at the time may have a lot to do with the different results in *Youngstown* and *Dames & Moore*: Truman was at a low point when he seized the steel mills; Reagan was new and popular in 1981.

But I think it has a lot more to do with the court trying to follow the essence of Justice Jackson's approach by asking whether President and Congress are basically in harmony on the action at issue. Although both cases involve congressional silence on the precise issue, it seems the Court has enough context to go on in drawing different implications from that silence.

B. The Power to Use Military Force

The doctrinal stuff really divides into two big sets of concerns.

- **Congress vs. the President:** These are a continuation of the separation of powers issues we've already been talking about. The big question, of course, is who has to authorize the use of military force.

- **War and Individual Rights:** There are a bunch of cases about suppression of political dissent in wartime, for instance.

We won't have time to do the straight-up individual rights cases, but in cases like *Merryman* and *Hamdan*, it's easy to see how the separation-of-powers issues bear directly on individual liberty.

There's also a more big picture set of questions:

- **Modern Goals/Old Constitution:** The provisions of the Constitution dealing with foreign affairs haven't been amended much, which means we're using a set of textual arrangements constructed for a small, weak country in a low-tech age to meet the security problems of the 21st century. We'll want to ask whether the apparatus we have is really up to it; more moderately, we'll ask to what extent we should rely on original understandings in this area.

1.   The Text

As I've said several times, there's no general "war power." Instead, the Constitution recognizes several different war powers and divides them between Congress and the President.

To Congress:

- to declare War
- to grant Letters of Marque and Reprisal, and make Rules concerning Captures on Land and Water

These are the legalized piracy powers.

- to raise and support Armies
- to provide and maintain a Navy

Note that there's no Air Force power – this is often one of the classic examples for why courts need to "update" the constitutional text. But maybe it's enough to note that the Air Force was originally part of the Army, and that the Army and Navy continue to have their own air forces.

- to make Rules for the Government and Regulation of the land and naval Forces.

This is where the authority to create a code of military justice comes from.

- to provide for calling forth the Militia to execute the Laws of the Union, suppress Insurrections and repel Invasions
- to provide for organizing, arming, and disciplining, the Militia

Note how prominent the militia is here – the Framers were deeply suspicious of standing armies. Their thought was that the point of a standing army was to use it on your own people.

To the President:

- The President "shall be Commander in Chief of the Army and Navy of the United States, and of the Militia of the several States, when called into the actual Service of the United States."

Note that there are also some powers expressly **prohibited to the States**:

- To engage in war (unless invaded or in imminent danger); and

- To keep troops or ships of war during peacetime.

This is in keeping with the Constitution's historical concern for monopolizing powers of war and peace in the Federal Government. But it's interesting that it's not absolute, isn't it? If the Canadians come pouring over the border, North Dakota can go after them on its own without waiting for approval from Washington.

2.   The Early Debates

There's some historical material, but not a whole lot, reflecting the Founding debate on war powers. In particular, there were frequent debates *after* ratification concerning war-related powers in connection with our efforts to stay *out* of the Napoleonic Wars between Britain and France. I think we can condense the relevant history into three points:

First, there's a lot of distrust of the Executive. Hamilton is at pains in the Federalist to show how much *less* power the President is given than the King of England had. This is another instance of constitutional meaning being shaped by what the Founders were reacting *against*. And Madison is pretty emphatic in his warning in the Helvidius essay: "War is in fact the true nurse of executive aggrandizement." This prefigures Justice Jackson's concern in *Youngstown* that the Executive will create military conflicts as a pretext for expanding his own powers. Madison says you can tell how free a country is by looking at how many checks there are on the Executive's ability to start wars.

Second, in particular, the evidence seems pretty strong that the Founders don't want the President to be able to *start* a war.

- At the same time, there's also pretty widespread agreement that the President needs to be solely in charge of conducting military operations.

3.   Three Positions

The two big positions on war powers correspond to sides in the struggle between the Congress and the President.

- The **Congress people** say that the history just discussed makes clear that the Founders didn't want to be able to commit troops without congressional authorization, outside a very narrow exception for responding to sudden attacks.

- The **Executive people** say either **(1)** the power to declare war was intended to be very narrow, so that its only consequences was to trigger certain legal conditions incident to wartime; or **(2)** that we just shouldn't be originalists on this because the world has changed.

- **Middle Ground (Prof. Ramsey):** Congress must authorize any action that explicitly or by action initiates a state of war with another nation. But the President may:

  1) Take military actions short of creating a state of war;

  2) Respond to an attack that initiates a state of war and prosecute the war to its conclusion; and

  3) Take actions, like deploying troops or severing diplomatic relations, that are likely to *provoke* an attack.

4.   Presidential War Powers

The materials on Presidential war powers raise at least three distinct questions:

- What war powers does the President have notwithstanding Congressional action? Does the President's power as "Commander in Chief" make war powers special, so that we shouldn't apply Justice Jackson's framework from *Youngstown*?

- In the absence of congressional authorization, does the President have power to initiate conflict?

- What is the nature of the President's power to repel "sudden attacks"?

a.   The President vs. Congress: *Little v. Barreme*, 6 U.S. 170 (1804)

We've already discussed how the *potential* scope of Presidential and Congressional power often overlap, so that the ability of the President to act will often be a function of what Congress has actually done. That's the basis of Justice Jackson's three categories in *Youngstown*, which suggest that the President has much greater power when he acts in concert with Congress than against it.

Little is a much older case but it suggests the same idea. This is another of the cases arising out of the undeclared war with France in the 1790s. Congress had passed a "non-intercourse" act prohibiting trade with France. It authorized seizure of any American vessel on the high seas traveling *to* French ports.

The *Flying Fish* was a Danish vessel captured by Captain Little in the U.S. frigate *Boston*. Little wants to sell the *Flying Fish* as a prize; the district judge, however, directs that the vessel be restored to its owners because it's a neutral vessel. The question before the Supreme Court is whether Barreme – the owner, I think – should also get *damages* against the U.S. naval officer for the wrongful seizure.

(Why was the seizure wrongful?)

Because the *Flying Fish* was bound *from* a French port to America, not the other way round. The statute only authorizes seizures of vessels bound *to* French ports. The Court reads this a prohibiting seizures of anyone else.

(Is that the only way to read the Act?)

Well, you could read it as just leaving the "traveling *from*" question open. Again, it's similar to *Youngstown* and *Dames & Moore*. Congress has authorized X; does that mean it prohibited Y?

Chief Justice Marshall does suggest that there's a broader seizure power for seizures in U.S. waters; maybe this strengthens his argument that Congress meant the high seas seizure provision to be more narrow. Maybe.

(What's Captain Little's best argument in defense?)

That he was acting under orders from the Secretary of the Navy which enjoined him to seize vessels going both ways.

Now, I think we can usefully distinguish between two questions here:

1. Do the instructions make the seizure *legal*?

2. Should Captain Little have to foot the bill when he was just following orders?

(Does Chief Justice Marshall have any doubts on the first question?)

No – Everyone seems to agree that the Executive's orders can't authorize a seizure that seems to be forbidden. That's the key holding of the case for our purposes; put in terms of the 20th century jurisprudence, it suggests that the basic *Youngstown* analysis applies even to war powers. Further, it suggests that this analysis applies not only to *initiation* of a war, which we've suggested is the most problematic question of presidential authority, but also to the *prosecution* of a war.

One counter-argument minimizing the importance of *Little* would go something like this: *Little* – like *Bas v. Tingy* – was a case about prize values for ships seized on the high seas. As such it falls squarely within a specific power allocated to Congress – that is, to make rules for captures. That being so, it might not tell us that much about cases that don't fall within a category that is explicitly delegated to Congress.

There's also the point that it's old and it doesn't explain very much. But that's a less compelling point when the old case is used to *confirm* the modern tendency under *Youngstown*.

(What about the other question? Is it fair to make Captain Little pony up here?)

You have an interesting opinion from the Chief Justice on this point. He says, I initially thought it's *not* fair – that Barreme should get his ship back, but that Little shouldn't have to pay damages. But I got talked out of that by my colleagues.

(What's the practical consequence of making individual officers liable in cases like this?)

It encourages them to question their orders, right? It makes them responsible, after all, for figuring out whether their orders are really correct and legal.

(Is that a good idea?)

Well, it's a tough call. In a case like this it doesn't seem like a great idea. We might worry that military officers won't carry out their duties zealously. But there's Nuremberg on the other side, in which the "just following orders" defense for war crimes didn't work out.

Note the similarity to Justice Scalia in *Morrison*: The effect of the Independent Counsel law was to render executive officials accountable to someone other than the President; so, too, does a damage award against Little. It's a tension between direct accountability and accountability *through* the President, which may be undermined if the President can't control his subordinates as well.

The general pattern today is two protect individual federal officers in two ways:

- For tort claims – which I'm assuming this is – the Federal Tort Claims Act provides that if an officer is acting within the scope of his duties, then the U.S. is automatically substituted as the defendant and pays any award.

- For other sorts of claims, the officer will have "qualified immunity," which means that he's only liable if the law he was violating was "clearly established."

The qualified immunity question might be a close call here. But it wouldn't be if, for example, your superiors ordered you to go gas a million civilians. Qualified immunity gives officers a cushion without absolving them for flagrant violations.

b.   Responding to Attack — *The Prize Cases*, 67 U.S. 635 (1863)

As the name suggests, this is another piece of litigation about captured ships – here, it's merchant ships that were trying to run the Union blockade of Confederate ports. (Remember, running the blockade is how Rhett Butler made his money in *Gone with the Wind*.) If it's a legitimate war, then the blockade is legal and the ships were subject to capture. So the question is whether President Lincoln had authority to take this action.

(Are all instances of insurrection wars?)

The Court's opinion suggests no. Certainly we wouldn't think of Dorr's Rebellion in Rhode Island or the Whiskey Rebellion in Pennsylvania under the Washington administration. At the low end, it's hard to tell the difference between an insurrection and something like the L.A. riots or Orville Faubus's defiance of the *Brown* decision in Little Rock, which caused Presdient Eisenhower to send in federal troops.

(Is the Court prepared to decide when an insurrection amounts to a "war," so that the President can take actions like imposing a blockade?)

No – It says that's not a justiciable question. "The proclamation of blockade is itself official and conclusive evidence to the Court that a state of war existed which demanded and authorized a recourse to such a measure."

(How does the Court describe the allocation of war powers between the President and Congress?)

Congress has the power to declare war, but if somebody *else* initiates a war, then "the President is not only authorized but bound to resist force by force."

This is the most important point: The President may respond to attack without awaiting authorization. Two questions then arise:

- What counts as an attack triggering the President's commander in chief power? (That's the question in *Durand*.)

- How far can the President go in responding? Can he prosecute the war to its conclusion?

The Court doesn't really decide either of these questions. But the *Prize Cases* are the best authority for broad presidential authority in response to an attack.

(The Court says all this, but does it really decide whether the President had the authority to institute the blockade on his own?)

They want to say they're deciding this, but it's arguably dicta. Justice Grier also points out that Congress had authorized Lincoln's actions in a number of ways, first simply by passing a variety of acts designed to support the war effort, and then by passing an act "approving, legalizing, and making valid all the acts, proclamations, and orders of the President,

&c., as if they had been issued and done under the previous express authority and direction of the Congress of the United States."

(Is this appropriate? Should Congress be able to authorize military force after the fact?)

You can understand why you'd need to have a retroactive procedure sometimes. On the other hand, the sheer cumbersomeness of the war declaration procedure – it's just like passing a statute – is itself a safeguard for peace. So you wouldn't want to have these after the fact authorizations too often, I think.

(What about Justice Nelson's dissent here? Does he say that President Lincoln doesn't have the authority to prosecute a war against the Confederacy?)

I don't think so. He doesn't seem to question the President's authority to use force in responding to sudden attacks or to a rebellion.

(Then what's the problem?)

He seems to think that the President lacks authority to transform the rebellion to a "war" within the meaning of international law. That's what is essential to resolve the case before the Court, which involves the obligations of neutrals to respect a blockade under the law of war. For Nelson, only Congress can do that. So, ironically, Nelson is defending the *narrow* reading of "declare war" in Art. I.

c.   A Theory of Powers to Initiate Hostilities

The $64,000 question, of course, is whether the President can *start* a war without Congressional action. On that point, I want to go back to Professor Ramsey's theory in a little more depth.

The argument *for* Presidential power to initiate a war would, ironically, be a textual one. Article I grants Congress the power to "declare" war. But we know that in the 18th century, as today, there were all sorts of *undeclared* wars. That suggests that "declaring" war is *not* synonymous with initiating military hostilities. If that's so, then the power to initiate hostilities is *not* exclusively allocated to Congress; rather, Congress has a monopoly over *one* way – the formal one – of starting a military conflict. Presidentialists then fall back on the notion of *residual* powers – that is, that the President has all those executive powers not exclusively allocated to someone else. If "declaring" war is a narrow power, then the President would retain all other war powers not delegated to Congress.

The problem with this argument is that it runs counter to all the historical evidence that the Founding Generation meant to keep the President from *starting* wars. Even Alexander Hamilton – who was the strongest advocate of executive power generally, and secretly yearned in his heart for a monarchy – didn't think the President had this power.

But it's hard to make too strong an argument from history without grounding it somewhere in the text. So we have to go back to what "declaring war" means. You should understand that there's lots of disagreement about this, but the most persuasive argument I've heard – from Professor Ramsey, who's cited in the notes – goes like this:

The 18th century practice recognized that there were "wars" that took place without formal declarations. They also believed – consistent with this fact – that war could be "declared" by words *or* action. There's a great quotation from the British Admiralty Court that war could be announced out of the mouths of cannons. If that's right, then when Congress is given the power to "declare war," that means that it's given the exclusive power to take actions that *amount* to initiating hostilities. This understanding thus provides some textual support for the Congressional power position.

It's important to recognize, however, that this reading of the power to *initiate* hostilities leaves some important powers to the President. It suggests, for instance:

- The President can take military actions that wouldn't place the U.S. in a state of "war" with another country. For instance, sending U.S. troops across the Mexican border, with Mexican permission or acquiescence, to chase bandits in the 19th century wouldn't amount to an act of war.

- Sometimes we're placed in a state of war by the act of another country that has attacked *us*. When that happens, the President doesn't need authorization to prosecute the war to its conclusion.

- Finally, the President can do things – like deploy troops or break off diplomatic relations – that are likely to *provoke* an attack, which would then allow him to prosecute the war to its conclusion.

Again, this is just one theory of war powers. But it at least offers one pretty coherent framework for analyzing these questions.

d.   Provoking Attacks: The Mexican-American War

What about if the President *provokes* the attack? You have some stuff in the notes about the initiation of the Mexican-American war in 1846. That war arises out of a boundary dispute concerning the border between Texas and Mexico. Mexico has moved its army to the south bank of the Rio Grande; in June 1845, President Polk moves his troops to the north bank – within the disputed territory – blockades the river, and aims his cannons at the other side. That causes military incidents in which at least some Mexican troops come across the river into what we claim to be U.S. territory.

On the basis of this, Polk states that a war exists and begins gathering troops. He then asks for a declaration of war and – probably more important – congressional action to raise a lot more troops.

He gets the declaration of war. But two years later, after the war is over, the House adopts a resolution stating that the Mexican-American War was "a war unnecessarily and unconstitutionally begun by the President of the United States." An obscure congressman named Abraham Lincoln voted for that resolution and opined afterwards that President Polk's position would make the President a king.

I think there are two questions here:

1. Were the initial actions taken by President Polk – ordering U.S. troops to the north side of the river – constitutional if he knew that they would provoke hostilities?

2. Once hostilities had begun, was the President limited to defending against Mexican incursions until he obtained congressional authorization for offensive operations?

(What do you think about the first question?)

Well, the textual argument I've sketched out for you suggests a fairly bright line – that is, that the President can take whatever actions he likes short of creating a state of war, and that we don't try to psychoanalyze why he took them.

(Is that a good rule? Does it obviate Congress's power?)

Let me give you a hypothetical. I think we could all agree that it would require congressional authorization for President Bush to order American armored units to strike north across the DMZ in Korea. Suppose instead he deploys short range missiles and strike aircraft just south of the DMZ, knowing that this will likely provoke the North Koreans to attack.

(Is that OK? Has Congress been circumvented?)

Arguably. But let me put it in a different light: Suppose he's afraid the North Koreans are going to attack anyway, so he shores up U.S. defenses while asking Congress to act on some kind of authorization. That might have the same provocative effect, but doesn't it seem like something he ought to be doing?

Let me give another example: North Korea has said that if the U.N. imposes sanctions, it will consider that an act of war and respond accordingly.

(Would that mean that sending Condoleeza Rice to the U.N. security council to ask for sanctions would *also* require authorization?)

Surely not. But this highlights that lots of non-military actions may be just as provocative as military ones, which makes it hard to hold out for a rule that any provocative action requires congressional action. Seems to me the only workable test is whether the President's own action created a state of war.

e.   Attacks on U.S. Citizens Abroad: *Durand v. Hollins*, 8 F. Cas. 111 (C.C.S.D.N.Y. 1860)

Everyone agrees that the President can respond to a sudden attack on the U.S. It's a somewhat tougher question whether the President can respond to attacks on others, such as private U.S. citizens or allies.

That's the question in *Durand*. American property in Greytown, Nicaragua, had been stolen and destroyed, and an American minister had been attacked. Hollins, the captain of the U.S.S. Cyane, bombarded the town. Durand, an American citizen living in Greytown, sued Hollins for damage to his property resulting from the bombardment. Hollins defended on the ground that the Secretary of the Navy – acting on behalf of the President – had authorized the bombardment.

(Does the President have power to authorize the bombardment based on the theory of presidential power I've been outlining? Is this a "sudden attack" within the meaning of that theory?)

I don't think so. The premise of that theory is that the reason you don't need congressional authority to respond to a sudden attack is that the attack itself creates the state of war between the U.S. and the foreign nation, so that no authorization to create such a state is required. It doesn't seem likely that the attacks on American citizens in Greytown was sufficient to create a state of war between the U.S. and Nicaragua.

You'd therefore need a broader view of the President's defensive power to justify the result here. Presidents have for a long time claimed the authority to protect U.S. citizens abroad without authorization from Congress, and they often cite *Durand* for that proposition.

Let's try some hypotheticals about the limits of such a power:

(If an American citizen is murdered in France, can the President invade? I know we're all looking for an excuse . . . .)

(What about terrorist attacks in Israel? If American citizens are killed, can we respond against the nation responsible?)

I think it's hard to say "yes" in these instances. That's not to say that the President can't take some military measures to protect U.S. citizens, short of military acts that would themselves be acts of war. I would think, for instance, that the President could deploy troops in Israel – with the government's permission – to protect U.S. citizens, and could respond if those troops were attacked.

(Can we justify the bombardment in *Durand* as this sort of protective measure?)

I doubt it – it seems like an act that itself creates a state of war with Nicaragua. If we think only Congress can authorize that, then *Durand* seems to overstep. Of course, that means that *Durand* is a counter-example to the theory. But no theory of war powers perfectly lines up all the cases.

(What's up with Justice Nelson in this case? In *Durand*, he seems to be for letting the President do just about anything. Can you reconcile that with his dissent in the *Prize Cases*?)

I think it's important to remember that the question in the *Prize Cases* is whether the blockade was legal as a matter of international law, so that neutral parties were bound to respect it. Two of the boats seized were a British barque, the Hiawatha, and a Mexican schooner, the Brilliante. Those are legitimate prizes under international law only if there was a legal blockade, and my understanding is that blockades are permitted under international law only if a formal state of war exists.

So, to repeat what I said earlier, the question in the *Prize Cases* is really whether the President has the power to initiate a *formal* state of war. Remember that one version of the Presidential position is that while the President can initiate hostilities however he likes, the function of a *declaration* of war is to formalize those hostilities. On this view, that's reserved to Congress under the Presidential theory.

So Justice Nelson could be consistent in saying that the President has the authority to order all sorts of military acts as a matter of domestic law – which is sufficient to defeat the claim of a U.S. citizen against an officer in *Durand* – but that only Congress can create a formal state of war, which is the issue in the *Prize Cases*.

f.   Post-September 11:   Non-State Foes and Preemptive War

The changed context of national security after September 11, 2001, suggests some final questions about the President's authority to initiate hostilities. One has to do with the notion of preemptive war.

It makes sense to start with the U.S. National Security strategy, which I asked you to read an excerpt from. This is a documented promulgated by the Bush Administration in September 2002 to express the basic aims of American foreign and defense policy.

One important aspect of the strategy is that it responds to new kinds of threats. There's a lot of talk about terrorists and WMDs – very different from the sort of security threats the Founders faced.

▶ blurs internal/external ("foreign"/"domestic")

▶ blurs law enforcement/military

▶ raises question of preemption – relation between int'l law and national interest.

But also—elsewhere in the document—there's a broader def'n of threat in other ways:

▶ poverty

▶ environment

▶ economic problems

Let's focus on the question of preemptive war:

(Can we extend the President's authority to defend against attack to preemptive action?)

It seems difficult.

(Think about the power to respond to attacks, however, and why that was vested in the President. What do you think the Framers would say about preemptive war under modern conditions?)

They might be more sympathetic. Remember that they were assuming nice big oceans separating us from most threats.

(What options do we have to deal with the issue of preemption?)

Well, it might be much better to authorize such action, but preemptive actions are also somewhat hard to anticipate; they may require surprise. So we either have no authorization or an authorization that's so broad it can't act as much of a check. We'll come back to this question whether an authorization can be over-broad when we look at the authorization for use of force in Iraq.

5. Declarations, Authorizations, and Uses of Force

There's a lot of fighting in American history, but only 5 declarations of war by Congress:

• the War of 1812

• the Mexican-American War of 1846-48

• the Spanish-American War of 1898

• World War I

• World War II

The book cites one study that counts 234 uses of force. Some of these were authorized by Congress without a declaration of war:

- Barbary Pirates (1802)
- Civil War (1861)
- Gulf of Tonkin Resolution (1964)
- Both Gulf Wars (1991 & 2003)

When you have these authorizations, the question becomes one of scope. That's particularly a problem with the Gulf of Tonkin Resolution. Note also that sometimes authorization comes retroactively, as in the Civil War case.

6.   The War Powers Resolution

Remember we finished the last chapter talking about how Congress sometimes enacts "framework statutes" to make the separation of powers more concrete in particular areas, and to provide procedural mechanisms for its enforcement. One of the most important and controversial examples is the War Powers Resolution, adopted after Vietnam.

a.   Provisions (50 U.S.C. §§ 1541-1548 (1973))

Don't be fooled by the title: It's a binding statute. Congress just thought "resolution" sounded cooler.

Constitutional Authorization

(What's Congress's basis for enacting this law?)

Congress relied on the Necessary and Proper Clause in combination with the various clauses granting powers to Congress and to the President dealing with war.

Limitation of Commander in Chief Power

Section 1541(c) purports to define the situations where the President may exercise his Commander in Chief powers. It limits those powers to three situations:

(a)   a declaration of war;

(b)   specific statutory authorization; or

(c)   a national emergency created by attack upon the United States, its territories or possessions, or its armed forces.

Note that this section is generally agreed simply to be a statement of Congress's view, not a provision having binding legal force.

(Should it be given binding effect? Would that be constitutional? How would it be enforced?)

Consultation Requirement

Section 1542 requires the President to consult with Congress, if possible before introduction of U.S. forces and regularly thereafter until they are removed.

The big question here is with whom does the President consult? The whole Congress? Key members? Which ones?

Reporting Requirement

The heart of the statute is the clock provisions requiring that troops be withdrawn if Congress does not approve their introduction within a certain period. But the clock only starts running when the President makes a report to Congress under § 1543(a)(1).

Section 1543 contemplates three reporting situations:

1543(a)(1)   U.S. forces are introduced into hostilities or imminent involvement in hostilities is clearly indicated.

1543(a)(2)   U.S. forces are introduced into foreign territories equipped for combat.

1543(a)(3)   U.S. forces are introduced in numbers that "substantially enlarge" U.S. forces equipped for combat already located in a foreign nation.

Note that most situations within (a)(1) would also fall within either (a)(2) and (a)(3). This means the President can avoid starting the clock by reporting under (a)(2) or (a)(3) instead of (a)(1).

What happened in practice for a long time was that the President *never* reported under any of these provisions. (Gerald Ford did *once* in connection with the *Mayaguez* rescue, but it was a minor operation that was over before he reported.) More recently, Presidents have submitted reports "consistent with" the Resolution, without acknowledging that they really have to do so.

Timing: The President must report within 48 hours of his action.

Contents: The report must state

(a)   the circumstances necessitating the introduction of U.S. forces;

(b)   the constitutional and legislative authority under which it occurred;

(c)   the estimated scope and duration of hostilities; and

(d)   "such other information as the Congress may request."

The Clock Provisions

A report under § 1543(a)(1) starts a 60 day clock. At the end of that period, Congress must terminate the use of U.S. forces unless:

(a)   Congress declares war or specifically authorizes the use of U.S. forces;

(b)   extends by law the 60 day period; or

(c)   is physically unable to meet as a result of an armed attack upon the U.S.

Objective Trigger: The clock also starts if a report "is required to be submitted" under § 1543(a)(1).   .

(Who decides this? Congress? The courts?)

Note that a court probably *can* decide this. There is no direct clash with the President, because the court's order would not need to require the withdrawal of troops. Instead, it could simply declare that the clock has started, thereby putting the ball back in Congress's court.

Extension: The President can extend the period by an additional 30 days if he determines and certifies to Congress in writing that "unavoidable military necessity respecting the safety of United States Armed Forces" requires continuing use of those forces to effect a safe withdrawal.

Congressional Removal Order

Despite the clock, § 1544(c) provides that at any time Congress can order the President to remove U.S. forces by concurrent resolution, which does not require Presidential approval.

(Is this provision constitutional? What's the problem?)

Chadha casts severe doubt on this provision, which is a legislative veto.

Definitions and Interpretation

The Resolution also contains some guides for construction.

(a)   Section 1547(a) provides that authorization for military action in a law or treaty must specifically mention the War Powers Resolution. This is a super-clear statement rule.

(b)   Section 1547(c) makes clear that the Resolution extends to use of our forces as advisors to foreign military forces.

(c)   Section 1547(d) says that the Resolution is not intended to alter anyone's constitutional powers.

(Is the statute protesting too much? Does it constrain the President beyond constitutional limits? Does it instead *expand* his power?)

b.   Constitutionality

(You have President Nixon's veto message explaining why he vetoed the Resolution. Why does he think it's unconstitutional?)

He gives two reasons:

- It purports to take away the President's constitutional war powers; and

- It allows Congress to act by concurrent resolution rather than by statute.

He's almost surely right about the second point, with respect to the Congressional removal orders.

(He's kind of vague about what Presidential powers are being taken away, however. Can you be more specific for him?)

I can think of four possible objections from the President's standpoint:

- If you think the President can initiate hostilities generally, then this is arguably a big limitation.

  That is, it's problematic if you take the strong Presidentialist position that the only power exclusively allocated to Congress is the power to make a formal declaration of war.

- It also seems to limit the President's authority to act in defense of U.S. citizens abroad, as in *Durand*, as well as defense of allies and interests.

- It would seem to limit the President's ability to respond to sudden attacks, by requiring a report and Congressional approval even in such cases.

  Remember, the theory of war powers I've suggested would say that once another country initiates a state of war, the President has full authority to prosecute the war to its conclusion.

- Finally, it also seems to limit the President's ability to use military force short of actually initiating a state of war.

  For instance, the deployment of U.S. marines in Lebanon was an "introduction of U.S. forces into a foreign territory equipped for combat"; it should have triggered an obligation to report. But it certainly wasn't an act of war and therefore didn't require congressional authorization.

Now, some of these objections are more important than others. For instance, it seems likely that most minor uses of force not amounting to war will take a lot less than 60 days, and therefore the Resolution isn't much of an impediment. Grenada's an example. The same is true of actions in defense of U.S. citizens abroad.

(Is the President the only person who should have a constitutional objection here?)

Probably not. Because what the Resolution effectively does is legitimize the use of force in the short term, as long as the President is willing to report. But that would mean that the President could initiate hostilities, as long as he reports to Congress afterwards. Constitutionally-speaking, he shouldn't have the power to do that.

c.   **Policy**

President Nixon's message spends more time talking about the *practical* difficulties created by the Resolution. He makes several arguments:

- The Resolution makes both allies and adversaries doubt our staying power in military operations.

- It may work to prolong a crisis.

   (Do you see why?)

- It may also escalate hostilities on our side – we have to win within 60 days.

- It undermines certain military operations, like peacekeeping.

   I think Nixon might be right in that these sorts of low-level operations are the most likely casualties of the War Powers Resolution – that is, they're the kind of thing where (a) they may take longer than 60 days, and (b) they don't generate the "rally round the flag" effect that ensures broad political support.

   (On the other hand, why *shouldn't* the President have to get Congress's approval for these sorts of operations?)

- It may undermine treaty commitments, like the obligation to defend NATO.

   That seems unlikely, since that sort of action will likely get plenty of support. If anything, it probably legitimates action in furtherance of those commitments in the short term before Congress can act.

(What do you think of these arguments? Is the Resolution a bad idea?)

A lot of people think the War Powers Resolution is problematic from the other direction – that it doesn't provide any real check on Presidential authority and instead basically gives the President *carte blanche* to commit the U.S. This is the "tacit deal" that Professor Ely talks about on p. 211 in the notes – that is, that "the president will take the responsibility . . . so long as he can make the decisions, and Congress will forego actual policy-making authority so long as it doesn't have to be held accountable (and can scold the President when things go wrong)."

(What does Nixon think Congress should have to do instead?)

He thinks that if Congress is against military action taken by the President, it should have to take affirmative action to stop that the President's exercise of force.

(Why is that important?)

Nixon says that this would guarantee full debate and deliberation; you could add that it would also force Members to take a vote that they could be held politically accountable for later on.

Let's say that the President initiates military operations in Iraq and the Congress is opposed. Both houses pass a bill directing the President to bring the troops home.

(What's the President going to do?)

Veto the bill, right? And it seems unlikely that you would be able to get enough votes to override the veto. So it's terribly important where you put the burden of inertia. If Congress has to act in order to *stop* the President, that's much more difficult.

(Is there any way in which Congress could stop an unauthorized war without passing a statute?)

Yes – The burden shifts on appropriations matters. There, Congress has to affirmatively *authorize* expenditures; the President can't veto a simple failure to pass an appropriations bill.

(What's the big difficulty with this?)

You have to wait until the next appropriations cycle, which could be months. Then you're really into *fait accompli* problems.

C.   Presidential Powers Incident to War

The last set of cases deal not with the direct military powers of the President, but his power to take actions incident to the contact of a war. We could talk about all sort of things here – for instance, the recent controversy over Presidentially-ordered surveillance in the context of the War on Terror. We're focusing on two related disputes, one from the Civil War and one "ripped from today's headlines". The first is the power to suspend the writ of *habeas corpus*, and the second is the power to detain suspected terrorists and try them through military commissions.

1.   Suspending the Writ—*Ex Parte Merryman*, 17 F. Cas. 144 (No. 9,487) (C.C.D. Md. 1861) (Taney, J.)

It's 1861, and the Union Army of the Potomac is eyeball to eyeball with the Confederate Army of Northern Virginia in the territory between Washington, D.C. and Richmond – which is now just a 90 minute drive down I-95 from the Nation's Capitol. To give you a sense of how close the fighting is, at the first Battle of Bull Run – the first major battle of the War (or "Wo-ah" as they say in Mississippi) – a bunch of well-dressed folks from D.C. came out in the carriages to the battlefield to watch the show. When the Union gets whipped at Bull Run, everyone realizes the capitol is in a lot of danger.

There's a big concern about being able to defend Washington under these circumstances, and the Union is rushing troops through Baltimore on their way to guard the District. Maryland, though, is a southern state and there are a lot of pro-secession sympathizers. A mob of these folks tries to prevent the Union troops from passing through.

President Lincoln authorizes the commanding general to suspend the writ of habeas corpus if there is any resistance along the line of march.

(What do we mean by "suspend the writ of habeas corpus"? What *is* the writ of habeas corpus, anyway?)

Well, the writ of habeas corpus is a common law writ that requires the government official who is holding a person in custody to come forward and provide the legal basis for holding him prisoner.

In the 20th century, the most important use for the writ of habeas corpus is as a mechanism by which prisoners in *state* custody can get a federal court to review the legality of their state court convictions. This is the way that the federal courts make sure that the state courts are respecting federal constitutional rights of criminal procedure, like the prohibition on forced confessions. The proceeding is basically a *second* bite at the apple in federal court for people who've already raised their constitutional argument once in *state* court.

But in 1861, the writ of habeas corpus hasn't been extended to cover persons in *state* custody. (That doesn't happen until 1867, directly as a result of our mistrust of state courts in the South following the Civil War.) Prior to 1867, the importance of the Great Writ is to help out prisoners in *federal* custody. And here, we're not usually talking about a second bite at the apple to get more judicial review of what happened at your initial trial. Rather, habeas corpus is pretty much the only tool available to people who are being held without any trial at all.

That's Merryman's situation – he's arrested for impeding the Union's troop movement, and he's basically being held by federal military authorities without having had a trial or anything. The situation isn't all that different from Mr. Padilla, the dirty bomber, who was arrested in Chicago on suspicion of being in league with Al Qaeda and is being held in military custody without a trial.

So now you ought to be able to see the importance of the ability to suspend the writ of habeas corpus. Habeas is the only legal tool that Merryman has to get judicial review of whether the government can legally hold him. If you can suspend the writ, you can basically make the government unaccountable for its actions.

(Can the writ ever be suspended?)

Sure. The Constitution specifically says so, in fact. It says "[t]he Privilege of the Writ of Habeas Corpus shall not be suspended, unless when in Cases of Rebellion or Invasion the public Safety may require it."

(Are the substantive conditions for that clause met here?)

Sure. If this isn't a "Rebellion" – and maybe an imminent "Invasion," too – then I don't know what is.

(So what's the problem?)

Justice Taney says only the Congress can suspend the writ – not the President, and certainly not some soldier to whom the President has delegated the power.

(How do we know it's Congress that can do it and not the President?)

Because the Suspension Clause in Article I, which is talking about Congress. The President's powers are in Article II.

(That's a decent argument, but can somebody argue it the other way? Is there a way to read this Clause as not limited to Congressional suspensions?)

I think you can. I'd make three points:

- The Suspension Clause is phrased as a *limit* on Congress's power, not as a power grant. Those limits surely apply to the government as a whole, not *just* to Congress. It may be placed in Article I simply because the Framers thought it had to go *somewhere*, and Congress was the part of the government most likely to *try* to suspend the writ.

  To illustrate, take the Suspension Clause's next door neighbor in Art. I, § 9 – the Titles of Nobility Clause. It says "No Title of Nobility shall be granted." Do you think that only limits *Congress* because the clause happens to show up in Article I? Since it's not in Art. II, can the *President* grant titles of nobility? Now this is actually an easy case because it says "No Title of Nobility shall be granted *by the United States*," which obviously takes in the government as a whole. But that just proves my point that at least some of the limitations in Art. I, § 9 apply to the whole government and not just the Congress.

- If that's right, and the Clause is a limit on the whole government, then it's not crazy to say that the *exception* to the limit – the authorization of suspension during war and rebellion – also presumptively applies to the whole government.

- The phrasing of the Clause itself in the passive voice arguably confirms this point. The Grammar Police always tell you not to use the passive voice, but there's times when it's really useful for lawyers – particularly when you want to avoid taking a position on who the subject of the

411

sentence is. For instance, sometimes you really want to just say "Mistakes were made" rather than "My client made mistakes," which is better grammatically but a lot worse in real life.

Here, the Suspension Clause says the Writ "shall not be suspended," but it doesn't say by whom. That leaves equally open who *can* suspend the writ in the situations that fall within the exceptions.

So I don't think President Lincoln was committing legal malpractice when he said in his address to Congress that "the Constitution itself, is silent as to which, or who, is to exercise the power" of suspension.

(Can anyone supplement Taney's textual argument with one based on separation of powers? Any functional reason to read the Suspension Clause as limited to authorizing *congressional* suspensions?)

I think that you can make a similar argument to the argument against non-statutory crimes – that is, that separation of powers protects liberty by requiring that at least two branches of the government concur before the government can do things that impose on the freedom of individuals. If only Congress can suspend the writ, then *two* things have to happen before you can be kept in jail indefinitely:

1. The Executive branch has to decide to put you there in the first place; and

2. Congress has to pass a statute suspending the writ.

Separation of powers is all about putting roadblocks in the way of potentially tyrannical actions, and having to get Congress's approval is a pretty good roadblock.

I think you could also argue that this roadblock is particularly important here since the whole point of suspending the writ is to take the *third* branch – the judiciary – out of the picture.

(Even if that's right, though, President Lincoln has another argument. What's his main point in his address to Congress, which at least implicitly responds to Chief Justice Taney's opinion in *Merryman*?)

He says, Look, we're in the middle of a Civil War here. One-third of the country is in open rebellion. I'm trying to take care that *all* the laws are faithfully executed in all those parts of the country. It's best to quote him:

"Must they be allowed to finally fail of execution, even had it been perfectly clear, that by the use of the means necessary to their execution, some single law [the statute authorizing writs of habeas corpus], made in such extreme tenderness of the citizen's liberty, that practically it relieves more of the guilty, than of the innocent, should, to a very limited extent, be violated? To state the question more directly, are all the laws, *but one*, to go unexecuted, and the government itself go to pieces, lest that one be violated?"

(What do you think of this argument?)

On one level, it's an appeal to substantive justice over legal niceties. Lincoln's just not a big fan of Justice Taney, who he thinks of as the genius who brought us the *Dred Scott* decision. (in fact, there's evidence that Lincoln nearly commanded Taney's *arrest* after *Merryman.*) And Lincoln is convinced that by doing whatever it takes to save the Union, he's doing what's best for the Country. Although he's an excellent lawyer in his own right, he's not inclined to let a few legal technicalities get in the way of the national interest.

But his statement can also be read as invoking this opposing tradition in foreign affairs law, that is, that in cases implicating foreign affairs and national security – and this is such a case even though we're in Baltimore, of all places – the constitutional rules are just different. We *aren't* just a government of limited and enumerated powers; the Nation has to be presumed to have whatever powers it needs, in extreme circumstances, to defend and preserve itself.

That's the claim you saw in *Curtiss-Wright*; it's the claim that Justice Taney explicitly rejects. He says "Nor can any argument be drawn from the nature of sovereignty, or the necessity of government, for self-defence in times of tumult and danger. The government of the United States is one of delegated and limited powers; it derives its existence and authority altogether from the constitution, and neither of its branches . . . can exercise any of the powers of government beyond those specified and granted."

(What authority does he invoke for this proposition?)

The Tenth Amendment, which says "the powers not delegated to the United States by the constitution, nor prohibited by it to the states, are reserved to the state respectively, or to the people."

We ordinarily think of this as a provision about *state*'s rights, but that's not the issue here. Taney's emphasizing the reservation of some rights "to the *people*." In other words, the People could have written emergency powers into the Constitution; because they didn't, we have to assume they reserved those powers to themselves.

(Who's right? Taney or Lincoln?)

2.   Military Commissions – *Hamdan v. Rumsfeld*, 126 S. Ct. 2749
        (2006)

Shortly after the September 11 attacks, President Bush issued an order
stating that suspected terrorists would be tried by military commissions
rather than given ordinary criminal trials in the Article III federal courts.

It's important to be clear about what a "military commission" entails: A
military commission is a military court – the judges are military officers,
not Article III judges with life tenure, and the jury is likewise composed of
military personnel. My understanding is that, in fact, rather than a judge
and jury you get a panel of officers who preside – essentially, it's like a
bench trial but to a multi-member court.

a.   The Key Questions

In the notes after *Hamdan*, I've organized the debate about military
commissions into three distinct sets of questions:

**(1)   Can suspected terrorists be tried in military commissions
          rather than in the ordinary civilian justice system?**

This is really an individual rights question – that is, the right of the
accused to a particular form of justice. Some more specific versions of this
question:

- Does due process require a civilian trial?

- Does international law require a civilian trial?

- *When* are military trials permissible, if they're not categorically
  prohibited?

The second and third questions are separation of powers question. The
first has to do with the President vs. Congress:

**(2)   May the *President* use military commissions to try suspected
          terrorists without new authorization from Congress?**

This is the central issue in *Hamdan*, and it breaks readily into two:

- To what extent do pre-existing statutes (e.g., the Uniform Code of
  Military Justice) allow military commissions for suspected terrorists?

- To what extent do those statutes require military commissions to follow
  ordinary courts martial procedures?

The other separation of powers question is about the President and
Congress vs. the Courts:

**(3)   To what extent must military commission proceedings be
          subject to challenge in and review by the Article III federal
          courts?**

This doesn't come up much in *Hamdan*, but it's the central question in *Boumediene* and *Al Odah*, which were argued today at the Supreme Court.

- Does Article III or Due Process require a federal court to be available to hear constitutional or other claims arising in the military commission process?

- Does Article III or Due Process require federal court review of the *factual* determinations (e.g., guilt or innocence) made by military commissions?

Remember from *way* back in the course that Congress's ability to restrict the courts' jurisdiction is one of the basic limits on the power of judicial review, but most people agree that this jurisdiction-limiting power is itself limited. We'll know a lot more about this issue in 6 months when today's cases come down.

Finally, there's another, more policy-oriented question:

(4)   Why use military commissions to try terrorists?

Let's take the last question first:

(Why use military commissions to try terrorists?)

I think there's several reasons:

- There might be a *lot* of these cases, and it's easier to come up with streamlined and specialized procedures.

- There's a lot of evidence involved that's highly sensitive to ongoing efforts to identify and thwart terrorists. Easier to keep that secret in a military commission proceeding.

- There's a fear that a civilian trial might turn into a circus. Remember the OJ trial?

- There may also be a sense that some of the procedural protections in civilian trials reflect balances that should be struck differently in this context.

Let's go back to the first *legal* question – whether use of a military process is OK.

(Is that in itself unconstitutional? Trying people in a military forum that's *within* the executive branch?)

Consider, for instance, the quote from Profs. Tribe and Katyal that I reproduced for you in the handout:

It is a "bedrock principle of our constitutional system" that "the body that defines what conduct to outlaw, the body that prosecutes violators, and the body that adjudicates guilt and dispenses punishment should be three distinct entities. To fuse those three functions under one man's ultimate rule, and to administer the resulting simulacrum of justice in a system of tribunals created by that very same authority, is to mock the very notion of constitutionalism and to make light of any aspiration to live by the rule of law."[50]

(That sounds really great – they're basically channeling Montesquieu and Madison. What's the problem, though?)

They've just described the FTC, the EPA, the FCC, etc. Almost all the administrative agencies have adjudicatory arms, prosecutory arms, and legislative arms. Maybe that ought to be unconstitutional, but that train left the station a long time ago. *I* might be willing to jump in front of it – to mix metaphors a bit – but I doubt the Supreme Court is.

(Should the fact that it's *military* make a critical difference?)

No – We have an extensive military justice system that tries our own servicemen when they're accused of crime, and it has withstood constitutional attack for centuries. Consider, for example, whether the fact that military judges work for the Executive is any worse than the fact that many *state* judges (and prosecutors) are *elected* by bloodthirsty, crime-hating voters.

A military commission is different from an ordinary court martial. Courts martial have very highly developed procedures, and they're designed to provide our servicemen with protections that are basically equivalent to what you'd get in the civilian system. Military *commissions* are more ad hoc – their structure and procedures are tailored to the particular circumstances where they're employed.

Military commissions are traditionally used in two situations:

- When the civilian courts are unavailable. They substitute for our domestic court systems during periods of martial law. And they may be used by temporary military governments over occupied territory, such as West Germany after WWII. That's *Milligan*,[51] from the Civil War, which disallowed use of a commission to try a civilian when the civilian courts were available.

---

[50] Neal K. Katyal & Laurence H. Tribe, *Waging War, Deciding Guilt: Trying the Military Tribunals*, 111 Yale L. J. 1259, 1259 (2002).

[51] *Ex Parte Milligan*, 71 U.S. (4 Wall.) 2 (1866): The Court holds that a military tribunal lacked jurisdiction to try a U.S. citizen, living in Indiana, of conspiring to aid the Confederacy.

- Military commissions can be used to try enemy combatants for violations of the law of war—even in times and places where the civilian courts are open and functioning. That's the *Quirin*.[52]

b.   Mr. Hamdan's Case

Salim Ahmed Hamdan is a Yemeni national alleged to have been Osama Bin Laden's bodyguard and driver.   He was captured in 2001 in Afghanistan and taken to Guantanamo Bay, Cuba.   He was eventually charged with conspiracy to commit war crimes and slated to be tried by one of the military commissions created by President Bush's post-Sept. 11 order, which is reproduced in the packet.   He filed a petition for a writ of *habeas corpus* in federal district court in D.C., asserting that a military commission would have no lawful authority to try him.

The Court (Stevens, J.) held that the commissions in question were not authorized by Congress.   This is the second question that I identified above.

The *Hamdan* opinions are overwhelmingly concerned with whether Hamdan's trial by military commission was permitted under various statutes—most importantly, the Uniform Code of Military Justice.   But there's another way of analyzing the case, reflected in some of the positions that the Administration has taken outside the context of this case.

Inherent Presidential Power: Proponents of broad Executive authority have often taken the position Article II's general language vesting "executive power" in the President confers power to do all sorts of things, including the power to detain suspected terrorists and try them before military commissions.   Moreover, this approach contends that Congress may not regulate the President's exercise of these constitutional powers.

The Government's brief in *Hamdan* argued both statutory authorization and inherent power, but it did *not* contend that any baseline authority that the President had on his own could not be restricted by Congress.   The Administration *has* taken that position in a few places, notably the infamous Torture Memo.   But it's unlikely that the Supreme Court would have embraced it.

Instead, the dominant framework is *Youngstown*:   The President's authority is largely a function of what Congress has authorized and prohibited.   As you've seen, what this framework does is turn most presidential power cases into cases about statutory construction: Whether the President can act depends on its consistency with any constraints that may be placed on such action by Congress.   Hence, the biggest separation

---

[52] *Ex Parte Quirin*, 317 U.S. 1 (1942): The Court upholds the use of military tribunals for German saboteurs apprehended in the United States.

of powers case in a generation turns largely on the meaning of *ordinary* laws.

c.　The Uniform Code of Military Justice

Under *Youngstown*, the Court has to work through the various statutory requirements bearing on military commissions.

(Where does the statutory authority for the President to convene a military commission come from?)

UCMJ Art. 21: "The provisions of this code conferring jurisdiction upon courts-martial shall not be construed as depriving military commissions . . . of concurrent jurisdiction in respect of offenders or offenses that by statute or by the law of war may be tried by such military commissions . . . ."

(What's the key limitation that the majority pulls out of this language?)

Commissions can be used only where the "law of war" permits.

(What's the "law of war"? Where does it come from?)

It comes from a variety of sources—some statutory, like the UCMJ itself; some treaty-based, like the Geneva Convention; and some of it is common law.

There are two distinct problems here: One substantive, the other procedural. The substantive problem, which only gets four votes (Justice Kennedy doesn't reach the question) is that the law of war doesn't seem to recognize "conspiracy" as a freestanding offense. The plurality determines this by looking at a variety of international treaties and practice.

Note that the MCA "cures" this problem by providing a statutory definition of war crimes punishable by military commissions, and explicitly including conspiracy on the list.

(Can Congress do this? Aren't war crimes defined by *international* law?)

Sure it can. It has explicit authority under Art. I, § 8, cl. 10, to "define and punish . . . Offences against the Law of Nations." The interesting question, I suppose, would be whether a court could review a statute like this and say, "Sorry, but we don't think that conspiracy is, in fact, an 'offence against the Law of Nations' and therefore the statute falls outside your power."

(Should a court be able to do that?)

I doubt it. The word "define" suggests Congress should get at least a great deal of deference when they interpret what "the Law of Nations" requires.

The procedural problems take both a general and a specific form.

(Putting aside problems with particular aspects of the commission procedure, what's the majority's more general criticism?)

The lack of parity with courts martial procedures.

Now, I think it's important to point out that the procedures established by the Department of Defense's regulations were surprisingly favorable to the accused, probably in response to public criticism of the use of commissions in the first place. Those rules required, for example:

- appointment of counsel

- proof of guilt beyond a reasonable doubt

- right not to testify, and to cross-examine witnesses

- juries of 3 to 7, with 7 in capital cases

- 2/3 vote to convict; unanimous in capital cases

- procedures similar to Uniform Code of Military Justice

The primary exceptions to the UCMJ, however, was loosened rules of evidence, including the use of evidence that may not be disclosed to the accused, and for which the accused may not be present when it is put on at trial. The Court doesn't categorically rule out such a procedure—it just says that the President hasn't made the necessary showing of justification for a departure from courts martial procedures.

d. The Geneva Convention

There's another problem, stemming from the Geneva Convention on Treatment of Prisoners of War. That convention has both rigorous provisions governing ordinary armed conflict between signatories and a more general provision, Common Article III, which governs "armed conflict not of an international character occurring in the territory of one of the High Contracting Parties." By relying on the fact that Afghanistan is a party, the Court doesn't have to decide whether Al Qaeda counts as a "state" for treaty purposes, etc.

Whenever you have a treaty claim, you have to worry about the extent to which it can be asserted in a domestic court. The Court doesn't have to answer that, because it holds that the Geneva Convention is part of the "law of war" incorporated by Article 21 of the UCMJ. It applies because Congress says it does.

Common Article 3's requirements are pretty general: It forbids "the passing of sentences and the carrying out of executions without previous judgment pronounced by a regularly constituted court affording all the judicial guarantees which are recognized as indispensable by civilized peoples."

The Court gets two things out of Common Article 3. The first is more support for the conclusion that you have to justify any departure from courts martial procedure. The other (which only gets 4 votes) is that the particular procedure of trying a defendant out of his presence is contrary to "judicial guarantees recognized as indispensable by civilized peoples."

     e.   **Congress Responds – the Military Commissions Act of 2000**

Congress responds to *Hamdan* by enacting the Military Commissions Act of 2006. This does several key things:

- It explicitly authorizes the use of military commissions to try suspected terrorists for war crimes.

- It defines the relevant crimes by statute, including conspiracy.

- It sets out detailed procedures for how the commissions will operate. According to colleagues who are otherwise quite critical of the prosecution of the War on Terror, they're quite generous to the accused.

- It restricts judicial review of the whole deal even more than the earlier statutes did.

Some of these provisions are being tested today, but it's likely we won't have any final resolution of the whole military commission question any time soon.

What can we say more generally, though, based on *Hamdan* and the other War on Terror cases? I think a couple of things:

- The Court's definitely sensitive to the imperatives driving the Executive to use things like military commissions. My guess is that the President will continue to get considerable deference on questions like exactly how much procedural protection suspected terrorists are entitled to.

But at the same time:

- The Court is definitely on the case here. It's not going to roll over or write the President a blank check. This is the same "activist" court that you say in *City of Boerne* and *Casey* – it believes that it has a crucial role to play in deciding the great issues of the day. And the President and Congress, while pushing back to some extent by restricting judicial review in certain ways, aren't about to try to cut the Court out entirely.

So we've come a long way from John Marshall's precarious situation in *Marbury*, yes? Judicial review is well-established and here to stay, even in the most fraught contexts of our times. For my own part, I find that pretty reassuring.